D1544204

DEATH IN THE DARK

DEATH IN THE DARK

MIDNIGHT EXECUTIONS IN AMERICA

John D. Bessler

NORTHEASTERN UNIVERSITY PRESS

Boston

Northeastern University Press

Copyright 1997 by John D. Bessler

Library of Congress Cataloging-in-Publication Data

Bessler, John D.
    Death in the dark : midnight executions in America /
John D. Bessler
      p. cm.
    Includes index.
    ISBN 1-55553-322-1 (alk. paper)
    1. Capital punishment—United States.   2. Executions and
executioners—United States.   I. Title.
HV8699.5.U5B47   1997
364.66'0973—dc21   97-8110

Designed by Gary Gore

Composed in Garamond by Letra Libre, Boulder, Colorado. Printed and bound by Maple Press, York, Pennsylvania. The paper is Maple Antique, an acid-free stock.

MANUFACTURED IN THE UNITED STATES OF AMERICA
01 00 99 98 97   5 4 3 2 1

To my mother and father

~ CONTENTS

ᕫ Acknowledgments

This book is the culmination of over five years of research. The idea for the book originated with a paper I wrote for Professor Joseph Hoffmann's death penalty seminar at the Indiana University School of Law in Bloomington. While writing this book, I received a great deal of assistance. I'd like to first thank my wife, Amy Klobuchar, for her patience while I worked on the project and for reading the manuscript and providing helpful comments on it. This book would have gone unwritten if not for her loving support. I'd also like to thank my daughter Abigail, my parents Bill and Marilyn Bessler, my in-laws Jim Klobuchar and Rose Klobuchar, and my five brothers—Bill, Greg, Brian, Andrew, and Anthony—for their encouragement and support. My brother Bill and his wife, Lori, deserve special thanks for helping me locate some hard-to-find nineteenth-century newspapers on microfilm.

I also need to thank the *William Mitchell Law Review* and the *Federal Communications Law Journal* for granting me permission to reprint portions of my previously published law journal articles. The staff of the *William Mitchell Law Review* (especially Hassan Saffouri, Eric Skytte, and Katheryn Ehler-Lejcher) deserve special credit for their assistance and editorial suggestions, which resulted in a much-improved manuscript. I am also grateful to my friends at the law firms of Faegre & Benson and Leonard, Street & Deinard who were supportive of this project. In particular, I would like to thank Tim Rank, who reviewed the manuscript and offered many helpful suggestions. I am also deeply indebted to Jim Volling, a truly first-rate lawyer who gave me the opportunity to represent death row inmates in Texas. Working with Jim has been one of the most rewarding experiences of my legal career. Hollis Fisher and Cindy Logergren also deserve mention for their expert secretarial skills, as does librarian Susan Rafter for imparting some of her research know-how.

I would also like to thank the following individuals who offered suggestions on the manuscript, provided materials for use in the book, or assisted me in some other way: Leigh Bienen, Doris Braendel, Greg

Braun, Karen Brown, Ross Corson, Watt Espy, Harriet Frazier, Samuel Freedman, Greg Gisvold, Sara Gurwitch, Michael Handberg, Hunter Labowitz, Michael Madow, Mike Miller, Kathryn Quaintance, Lisa Queen, David Skover, H. Mark Stichel, Dick Sullivan, Kellye Testy, Jenny Wahl, and Scott Walker. In addition, I am grateful to the staff of the Minnesota Historical Society, the Minneapolis Public Library, the University of Minnesota Law Library, and the staffs of other libraries and historical societies across the United States who provided research assistance to me. The staff of the interlibrary loan department at the Minneapolis Public Library, who processed dozens of requests for books and microfilm for me, deserve special recognition for their extraordinary efforts.

I would also like to thank Sister Helen Prejean, who recommended Northeastern University Press as a possible publisher for my manuscript, and the Director of the Press, William Frolich, who agreed to take on the project. My editor at Northeastern University Press, Scott Brassart, and the production director, Ann Twombly, also deserve special thanks for their invaluable editorial assistance. Finally, I am forever indebted to my law school classmate Bruce Beddow, who inspired me to write this book and who aided me at every turn in preparing the manuscript for publication. I could not ask for a better friend.

DEATH IN THE DARK

❧ INTRODUCTION

Was it not better that [the condemned] man should be slid off in the night away from the sight and view of the crowd than that the execution of the law should be made the occasion of a gala day and a circus?

> —John Day Smith, author of Minnesota's
> "midnight assassination law" requiring private,
> nighttime executions (1889)

Our courts of justice must be open to the public; the deliberations of our legislature must be public; not even a poor freemasonry society is to be tolerated because its ceremonies are secret; but when life is to be taken, when a human being is to be smitten down like an ox, when a soul is to be violently hurled into eternity, the most solemn occasion that can be witnessed on earth, then the public must be excluded. But the American public will not long submit to this. If business of this nature is done at all, it must be done in the light of day; if the continuance of capital punishments depends on their being inflicted in private, it may be regarded as certain, that they cannot long exist in this country.

> —Thomas Upham, a Congregationalist
> minister and professor of moral philosophy
> at Bowdoin College (1836)

Gary Gilmore. Ted Bundy. John Wayne Gacy. These are just three of the more notorious names of the 313 death row inmates who were executed in the United States from 1977 to 1995. Other names—John Young, Larry Smith, Edward Johnson, and James Clark—are less recognizable, but all 313 executions share a common feature.[1] They were all hidden from public view. State laws, in fact, require that executions take place within prisons, and most states limit public attendance at executions to only six to twelve "reputable" or "respectable" citizens. The number of journalists who can attend executions is also severely restricted, and television cameras are universally forbidden in execution chambers.

Capital punishment is cloaked in added secrecy because executions are often performed in the middle of the night. Indeed, many states mandate that executions take place after midnight. Delaware and Louisiana authorize executions only between midnight and 3:00 A.M., and South Dakota executions must occur between 12:01 A.M. and 6:00 A.M. Other states, like Wyoming and Indiana, require executions "before the hour of sunrise."[2] One minute after midnight is one of the most popular times to schedule an execution, and in the past two decades only rarely have executions occurred during daylight hours.

Recently, attempts have been made to expose the innermost workings of capital punishment. In 1991, U.S. Senator Mark Hatfield proposed a bill to require public executions for federally imposed death sentences. That same year, California legislators also debated whether to mandate cameras in the execution chamber. Lawsuits seeking to televise executions also have been filed by death row inmates and media representatives, most recently by Phil Donahue.[3] These legislative initiatives and court challenges, however, have all failed. Executions remain private affairs.

The privatization of executions is a relatively recent phenomenon. Hangings were once frequently performed in public squares or commons. At these well-attended events, sermons were delivered and printed messages distributed to spread the execution day message. Only in response to a movement in the 1830s to abolish capital punishment, and to a growing concern among civic leaders that public executions were unwholesome spectacles, did states begin privatizing executions. The transition was not complete until 1936, when the last public execution in the United States took place in Owensboro, Kentucky.[4]

With America's last public execution having occurred over sixty years ago, this book attempts to answer two historical questions. First, what propelled executions out of the public squares and into prison execution chambers? Second, why did Americans start executing people at night? The book also delves into several more topical questions.

Why is capital punishment so popular, as expressed in some public opinion polls? Why does the public blindly accept the fact that executions are hidden from public view? What is the media's role in America's death penalty debate? And should television stations be allowed to televise executions?

To frame the discussion, Chapter 1 explores the unusual case of Robert Alton Harris. Most death row inmates are executed with little fanfare, but as Harris's execution date neared in April of 1992, the media flocked to northern California. Harris would be the first person executed in that state in twenty-five years, and death penalty opponents were fearful. If Harris's execution at San Quentin went forward, it might open the floodgates to more executions in California—a state with numerous inmates on death row.

The battle over Harris's life was waged on the night of April 21, 1992. Vigorous attempts made to block the scheduled 12:01 A.M. execution resulted in a short postponement, but Harris was eventually gassed at daybreak. Harris died, however, only after four last-minute stays were issued, and the U.S. Supreme Court took the unprecedented step—at 5:45 A.M. California time—of enjoining lower courts from further interfering with the execution. The Supreme Court ruled that no further stays could be issued "except upon order of this Court." The Justices had pulled an all-nighter to ensure that Harris did not get another last-minute reprieve.

The Harris case is unique for an additional reason. A year before his execution, a battle was fought in federal court by KQED, a San Francisco public television station, over whether Harris's execution could be filmed. This dispute pitted KQED against the warden of San Quentin, Daniel Vasquez. Ultimately, a federal judge ruled that television cameras could be excluded from the execution chamber, although the judge refused to permit Warden Vasquez to exclude all journalists from attending the execution. Because KQED never appealed the ruling, many legal issues surrounding the constitutionality of laws barring television cameras from execution chambers were left unresolved.

After recounting the two legal battles surrounding Harris's execution, Chapter 2 goes back in time to examine the phenomenon of public executions in America from colonial days until the mid-1930s, when public executions ended. It describes the ritual of execution day, and the large crowds and frequent mayhem often associated with such events. Through historical accounts of actual hangings, it focuses specifically on why condemned prisoners used to be hung publicly in this country at midday.

In contrast, Chapter 3 traces the rise of private execution laws in the United States. These laws, first enacted in the 1830s, required that executions take place behind prison walls or within other suitable enclosures. They sharply limited the number of execution spectators and sometimes barred the attendance of women and children altogether. The most restrictive laws actually forbade newspaper reporters from attending executions and prohibited newspapers from publishing any execution details. The only information that newspapers could lawfully print was the mere fact that the execution had occurred.

Chapter 4 explores the historical origins of statutory provisions requiring nighttime executions. In 1994, Delaware became the newest state to require executions after dark, although Ohio, Minnesota, and Indiana enacted laws requiring nighttime executions as early as the 1880s. In the last few years, the vast majority of executions have taken place in the middle of the night. From 1977 to 1995, over 82 percent of all American executions were carried out between the hours of 11:00 P.M. and 7:30 A.M., with over 50 percent of the 313 executions during that period occurring between midnight and 1:00 A.M.[5] In uncovering the legislative rationales that gave birth to laws mandating nighttime executions, Chapter 4 sheds light on why executions are now commonly performed at night.

In Chapter 5, the history of Minnesota's "midnight assassination law"—as contemporaries to its passage called it—takes center stage. The "midnight assassination law" was the only private execution law ever attacked as unconstitutional by the press in American courts prior to 1976. Enacted in 1889, this law required that executions be conducted privately and "before the hour of sunrise." It prohibited all press attendance at hangings and barred newspapers from printing any execution details. Any sheriff or reporter who violated the law could be criminally prosecuted.

After its passage, the "midnight assassination law" went unenforced for over sixteen years. However, in 1906, three Minnesota newspapers were indicted by a grand jury for publishing details of the botched hanging of William Williams—the last person executed in Minnesota. The newspapers fought the indictments, asserting that the law infringed on their constitutional rights of freedom of the press. The case ended up in the Minnesota Supreme Court, which ultimately rejected the newspapers' legal challenge to the law, although the press exposure of the horrific details of Williams's death eventually led to the abolition of capital punishment in Minnesota. The history of this Minnesota law—like the history of no other American law—shows how laws requiring private, nighttime executions dramatically affected America's death penalty debate.

The book then turns to the politics of capital punishment in America. Chapter 6 describes how the U.S. Supreme Court and lower courts are abandoning review of death penalty cases at the same time that state governors are adamantly refusing to exercise their clemency powers. After analyzing public attitudes toward capital punishment, and how those attitudes have changed over the past three decades, Chapter 6 examines the increasing propensity of politicians to trumpet the use of the death penalty as a get-tough-on-crime measure. Finally, the chapter explores how the popularity of capital punishment—as expressed by many public opinion polls—has affected the actions of elected prosecutors and judges, particularly in southern "Death Belt" states like Texas and Florida.

The final chapter reviews modern-day attempts to bring cameras into execution chambers. It details how journalists and death row inmates alike have sued, alleging that laws barring television cameras from execution chambers are unconstitutional, and how politicians on both sides of the death penalty debate have argued for televised executions. Chapter 7 also describes the universal failure of these lawsuits and legislative initiatives, including Phil Donahue's failed attempt in 1993 to televise David Lawson's execution. Finally, Chapter 7 discusses whether executions *should* be televised and whether laws banning television cameras from execution chambers are unconstitutional.

This book concludes by addressing some fundamental questions. Does the government have the right to censor film footage of newsworthy events like executions? Or should journalists be given full access to executions, just as they are given unrestricted access to other governmental proceedings? What obligation does the press have to the public to do hard-hitting news stories about capital punishment and the alternatives to it, such as life imprisonment without the possibility of parole? Should television stations refuse to televise executions because of their graphic nature, even if they are given the opportunity to film them? Or are broadcasters ethically obligated to bring execution film footage into citizens' living rooms, even though some commentators, like George Will, predict that televised executions will only "coarsen American life"?[6]

The answers to these questions are of grave importance. Over three thousand inmates now sit on death row, and a record number of executions, fifty-six, took place in 1995. That is the highest number of executions in any year since 1957, when sixty-five people were executed. The federal death penalty was expanded in 1994, prisoners' habeas corpus rights were severely curtailed by Congress in 1996, and the reinstatement of capital punishment in New York brings the number of states with death penalty laws to thirty-eight. Given these recent federal developments and the size of New York, Americans are sure to see even more executions in the years to come.[7] As Americans execute more and more people each year, journalists should feel compelled to reevaluate the quality of their news coverage of executions. More important, because the death penalty is being used so frequently, Americans should pause to consider whether executions should remain hidden from public view.

ᐁ 1

On the Dark Side

The Macabre Legal Circus

As night approached on April 20, 1992, Robert Alton Harris, convicted of killing two high school kids that he and his brother abducted from a parking lot in San Diego in 1978, prepared to die in San Quentin's gas chamber. California officials had already made the necessary preparations. The execution was scheduled to take place at one minute after midnight. All parking within two miles of the prison had been banned to reduce the number of demonstrators, and invitations had been extended to forty-eight witnesses, including eighteen members of the press. On April 16, Governor Pete Wilson—undoubtedly aware of polls showing that 80 percent of Californians held pro–death penalty views—had denied Harris's clemency petition, removing the final obstacle to the death row inmate's execution. Wilson announced his decision live on statewide television, noting that Harris had suffered "monstrous child abuse," but finding that Harris's own victimization did not alter his responsibility for his acts. As California neared its first execution in twenty-five years, the whole nation anxiously watched and waited.[1]

Although parking was restricted, five hundred death penalty opponents hiked to the prison by midnight with signs that read "Abolish the Death Penalty" and "Don't Kill In My Name." Two of the marchers, David Magris and Dennis Tapp, made strange bedfellows. Magris was on San Quentin's death row in the 1970s after killing one man and partially paralyzing another. Tapp was the man Magris disabled. These men, who had earlier reconciled on a television program, came to San Quentin to protest Harris's execution. Another three dozen demonstrators joined them, marching twenty-one miles to the prison from San Francisco. Outside the prison, hordes of journalists assembled to report about Harris's impending death, the state having granted only 18 of 150 applications by journalists to watch Harris die in the gas chamber.[2]

People were debating the merits of capital punishment all along Main Street in San Quentin Village, a small neighborhood near the prison. A schoolteacher took his class to the prison as part of a classroom debate on capital punishment. Another man, the father of a victim whose murderer resided on death row, carried a sign urging "Justice for Victims." He stood by the prison gate, telling reporters he would suffer until his daughter's killer died. Other death penalty proponents held homemade signs expressing their views. One poster, a mock advertisement for "Alka Cyanide," proclaimed, "Plop Plop Fizz Fizz, Oh, What a Relief It Is!"[3]

Despite meticulous planning, Harris's execution did not occur on schedule. At 6:30 P.M., the U.S. Court of Appeals for the Ninth Circuit issued a stay of execution, or postponement, based on Harris's federal habeas corpus petition. That petition alleged that newly discovered evidence existed about Harris's brother's involvement in his crime that diminished Harris's culpability. A second stay was subsequently ordered by ten Ninth Circuit judges at 10:30 P.M. That stay was issued as a result of a class action lawsuit brought by the American Civil Liberties Union on behalf of Harris and California's other 330 death row inmates. The ACLU's lawsuit alleged that death by lethal gas was a "cruel and unusual punishment" that violated the Constitution's Eighth Amendment. A miscommunication among the twenty-eight Ninth Circuit judges, located all over the West, resulted in the Ninth Circuit issuing a third stay—also related to Harris's cruel and unusual punishment claim—at 11:45 P.M.

Twenty minutes before this third stay was issued, the U.S. Supreme Court lifted the Ninth Circuit's first stay of execution. The Supreme Court would not hear allegations of newly discovered evidence at such a late hour. The Justices also nullified the Ninth Circuit's second and third stays by 7–2 votes at 2:30 and 3:00 A.M., respectively. The Supreme Court refused to address the merits of Harris's cruel and unusual punishment claim, ruling that this claim "could have been brought more than a decade ago." Justices Stevens and Blackmun dissented, arguing that Harris's claim had merit. They relied on eyewitness accounts of gas chamber executions, opining that "execution by cyanide gas is extremely and unnecessarily painful."

After the Supreme Court vacated the third stay, Harris was strapped into the gas chamber. The door was shut, and sulfuric acid began filling the two vats beneath Harris's seat. At 3:51 A.M.—just seconds before cyanide pellets would drop into the vats to form lethal gas—a telephone next to the gas chamber rang, bringing news of a fourth stay. This stay was issued by Ninth Circuit Judge Harry Pregerson, an ex-marine, who had never received the Supreme Court's orders vacating the Ninth Circuit's prior stays of execution. Having been awakened by a phone call from Harris's lawyers, Judge Pregerson ruled that Harris's claims required further examination. Accordingly, the acid was drained from the vats, and Harris was returned to a nearby cell. Harris had spent eleven minutes in the gas chamber. Outside the prison, the twenty remaining anti–death penalty protestors sang "We Shall Overcome." One death penalty proponent held up a sign that read, "Take a deep breath, Bob."

In an unprecedented ruling, the U.S. Supreme Court vacated Judge Pregerson's stay. Still awake at 8:45 A.M. Eastern time, a majority of the Justices ruled that the lower federal courts could enter no further stays "except upon order of this Court." The two Justices who had previously dissented were not consulted. At 6:00 A.M. Pacific time, Harris was again strapped into the gas chamber chair. Cyanide pellets were dropped into the sulfuric acid at 6:10 A.M., and Harris was pronounced dead eleven minutes later. His last words, "I'm sorry," were mouthed to the father of one of Harris's victims, who peered through the gas chamber glass six feet away.[4]

When Harris was pronounced dead shortly after daybreak, over two hundred journalists were still awaiting word outside the prison. These journalists easily outnumbered the dozen death penalty opponents who remained. Amidst the sound of birds, these capital punishment foes joined in a circle and hugged. The ACLU's spokesman, David Hinkley, said gravely: "As a child, Robert Harris was beaten within an inch of his

life. Now California has taken the last inch." Elsewhere, the mood was
not so somber. A San Diego disc jockey, on hearing of Harris's death,
played a popular Rolling Stones tune with the chorus "But it's all right
now, in fact it's a gas. . . . I'm Jumping Jack Flash, it's a gas gas gas." A
livid listener called in to say she would not listen to the station again.
She was followed by a cheering caller.[5]

In the aftermath of Harris's execution, California Attorney General
Dan Lungren called the execution a solemn act that showed the state's
ability to "respond to the true needs and concerns of victims." Governor
Pete Wilson described the evening as a "macabre legal circus" performed
by "manipulative lawyers and indulgent judges." However, having earlier denied Harris's clemency appeal, Wilson also quickly praised the use
of capital punishment. By overseeing Harris's execution, he had fulfilled
a campaign pledge to bring executions back to California. In fact, in his
1990 gubernatorial race against Dianne Feinstein, Wilson frequently
stressed that he helped lead the campaign to remove Chief Justice Rose
Bird from the California Supreme Court. Voters ousted Bird and two of
her fellow justices, Cruz Reynoso and Joseph Grodin, after a bitter advertising campaign targeted them for their votes on death penalty cases.
Thirty-second television commercials urged voters to cast three votes for
capital punishment: "No on Bird," "No on Grodin," and "No on
Reynoso." Other commercials stressed that "all three justices needed to
lose if the death penalty is to be enforced." Bird had voted to overturn
death sentences in each of the sixty-one cases that she participated in on
the court. Wilson had also made his pro–death penalty views a central
theme of his 1982 campaign for U.S. Senate.[6]

KQED v. Vasquez

Prior to the lawyers' last-ditch efforts to save Harris's life, another
legal battle related to Harris's execution had already been fought in California's federal courts. This skirmish was between San Quentin's warden, Daniel Vasquez, and KQED, San Francisco's largest public television station. KQED wanted to film Harris's execution as part of a
documentary on capital punishment. Harris himself expressed no objection to television cameras recording his execution. "I have no problem with that at all," he said.[7]

The battle lines were drawn in February 1990, over two years before Harris's actual execution date. At that time, Warden Vasquez issued revised guidelines prohibiting reporters from carrying any equipment into Harris's execution. This prohibition extended to cameras and recording equipment, as well as to pencils and notepads. Warden Vasquez also announced that only fourteen media representatives would be allowed to witness the execution. In sharp contrast, some forty reporters witnessed the 1967 execution of Aaron Mitchell, California's last gas chamber execution. Finally, Warden Vasquez announced that the selection of media representatives would be delegated to Governor Wilson's press secretary, Robert Gore.

From hundreds of statewide applicants, Gore selected media witnesses who were unlikely to write anti–death penalty articles or editorials. For instance, Gore added the *Sacramento Union* to the list, passing over the *Sacramento Bee*. The politically conservative *Union* had not even applied to witness the execution, while the *Bee,* which had applied, boasted a circulation of four to five times that of the *Union*. Gore later claimed that he could not remember why he chose the *Union* over the *Bee,* although he admitted that he was well aware of the extremely negative columns that the *Bee*'s political columnist had written about Governor Wilson.[8]

Warden Vasquez's actions in allowing Gore to select execution witnesses and in refusing to allow cameras into the execution chamber prompted KQED to file a lawsuit against Vasquez. That lawsuit, lodged in federal district court, alleged that the process for selecting execution witnesses was unconstitutional. The selection process should be a "neutral, objective one," KQED argued, rather than one based on "politics, personal favoritism or other improper factors." Vasquez himself conceded that his selection criteria for nonpress witnesses included their disinclination to talk with reporters. Afraid that reporters might "try to extract" interviews or comments from selected witnesses, Vasquez advised them that he would try "to contain the media."[9]

KQED's lawsuit further alleged that Vasquez had unlawfully discriminated against television broadcasters by excluding cameras from the execution chamber. In court briefs, KQED argued that the public has "a right to view the event as the 'ultimate sanction' of the criminal justice system." Modern technology permitted cameras to record an execution unobtrusively, KQED contended. California officials countered that televised executions would jeopardize prison security. Such broadcasts would reveal the identity of prison staff and execution witnesses "who might later be subject to harassment or threats."[10]

Initially, U.S. District Court Judge Robert Schnacke refused to dismiss the suit. He concluded that there must be "appropriate balancing" between security concerns, an inmate's privacy concerns, and the rights of a free press. Just five days before the trial was scheduled to begin, though, Warden Vasquez barred *all* journalists from attending future executions. This action, taken with Governor Wilson's approval, prompted Judge Schnacke to declare on the first day of trial that KQED's lawsuit might be moot. Judge Schnacke said that neither the press nor the public appeared to have a First Amendment right to attend executions.[11]

Reserving final judgment, however, Judge Schnacke began the trial—in which he, not a jury, would decide the outcome—on March 25, 1991. KQED's first witness was Michael Schwarz, the station's news director and a proponent of capital punishment for particularly heinous crimes. Schwarz's testimony focused on the objectivity of a camera's lens. "I think a camera alone can provide a true and clear and complete and accurate picture that is unmediated by an individual's personal interpretation of that event," he declared. Schwarz's testimony later took on a more political tone: "I think the videotape would enable us to speak to the central question raised by executions, which is whether or not this is an appropriate punishment to carry out for the most horrible crimes that people commit in society." He added: "The death penalty tells us who we are as a people. And I think that in order to examine that event most fully, in all its complexity, it's very important for us to be able to look at it."[12]

During Schwarz's testimony, Judge Schnacke frequently questioned Schwarz's journalistic motives. "If you got a scream, that would be a lot more saleable, wouldn't it?" he inquired. When Schwarz reminded him that KQED lacked commercial motives, Judge Schnacke remarked sarcastically that Schwarz was "speaking on behalf of every potential television station," including the Playboy channel. He pointed out that other television stations might not have such "extraordinarily high motives." Mimicking the words of H. L. Mencken, Judge Schnacke then remarked that "no one ever went broke underestimating the taste of the American people." When asked who would be the "supreme arbiter" of good taste in airing the film, Schwarz replied, "the public." Schwarz added that KQED planned to show the film late in the evening to avoid exposing young viewers to it.[13]

The next day, Raymond Procunier took the stand for KQED. The head of Nevada's prison system and a former prison director in California, Texas, Utah, and Virginia, Procunier had supervised several executions. He testified that reporters and their equipment posed no security risk at an execution. "Corrections people have a tendency to set moral standards and meddle in areas that are none of their business," he said. When asked if televised executions would present a security problem if death row inmates were watching, he replied bluntly, "If it did, they're not running San Quentin Death Row properly." He added that the state's concern that a broadcast journalist might hurl a camera against the gas chamber windows to try to stop an execution "bordered on the bizarre." On cross-examination, Procunier was asked whether a camera thrown at the gas chamber windows could crack the glass. This question prompted Judge Schnacke to interject that "there may be such a thing in this world as a suicidal cameraman." Procunier countered that a camera stand could easily be secured to the floor. He emphasized that reporters are already permitted to bring cameras on prison tours and that, in forty-three years of correctional work, he had never seen a camera operator hide contraband in equipment.[14]

The following day, Warden Vasquez testified that televised executions should be prohibited for a "host" of reasons. First, televised executions might cause "radicals" to identify guards and take revenge. "If we're talking about the lives of human beings, I'm afraid that some radicalism might be directed against my staff," he said. Second, cameras would disrupt the decorum of executions. He did not want executions to be "a spectacle." Executions require "tactfulness and precision," he said, calling for "a procedure that is as respectful as possible." Finally, Vasquez renewed the concern that a camera operator might throw a camera at the gas chamber's windows. "What if he decided he was going to throw it against the glass?" he asked rhetorically. "What if there was something in it and he was going to throw it and try and stop the execution?"[15]

In June 1991, Judge Schnacke upheld the ban on cameras in the execution chamber. His ruling, issued before a packed courtroom, reiterated the same prison security concerns raised by Warden Vasquez. Executions seen on television by inmates could spark a severe reaction or cause prison riots. Cameras might identify guards or staff members, thereby jeopardizing their safety or the safety of their families. "[N]o rational way appears to prevent cameras . . . from getting either intentionally or inadvertently photographs of the prison personnel," he ruled. Judge Schnacke further credited the testimony that photographers' heavy equipment might be used to break the glass shielding the gas chamber. "The warden is not required to trust anybody," he ruled. "It's no answer to say the press are all nice people and would never do anything irrational." "Prison officials are the experts," he concluded. "Their reasonable concerns must be accommodated. They not unreasonably see risks permitting cameras. Prohibition of cameras is a reasonable and valid regulation." Despite KQED's evidence of impropriety, the selection process for media representatives was also upheld as "reasonable and appropriate."[16]

However, Judge Schnacke decided that it was "irrational and capricious" to bar all reporters from executions. "The press has always been there," he said, "and the First Amendment makes it pretty clear it is important to have a process of news gathering." Describing the warden's actions in barring all press attendance as "more emotional than rational," Judge Schnacke recognized that the press have traditionally attended executions. "It does appear that where there is a long custom and practice of accommodating the press, and where that has not caused any intrusion of any sort, it is probably irrational, unreasonable and capricious to bar the press at this point."[17]

On September 4, 1991, KQED announced that it would not appeal Judge Schnacke's ruling. Its decision was fueled by the lost donations and membership cancellations that followed KQED's filing of the lawsuit against Warden Vasquez. As of March 1991, roughly 200 of KQED's 250,000 members had cancelled because of the lawsuit. "[T]he angry letters accompanying these cancellations," noted one commentator, "followed a predictable how-can-you-be-involved-in-such-sleaze pattern." KQED's member services supervisor, Karen Laird, said that no other issue had ever generated such a strong membership response.[18]

Although KQED's lawsuit failed to get Harris's execution on television, the ACLU actually received last-minute court approval to have Harris's execution videotaped to preserve "critical evidence." The ACLU's request to film Harris's execution was associated with its pending class action lawsuit alleging that death by lethal gas was a cruel and unusual punishment in violation of the U.S. Constitution's Eighth Amendment. The ACLU's request was granted by U.S. District Court Judge Marilyn Hall Patel to help resolve this constitutional issue. Judge Patel ruled that evidence critical to the ACLU's lawsuit would be irretrievably lost unless Harris's execution was filmed. "Videotaping the execution," she ruled, "is necessary to preserve material evidence not otherwise available from any other source." After being taken, the film footage—made by California authorities under court order—was quickly sealed in a court vault. Judge Patel had specifically ordered that no copies of the videotape were to be made "except by order of the court." The videotape reportedly depicted Harris's lifeless body being blasted with water to remove any lingering lethal gas and being rammed with a broom in the chest to expel any fumes in his lungs. A prison spokesman, however, refused to divulge or confirm what was depicted on the videotape, saying that information was "confidential, not public information."

In fact, California authorities vigorously and successfully fought efforts by a death row inmate in Maryland to obtain a copy of the videotape. That inmate, Donald Thomas, wanted to introduce the videotape as evidence in his legal challenge to the constitutionality of Maryland's gas chamber. Judge Patel refused to release the videotape to Thomas's lawyer, H. Mark Stichel, even though a Maryland judge had promised to enter a protective order to restrict access to the tape.[19]

The ACLU's Class Action Lawsuit

The ACLU's class action lawsuit attacking the constitutionality of California's gas chamber was eventually tried on the merits in 1993 after Harris's execution. The trial, presided over by U.S. District Court Judge Marilyn Hall Patel, lasted eight days. The question at hand was whether the use of lethal gas constituted a cruel and unusual punishment in violation of the Eighth Amendment of the U.S. Constitution. United States Supreme Court precedents had already established that shooting and electrocution were constitutional methods of execution. Before Judge Patel issued her ruling, the Ninth Circuit had also ruled that hanging was a constitutional method of execution.

In the latter case, death row inmate Charles Campbell challenged the constitutionality of Washington's law requiring death by hanging. In his habeas corpus petition, Campbell alleged that hanging violated the Eighth Amendment's guarantee against cruel and unusual punishments. Hanging involves the infliction of unnecessary pain, he pled, relying primarily on a legislative trend disfavoring the use of the gallows. He emphasized that only two states, Washington and Montana, allowed hanging. The Ninth Circuit rejected Campbell's constitutional attack. The court ruled that hanging does not involve "lingering death, mutilation, or the unnecessary and wanton infliction of pain." Hanging causes "rapid unconsciousness and death," the court said.[20]

Thus, in challenging the constitutionality of the gas chamber, the ACLU knew it faced an uphill battle. The Eighth Amendment had been interpreted as forbidding punishments of torture like beheading, disembowelment, and burning at the stake. However, American courts had never struck down a modern-day execution method. In attempting to show the torturous nature of lethal gas, the ACLU therefore presented its case through medical experts, execution eyewitnesses, and two former prison wardens—one of whom was Daniel Vasquez, who had presided over Robert Alton Harris's execution. California officials countered with medical experts of their own. Indeed, prior to trial, California Attorney General Dan Lungren had actually proposed, unsuccessfully, to commission a study by Michigan State University's College of Veterinary Medicine to help gather medical evidence that gas chamber executions do not inflict needless pain. The "colon balloon distension" study, to cost taxpayers an estimated $13,952, was originally proposed by Lungren in court papers filed with Judge Patel. The proposed study called for the insertion of balloons in the anuses of sixty rats, and for the balloons to be inflated until the rats squealed, with instruments measuring the decibel levels of the squeals. The tests would then be rerun after the rats had been injected with cyanide to try to establish any pain-killing benefits of this poison.[21]

At trial, the ACLU's medical experts testified that cyanide inhalation kills human beings by depriving the body's cells of oxygen. They described this cellular suffocation as analogous to death by drowning or strangulation. The experts further maintained that cyanide inhalation can cause tetany, a painful sustained muscular spasm. They concluded that a gassed inmate may remain conscious for several minutes while the execution is taking place. In contrast, the state's experts testified that unconsciousness occurs within at most thirty seconds of inhalation. They testified that cyanide gas quickly eliminates brain function, which causes a rapid loss of consciousness.

Against this backdrop of scientific debate, the ACLU presented numerous eyewitness accounts of executions. The ACLU introduced records made by San Quentin's medical personnel since 1937, as well as media and spectator accounts. The attending physicians at San Quentin recorded that it took anywhere from fifteen seconds to five minutes for "certain unconsciousness" to occur after lethal gas reached an inmate's face. Lay witness accounts confirmed that inmates often remained conscious for significant periods of time. Media reports of Robert Alton Harris's execution reported that Harris raised his head and looked around more than two minutes after he inhaled the lethal gas.[22]

Because the state agreed not to contest the ACLU's eyewitness accounts of Harris's execution, the ACLU never introduced into evidence the videotape depicting Harris's death. "If there was going to be any dispute about what people saw, we certainly would have been willing to introduce that videotape," said ACLU lawyer Michael Laurence. The videotape was thus never shown in court or made public. Indeed, the tape was later destroyed pursuant to an order issued by Judge Patel, who reportedly never watched the tape. KQED's lawyer, William Bennett Turner, strongly criticized the court's destruction order. "It's the only videotape of an American execution ever," he said. "I don't understand the reasons for its destruction."[23]

On October 4, 1994, Judge Patel issued her long-awaited ruling. Her seventy-two-page opinion declared that California's use of lethal gas was unconstitutional. She found that "inmates who are put to death in the gas chamber at San Quentin do not become immediately unconscious upon the first breath of lethal gas. . . . [A]n inmate probably remains conscious anywhere from 15 seconds to one minute." She further noted that "there is a substantial likelihood that consciousness, or a waxing and waning of consciousness, persists for several additional minutes." She concluded that during this time "inmates suffer intense, visceral pain, primarily as a result of lack of oxygen to the cells." She described this experience of air hunger as "akin to the experience of a major heart attack, or to being held under water."[24]

In interpreting the Eighth Amendment, Judge Patel explained that "the amendment is not tethered to modes of punishment that were thought to be cruel and unusual at the time the Bill of Rights was adopted." Citing controlling U.S. Supreme Court precedent, she wrote that the Eighth Amendment must be interpreted in a "flexible and dynamic manner." This approach lets sitting judges decide what punishments their own present-day society finds cruel and unusual and rejects the notion that the Constitution should be read as expressing only the expectations of the particular statesmen who wrote and voted for the Bill of Rights. In the U.S. Supreme Court's own words, the Eighth Amendment "must draw its meaning from the evolving standards of decency that mark the progress of a maturing society."[25]

Applying this approach, Judge Patel concluded that a "societal consensus" exists that death by lethal gas "is inhumane and has no place in civilized society." She emphasized the legislative trend toward lethal injection, noting that no state currently authorized lethal gas as the sole means of execution. She also found that states' legislative histories indicate that "the flight from gas" is influenced largely "by the belief that lethal gas is a cruel and inhumane way to put a person to death." The U.S. Court of Appeals for the Ninth Circuit later affirmed Judge Patel's ruling, holding that "[t]he district court's findings of extreme pain, the length of time this extreme pain lasts, and the substantial risk that inmates will suffer this extreme pain for several minutes require the conclusion that execution by lethal gas is cruel and unusual." Ironically, the U.S. Supreme Court, in refusing to address the merits of Harris's appeal, had allowed a man to die in the gas chamber, a punishment Judge Patel and the Ninth Circuit now found unconstitutional.[26]

After Judge Patel's ruling was released, California Attorney General Dan Lungren held a press conference at which he announced Judge Patel's order would be appealed. He called the ruling "a tragic day for victims of crime and their families." Governor Pete Wilson also criticized the ruling. He stressed that California's death penalty law—which, in response to the ACLU's lawsuit, was amended to authorize lethal injection—remained in place. "Killers have no place in society," he said. "I will do everything in my power to see to it that the people of California remain protected by the death penalty."[27]

Governor Wilson even tried to exploit Judge Patel's ruling for political gain. With less than five weeks before Election Day in his bid for re-election, Wilson linked Judge Patel to former California Governor Jerry Brown, the brother of his Democratic challenger, Kathleen Brown. Wilson's campaign manager, George Gordon, called Judge Patel "a dangerously lenient judge" and noted that Jerry Brown had appointed her to the Alameda County Municipal Court before President Carter elevated her to the federal bench in 1980. "As long as a Brown appointee remains on the bench, California's death penalty is not safe," Gordon maintained. Steve Glazer, a senior advisor to Kathleen Brown's campaign, responded by saying that his candidate "has nothing to do with Judge Patel so it's another example of Pete Wilson's effort to smear Kathleen Brown."

Earlier in the campaign, Kathleen Brown had held an emotional news conference at the old governor's mansion, where her father, Pat Brown, had agonized over death penalty cases. At the news conference, she told reporters that she was personally opposed to capital punishment "because my father taught me it was wrong and the religious experiences I had reinforced that." However, she pledged to enforce California's death penalty law because "the people and the courts have spoken." Brown added that she agreed with Governor Wilson's decision not to commute Robert Alton Harris's death sentence. The old governor's mansion was chosen as the site for the forty-five-minute press conference to remind voters that Kathleen Brown's father had opposed capital punishment but nonetheless had let thirty-six people go to the gas chamber in his eight years as governor. Wilson found the mansion "an interesting choice" for Brown's news conference because it would remind voters "who may have forgotten that her father in the exercise of his conscientious view" commuted twenty-three death sentences. Wilson suggested that, if Kathleen Brown were elected, she would use the governor's clemency powers to spare the lives of death row inmates. Pete Wilson won the election.[28]

Ruminations on the Harris Case

The saga of Robert Alton Harris and the legal battles surrounding his execution draw into focus several aspects of capital punishment in

America. First, executions are conducted in private, and governmental officials clearly want to keep it that way. Many members of the press are excluded from watching executions, and the prospect of televised executions is unthinkable to most governmental officials. Second, executions are frequently performed at night. Although Harris died shortly after sunrise, his execution was originally scheduled for 12:01 A.M. Only a series of last-minute stays prevented Harris from dying in the middle of the night.

Third, the U.S. Supreme Court is anxious to speed up the execution process. The members of the Court are fully aware that many convicted killers are spending several years on death row before being executed, and the Justices are trying to reverse that trend. The eighteen inmates executed in 1985 had been on death row an average of five years and eleven months, while the fifty-six men executed in 1995 had spent an average of eleven years and two months on death row. The Supreme Court will no longer tolerate last-minute appeals, as evidenced by its unprecedented order enjoining the lower federal courts from further interfering with Harris's execution. Finally, most politicians are equally anxious to capitalize on the growing popularity of capital punishment, as reflected in public opinion polls showing that around 70 percent of Americans favor capital punishment. These public officials view their pro–death penalty stances as a way of demonstrating their ability to "get tough" on crime.[29]

The rest of this book grapples with the history and politics of capital punishment in America and the questions raised by Robert Alton Harris's execution. Why are executions generally conducted at night and behind thick prison walls? What explains the U.S. Supreme Court's desire to expedite death penalty appeals? Why are politicians quick to trumpet the use of capital punishment, yet so reluctant to let Americans watch executions? Should cameras be allowed into execution chambers? And finally, are laws and regulations barring television cameras from execution chambers constitutionally permissible?

2

Public Executions in America

In Public Commons, on Gallows Hills

Public executions were once a fixture of American society. Such spectacles usually took place in the afternoon in the public square and were designed as "an awful and effecting demonstration of the danger of sin." Many counties had hangings on so-called gallows hills or at the bottom of ravines so that the entire community could watch them, and some localities even purchased the surrounding land because "the concourse of spectators at public executions was so great that the property of individuals was necessarily trespassed upon." Literally thousands of people—including "[e]ntertainers, vendors, pick-pockets, promoters, evangelists, sight-seers, peddlers and medicine men"—turned out at public hangings. On May 19, 1837, an estimated twenty thousand people gathered in Philadelphia to watch nineteen-year-old James Moran hang from the Bush Hill gallows. The afternoon hanging of John Lechler on October 25, 1822, in Lancaster, Pennsylvania, drew between twenty and thirty thousand people. And over ten thousand people attended the hanging of Samual Godfrey on February 18, 1818, in the tiny hamlet of Woodstock, Vermont. When an execution took place, pamphlets and broadsides containing the dying confessions of the condemned criminal were sold to disseminate the execution day message throughout the community.[1]

Early Americans traveled great distances to attend public hangings and sometimes even camped out for days in advance to ensure a good view. For example, on March 1, 1861, Henry Kriegler was hanged "on the Commons" in the Village of Albert Lea, Minnesota, before an estimated crowd of between thirteen hundred and two thousand people. Despite "clouds and fog and melting snows," people traveled "some twenty, thirty, and some fifty miles to witness the execution." In fact, the hordes of people who flocked to executions were greatly disappointed if they arrived late or missed them. One account reports that "[a]n old woman walked near seventy miles to see the execution" of William Welsh in 1784. "Being fatigued, a little before the execution, she fell asleep and did not wake up until it was over, when she cried most bitterly."[2]

Public executions were attended by all members of the community regardless of social class. As three scholars who have studied Texas's public executions have written, "These hangings were by design a public show, 'carefully arranged beforehand and attended not only by the rabble, but by persons of rank and fashion, of intelligence and sensibility.'" Women and children were no exception. On June 19, 1857, in Chicago, Illinois, five to six thousand people "of every age, sex, color and condition" crowded the streets to watch William Jackson hanged. According to one account, "Excited mothers and fathers boosted their small children high over their heads so the youngsters could get a better look as the condemned man . . . mounted the platform." Before Israel Wilkins was hanged in Amherst, New Hampshire, in 1820, "youngsters were called in from the playing field to prepare to go to the hanging."[3]

At some public executions, military personnel were necessary to preserve order or proclamations were issued to deter alcohol consumption. For example, when John Lechler was hanged, the mayor of Lancaster urged tavern owners "for their honour . . . to prevent gambling, dancing and all immoral transactions within their houses." Likewise, the preservation of public order was a major concern at what remains the largest mass hanging in U.S. history, when thirty-eight Dakota Indians were hanged on December 26, 1862, in Mankato, Minnesota, for their participation in the Dakota Conflict of 1862, which claimed the lives of over five hundred white settlers. A large number of troops were brought into Mankato in anticipation of the mass hanging, and an order was widely circulated proclaiming that the executions would occur in the public square at 10:00 A.M. Martial law was imposed, and all intoxicants were banned until a day after the hanging for fear of a "serious riot or breach of the peace." A "vigilant patrol" was organized to enforce this ban, with violations punished by "the immediate seizure and destruction of all the liquors of the offender."[4]

On execution day, the Dakota Indians began chanting their death songs early in the morning. This ritual continued while their arms were bound with cords and white caps were placed on their heads. At around 10:00 A.M., the thirty-eight prisoners were ushered to the diamond-shaped scaffold, designed to hang ten prisoners on each side, now surrounded by more than fourteen hundred soldiers. Three thousand curious citizens crowded the streets, occupying all eligible places, including rooftops. While chanting their "Hi-yi-yi" death song, the prisoners ascended the gallows, and the caps were rolled down over their faces. At the third drum roll, William Duley, a Dakota Conflict survivor, cut the triggering rope. Almost instantaneously, all but one of the thirty-eight men were suspended by the neck. The man whose rope broke was immediately strung up again. As the drop fell, there was "one, not loud, but prolonged cheer" from soldiers and citizens alike.[5]

County sheriffs in early America did little to discourage attendance at hangings. As law professor Michael Madow has written, local officials "deliberately arranged the proceedings to enhance, if not maximize, their public visibility." These spectacles, Madow concludes, were "organized on the theory that the larger the number of people who witnessed an execution the greater would be its salutary deterrent effect." The only thing that was sometimes kept secret at early American executions was the executioner's identity. At some executions, professional executioners wore disguises or hideous masks or had their faces blackened, and were generically called "Jack Ketch" after a famous seventeenth-century English hangman. In preparation for their grim task, hangmen were occasionally furnished with "strong drink to bolster up their courage."[6]

Civil Ceremony, Religious Event

According to historian Louis Masur, public executions served two functions: one civil, one religious. "As a civil ceremony," Masur writes, "the execution exhibited the authority of the state. It sought to bolster order and encourage conformity to a republican code of social values." Thus, the overarching civil theme of execution day was "the preservation of order," with public executions designed "as a demonstration of the power of government and a warning to those who violated the law." Society must punish, one minister explained, "for the great purpose of preserving, in peace and safety, our property, our life, our civil and sacred rights and privileges." Another person feared the consequences of social disorder without executions: "In civil society, the wicked would walk on every side, and the cry of the oppressed be in vain, the foundations be destroyed, confusion and misery would prevail were punishment, capital punishment, never inflicted."[7]

"As a religious ceremony," Masur explains, "ministers used hanging day to remind the crowd of its own mortality and to demonstrate that God alone could redeem the sinful." Thus, the "religious meaning" of public executions focused on "the eternal life of the condemned," and on spiritual leaders conveying a message of repentance to the execution day crowd. As Masur finds in his book *Rites of Execution,* "Ministers instructed spectators that the truly penitent could earn salvation." "By linking the crowds with the criminal," Masur writes, "preachers tried to persuade the spectators at executions to see themselves as participants in the ceremony who were required to alter their ways." On hanging day, spectators were urged to "be afraid of sin, and a life of ungodliness." One pastor, Nathan Strong, preached a particularly directed message to his congregation: "Unless we repent, we shall all likewise perish."[8]

At public executions, condemned criminals were frequently encouraged and cajoled by religious authorities to convey a message of penitence and redemption. Oftentimes, so manipulated, the prisoners' last words to the gathered crowd served as warnings that buttressed the ministers' sermons. One criminal hoped that "all people will take warning by my evil example and shun vice and follow virtue." The vices that led to his "ignominious death" included "bad company, excessive drinking, . . . swearing, shameful debauchness, disobedience to parents, [and] the profanation of the Lord's Day." A teenager executed at Dedham, Massachusetts, similarly implored the crowd with his dying words: "Do not cheat—Do not steal—Do not lie—Do not commit adultery—Especially, do not destroy virgin innocence—and, above all, do not kill." Another teenager hoped his "unhappy Fate . . . will be a Warning to all young Men to abstain from excess of Liquor, bad company, and lewd women, which have brought me to this untimely end."[9]

The mutually reinforcing interplay of the civil and religious themes of execution day is evident in many execution ceremonies. On the afternoon of October 20, 1790, a twenty-two-year-old black man, Joseph Mountain, was executed before a crowd of thousands in New Haven, Connecticut. Before the execution, Mountain was led from the jail to the First Church, where Reverend James Dana delivered a sermon entitled "The Intent of Capital Punishment" to a packed assembly. His words were taken from Deuteronomy: "So shalt thou put evil away from among you. And those who remain shall hear and fear, and shall henceforth commit no more any such evil among you." He then preached directly to the prisoner. "In about three hours," he told him, "you must die—must be hanged as a spectacle to the world, a warning to the vicious." After the church service, a large procession led Mountain to the gallows in New Haven's public green. The condemned man walked to the gallows with a coiled rope around his neck, accompanied by the sheriff and his deputies on horseback. A cart containing a coffin followed Mountain, as did a throng of people. Once at the gallows, the sheriff read the death warrant and a chorus sang hymns. A white cap was pulled over Mountain's face by the sheriff before the prisoner was "launched into eternity."[10]

In November 1825, seaman James Reynolds, who had murdered his ship captain, was likewise publicly hanged in New York City. As one newspaper reported, starting at 9:00 A.M. on execution day crowds of people gathered near the Lower Manhattan prison in which Reynolds was confined. By 10:00 A.M., an infantry battalion and a company of dragoons had arrived to ensure order. Reynolds, dressed in white trousers and a matching white frock and cap with black trim, was led into the prison yard thirty minutes later. After Reynolds was seated on a small stage, the prison chaplain gave a "very solemn and affecting" sermon to which Reynolds "listened attentively" throughout. When the prison service had concluded, a procession led by the sheriff and his deputies on horseback ushered Reynolds out of the prison yard. Joined by the military guard and a wagon bearing an empty coffin, the procession took more than an hour to traverse the over two miles to the execution site. At the scaffold, the sheriff read the execution warrant, and Reynolds warned the crowd to heed "the awful spectacle" and "shun the paths of vice." Two clergymen addressed "the multitude" before the drop fell at 12:45 P.M., ending Reynolds's life.[11]

At John Stone's execution in Chicago on July 10, 1840, nearly two hundred "citizens on horses, and about 60 armed militia assembled at the public square . . . as a guard to accompany the prisoner to the place of execution." Accompanied by law enforcement officers, Stone rode in a four-horse carriage with the officiating clergyman, Reverend Hallam of the Episcopal Church. After the procession traveled three miles to a spot on the lakeshore and Reverend Hallam performed a "solemn" church service, the death warrant was read aloud at about 3:15 P.M. A cap was then pulled over Stone's head, and, still protesting his innocence, he was "swung into another world [while] the lakefront crowd gaped in amusement." In contrast to these elaborate ceremonies, modern-day executions are largely without pomp and are usually over in a matter of minutes.[12]

Unintended Consequences

Although public executions were well orchestrated, they did not always go as planned. Sometimes they were botched because the rope broke or some other mishap occurred. At the last public hanging in Cooperstown, New York, on December 27, 1827, a stand erected for spectators collapsed, killing two people and injuring others. Moreover, public executions did not always serve their intended purposes, with anecdotal evidence abounding that such hangings did not deter, but only incited, criminal activity. After observing John Lechler's execution in Pennsylvania, "[f]ifteen persons were committed to prison, one for murder, one for larceny, the rest for vagrancy." The murderer was John Wilson, who stabbed a man in a drunken brawl at a tavern after both men had just watched Lechler hang. Similar stories are abundant. In 1894, Kansas City resident Martin Reed was hanged for slaying his wife, and five years later, his son was hanged from the same gallows for killing his girlfriend. An experienced hangman, Sheriff George Swearingen of Cumberland County, Maryland, was also hanged from his own gallows for murdering his wife in 1829. In Ohio in 1836, "on the day on which a man was executed for the murder of his wife, under circumstances of particular cruelty, another man, near the place of execution, murdered his wife in the same manner." One writer went so far as to conclude that a "hundred persons are made worse, where one is made better by a public execution."[13]

Many people actually opposed public executions based on the widespread belief that such spectacles caused more crime. Anti–death penalty advocate Marvin Bovee wrote in 1878: "The law of capital punishment, when executed, can have no other effect upon the criminally-inclined than to arouse the bloody instincts, and to excite those baser propensities which are the dark precursors of bloody deeds. . . . The testimony is overwhelming, that the gallows ever incites to crime, and is, in no case, promotive of virtue." Skull-measuring practitioners of the "science" of phrenology, which enjoyed significant popularity in the nineteenth century, lent credence to this view. In his 1847 essay *Thoughts on Capital Punishment,* phrenologist George Combe wrote that the "bloodthirsty man becomes excited by executions." Combe concluded that "the direct effect of witnessing acts of killing . . . is to stimulate the desire to kill in those in whom the propensity is naturally strong; and that hence executions operate as the natural fuel of murders."[14]

Even if the hanging was not bungled by the county sheriff, other things often went wrong. For instance, condemned criminals frequently failed to accept their role on execution day. In 1797, a man named Young was hanged in New York City for killing a deputy sheriff who tried to arrest him for nonpayment of debt. Instead of acting penitent on the scaffold, Young "transformed the literary form of the dying speech and last confession into an attack on those who used credit to destroy the honest working man." Young's final warning was not to let one's papers fall into the "hands of those tolerated leeches that call themselves sheriffs' officers." Many other condemned men also chose to "die game," an expression that meant to go to the gallows in a "joking, unrepentant, defiant, or indifferent" manner.[15]

On some occasions, execution day crowds also misbehaved by drinking alcohol, gambling, or engaging in other vices. Booths were commonly erected along the path of the execution day procession "for the sale of confectioneries, eatables and intoxicants," and curiosity seekers gathered around the scaffold. As one nineteenth-century commentator wrote about public executions: "Rioting, drunkenness, and every species of disorderly conduct prevail. . . . There is on most occasions that draw people together in large bodies, some attention to decorum, some regard to character, some appearance of feeling; but all these are banished for a time by the thousands who flock together to witness a public execution." Execution day, the commentator concluded, "blunts moral sensibilities . . . and brutalizes people by the barbarity of the example."[16]

These activities frequently turned public executions into public embarrassments. On December 29, 1854, a Dakota Indian named U-ha-zy was hanged on the outskirts of St. Paul. A former officer in the Mexican War, newly appointed territorial Governor Willis A. Gorman approved of the whole affair, at least initially. Just a day before the scheduled hanging, he denied a petition from forty of the "most respectable ladies of St. Paul" to pardon U-ha-zy. Invoking "duty to country," he wrote that he could find no just reason to commute U-ha-zy's sentence. The Dakota Indian had killed a white woman "without a shadow of excuse." She had been "murdered by the side of a poor, but no doubt fond and devoted husband," Governor Gorman proclaimed.[17]

However, Governor Gorman did not anticipate the public spectacle that would accompany the execution. One newspaper account reported that "Total Depravity" was out early in the morning on execution day. The night before, in fact, "Total Depravity appeared not to have gone to bed at all." That night, sleeping residents were "frequently disturbed by the firing of guns and pistols" around the jail where U-ha-zy had been confined for two years. By 9:00 A.M., Ramsey County Sheriff Abram M. Fridley appeared a "strong friend of Total Depravity," for he started erecting the scaffold in one of St. Paul's most public places. The boisterous crowd applauded the sheriff's actions, and cheered loudly at learning that the law did not prohibit public hangings. "Crucify him!" the mob cried out.[18]

Only through the "determined interposition of Gov. Gorman and many right minded citizens" was the gallows taken down from the center of St. Paul. The execution, urged city authorities, simply could not take place within the public quarter. Eventually, Sheriff Fridley relented, and the crowd marched with "great pomp and noise" behind the sheriff and the prisoner to an uninhabited prairie. "Men, women and children thronged the gallows on St. Anthony Hill, and followed the victim with howls and cheers as though it was to be a delightful entertainment," reported the *St. Paul Pioneer*. After the scaffold was reerected, U-ha-zy was hanged at around 3:00 P.M. According to one newspaper account:

> Liquor was openly passed through the crowd, and the last moments of the poor Indian were disturbed by bacchanalian yells and cries. The crowd revealed the instincts of brutes and was composed of ruffians. A half drunken father could be seen holding in his arms a child, eager to see all; giddy, sense-less girls and women chattered gaily with their attendants, and old women were seen competing with drunken ruffians for a place near the gallows.

The crowd left the scene "satisfied and in high glee."[19]

Newspapers later condemned the public spectacle created by U-ha-zy's execution. The *Minnesota Republican* reported that the hanging represented a "disgusting" scene, and the *Daily Minnesota Pioneer* remarked on the "barbarity" displayed by those in attendance. These "fiends incarnate" disturbed U-ha-zy's final moments with "laughs and jeers," and the "debauched in the crowd" acted "much more like savages" than the condemned man. The editors of the *Daily Minnesota Pioneer* concluded that "[s]uch conduct should be frowned upon by every lover of decency in the community." Likewise, the *Daily Minnesotian* declared that no future attempts should be made "to hang even a dog in the public streets of St. Paul" or in "any other civilized town or city." "The sooner the scenes connected with that transaction are forgotten," the *Daily Minnesotian* wrote, "the better for the reputation of St. Paul and all Minnesota." Although public executions were not prohibited by law in Minnesota until 1889, many American states had already passed laws requiring executions to be conducted away from public view by the time of U-ha-zy's hanging in 1854. The transition from public to private executions began in the 1830s and was completed in the 1930s, when America's last public executions took place.[20]

The End of Public Executions

A dispute has arisen about the site of America's last public hanging. Some people claim that Roscoe Jackson, hanged on May 21, 1937, in Galena, Missouri, before fifteen hundred spectators, was the last person publicly executed in the United States. Jackson had killed a traveling salesman, Pearl Bozarth, after Bozarth picked Jackson up in his automobile. However, Jackson's hanging was not public, at least not technically speaking. The execution took place inside a high, forty-foot-square stockade, and only people with special passes were admitted. Some spectators came from as far away as Arkansas and Oklahoma to purchase tickets to attend the hanging.[21]

The last truly public execution in America took place in Owensboro, Kentucky, on August 14, 1936, when a twenty-two-year-old black man, Rainey Bethea, was executed for allegedly assaulting and murdering a seventy-year-old white woman. Although state law made it optional with county officials as to whether the hanging be public or private, officials decided on a public hanging without announcing their reasons. Between ten and twenty thousand "jeering" and "festive" spectators, some perched on a telephone pole to get a better view, watched as a prayerful Bethea was executed on Owensboro's "pit and gallows."

The hanging of Rainey Bethea in Owensboro, Kentucky, in 1936. This was the last public execution in the United States. (Acme News Photo, UPI/Corbis-Bettmann)

Crowd members, who were predominantly if not all white, shouted, "Take him up! . . . Up on the scaffold where we can see him! . . . Let's go!" Once on the gallows, an execution assistant bound Bethea and slipped a black hood on him. The county sheriff, Mrs. Florence Thompson, did not appear publicly before the crowd in the three-acre lot; it was a former Louisville policeman, Arthur L. Hash, who sprung the trap. Despite the presence of guards who cordoned off the gallows, a few persons near the scaffold managed to grab bits of the hood as souvenirs after Bethea was pronounced dead at 5:44 A.M. The night before Bethea's execution, some spectators had participated in "hanging parties."[22]

Decades before Bethea's hanging in Kentucky, Michael Barrett became the last person publicly hanged in England on May 26, 1868. In that country, public executions used to be announced by the ringing of church bells and hawkers selling thousands of copies of execution ballads and "last dying speeches." The penny press, with its large circulation, also excited widespread interest in English executions by printing gory details about crime. State authorities at first embraced public executions. Indeed, from the days of King Henry VIII in the sixteenth century, when criminals were publicly boiled to death, conventional wisdom had it that "[t]he more public the punishments are the greater effect will they produce upon the reformation of others." Not only were murderers in England publicly hanged, but they were often sentenced to be publicly dissected in Surgeons' Hall, where spectators crowded the galleries. In other instances, the executed criminal's body was ordered to be hung in chains near the crime scene as a warning to others. Literally thousands of citizens would gather to watch the frequent public executions that took place at Tyburn, on Tower Hill, and later in front of Newgate prison. It is estimated that fifty thousand people were publicly hanged at Tyburn, one of England's most notorious execution sites. Only on rare occasions, when authorities feared rioting, were certain "ladies" and royalty hanged privately within the Tower of London.

However, all public executions were abolished in England in 1868, "largely due to official fear of the crowds," which were often unruly on execution day. At the execution of the "Five Pirates" in 1864, crowds swarmed into London "on foot, by omnibuses, and by the Metropolitan Underground Railway" to watch the hangings. According to one account: "Windows in the surrounding houses were filled with expectant faces and people were even clinging to chimney pots to the roofs of nearby buildings. Rented out upper rooms had been occupied by 'swells' who passed the night drinking and playing cards." Indeed, in the early and mid-nineteenth century, public executions were commonly attended by tens of thousands of spectators, among them "hordes of thieves and prostitutes." At a triple execution in England in 1807, there were so many spectators that "some fell, and others tumbled over them; till there were two or three heaps of persons in this situation, all struggling with each other to extricate themselves." Thirty people died, and fifteen others were injured. Similarly, in 1818, a riot ensued after the botched hanging of a robber.

Beginning in the 1840s, the concept of private executions was first seriously considered by English authorities. Most abolitionists fought the idea, believing that the advocates of private executions only sought "to prolong capital punishment by hiding its objectionable public example from view." One member of Parliament and an ardent abolitionist, Charles Gilpin, expressed particular disdain for private executions. "If hanging be acknowledged to be so unclean a thing that it is no longer to be tolerated in the broad sunlight," Gilpin argued, "the English people will have none of it." Instead of advocating what they called "secret murder" or "private strangulation," most abolitionists fought vigorously for a complete end to capital punishment. For example, William Ewart, who made the first proposal to abolish capital punishment entirely in 1840, acknowledged the "demoralizing" and "degrading spectacles" of public executions. However, he believed that private executions were "contrary to the genius of the constitution and the habits of the people." With the passage of time, though, some abolitionists came to favor private executions, either because they found public executions revolting or believed that private executions would bring them one step closer to total abolition.

The public execution controversy in England, and the abolitionists' growing ambivalence toward private executions, is vividly illustrated by a series of letters that novelist Charles Dickens wrote to London newspapers in the 1840s. In editorials written for the *Daily News* in 1846, Dickens denounced the "ribaldry, debauchery, levity, drunkenness and flaunting vice" at public executions and urged the total abolition of capital punishment. However, after watching the 1849 execution of Frederick and Maria Manning, the first husband-wife execution since 1700, Dickens wrote to the *Times* on November 14, 1849, to condemn public executions alone, and not to "discuss the abstract question of capital punishment." Dickens was shocked at the demeanor of the thirty thousand people who assembled to watch the double hanging, and because most abolitionists opposed private executions, Dickens's letter to the *Times* sparked enormous controversy. One abolitionist newspaper accused Dickens of being willing "to forego his well-known desire for the abolition of the death penalty altogether," and abolitionist Charles Gilpin invited Dickens to appear at an abolitionist meeting.

In replying to Gilpin's invitation, Dickens predicted that capital punishment would never be abolished in England and that the "right course" was to advocate private punishments that could be "solemnly inflicted." "We know," Dickens wrote to Gilpin, "what a fearful and brutalizing sight a public execution is, and when we know that we must do a great national service by bringing it to pass that such a sight shall never take place again." In another letter to the *Times* on November 19, 1849, Dickens publicly split with the abolitionists, whom he criticized as too dogmatic for being unwilling to accept anything less than total abolition. The abolitionists were outraged. The day after Dickens's second letter appeared in the *Times,* a large crowd of abolitionists assembled at the Bridge House Hotel and impugned Dickens's intentions. The meeting's chairman, Charles Gilpin, was emphatic that the friends of the movement would "never advocate assassination instead of public execution." After the crowd roared its approval, Gilpin read a letter from a fellow abolitionist, Richard Cobden, who urged those present to "take heed of the new dodge—private executions." William Ewart then addressed those assembled. Ewart spoke of his own repugnance toward public executions but said that abolitionists must reject private executions as an "evasion of the main principle for which they were agitating—the abolition of capital punishment without any qualification whatsoever."

Nevertheless, the proponents of private executions eventually prevailed. Although in 1841 only two members of the House of Commons supported the notion of private executions, when the bishop of Oxford proposed using America's system of private executions in 1856, the House of Lords created a Select Committee on Capital Punishment to

examine public executions. Testimony given to the Select Committee by
J. P. Kennedy, former Secretary of the Navy in President Fillmore's cab-
inet, aroused intense interest in America's new method of executing
criminals. Kennedy told the Select Committee that the use of private executions in many American states was so successful that this method
would soon be employed in all of the states. The Select Committee concluded that public executions had no deterring effect and recommended
that executions take place behind prison walls as they already did in
Prussia and the United States. The bishop of Oxford argued to his colleagues that in America, where the English system at first prevailed,
there had been substituted for it the method of carrying out executions
before prescribed witnesses. Although the bishop reported that there had
been some prejudice against this system at first, an eminent American
citizen had assured him that "there was not a single person present in
America who would return to the old system of conducting executions."
However, the Select Committee's report was condemned by English
abolitionists and conservatives alike. The *Times,* voicing conservative
opinion, accused the Select Committee of seeking to undermine the
English system of government "by doing away with publicity, one of the
cherished bulwarks of English freedom." Attacked from both sides, the
Select Committee's proposal went nowhere.

Following the sensational execution of the "Five Pirates" in 1864,
though, there was renewed interest in private executions. A Royal
Commission was appointed in that year to study the question of capital punishment, and that Commission recommended in an 1866 report
that executions be carried out within prison grounds. The current
Home Secretary, Sir George Grey, was particularly enamored of private
executions from hearing stories of successful accounts of them in America and Australia. "The letters which I have, as to America, state that a
certain number of persons are required to be present," Sir Grey reported, "and that the regulations there existing (and I believe the same
in the case of Australia) completely satisfy the public the executions
take place." Many people who testified before the Royal Commission
believed that newspaper reporters should still be permitted to attend
executions, although one professor believed that even the publication
of details of private executions would be demoralizing. Five members
of the twelve-person Commission, four of them vocal abolitionists, dis-

sented from the Royal Commission's recommendation to privatize executions. The four abolitionists on the Commission urged in a minority report that capital punishment be abolished at once.

Although the abolition of capital punishment was suggested by Charles Gilpin in 1868 as an amendment to the Capital Punishment Within Prisons Bill, that proposed amendment was defeated by a vote of 127–23, and the bill went on to passage. Abolitionists like Gilpin and Ewart, who had unsuccessfully introduced bills to abolish capital punishment in 1849, 1850, 1856, and 1864, had lost the support of some fellow abolitionists and conservatives who previously favored public executions. For example, abolitionist George Denman favored the Capital Punishment Within Prisons Bill to avoid "the horrible and disgusting scenes" of public executions and because he believed that private executions would guarantee the abolition of capital punishment. "It will not be long," Denman confidently predicted, "before public opinion will declare that a secret act of assassination within the gaol is not necessary nor expedient."

In his 1885 book, *The Punishment and Prevention of Crime,* Sir Edmund DuCane offered this explanation for the demise of public hangings in England: "It was decided after full consideration that the scenes at a public execution were so demoralizing that they could no longer be tolerated; they collected all the scum of the neighborhood, and were little less disgusting than the former practice of the procession to the distant place of execution." A more contemporary observer noted that "British society of the 1800s was particularly fearful of mobs as a social phenomenon." This scholar concludes that, because nineteenth-century crowds were "a symbol of lower class disposition and unrest," it is not surprising that public executions were outlawed in 1868 to bring "to an end the mobs of lower-class Londoners who gathered for executions." As another commentator, E. Roy Calvert, observed: "Each succeeding public execution became the excuse for an increasing debauch in brutality which eventually compelled the authorities to abandon the practice." Public executions were also abolished by the Canadian Parliament in 1869 after an unruly crowd gathered to watch the hanging of convicted assassin Patrick Whelan on February 11, 1869.[23]

Although executions were privatized in England and Canada in the late 1860s, capital punishment was not abolished in those countries until 1965 and 1976, respectively. This fact leads one to question whether the privatization of executions may only have perpetuated the death penalty in those nations beyond when capital punishment might otherwise have been abolished if executions had remained public spectacles. Obviously, one can only speculate as to the answer to this question. However, it is interesting to note that, at least in England, vigorous governmental efforts were made to prevent the public from getting access to reliable information about capital punishment once public executions were outlawed. Newspaper reporters were excluded from English executions beginning in 1888, and the Official Secrets Act was extended in the mid-1930s to prevent the disclosure of execution details by prison officials. Executioners were required to sign monetary bonds promising that they would not disclose "any information or particulars" about executions "to any unauthorized person."

English officials barred journalists from executions because newspaper accounts of hangings were considered harmful to public morals. In the 1920s, it was even suggested that Sunday papers that published information about executions be banned. Abolitionists, who had predicted that private executions would not correct the evils of public executions, concurred. As abolitionist Frederic Hill wrote, "the brutalizing effect of an execution is but diminished not banished" because newspaper accounts of executions are "eagerly read by all who are . . . attracted by baneful excitement." In 1929, a member of Parliament, W. J. Brown, actually called for the abolition of the death penalty because "sadistic" newspaper reports of executions only led to "imitative crime."

Confidential Home Office instructions even ordered English prison governors to be as brief as possible in any references to the way in which hangings took place. The Home Office instructions suggested standard responses to reporters' inquiries about an execution, like "[i]t was carried out expeditiously and without a hitch." When the Home Secretary was questioned about these instructions in the House of Commons in 1927, he made the disconcerting remark that "it is preferable to draw a veil over these cases." This remark was so disquieting because press coverage of executions had admittedly influenced public opinion. For example, former English executioner Albert Pierrepoint notes that "[i]t was in fact because newspapers were represented at executions, and reporters wrote their accounts without excessive reverence for the authorities, that the whole technique of hanging was improved." "When an execution was bungled," Pierrepoint wrote, "the newspapers had no hesitation in reporting it" and "it was the influence of newspaper reporting on public opinion and particularly parliamentary opinion which spurred the Home Office into much more serious research into instantaneous killing and the preparation of a standard table of drops, which was recommended in 1888."[24]

If public executions in England and Canada were prohibited because of their demoralizing and brutalizing influences and over concerns about out-of-control mobs, one naturally wonders whether public executions in America ended for similar reasons. Did Americans, like their northern neighbors or the English, find public executions to be demoralizing and threatening to the fabric of society? Or did state legislators in America have different or additional reasons for banning public hangings? Also, after catching a glimpse of English history, one is compelled to ask whether American abolitionists, like their English counterparts, resisted the passage of private executions laws? Or, in America, were abolitionists supportive or ambivalent about the enactment of such laws? The next chapter provides answers to these important historical questions.

~ 3

The Passage of
Private Execution Laws

The Doctor's Orders

Dr. Benjamin Rush, a signer of the Declaration of Independence, was one of the first Americans to advocate private punishments. In a speech delivered in Benjamin Franklin's living room in 1787 to the Society for Promoting Political Inquiries, Rush declared that "crimes should be punished in private, or not punished at all." A death penalty opponent, Rush was a citizen of Philadelphia, and his interest in private punishments grew out of an accidental meeting with a group of "wheelbarrow men." These Pennsylvania prisoners, who wore distinctive prison garb and had their heads shaved as a form of humiliation, worked on public projects like digging ditches or repairing roads. Rush scorned all forms of public punishments, including public hangings. "How often do we find pockets picked under a gallows, and highway robberies committed within sight of the gibbet?" Rush asked rhetorically.[1]

Because of Rush's activities, it is not surprising that the Pennsylvania Senate became the first legislative body in America to pass a resolution to "explore the propriety of executions in the prison yard." In February 1824, the Pennsylvania Senate entertained a motion that public executions were "inexpedient, highly demoralizing, and a great and unnecessary waste of public time and labor." The legislature's interest in the subject was sparked by John Lechler's hanging in Lancaster, Pennsylvania, in 1822, which drew as many as thirty thousand people. Although

Pennsylvania took no legislative action in 1824, states nearby soon passed legislation either encouraging or mandating private executions. In 1828, New York gave sheriffs the discretion to hold executions in prisons, in jail yard enclosures, or "in the manner heretofore accustomed." In 1830, Connecticut passed a law requiring the punishment of death to be inflicted "within the jail, or within an enclosed yard, so as to prevent public observation."[2]

In the next few years, five northeastern states—Massachusetts, New Hampshire, New Jersey, New York, and Pennsylvania—followed Connecticut's lead, enacting laws expressly prohibiting public executions. The Pennsylvania law, passed in 1834, required that death be inflicted "within the walls or yard of the jail" in the county of the criminal's conviction. The sheriff was permitted to select the witnesses, although he had to include at least one physician, the attorney general, and "twelve reputable citizens." A riot at an 1833 hanging in Mount Holly, New Jersey, fueled the call for an end to public hangings in some of these northeastern states. The passage of these laws ran counter to the long-standing European tradition of holding executions in public. Executions in Europe were only occasionally carried out in secret, as happened in 1672 when a council treasurer was beheaded in a small yard in Nuremberg, Germany, "probably because the Council did not wish the public to witness the disgrace of one of its officials." To deceive would-be spectators, a dummy scaffold was erected elsewhere.[3]

In New York, the first bill to abolish public executions was introduced in 1834, although public executions were not abolished until the following year. That bill was introduced by Assemblyman Carlos Emmons after attempts in 1832 and 1834 to abolish capital punishment had failed, and after it became clear that New York's 1828 law—permitting, but not mandating, county sheriffs to conduct private executions—was totally ineffective. The 1828 law had sought to "avoid the consequences frequently attending the parade of public executions" while preserving "the solemn and monitory example" of hangings, yet no sheriff had ever held a private hanging under that law. Sheriffs were too concerned with favoring certain towns with the business associated with public executions. Under Emmons's bill, which sought to end "the vicious assemblages and demoralizing tendencies of public executions," county sheriffs would no longer have the discretion to hold public executions.

Emmons's 1834 proposal to abolish public executions, however, was vehemently opposed by two legislative groups. One faction liked public executions and felt that the practice should be continued. Two legislators even asserted that private executions would not satisfy the public, which wanted proof that hangings were actually being carried out. The other faction was led by men, such as Samuel Bowne, who wanted to abolish capital punishment. Bowne argued that if executions were to exist at all, he wanted them to be public so "that their consequences and enormity might be more vividly impressed on the public mind." The disgust they produced would soon lead "to the entire abolition of capital punishment." Bowne's ally, Amasa Parker, concurred. He believed "public executions would be ultimately instrumental in abolishing capital punishment." Besieged on two sides, Emmons's bill never reached a final reading.

Although Emmons's proposal failed in 1834, Senator Ebenezer Mack renewed the fight to abolish public hangings in the next legislative session. On March 28, 1835, Mack proposed that a committee inquire "into the propriety of abolishing public executions." Most legislators now realized that there was little hope that county sheriffs would ever conduct executions away from public view on their own accord, as permitted by New York's 1828 law. Indeed, one state senator had recently failed to convince the Saratoga County sheriff to hold a private execution. The sheriff worried that a private hanging "would draw down upon him, the ill will of the multitude of grocers and tavern keepers and merchants who always anticipate great profits from these executions." At Senator Mack's request, the senate formed a committee to explore the propriety of abolishing public executions, and Mack delivered the committee's report ten days later.

Senator Mack's report first summarized what was seen as the best defense of public hangings: "that if punishments were privately inflicted, it could not be known whether they were actually, and justly and properly, inflicted upon the persons condemned, or that innocent persons had not become victims." Using phrenological principles, however, the report concluded that "public executions . . . are of a positively injurious and demoralizing tendency" and tend to "harden and brutalize the feelings of the populace, to familiarize them with scenes of blood, to incite disgust instead of terror or respect for the laws, and to increase offenses both in number and severity." After pondering whether execution spectators were simply those "whose animal feelings are to be excited," the report recommended that private executions be substituted for public hangings and that newspapers be used to disseminate execution day information. Newspaper accounts could be published by "respectable citizens who would attend the execution not as private spectators but as public witnesses," and these newspaper accounts would protect against any "evasion, perversion, or abuse" despite the absence of "ocular evidence" of the execution. That May, the senate easily passed a bill forbidding public executions, and the assembly, which rejected the total abolition of capital punishment earlier in the session, quickly concurred by a vote of 66–20. The enacted law, requiring "twelve reputable citizens" to witness executions "within the walls of the prison" and mandating the publication of a certificate of execution in "the state newspaper," took effect on May 9, 1835.[4]

Legislative reports from the 1830s through the 1850s provide further evidence of the original intent of private execution laws. One Massachusetts report, penned in 1836, states that "[t]he spectacle of capital punishments is most barbarizing, and promotive of cruelty and a disregard for life." It concludes that, after public executions, "the spectators go away with their virtuous sensibility lessened, their hearts more callous, and with less power of resistance, if any strong temptation shall urge them to a deed of blood." That report cites a New Hampshire execution where rioting caused "the death of a tender wife, daughter and mother." Another Massachusetts report written fifteen years later reached the same conclusion. "The baneful effects of public executions are not now generally denied," that 1851 report concluded, noting that "any amount of evidence might be adduced to show the positively injurious influence of such exhibitions."[5]

An 1841 legislative report that recommended the abolition of capital punishment in New York made similar findings. "The demoralizing effect of public executions on the public mind," the report observed, "is a fact to which a testimony perfectly unanimous seems to be borne by all who have given the subject any consideration." The report also answered why New Yorkers had already done away with public executions in 1835: "Why, when the object of the law is to strike the public mind with the terror of its infliction, why have we denied the public access to the fearful spectacle of its infliction, instead of endeavoring on the contrary to congregate the whole community to witness the scene? The chief answer is, that it tends to harden and brutalize the hearts of men." An 1835 legislative report from Maine also complained about the "drunkenness and profanity" at public executions and the persons "who came to profit by the solemn scene" of such spectacles.[6]

Abolitionists and Privatization

In 1839, Mississippi became the first southern state to pass a private execution statute, and in the next two decades, thirteen states—Alabama, California, Delaware, Georgia, Illinois, Indiana, Iowa, Kansas, Maine, Michigan, Ohio, Vermont, and Virginia—all passed their own private execution laws. Many of these laws required county sheriffs to invite twelve "reputable" or "respectable" citizens to attend hangings. Although private execution laws usually forbade public hangings, the laws of the three southern states—Alabama, Georgia, and Virginia—merely gave the trial judge or the sheriff the discretion to make an execution private. Georgia's law, for instance, allowed the sentencing judge to order "the execution to be in public, if he sees proper." Those three southern states would not mandate private executions until the end of the nineteenth century.[7]

The 1830s through the 1850s, when many states passed private execution laws, was the height of America's abolitionist movement. Governors and legislators pushed for the abolition of capital punishment, special legislative commissions were formed to consider the issue, and anti-gallows societies were organized in the mid-1840s in Massachusetts and New York. A national organization, which elected U.S. Vice President George M. Dallas as its leader, was started in 1845. By the 1850s, anti-gallows societies also existed in Alabama, Indiana, Iowa, Louisiana, Ohio, Pennsylvania, and Tennessee. A member of the Massachusetts anti–death penalty movement, Reverend Charles Spear, even founded a weekly paper for agitation purposes called the *Hangman*. These efforts produced successful results. Michigan became the first state to abolish capital punishment in 1847; Rhode Island and Wisconsin abolished the death penalty in the early 1850s.[8]

Many abolitionists actually fought to outlaw public executions, seeking to deprive death penalty proponents of the argument that capital punishment deters violence. As an 1851 Massachusetts legislative report logically concluded, the privatization of executions was "a virtual abandonment of the argument that capital punishment is calculated to deter from the commission of crime." The 1841 New York legislative report, which recommended the death penalty's abolition, concluded that the abolition of public executions was a "very proper reform." However, that report emphasized that conducting executions in private merely diminished "their demoralizing tendency . . . in degree." It concluded: "[A]ll the arguments of policy and humanity which dictated to our legislation the abolition of the public spectacle of the execution of a fellow-creature, command us to go forward, and consummate the same wise and humane movement thus begun, by the total abolition of the execution itself."[9]

In fact, as Marvin Bovee's biographer writes, "Making hangings private affairs was often used as an entering wedge [by abolitionists] to take more sweeping action." As that biographer notes, Bovee, a Wisconsin state senator who led that state's fight to abolish capital punishment and who became a national abolitionist leader, crusaded against capital punishment in Illinois in 1859. Many anti-gallows petitions were generated, but the Illinois legislature only passed a bill abolishing public executions, prompting Bovee to comment that "[t]his was a point gained, but not all that was desired." Seven years later, Bovee penned an open letter to Illinois Governor Richard Oglesby in a Chicago newspaper stressing that, by abolishing public executions, Illinois had "tacitly admitted its failure to minister to the moral welfare of her people." Echoing the same sentiments as the 1841 New York legislative report, Bovee's letter continued:

> [I]f the death penalty, as some allege, possess a restraining influence upon the vicious, why not erect the gibbet in your public marts, and beside your churches, that the rising generation may profit by the moral lessons which the friends of the gallows claim it inculcates? But, sir, we are all too well aware of the debasing influence and demoralizing effects of public executions, and what is true of these public executions is also true of private executions, only in a lesser degree.[10]

Although America's abolitionist movement of the 1830s through 1850s had many prominent supporters and much strength, the bloodiest conflict in U.S. history, the Civil War, stopped the abolitionist movement in its tracks. That war claimed the lives of over 600,000 men, and soldiers were routinely executed in public for desertion. It is hardly surprising, then, that historian David Brion Davis finds "no mention of capital punishment in the legislative journals" during the Civil War. As Davis writes, "It was difficult for rationalist reformers to preach against the violence of capital punishment when reformers themselves advocated the shedding of blood." Abolitionist Marvin Bovee even delayed publication of his book *Christ and the Gallows* until 1869—four years after the Civil War ended. The publication date had originally been slated for 1861, but the Civil War broke out before the book was ready for printing. "To have presented a work of this kind during the continuance of such a struggle would have been 'ill-timed,' to say the least," Bovee wrote in the book's preface when it was finally published. As David Brion Davis concludes, after the Civil War, "men's finer sensibilities, which had once been revolted by the execution of a fellow human being, seemed hardened and blunted."[11]

The end of the Civil War, however, did not mark the end of the passage of private execution laws. On the contrary, from 1868 to 1887, eighteen more states passed such laws in one form or another. Like their predecessors, many of these new laws required the attendance of a small number of "reputable" or "respectable citizens." A New Jersey statute enacted in 1878 permitted "twelve respectable persons" to attend executions and made sheriffs "liable to punishment as for a contempt of the court" if more persons than allowed by law were permitted to watch them. After the execution, the official witnesses were required to "unite in a report" setting forth "the time, place and manner of the execution." An unusual Kentucky law passed in 1880 allowed "not exceeding fifty persons" to attend executions, but specifically guaranteed that "[n]o fee shall be charged to any person or persons that are permitted to witness such executions." Pre-existing private execution laws also were amended or slightly modified during this time period or shortly thereafter. A Tennessee law enacted in 1889 added one new twist to that state's law by providing that the convict had to be "carried to the place of hanging in a covered vehicle, so that he may not be seen by persons outside the [execution] inclosure."[12]

New York's Gag Law

After New York banned public executions in 1835, executions there still attracted widespread public interest. At a hanging in 1842, a New York City prison "was literally besieged by a mob, blocking every street around it, all assembled not with the hope of getting admission, but to gaze eagerly at the walls that contained the miserable prisoner and to catch what rumors they could of what was going on within them." In another instance, in 1858, the roofs of the buildings overlooking the prison yard were "jammed with human beings, some of whom, clinging to the chimneys and railings, appeared to be in great danger of falling." Spectators paid anywhere from ten to fifty cents for the most coveted positions, which had only a "tolerable view" of the gallows. At subsequent executions, public officials often resorted to stretching a canvas awning over the gallows or stationing policemen on the roofs of buildings adjoining the jail yard to prevent would-be spectators from watching executions.[13]

New Yorkers' "morbid curiosity" surrounding executions, as well as a desire to find a more humane method of execution than hanging, eventually led to the creation of New York's Gerry Commission in 1886. That legislative commission, chaired by prominent New York City lawyer Elbridge T. Gerry, was appointed to investigate and report on "the most humane and practical method known to modern science of carrying into effect the sentence of death in capital cases." In its ninety-five-page report issued in January 1888, the Gerry Commission made several wide-ranging recommendations, the primary one being that criminals be electrocuted instead of hanged. The commission made this proposal because it considered death by electricity more humane than hanging and because electrocutions could be inflicted in a "strictly private" fashion. The commission also proposed that state prison authorities, instead of county sheriffs, conduct executions to effectively bar members of the press from attending them. This change would also be beneficial, the commission argued, because it would hinder the ability of the condemned criminal's friends from gathering outside the prison on execution day to "evince their sympathy for the condemned in a manner . . . discreditable to public decency and dangerous to the public peace."[14]

In addition, the Gerry Commission recommended several antipublicity measures aimed at stopping the "demoralizing tendencies" of executions. First, the commission proposed keeping the condemned inmate in solitary confinement from his arrival at the state prison until his execution date. No one would be allowed to visit him without a court order except his family members, his attorney, his physician, and a clergyman. By excluding reporters and members of the public from visiting condemned inmates, the commission hoped to end the "glorification" of murderers. Second, the commission recommended limiting to seven the number of "special deputies" the warden could have present at executions. In the past, county sheriffs had invited hundreds of friends, political cronies, and constituents to executions under the guise of their being "special deputies." These "deputies" had no responsibility at executions, and they usually just "lounged around, cracking jokes, smoking segars, and indulging in other festivities." Some of these invited guests even sold their tickets for "very tidy sums."[15]

Finally, the commission proposed making it a crime for any newspaper to publish the details of an execution. The commission railed against sensational newspaper articles that "always appear on the same day or the day following" an execution, giving lurid details "of the agonies and struggles of the dying wretch." The result is that "the execution, instead of operating as a deterrent, creates with many a vicious and morbid description, and has been known even to stimulate others to the commission of crime." Accordingly, the commission proposed that newspapers be limited to printing "a simple statement . . . to the effect that the sentence of the law had been duly carried into effect." The commission believed that this proposal, intended to contribute to the "moral and deterrent effect" of executions, would meet with the "hearty approval" of the press. In fact, the commission insisted that it was far from recommending legislation that would even indirectly curtail the liberty of the press.[16]

The Gerry Commission's recommendations were adopted almost verbatim by the New York legislature and resulted in the passage of the Electrical Execution Act of 1888. That law, which took effect on January 1, 1889, required that convicted criminals be electrocuted "within the walls of the State prison" or an adjoining enclosure. The law allowed the warden to have present at the execution "seven assistants or deputy sheriffs," and permitted the warden to select the time of the electrocution. However, the law specifically provided that "no previous announcement of the day or hour of the execution shall be made, except to the persons who shall be invited or permitted to be present" at it. The law further provided: "No account of the details of any such execution, beyond the statement of the fact that such convict was on the day in question duly executed according to law at the prison, shall be published in any newspaper. Any person who shall violate or omit to comply with any provision of this section shall be guilty of a misdemeanor."[17]

Some abolitionists like Marvin Bovee, who died in 1888, probably would have applauded the passage of New York's gag law, which restricted the publication of execution details. In his book *Reasons for Abolishing Capital Punishment,* Bovee wrote that the "horrid and disgusting details" printed in "newspaper accounts of executions . . . can subserve no good purpose." However, the New York press was outraged by the passage of the gag law. The *New York Times* wrote that the state should not have the right to regulate journalistic "decency" or "good taste" using criminal sanctions. The *New York Times* agreed that it would "probably be better for everyone if newspapers gave but a bare announcement of the execution of ordinary murderers." The paper argued, though, that certain executions—like that of President Garfield's assassin—were important historical events, and that it would be "despotic" and "absurd" to restrict newspapers' ability to fully report about them. The *New York Times,* concluding that it was impossible to draw a "hard-and-fast line" between these two categories of executions, believed that newspaper editors alone should decide what to print.[18]

On August 6, 1890, William Kemmler became the first person to die in New York's electric chair under the auspices of New York's new death penalty law. Although state prison warden Charles F. Durston tried to keep the exact date and time of the execution a secret, his efforts failed. Moreover, New York's newspapers blatantly ignored the gag provision of the state's new capital punishment law by printing detailed accounts of Kemmler's death. These accounts were based on statements extracted from eyewitnesses, as no newspaper reporters were permitted to watch the execution. Contrary to claims made by state physicians and official witnesses that Kemmler's death was swift and painless, these newspaper accounts reported that Kemmler's electrocution had been terribly botched. The *New York World* reported that Kemmler was "slowly roasted to death," the *New York Herald* believed Kemmler endured "death by torture," and the *New York Times* wrote that "no murderer of modern times [had] been made to suffer as Kemmler suffered."[19]

Although one editorial writer for the *Evening Post* had urged state authorities to prosecute "every New York editor who prints a fuller account of [Kemmler's] execution than the law allows," no prosecutions were initiated against violators of the gag law after Kemmler's electrocution. In fact, amongst newspapers, the *Evening Post* stood virtually alone in defending the gag law. For example, an editorial in the *New York Sun* proclaimed that "the publication by the New York newspapers of all the details concerning the awful death of Kemmler [was] one of the most valuable services which a free press ever rendered to the cause of civilization." Had this "foolish and unconstitutional" law been obeyed, the editorial concluded, "the horrible circumstances" of Kemmler's execution would have gone undisclosed.[20]

No newspapers would be prosecuted under New York's gag law until two weeks after four convicted criminals were electrocuted in Sing Sing Prison in the summer of 1891. At that quadruple execution, the prison warden made all of the official witnesses swear not to disclose what transpired in the death chamber. He also stationed guards and dogs outside the prison to keep reporters out and told the guards to shoot any reporter who attempted to cross a designated "dead line." Although no reporters were allowed inside the prison, the warden did agree to hoist a different color flag after each prisoner was electrocuted. The warden assigned a black flag to the sole African American prisoner, stressing that "it was good enough for a coon." Despite the warden's precautions, however, newspaper reporters easily persuaded eyewitnesses to break their oaths and reveal what had happened inside the prison. The resulting news stories reported that the electrocutions were "repetitions of the Kemmler horror," even though some official witnesses insisted that the executions had gone off "without a hitch."[21]

Because of the violations of the gag law, New York District Attorney DeLancey Nicoll sought an indictment against *New York Daily News* editor Charles Hennessey to test the constitutionality of the Electrical Execution Act's antipublicity provision. Nicoll announced that he disapproved of the ban on the publication of execution details, but he felt obligated to bring a test case to determine the provision's constitutionality. A week after Hennessey was indicted by a grand jury on July 23, 1891, and promptly arrested, Nicoll also secured a second indictment against James Gordon Bennett, the publisher of the *New York Herald.* That newspaper, delighted to have been indicted to enable it to defend the liberty of the press and the public's right to know, proudly ran the headline "THE HERALD INDICTED FOR PRINTING NEWS." Eight other New York City newspaper editors or publishers were later indicted by Nicoll, prompting a vigorous debate among journalists and lawyers as to the constitutionality of New York's gag law.[22]

Before any action was taken on the indictments, one of the indicted newspapers, the *New York Sun,* announced on August 3, 1891, that it would make the gag law a major issue in the upcoming November elections. The *Sun* urged that "every candidate for executive or legislative office" answer the following question: "Is he in favor of the gag law which now disgraces the statutes, or is he for its immediate and unconditional repeal?" Its editorial continued: "For any office from Governor down, the *Sun* is prepared to support the man who comes out squarely for free speech and unshackled newspaper press, as against the man who believes in the gag law." This strategy produced concrete results. On the same day the *Sun's* editorial appeared, the *Sun* published a front-page story reporting the responses of a dozen candidates and elected officials as to whether they favored repeal of the gag law. Not a single one opposed repeal, and the Democratic nominee for governor, Roswell Flower, specifically pledged to repeal the law if elected. A similar promise was later obtained from Jacob Fassett, his Republican opponent.[23]

After Roswell Flower won the election, he fulfilled his campaign pledge. In his first annual message, he asked legislators to repeal the gag law so that members of the public could secure "the most unbiased information" about New York's new method of execution: electrocution. He told legislators that "the adoption of so novel a method of inflicting the death penalty as electricity naturally excited world-wide attention and aroused both popular and scientific curiosity." The public's desire to know "the actual results of the experiment," Flower added, "did not spring from morbidity, but from wholesome interest." A week after this address, the Gerry Commission submitted a supplemental report reminding legislators that the chief purpose of the gag law was to prevent the "criminal classes," whose minds are easily "stimulated to fresh acts of violence," from reading the "disgusting details" of executions. The commission's supplemental report also opined that the gag law did not "restrain or abridge" the liberty of the press. The state legislature, however, quickly repealed the provision of New York's law making the publication of execution details unlawful. As a result, the indictments against New York City's newspapers for violating the now-rescinded gag law were dismissed by the New York district attorney. In fact, after the gag law was repealed, eight reporters were allowed to attend New York's next electrocution to satisfy public curiosity about this new mode of killing.[24]

The U.S. Supreme Court and Colorado's Gag Law

One year after New York's gag law was enacted in 1888, Colorado passed a similar law. That 1889 law required executions to take place "within the walls" of the state penitentiary in "a suitable room or place enclosed from public view." After arriving at the penitentiary, the condemned man had to be kept in solitary confinement until his execution date, and no person could see him except his counsel, his physician, and a spiritual adviser, and "then only in accordance with prison regulations." The warden was obligated to fix the date and hour of the execution within a one-week period, and the time fixed by him was to be "kept secret and in no manner divulged, except privately to the persons" invited to attend the execution. A maximum of eight official witnesses, along with "six reputable citizens," were permitted to attend the execution, although all execution spectators were required to "keep whatever may transpire thereat secret and inviolate." The law provided that "[n]o account of the details" of any execution, "beyond the statement of the fact that such convict was on the day in question duly executed," could be published "in any manner" in the state. Any person who violated the law was guilty of a misdemeanor and could be imprisoned for thirty days to six months or fined $50 to $500.[25]

After Colorado's gag law took effect on July 19, 1889, two convicted murderers, James Medley and James Savage, challenged the law's constitutionality. Both men had been convicted of murders that occurred before the gag law's effective date, but had been sentenced to death in accordance with the new law. Because the law imposed the new requirement that convicted murderers be kept in solitary confinement before being executed, Medley and Savage argued that it was an unconstitutional ex post facto law as applied to them. They also argued that the gag law was an unlawful ex post facto law because it imposed the new requirements that executions be "enclosed from public view" and that newspapers be prohibited from printing any execution details. Pointing out that the gag law contained a clause repealing Colorado's prior murder statute, Medley and Savage asserted that their death sentences were void and that they should be released from prison immediately. Medley and Savage argued that the gag law's repealing clause meant that they could not be retried for murder because the murder statute under which they had originally been convicted was no longer in effect.[26]

Not surprisingly, Colorado officials contended that the new gag law was not an unconstitutional ex post facto law, arguing that the law's new provisions did not unlawfully increase Medley's and Savage's punishment for murder after their crimes were already committed. The Colorado Supreme Court agreed, ruling that the gag law's requirement that prisoners be kept in solitary confinement did not impermissibly increase Medley's or Savage's punishment. The court emphasized that the gag law made provision for a condemned prisoner to be visited by family members, his attorney, his physician, and a clergyman. The Colorado Supreme Court also rejected the argument that the gag law was an impermissible ex post facto law because it required private executions and prohibited newspapers from publishing any execution details. The court ruled:

> It is a part of the public history of the State that prior to the passage of this act the death penalty with us was usually inflicted in public at a previously advertised hour, in the presence of a large concourse of people and the particulars of the execution published in the public journals. In deference to the wish of many good citizens who were of the opinion that the tendency of such proceedings was detrimental to the public morals, the recent statute was passed, requiring executions in the future to be conducted privately at the penitentiary, enjoining secrecy upon the few persons required or permitted to be present; and making it a misdemeanor pun-

ishable by fine for such persons to disclose the details of the
execution, or for the press to publish the same. To accomplish the desired change, it became necessary to change certain incidents connected with the punishment, but no attempt was made to change the punishment itself. This
remains the same as before the passage of the act.[27]

On appeal to the U.S. Supreme Court, Medley and Savage, making
the same arguments that they had made previously, argued that the Colorado Supreme Court's ruling was in error. Colorado officials, however,
continued to assert that the gag law was not an unconstitutional ex post
facto law. First, they reiterated that the law's solitary confinement provision did not increase the punishment for murder as the law actually
guaranteed prisoners the right to receive certain visitors. Second, they asserted that the privatization of executions did not unlawfully increase
the punishment for murder, making the following argument in the
state's appellate brief:

> [A]t no time and by no law has there been any direction or
> command that executions shall be public. All this is left to
> the discretion of the sheriff, who provides the place and
> manner thereof. That he may have been accustomed to make
> executions public, in no wise deprived him of the discretion
> to make them private, or to restrict the number of those who
> may be present. Before this objection could avail, in any
> event, it must appear that there was a legal right to a public
> execution. Had the law been changed in this particular
> alone, of providing for private executions, leaving all else un-
> changed, we conceive that this ground of challenge would
> never have been seriously entertained. But the reasons for
> the change are so clearly referable to penal administration,
> and not to change in the punishment, that no good reason
> can be assigned against the law.[28]

Colorado officials were equally dismissive of the argument that the punishment for murder had been unlawfully increased after Medley's and
Savage's crimes were committed because Colorado's gag law prohibited
newspapers from publishing any execution details. According to the
state's brief:

It is difficult to conceive how this objection affects the rights of the prisoner. Whether his execution be private or public, newspaper comments are so decidedly ex post facto, as to the particular occasion, that it can have not the slightest effect on the condition of the prisoner. Besides, it cannot be, and is not the policy or intent of this law, that acts of barbarism, cruelty or any other legitimate grounds of reprehension against the executioner, should forever be excluded from the cognizance of the proper tribunals, or to forbid that punishment be meted out to those guilty of unmerciful acts on so awful an occasion. Witnesses are required to be present for the purpose of seeing that the execution is entirely according to law. The inhibition is directed against the too common practice news-mongers have of parading sickening details under the disguise of enterprise.[29]

After reviewing these arguments, the U.S. Supreme Court found it "unnecessary" to examine the clashing contentions about whether Colorado's gag law was an unconstitutional ex post facto law because it privatized executions and prohibited the publication of execution details. The Court focused instead on the parties' arguments about whether the state's imposition of solitary confinement rendered the statute an unconstitutional ex post facto law. In this regard, the U.S. Supreme Court took issue with the Colorado Supreme Court's ruling, noting in its March 3, 1890, decision that the "matter of solitary confinement is not . . . a mere unimportant regulation." Indeed, the Court specifically ruled that solitary confinement is "an additional punishment of the most important and painful character, and is, therefore, forbidden by . . . the Constitution" as applied to Medley and Savage. Accordingly, the U.S. Supreme Court ordered that Medley and Savage be released from Colorado's state penitentiary. A strongly worded dissent lamented that two convicted murderers who deserved death were now being "turned loose on society."[30]

The first person executed under Colorado's new gag law, Noverto Griego, was not hanged until November 8, 1890. Although the state prison warden was "besieged by newspaper representatives without number for permission to be present," none whatsoever were admitted to watch Griego die. In accordance with the new law, the time fixed by the warden for the execution was kept secret—creating much speculation as to when the execution would actually take place—and the prison guards were "cautioned to keep the utmost secrecy." Indeed, only after the execution was it "readily ascertained who the witnesses were" by members of the press, who then obtained and printed detailed accounts of the execution in violation of the gag law.[31]

The Holden *Decision and Its Aftermath*

The same year that Colorado enacted its gag law, Minnesota passed a similar law authored by Minneapolis legislator John Day Smith. Dubbed the "midnight assassination law" by local newspapers, that law required that executions take place in jail yards or other suitable enclosures "before the hour of sunrise" and severely restricted the number of execution spectators. The John Day Smith law, as it was also known, also prohibited newspaper reporters from attending hangings and forbade newspapers from printing any execution details. Only the minimal fact that the execution occurred could be lawfully printed. Sheriffs or reporters who violated the law could be criminally prosecuted and fined or imprisoned.[32]

John Day Smith, author of Minnesota's "Midnight Assassination Law." (Minnesota Historical Society)

On December 8, 1890, in *Holden v. Minnesota,* the U.S. Supreme Court actually commented about the constitutionality of John Day Smith's "midnight assassination law." That case pitted the state of Minnesota against Clifton Holden, a man convicted of first-degree murder in Redwood County, Minnesota, on May 28, 1889. Holden's jury determined that he had shot a man in the head with a pistol in November 1888, and Holden was sentenced to death in February 1890 after the Minnesota Supreme Court refused to grant his request for a new trial. Holden's death warrant, mandating compliance with the provisions of the John Day Smith law, was issued by Governor William Merriam on May 21, 1890. That warrant directed that Holden be "confined" in the county jail until his execution date and that he be executed "before the hour of sunrise" in accordance with the Smith law.[33]

The issuance of Holden's death warrant prompted Holden's attorney, Charles C. Willson, to file a habeas corpus petition in federal court against the state of Minnesota asking for Holden's immediate release from prison. The petition asserted that the law in effect at the time Holden committed the crime of first-degree murder was death without any solitary confinement prior to execution. He then contended that the Smith law, which required solitary confinement before execution, was an unconstitutional ex post facto law, thereby voiding Holden's death sentence. In addition, Holden asserted that Smith's law contained a provision that repealed all prior inconsistent laws, arguing that this repealing clause granted him complete amnesty for any crime committed prior to the passage of the Smith law. That legal argument was not pure invention. The U.S. Supreme Court, after all, had recently decided that Colorado's 1888 death penalty law was an impermissible ex post facto law because it added solitary confinement as punishment for murder.[34]

In response to Holden's habeas corpus petition, Minnesota Attorney General Moses E. Clapp asserted that the Minnesota law under which Holden had been convicted "has never been repealed." Clapp further denied that Holden was being kept in solitary confinement, pointing out that Holden had been "permitted to mingle with the other prisoners during the daytime as freely as any person therein confined," and that "no restriction had been placed upon Holden's ability to receive visitors." After reviewing Holden's petition, the U.S. Circuit Court for the District of Minnesota denied Holden relief on July 3, 1890. The court held that Holden's death warrant "is not contrary to law or in violation of the Constitution of the United States, and that . . . Clifton Holden is not entitled to his liberty." That decision forced Holden to take his case all the way to the U.S. Supreme Court.[35]

In his appellate brief, Holden acknowledged that an "issue of fact in the Court below" was whether the law enforcement officials had "disobeyed" the John Day Smith law by giving him "the liberties of the jail." However, Holden found it unimportant whether or not he "had actually been kept in solitary confinement." The Smith law had "full force and operation," Holden argued, taking the position that "the actual manner of his imprisonment is irrelevant to the question in debate." To Holden, the Smith law—which Holden viewed as not unconstitutional in and of itself—impermissibly increased his punishment by adding solitary confinement, rendering the Smith law an unconstitutional ex post facto law as to his case. Thus, it was inconceivable to Holden that his jailor could, "by the manner of confining his prisoner, cause his execution or his discharge," making the jailor "a most important man in the administration of the criminal law." Also, Holden contended again that because the Smith law did not contain "a saving clause" to continue the repealed murder statute in force, he was entitled to amnesty.[36]

In his brief, Minnesota Attorney General Moses Clapp countered that the John Day Smith law did not repeal the law under which Holden was convicted of first-degree murder. Clapp further argued that the Smith law was not an unlawful ex post facto law, emphasizing that it "in no wise affects the pre-existing law as to the imposition of the sentence, but appertains wholly to the mode or manner of inflicting the penalty" for first-degree murder. The state's brief noted that the Smith law "breathes throughout its text a spirit in harmony with the greater light and broader humanity of the age," adding:

> With wise prudence, it seeks to forestall the gathering of the thoughtless disorderly mob too frequently an incident to such occasions; it strives to minimize the evils of too much publicity of such awful scenes, and excludes all representatives of the press; it is tenderly regardful of the abject condition of the accused, and assures him the ministration of friends and the consolations of religious advisors.[37]

After hearing oral arguments, the U.S. Supreme Court decided in Minnesota's favor. In its decision of December 8, 1890, the Court ruled that Holden failed to prove that he was actually being held in solitary confinement. His habeas corpus petition made this allegation, but the state denied it, and the Court could find "no proof in the record upon the subject." In addition, the Court found that the Smith law did not repeal the law under which Holden was sentenced to death. Although the Court flatly rejected Holden's arguments, it also briefly commented in dicta about the constitutionality of the provisions of the Smith law requiring private, nighttime executions. The Court stated:

> Whether a convict, sentenced to death, shall be executed before or after sunrise, or within or without the walls of the jail, or within or outside of some other inclosure, and whether the inclosure within which he is executed shall be higher than the gallows, thus excluding the view of persons outside, are regulations that do not affect his substantial rights.

The Court added: "The same observation may be made touching the restriction . . . as to the number and character of those who may witness the execution, and the exclusion altogether of reporters or representatives of newspapers." "These are regulations which the Legislature, in its wisdom, and for the public good, could legally prescribe in respect to executions," the Court declared.[38]

After the U.S. Supreme Court's ruling in *Holden*, several states passed laws requiring private executions. In 1893, Connecticut passed a law requiring executions to "be inflicted within the walls" of the state prison, and in 1898, Massachusetts enacted a law requiring executions to take place at the state prison "within an enclosure or building." In 1899, West Virginia and Idaho passed laws that required executions to be conducted within enclosures as to exclude "public view." Washington passed its own law requiring executions "within the walls of the penitentiary" in 1901, and New Mexico enacted legislation in 1903 requiring private executions that would be "not open to the public." In 1903, Oregon also passed a law requiring that "all executions should take place within the walls of the penitentiary, out of hearing and out of sight of all except officials." This law was necessary, Oregon Governor George Chamberlain asserted, because of the "demoralizing scene" at a public execution in Portland on January 31, 1902.[39]

Crimes and Misdemeanors

In 1906, three newspapers were prosecuted in St. Paul, Minnesota, for publishing detailed accounts of the botched hanging of William Williams in violation of Minnesota's "midnight assassination law." The antipublicity provisions of that law, passed in 1889 and making it a misdemeanor to publish any execution details, had gone unenforced for over sixteen years. The three newspapers fought the indictments, asserting that the law infringed on their constitutional rights to freedom of the press, and the case eventually ended up in the Minnesota Supreme Court. That court, which rejected the newspapers' legal challenge, found in 1907 that the "evident purpose" of the law was "to surround the execution of criminals with as much secrecy as possible, in order to avoid exciting an unwholesome effect on the public mind." As a result of the ruling, the three newspapers were found guilty of violating Minnesota's "midnight assassination law" and fined $25 each.[40]

The Minnesota Supreme Court's ruling sent a clear signal to the nation's lawmakers that laws permitting private executions and prohibiting the publication of execution details were constitutionally permissible. Thus, in 1908, Virginia passed a "progressive" law substituting electrocution for hanging as the method of inflicting death and moving all executions to the state penitentiary. The Virginia law permitted only "twelve respectable citizens" to attend executions and specifically provided: "No newspaper or person shall print or publish the details of the execution of criminals under this act. Only the fact that the criminal was executed shall be printed or published." In 1909, Washington also passed a law—which was not repealed until 1982—that made the publication of execution details punishable as "obscenity." That law was enacted in the midst of strong abolitionist sentiment. In fact, after unsuccessful efforts were made in Washington to abolish the death penalty in 1897, 1899, 1901, 1907, and 1911, the Washington legislature voted to abolish capital punishment in 1913.[41]

In the case of Virginia, historical evidence indicates that Virginians privatized executions in 1907 for three reasons. First, at least one Virginia legislator, echoing concerns expressed in the 1800s, believed that "it is a well-known fact" that public executions do not prevent crime. Second, some state residents felt that public executions were "demoralizing" and wanted to spare young or sensitive minds from "the horrible impression which is necessarily produced by . . . public executions." Finally, at least one state senator believed that private executions "would much more impress the imagination of the negroes." The *Richmond Times-Dispatch* flushed out this line of argument as follows:

The *Times-Dispatch* had long contended that the publicity,
the excitement and the general hurrah-and-holiday air attending the old-time hanging were a positive allurement to
the negro. His strong theatrical sense reveled in a final melo-
drama in which he was the conspicuous central figure. The
electric execution wholly does away with that. The time set
for turning on the death current is unannounced, the public
is rigorously eluded, and the whole affair is conducted with
secrecy and mystery, well calculated to inspire terror in the
heart of the superstitious African.

In contrast, a few state senators opposed Virginia's private execution law
because "local hangings served to impress the negroes, and in this way
to prevent more of the 'unmentionable crimes.'"[42]

The first person executed under Virginia's new law was Henry
Smith, who was electrocuted at the state prison in the early morning of
October 13, 1908. Smith, a twenty-two-year-old black man, had been
convicted of raping "an aged white woman." The exact hour of Smith's
execution was not made public in advance by prison superintendent
E. F. Morgan, and prison officials did not release any details about the
execution after it occurred. Superintendent Morgan "particularly en-
joined the jury of viewers to reveal but little of what they had seen," and
newspaper reporters were requested to abstain from revealing even the
names of the twelve citizens who saw Smith die. After the execution, officials only told reporters that there had been "no hitch." In the wake of
Smith's death, the *Richmond Times-Dispatch* correctly reported that
"[t]here is no penalty for violation" of Virginia's new law prohibiting the
publication of execution details. However, that newspaper pointed out
that "the press has observed the spirit, if not the letter, [of that provision]
for the wholesome effect it will unquestionably have in Virginia." The
paper emphasized that it had previously urged that "all prisoners be executed in the penitentiary, mainly for the reasons that it would free the
various communities of the excitement, the morbid curiosity and the
maudlin sentiment connected therewith."[43]

Although the *Richmond News Leader* believed that Virginia's gag law
was probably unconstitutional, that newspaper did not print any details
of Smith's execution, finding the law to be "right and wise." "We have a

very strong hope that the privacy . . . of the execution . . . will tend to make the law more terrible and to diminish crime," the paper editorialized. The newspaper added: "The death penalty was inflicted decently, secretly, mercifully, relentlessly. Let every citizen reflect how much better this is, how much more creditable to the dignity of the Commonwealth and the character of our people, than the noisy, hasty, lawless and bungling work of a mob."[44]

Following Virginia's lead, Arkansas passed a law in 1913 requiring convicted criminals to be electrocuted at the state prison. That law, recommended for passage by the Arkansas Sheriffs' Association and the Prosecuting Attorneys' Association, permitted only six to twelve "respectable citizens" to witness executions. In language identical to Virginia's law, the Arkansas law specifically provided: "No newspaper or person shall print or publish the details of the execution of criminals under this Act. Only the fact that the criminal was executed shall be printed or published." During house debate, one state representative argued in favor of execution publicity, which he said would have "the effect of checking crime." He asserted that "under the bill as drawn the public generally would not be informed as to what had been done." The bill's author responded that "publicity is not prohibited, as the facts could be printed and the details left out, and the people generally do not care for details of that kind of news." He pointed out that "the more progressive states had taken up the idea, which he declared to be a step forward." Another representative who favored the bill was opposed to capital punishment entirely but favored a "more humane" form of punishment "until that time comes."[45]

As in Virginia, the first person electrocuted under the new Arkansas law was a black man convicted of raping a white woman. The condemned man, Lee Simms, was executed on September 5, 1913, at the Arkansas State Prison before only official witnesses. Individuals who telephoned the penitentiary seeking invitations were refused admission. After the execution, the *Arkansas Democrat* merely reported that Lee Simms, "a negro, who criminally assaulted a white woman, in Prairie County July 28, was electrocuted at the State Penitentiary at 9:18 o'clock Friday morning." "Under the law passed by the last legislature the above is all the newspapers are permitted to publish," the newspaper declared. The *Arkansas Democrat* noted that it had sought an official opinion of the law from the attorney general's office, but that "that official has been out of the city for several days." The newspaper wrote: "The newspapers of the State have no desire to evade the law, but they are concerned in knowing just how far it is possible for the legislature to go in prohibiting the publication of news." The newspaper emphasized that a violation of the law, which was intended "to prohibit the publication of sordid details of execution," was punishable by up to one year in jail.[46]

Legislative attempts to pass death penalty gag or muzzle laws directed at the press were not always successful. A bill introduced in Michigan in 1889 to reinstate capital punishment and exclude all newspaper reporters from executions failed to pass, as did a bill introduced in Maryland in 1916 to forbid the publication of execution details. The Maryland bill would have made anyone who violated the law guilty of a misdemeanor.[47]

Censorship and State Control

Some county sheriffs took it upon themselves to conduct executions in a semiprivate manner even before the passage of private execution laws. For example, on March 6, 1868, farmer Andreas Roesch was hanged in St. Peter, Minnesota, for killing a neighbor's sixteen-year-old boy. At the governor's urging, a "close board fence, sixteen feet high," was built around three sides of the jail, with the gallows constructed within the enclosure. The county sheriff invited only law enforcement officials, clergy, and newspaper reporters to attend the hanging, and because he wanted it to be "as private as possible," the sheriff came for the prisoner earlier than anticipated. Despite his early arrival, approximately one hundred to three hundred people, some perched on house tops, had already gathered around the jail when Roesch was brought out at around 10:30 A.M.[48]

When Roesch fell through the scaffold trap, he "bounced back" when he reached the end of the rope, prompting some boys outside who were looking through the fence's cracks to shout: "He's twitched up," "He's gone," and "That's all of him." Because the hanging was "a good deal earlier than the country people expected it would be," it was not attended "by as many persons as it otherwise would have been." Although only forty people were admitted into the enclosure to witness the execution, newspapers went to great lengths to quickly disseminate the news of Roesch's death. The *St. Paul Dispatch* reported: "Our special correspondent was present at the execution, and by rapid driving reached Le Sueur with his report in time to telegraph it in full to this evening's *Dispatch*. This is but a moderate sample of the enterprise the *Dispatch* will display in gathering news for its readers." After the execution was over, many heavily loaded "teams" carrying disappointed would-be spectators were seen coming into St. Peter.[49]

Other executions were not so private, even though enclosures were built for them. When Anne Bilansky was hanged on March 23, 1860, in St. Paul, Minnesota, a fence was erected around the gallows in St. Paul's courthouse square. The notorious Mrs. Bilansky was convicted of killing her husband with arsenic to either marry or have "more unrestrained intercourse with her paramour," a young carpenter named John Walker. The building of the fence drew many curious onlookers, although the gallows-posts were still visible to people on the street when the structure was finished. In fact, spectators only a few feet above street level had "a fair view" inside the enclosure. No law required private executions, but the county sheriff decided to exclude the general public from the execution, and later would be applauded for "rendering the execution as private as the means at his command permitted."[50]

On execution day, the crowd assembled early in the morning. "[T]hey took possession of the stone piles, the roofs of the various buildings in the neighborhood, and every elevation which offered an opportunity of viewing within the enclosure." At 10:00 A.M., soldiers wearing heavy overcoats and fatigue caps marched into the square and, after a "great deal of trouble," cleared the crowd from the vicinity of the fence. A line of sentinels then formed, whose duty it was to keep all spectators at least twenty feet away from the enclosure. At 10:15 A.M., Mrs. Bilansky, wearing a black robe and a brown veil over her head, was led out of the jail. "Don't let a crowd see me," she pleaded with an escort before leaving the jail. "I am willing to meet my God, but I don't want to have a crowd see me die." The crowd outside, however, had already swelled to between fifteen hundred and two thousand people. The short procession from the jail to the enclosure, located just across the public square, would be anything but private.[51]

Once within the enclosure, the heads of those on the scaffold platform were visible to anyone at street level. Others, who had positioned
themselves atop roofs, carriages, and hay wagons, enjoyed an unobstructed view of the entire proceedings inside. In all, about one hundred persons, including twenty-five to thirty women, entered the enclosure. The women, "falling in the rear," had gained admittance
"before the gate could be closed." Some of them carried infants, who
"kept up an innocent crying, in unison with their mothers." Additional
crowd members, not gaining admittance, "ran the guard" to obtain positions at the fence. Through numerous small openings, these spectators were able to get "as good an opportunity of witnessing the execution as those inside enjoyed." Many women in the crowd attempted to
"run the guard," but they were usually turned back, and only "a few of
the 'tender sex' obtained the coveted position." After Mrs. Bilansky was
hanged, a few onlookers took pieces of the rope for mementos or as "a
remedy for diseases."[52]

Although county sheriffs once decided whether to hold public or
private executions, all of the states permitting capital punishment eventually adopted private execution laws, which should have ensured the
end of public and semipublic executions. However, public executions
still occasionally took place. For example, although an 1882 Maryland
law obligated sheriffs to conduct executions "in as private [a] manner as
possible," a 1902 execution in that state was open to the public. Likewise, although an 1859 Kansas law required private executions, at least
two public executions occurred in that state after that time. At one of
them in 1863, no attempt whatsoever was made to construct an execution enclosure, and many spectators, including "dozens of women,"
came to watch the noontime hanging. In other instances, county sheriffs admitted large number of spectators into execution enclosures.
When Richard Jackson was hung in a New York City jail yard six
months after New York's 1835 private execution law took effect, more
than five hundred persons were present.[53]

Public and semipublic executions were not fully curtailed in America until county sheriffs lost control over executions to state prison wardens. "With the growth of state penal institutions and the centralization
of penal authority after the Civil War," death penalty expert William
Bowers explains, "States began to require that all executions within their

boundaries be performed under state authority at a single state facility."
This movement, which began in 1864 when Vermont and Maine first
imposed executions under state authority, continued over the next century. In the 1890s, 86 percent of executions were performed by local authorities, but by the 1920s, nearly eight out of ten executions were conducted by state officials. When the nearly decade-long moratorium on
executions in America began after Louis Jose Monge was hung at the
Colorado State Prison on June 2, 1967, only two states, Delaware and
Montana, had not transferred the authority to perform executions to
state prison authorities.[54]

Private execution laws varied as to whether journalists were authorized to attend executions. Some laws—in places like Connecticut,
Ohio, and Pennsylvania—specifically authorized newspaper reporters to
attend executions, although other laws, like Alabama's 1923 statute, authorized the entry of only "such newspaper reporters as may be admitted by the warden." Still other statutes expressly forbade the attendance
of journalists or strongly implied that they could not attend executions
by not listing them among the statutory list of authorized official witnesses. However, these restrictions on press attendance were rarely enforced. For instance, newspaper reporters frequently attended hangings
in Minnesota after 1889, when reporters were statutorily barred from attending them, or creative journalists found ways to attend them in violation of the law.[55]

While American journalists were occasionally excluded from nineteenth-century executions, media representatives have traditionally been
allowed to attend such proceedings. For example, even though New
York's 1835 law did not include reporters in its list of authorized spectators, journalists were regularly admitted to New York prisons for hangings after 1835. Indeed, historical evidence indicates that "the New York
press succeeded in establishing for itself what might fairly be called a de
facto right of access to executions." Likewise, although California's 1858
law outlawing public executions did not authorize the attendance of
newspaper reporters at executions, journalists in that state also were routinely allowed to attend them. In other instances, journalists actually
fought legislative battles for the right of attendance. For instance, an
1879 New Jersey law did not authorize the attendance of journalists at
executions, but that law was amended in 1882 to require the presence of

two Associated Press reporters and "the accredited representatives of the local press of the county, not to exceed three in number."[56]

The Intent of Private Execution Laws

At least three factors led to the passage of private execution laws in America. First, public executions were outlawed for cultural reasons that sought to make executions more "civilized." As historian Louis Masur concludes, the abolition of public executions was the product of a growing "middle-class culture that dreaded vice, craved order, advocated self-control, and valued social privacy." Beginning in the 1820s, middle- and upper-class Americans began to find public executions "revolting" and no longer wanted to be "associated with such disturbing scenes." This was part of a larger upper- and middle-class trend toward withdrawal from the public sphere and a turning inward "to the private realm of the sanctified home." The ascendancy of these privacy-oriented sensibilities, coupled with a growing societal insistence on a "strict segregation of the 'masculine' and 'feminine' realms," Masur argues, "altered attitudes toward public rituals and gatherings and made certain events in the public realm, such as executions, intolerable." "Disgusted by public executions, but unwilling to advocate the abolition of capital punishment entirely," Masur concludes, "legislators in the 1820s proposed a new solution to the problem—private executions."[57]

By the time of America's last public hangings in the 1930s, most state legislators had come to view public executions as degrading and embarrassing. For example, when the Missouri legislature passed a bill in 1937 abolishing public hangings, its proponents called public executions "uncivilized" and "sadistic." Proponents were concerned that, in at least three instances, small communities had become "carnival spots" that attracted the "idle curious" on execution day for "a picnic lunch." The bill's sponsor, state senator Paul Jones, represented a constituency where one such "revolting" spectacle took place. According to a newspaper account, these well-attended public hangings "shocked and embarrassed Missourians who believe that an execution is no occasion for a Roman holiday." Kentucky was also shamed into abolishing public executions in 1938, only two years after the unsightly spectacle at Rainey Bethea's public hanging in Owensboro, Kentucky. As historian George Wright notes,

A photograph of the April 30, 1896, hanging of William Taylor in Carroll County, Missouri, taken by local photographer D. S. Cole. Although an estimated 10,000 people gathered in Carrollton, Missouri, for Taylor's 10:56 A.M. execution, only 300 people were admitted to the jail-yard stockade to watch Taylor hanged. A lawyer, bank cashier, and former state representative, Taylor and his brother were convicted of killing four members of the Meeks family in an attempt to cover up their own involvement in criminal activities. The photograph is entitled "Before the Drop." (Library of Congress)

"Several organizations, concerned about the state's image, lobbied for an end to the practice."[58]

The elitist and paternalistic nature of private execution laws is evidenced by the fact that, after their passage, women and children were regularly excluded from execution proceedings. Many private execution laws prohibited the attendance of minors, and Connecticut's 1893 law only permitted "adult males" to attend executions. Even when laws did not expressly forbid women from attending executions, county sheriffs usually made certain that only men watched them. At the 1858 execution of Ira Stout in Rochester, New York, antislavery activist Lucy Coleman reported that "not one of my sex was invited." "Man has come to know that a woman's presence is objectionable at such a place," Coleman wrote, pointing out that invitations were extended only to "professional and public men" like attorneys, physicians, and clergymen. Likewise, after Texas's private execution law took effect on February 8, 1924, dozens of people were executed before the first female newspaper reporter was permitted to attend an execution in 1927. Even in the 1940s, New York executioner Robert Elliott wrote that "[m]ost wardens . . . will not invite female witnesses." Elliott commented that those decisions were "based on the fact that women, as a rule, cannot stand up under the strain."[59]

When women did gain entry to executions, the predominantly male press reporters were appalled. One newspaper described the "most disgusting feature" of Anne Bilansky's 1860 hanging in Minnesota as "the eagerness and persistency with which females sought to obtain eligible places to view the dying agonies of one of their own sex." Remarking on the women who gained admittance to the execution enclosure, the paper editorialized: "What could have induced these women to voluntarily witness a spectacle so harrowing to the feelings of even the 'sterner sex,' we cannot imagine." In short, while public executions were attended by both sexes and persons of all ages and social classes, private executions quickly became "a theatrical event for an assembly of elite men who attended the execution by invitation while the community at large was excluded."[60]

Fear of rioting and social disorder, and the related concern that public executions only caused crime, was the second factor that led to the passage of private execution laws. In fact, there was a sharp rise in the reported incidents of rioting and other disturbances in America from 1833 to 1835, corresponding exactly with the abolition of public executions in Pennsylvania, New Jersey, and New York. One essayist in 1835 even declared that "the years 1833 and 1834 will be remarkable in the annals of our country for disregard of the law and illegal violence to persons and property." North Carolina's private execution law, enacted in 1868, made the point explicit. That statute specifically provided: "As the ends of justice, public morals and the preservation of order, demand that the execution of all capital offenders should be made private and invested with the solemnity appropriate to the final act of penal law, any sheriff . . . shall be required to provide for the execution of such criminal within the jail yard enclosure, and as much removed from public view as the means within his control will allow." Public executions in Louisville, Kentucky, also were stopped by local authorities in 1880 after a riot nearly broke out at a public execution attended by as many as twenty thousand people. After 1880, residents of Louisville had to obtain special tickets to attend executions. As Louis Masur concludes, "One response to the perception of disorder was legislation that abolished public executions."

The concern that well-publicized executions only caused crime helps explain why legislators passed laws explicitly prohibiting the publication of execution details. As abolitionist Raymond Bye wrote in 1919:

> The use of capital punishment in any form involves a dilemma. If it be made absolutely secret, and no details of the event be allowed to reach the public other than the mere announcement of execution, the force of the example is by so much weakened. If, on the other hand, the full details of an execution are allowed to be published in the public press, even though but few persons are allowed actually to witness the event, there is the danger of brutalizing the public mind and of suggesting crime to those easily impressionable persons of weak mental calibre who make up a large part of the criminal classes.

"A vivid newspaper account, with the dramatic coloring of modern yellow journalism," Bye noted, "may have almost as bad a result as a public execution." Bye added that "[t]he effect of newspaper sensationalism upon the occurrence of crime has long been recognized."[61]

The popularity of phrenology in nineteenth-century America also provides a legitimate explanation for why many Americans believed that public executions caused, rather than deterred, crime. This psychological theory, which analyzed behavior "by viewing the brain as the mind's organ," was developed by two Austrian physicians, Johann Spurzheim and Franz Joseph Gall, and popularized in America by George Combe. In his writings, Combe argued that public executions would effectively deter only "all favorably constituted men," reasoning that such spectacles would "operate with least effect precisely on those on whom it is most needed, viz., on such as by nature and circumstance are most prone to fall before temptation." Horace Mann, a Massachusetts legislator who first proposed abolishing public executions in that state, was so devoted to phrenology that he named a son after George

Combe. Another American phrenologist, Charles Caldwell, went so far as to argue that all executions, whether conducted publicly or privately, awaken "in persons of suitable temperament who either witness the deed or learn it by report . . . the instinct to destroy human life." Thus, as Louis Masur concludes, "In the 1830s phrenology provided a compelling argument against public hangings at a time when social authorities increasingly feared a crisis of public order."[62]

Third, the move to exclude the public from executions was motivated, as another scholar notes, by "a fear that well-publicized executions would fan sentiment to abolish capital punishment altogether." In this regard, it is significant to note that many private execution laws were enacted in the midst of credible legislative attempts to abolish capital punishment entirely. Many private execution laws were passed between 1897 and 1917, the so-called Progressive Era, when ten American states abolished the death penalty. The passage of private execution laws thus can be seen as an attempt to appease abolitionists, many of whom actually supported the passage of such laws to bolster their own anti–death penalty arguments. In the 1830s, many abolitionists firmly believed that the elimination of public executions would eventually lead to the abolition of capital punishment. After all, if executions were no longer public, how could death penalty proponents persuasively argue that the death penalty deters crime? As one legislative report concluded: "Nearly the whole force of this deterrent influence is now lost by the almost universal infliction of the death penalty in private. Public opinion, in banishing the gallows from the public gaze, has really abandoned the argument."[63]

In the early twentieth century, some abolitionists continued to argue that the private nature of executions was an admission that the death penalty was not a deterrent. Arizona Governor George Hunt, the man who successfully led that state's abolitionist campaign in 1916, made this very argument in a speech delivered in 1914. Hunt stated: "[T]he entire abandonment in recent years of public executions in this country, as in others, must be attributed directly to the realization upon the part of the people that applications of the death penalty in city squares, or court house yards, have had the opposite effect from that which they were intended to produce." "It has been recognized, beyond all possibility of doubt," Hunt continued, "that the public execution is brutalizing and that it engenders in the minds of the people who behold it, emotions and ideas more dangerous to society than the condition which it is designed to correct."[64]

The State of the Union

Modern-day laws still mandate that executions take place behind prison walls. For example, New Jersey law requires that executions take place within "a suitable and efficient facility enclosed from public view, within the confines of a designated State prison." The number of execution spectators also remains the subject of tight governmental control. Typically, only official witnesses and a small number of "respectable" or "reputable citizens" may attend executions. Thus, Pennsylvania and North Carolina allow only six such citizens to attend, and New Hampshire restricts attendance to "reputable citizens not exceeding 12." Attendance is restricted to between six and twelve "respectable citizens" in Arkansas and Maryland, between six and nine "reputable citizens" in Nevada, and "not more than two respectable citizens" in South Carolina.[65]

Although some states do not require execution witnesses to be "respectable" or "reputable," all states restrict the number of execution spectators. The number of authorized citizen-observers generally ranges from three in Massachusetts to twelve in Montana, although Colorado authorizes slightly more, permitting the attendance of "such guards, attendants, and other persons" as the director of corrections "deems desirable, not to exceed fifteen persons." Typically, the warden or prison superintendent has the statutory power to invite or designate witnesses, or attendance is contingent on "the approval of the superintendent." Criminal sanctions are sometimes employed to ensure compliance with these laws. In Tennessee, the warden of the state penitentiary commits a Class C misdemeanor if anyone other than official witnesses or the condemned's family members are allowed to attend an execution. Likewise, an Arkansas law mandates a $100 penalty for any governmental officer who carries out a public execution.[66]

Aside from official observers invited by prison officials, states generally permit the presence of a few additional witnesses. A priest or minister can usually attend executions,[67] and the condemned prisoner can usually invite not more than five friends or relatives.[68] Only Indiana and Wyoming authorize the attendance of up to ten relatives or friends, and only New Jersey prohibits "any person who is related by either blood or marriage" to the condemned prisoner from being present at the execution.[69] The condemned's attorney is specifically permitted to attend the execution in several states, although sometimes prison officials have attempted to bar an attorney's presence. At Walter Key Williams's execution in 1994, Williams's counsel, Joan Cheever, was told that she could not witness the execution. The director of the Texas Department of Corrections, Wayne Scott, told her that she could not attend because her name did not appear on a witness list fourteen days in advance. "Rules are rules, Miss Cheever," he said. Only after Cheever threatened to sue Scott to prevent her client from dying without any friends or family members present was she allowed to witness the execution.[70]

In recent years, victims' families have successfully lobbied in a few states for the right to attend executions. In 1993, for instance, a bill was introduced in Virginia to allow relatives of victims to witness executions. That bill failed to pass, but Governor George Allen pledged to change the Department of Corrections' rules, and the rules were eventually altered. Today, seven states—California, Illinois, Louisiana, Oklahoma, Texas, Virginia, and Washington—allow victims' relatives to watch executions, either live or via closed circuit television. Prison officials in Illinois changed their policy to allow victims' families to watch executions following complaints at the 1994 execution of convicted serial killer John Wayne Gacy. "There was a hue and cry about victims' families not being able to view the execution," said Nic Howell, a spokesman for the Illinois Department of Corrections.[71]

The least restrictive private execution laws authorize press attendance, although the number of reporters who can cover such events is usually severely restricted. California admits no more than twenty-five press representatives, Mississippi admits no more than eight, and South Carolina limits access to only "five representatives of the South Carolina media." South Dakota merely requires the attendance of one member of the news media. Other states admit press members on the sole condition that they serve as a "pool" for other reporters. Utah law gives access to nine reporters, so long as they act as a pool for other press representatives, and New Jersey contemplates that the eight press witnesses will hold a press conference after the execution to brief other reporters about its details. Pennsylvania and Connecticut limit execution access to print reporters. For example, only six "duly accredited representatives of the daily newspapers" are authorized to attend Pennsylvania executions. In Arkansas, it is still unlawful for any newspaper or individual to print or publish the details of an execution. Only the fact that the criminal was executed can be published without violating the law.[72]

Although radio and television reporters are frequently permitted to attend executions, no state authorizes audio or video recording of them. Not only are journalists prohibited from filming executions, but they are frequently denied full access to death row inmates prior to execution day. Thus, some states strictly curtail death row inmates' visitation rights immediately before their execution dates. For instance, Florida's administrative regulations normally permit media interviews with death row inmates each week on Tuesday, Wednesday, and Thursday, between the hours of 1:00 and 3:00 P.M. During the week preceding the execution, though, the death row inmate is allowed only one group interview with not more than thirty media representatives and one individual interview with a single reporter. Each of these interviews may not exceed one hour. Other states have similar provisions limiting access to inmates under a death warrant.[73]

Procedures for selecting media representatives vary widely. In California, South Carolina, and South Dakota, the warden or correctional officials have wide discretion to select media representatives. In other places, witnesses are selected by lot or on a first come, first serve basis. When Keith Wells was killed by lethal injection in Idaho in 1994, eighty-nine media representatives crowded into the prison's visitor room, but only seven reporters were selected by lottery to watch Wells die. However, neutral selection procedures often fall by the wayside in favor of political selection methods. When Robert Alton Harris was executed in 1992, San Quentin's warden, Daniel Vasquez, delegated his selection duties to California Governor Pete Wilson's press secretary, Robert Gore, who gave preference to conservative media representatives in extending invitations.[74]

Occasionally, journalists are excluded from execution chambers altogether. No reporters were allowed to attend Indiana's 1981 execution of Steven Judy, Indiana's first execution in twenty years. Although media representatives are usually permitted to attend executions by custom and tradition, if not by law, they are sometimes given little to watch. John Spenkelink was already strapped into the electric chair before the venetian blinds that blocked spectators' views were raised at his 1979 execution in Florida. At John Wayne Gacy's execution in 1994, a curtain separating the witness room from the execution chamber was hastily closed by prison officials during the execution itself while an equipment malfunction was being repaired. And in 1988, Texas prison officials quickly closed the curtains between the spectators' area and the gurney midway through Raymond Landry's execution when a needle popped free from an intravenous tube, spewing forth deadly chemicals. The curtains were not reopened for fourteen minutes, during which time witnesses heard doors opening and closing and at least one groan. When the curtains were finally reopened, Landry appeared to be unconscious, although he was not pronounced dead for another six minutes. Amnesty International's call for an investigation went unheeded by the Texas Attorney General's Office, which accepted prison officials' explanation that they did the right thing by closing the curtains.[75]

Declining Interest

The first execution in a state often draws a large number of protestors, but subsequent executions rarely attract the same level of interest. For example, Robert Alton Harris's execution in 1992, the first execution in California in twenty-five years, attracted more than fifteen hundred people. As *USA Today* reported, "The whole region throbbed with news conferences, marches and candlelight vigils." In stark contrast, California's next execution, of David Mason in 1993, drew only six hundred demonstrators at its peak, and only about three hundred people were on hand when Mason was pronounced dead at 12:23 A.M. Executions in Texas, which are now commonplace, draw even fewer demonstrators. The 1993 execution of Ramon Montoya, the first Mexican citizen executed in Texas in fifty years, drew just over two dozen protesters. The demonstration at Montoya's midnight execution was later called "the largest in several years for a Texas execution."[76]

The media show up in reduced numbers too for a state's subsequent executions. Only a third of the number of reporters that covered Robert Alton Harris's execution showed up when the next man, David Mason, was executed in California. San Francisco reporter Manuel Ramos of KPIX predicted that even fewer press members would attend the next execution. "I doubt we'll do much at all next time," he said. One of the few protestors at Mason's execution, Tom Cooper of Amnesty International, aptly summarized why Mason's execution drew less interest. "The attention span of people is short," he said. "It's hard to keep them involved." Texas Attorney General Jim Mattox agrees, stating that executions have "gone from being a real novelty to something that is more a matter of fact." At early Texas executions, two hundred to three hundred reporters gathered at the prison, and "it was absolute bedlam" recalled a spokesperson for Mattox. In contrast, most of the recent Texas executions have drawn three or fewer reporters.[77]

The declining interest in executions must be attributed largely to their private and secretive nature. Executions are conducted behind thick prison walls, and only a limited number of official witnesses and reporters are permitted to attend these proceedings. The timing of executions is sometimes kept secret by prison wardens, and press access to death row inmates prior to execution day is often greatly curtailed. Executions also frequently take place in the middle of the night in remote locations, where penitentiaries tend to be built, making it extremely burdensome for interested citizens to demonstrate outside prisons when executions occur or for reporters to attend these events. Perhaps most important, television cameras are forbidden in execution chambers, even though most Americans rely on television for news.[78]

In the nineteenth century, public executions were abolished, largely due to the adolescent behavior of execution day crowds. However, modern-day executions, even though privately conducted, are rarely solemn occasions either. When John Wayne Gacy was executed, death penalty proponents sang and danced outside the jail in Joliet, Illinois, some people dressed as clowns or wore black hoods, and street vendors sold T-shirts with the slogan "No Tears for the Clown." Before John Brewer was lethally injected in Arizona shortly after midnight in 1993, two off-duty prison guards hawked pro-death penalty T-shirts outside the prison in Florence. The T-shirts depicted a syringe and the slogan "For All You Do This Shot's for You. Arizona Execution 1993."[79]

These unseemly acts bear striking resemblance to activities at some executions in early twentieth-century America. Before a woman's scheduled execution in Vermont in 1905 where executive clemency was possible, one newspaper reported: "The element which bets on the horse trots in the fall and the maple sugar crop in the spring is laying wagers freely as to whether the woman will hang. The odds are three to one on the hanging. The risks run from a 10-cent plug of tobacco to $2 in cash or groceries." Another newspaper described a 1921 execution as an "orgy" after reports circulated that some of the twenty-two execution witnesses "indulged in a drinking bout." Before a Pennsylvania execution in 1912, two men even got themselves arrested for drunkenness and refused to pay fines to gain their release in an attempt to witness the hanging, which was to take place in the county jail. They paid the fines and were released only after discovering that prisoners were not permitted to watch hangings.[80]

Although ordinary Americans are prohibited by law from watching executions, official witnesses often find execution proceedings memorable, if not highly emotional and dramatic. At Donald Harding's execution in 1992, Harding "flipped the bird repeatedly" at Arizona Attorney General Grant Woods. Likewise, on August 3, 1994, Hoyt Clines, Darryl Richley, and James Holmes (all convicted of killing a man during a robbery) were executed in Arkansas within hours of one another on the same gurney. State officials originally planned to execute the men by their prison serial numbers—Clines SK886, Holmes SK887, and Richley SK888. However, the U.S. Supreme Court's last-minute consideration of Holmes's appeal forced prison officials to execute Holmes last. Arkansas officials report that multiple executions are conducted to reduce overtime pay and staff stress. "It is an emotional toll on everyone involved. Better one night of tension in the prison than three," remarked a spokeswoman for the Arkansas Department of Corrections. The condemned inmate's dying words or the presence of the murder victim's family also contribute to the dramatic nature of executions.[81]

Moreover, executions today, as in the past, are frequently bungled or downright gory to watch. A recent study found that 12 of 150 American executions since 1977 were "botched," and Justice William Brennan's dissent in *Glass v. Louisiana* vividly illustrates how gruesome a typical electrocution can be:

> "The hands turn red, then white, and the cords of the neck
> stand out like steel bands." The prisoner's limbs, fingers,

toes, and face are severely contorted. The force of the electrical current is so powerful that the prisoner's eyeballs sometimes pop out and "rest on his cheeks." The prisoner often defecates, urinates, and vomits blood and drool. Sometimes the prisoner catches fire, particularly "if [he] perspires excessively." Witnesses hear a loud and sustained sound "like bacon frying," and "the sickly sweet smell of burning flesh" permeates the chamber. This "smell of frying human flesh in the immediate neighborhood of the chair is sometimes bad enough to nauseate even the Press representatives who are present." . . . The body frequently is badly burned and disfigured.

Two surges of electricity, in fact, are often needed to kill a death row inmate because of human error. Even the most clinical lethal injections usually are not without incident or drama. In April 1992, it took executioners forty-seven minutes to locate Billy Wayne White's vein to conduct the lethal injection. White finally had to assist executioners in finding his own vein so that the execution could go forward.[82]

While many Americans shudder at the idea of returning to public executions, these events did have a rather democratic air to them. All citizens, regardless of gender, age, race, or social class, were permitted to attend these events; public officials and religious leaders spoke freely about their intended effect, that is, to deter crime and sin; and the condemned inmate was allowed to publicly make a last statement for all to hear. He or she could choose to die penitent by confessing to the crime and asking for forgiveness or to "die game" or rail against the criminal justice system for condemning an innocent person to death. In contrast, private executions seem rather undemocratic. The American public is forced to rely on secondhand accounts of executions to get information about them, and only "respectable citizens" who are handpicked by governmental officials are permitted to watch them.

The effect that public executions would have on crime rates and America's death penalty debate is unclear. Because no American execution has ever been broadcast on television, it is nearly impossible to predict whether televised executions would deter crime, incite criminal activity, or lead to the abolition of capital punishment. What is clear is that the passage of private execution laws greatly affected America's anti-gallows movement. As law professor Michael Madow writes, for example, New York's abolitionist movement "gradually began to lose momentum" after executions were moved indoors in 1835. "While abolitionist agitation did not peak until the 1840s," Madow observes, "privatization may well have 'saved' capital punishment in New York and elsewhere in the northeast." The historian Philip Mackey similarly observes that the privatization of executions in New York decreased the supply of anti-gallows reformers "by ending the recurrent scenes which had turned so many against the death penalty," and "almost certainly relieved the current pressure for total abolition" by giving "current reformers the impression that the government had met them half way." Indeed, an anonymous New York writer observed in 1836 that the abolition of public hangings had "subtracted much of the force from the anti–death penalty movement." While some states temporarily abolished capital punishment in the 1870s and immediately prior to World War I, the abolitionist movement never again recaptured—as the historian David Brion Davis puts it—"the widespread enthusiasm and evangelical fervor of the 1830's and 1840's."[83]

Although a few nineteenth-century abolitionists vigorously opposed the passage of private execution laws, believing that public executions would be instrumental in abolishing capital punishment, most abolitionists supported their passage. "Only in the 1840s," writes historian Louis Masur, "did [abolitionists] begin to realize their error. The abolition of public executions not only left capital punishment intact, it also neutralized the argument that the spectacle of executions disordered society." As Masur persuasively argues: "[T]he elimination of public executions had deprived opponents of capital punishment of a critical argument: that such spectacles demoralized the population." Many Americans originally opposed outlawing public executions, but Masur concludes that the widespread newspaper reporting about executions served to deflect popular opposition to their privatization. As another scholar suggests: "The presence of reporters—especially reporters from the new 'penny press,' which catered to the informational needs and interests of the laboring and artisanal classes—'permitted the appearance of openness, the illusion that the public had access to events that, in reality, had been shut off to them.'"[84]

Obviously, it is impossible to speculate whether the thirty-eight states currently permitting capital punishment would have abolished it by now had American executions not been privatized in the nineteenth and early twentieth centuries. However, it is feasible to ask several non-hypothetical questions. Why do Americans still blindly accept the fact that executions are hidden from public view? Should today's executions be conducted publicly via television broadcasts to restore public partic-ipation in America's death penalty debate? And would such television broadcasts, if allowed, help educate the public about executions and other issues surrounding capital punishment? These important ques-tions will be explored in detail in Chapters 6 and 7 after readers learn more about the origins of laws requiring private, nighttime executions in the next two chapters.

ᴄᴇ 4

After Midnight, Before Sunrise

At the Midnight Hour

Executions in America, conducted behind prison walls, are cloaked in added secrecy because they frequently occur in the middle of the night. Of the 313 executions that took place in the United States from 1977 to 1995, over 82 percent of them were carried out between 11:00 P.M. and 7:30 A.M., and more than half of them happened between midnight and 1:00 A.M. Because television audiences are largest when people return home from work or school—viewership levels peak from 8:00 to 11:00 P.M.—many executions occur after most Americans are already sound asleep. In the last few years, only a few executions were actually scheduled for "prime time," when an estimated 96 million people are watching television in an average minute. As viewers go to bed, television audiences gradually decline and then drop off sharply at 11:30 P.M. following late newscasts, meaning that midnight executions happen too late to make nightly news programs. Consequently, live film footage of anti–death penalty rallies, candlelight vigils, or pro–death penalty demonstrations outside prisons regularly goes unwatched by millions of slumbering Americans.[1]

Many state laws, in fact, explicitly require nighttime executions. In Delaware and Louisiana, every sentence of death must be imposed between the hours of midnight and 3:00 A.M., and South Dakota executions must be performed between the hours of 12:01 and 6:00 A.M. Laws in Indiana, Kentucky, and Wyoming specifically mandate that executions take place "before sunrise," and until 1995, Texas also required executions to take place "before sunrise." In 1995, Texas legislators passed a law requiring lethal injections to occur "at any time after the hour of 6:00 P.M. on the day set for the execution."[2] This change, which in no way made executions themselves more open and accessible to the public, was merely intended to accommodate lawyers and judges, who are more available during the day. Other states, like Mississippi, schedule executions for 12:01 A.M. by custom. Nighttime executions can also occur under federal law because any federally imposed death sentence must be carried out "in the manner prescribed by the law of the State in which the sentence is imposed."[3]

Even where nighttime executions are not mandated by statute, prison wardens or governmental officials frequently schedule executions for the middle of the night. For example, although the exact hour has been subject to change over time, executions in Maryland have taken place at night for decades. In the 1940s and early 1950s, Maryland executions were performed shortly after midnight. Convicted rapist Eugene James was hanged on August 12, 1949, at the Maryland Penitentiary at 12:21 A.M., and the scaffold trap was swung open on convicted murderer Lott Glover on August 25, 1953, at 12:04 A.M. "At midnight," Maryland Penitentiary Warden Vernon Pepersack stated, "right as City Hall strikes twelve, we start to work." Beginning in 1957, executions in Maryland were temporarily moved to 10:00 P.M., although executions were later moved back to shortly after midnight for unknown reasons. "This change in time," Warden Pepersack said, commenting on the temporary change to 10:00 P.M. executions, "will work better in relation to institution operations and it will cause less of a hardship on those persons assigned as legal witnesses to the execution."[4]

Executions are timed to occur shortly after midnight to avoid unwanted protestors or to ensure that enough time exists, because of possible last-minute stays and appeals, to carry out a death warrant—the legal document that lists a specific date on which the execution must occur. For example, to avoid the impact of death penalty protestors on traffic and neighborhoods near San Quentin, Robert Alton Harris's execution was originally scheduled for April 3, 1990, at 3:00 A.M. "We want to minimize as much as possible the impact on the lives of the people who live in Marin County—and at that hour, there's not much traffic," San Quentin Warden Daniel Vasquez declared. Even though most Americans are sound asleep at 3:00 A.M. and executions used to traditionally occur at San Quentin at 10:00 A.M., Vasquez denied the charge that the timing change was meant to restrict freedom of speech. "Those strong in opposition are going to come out here anyway and demonstrate," he said. Likewise, executions must take place on the exact date listed on an inmate's death warrant or the state can be held in contempt of court. Indeed, Mississippi State Penitentiary's former warden, Donald Cabana, admits that executions often take place at midnight because if "there's a last-minute stay, the state still has 24 hours to rush through legal maneuvers and try to do the deed before midnight of the next day."[5]

Some state laws actually prohibit prison wardens or execution spectators from disclosing when an execution will take place. For example, four states—Colorado, Maryland, Massachusetts, and South Dakota—have laws requiring executions to take place at any time within a one-week period, leaving the exact date and time of the execution to be set by correctional officials. In South Dakota, the time fixed by the warden is to be "kept secret" and in "no manner divulged," except to official witnesses. No previous announcement of the date or time of the execution can be made, and it is a crime for invited spectators to disclose their invitation or the execution time. In Colorado, the timing decision of the head of the department of corrections must "not be made public by him," and in Massachusetts, no "previous announcement" of the execution time is permitted, except to official witnesses. A Massachusetts court ruling from 1901 called this procedure "humane," even though the prisoner was not required to be notified in advance as to when the execution would take place. The court found that the law was not intended to "aggravate the prisoner's distress by enhancing his suspense." A law passed in Nevada in 1920 actually called for the condemned inmate to be executed by means of lethal gas "without warning and while asleep in his cell."[6]

The Maryland law, giving the warden discretion to set the execution time, was closely adhered to by prison officials in 1994 for that state's first execution in nearly thirty-three years. Under that law, "No previous announcement of the day or hour of the execution shall be made except to the persons who shall be invited or permitted to be present at the execution." At the execution, death row inmate John Thanos got just a one-hour warning before he was executed by lethal injection at 1:10 A.M. on May 16, 1994, depriving Thanos of a special last meal. The execution team, led by Frank Mazzone, tried extremely hard to keep the execution time secret. In fact, the six invited journalists were required to sign statements that they would not notify their news organizations when they were summoned to the prison just three hours before the execution. Reporters said later that "logic rather than leaks from within the prison system made the advance coverage possible."[7]

Into the Night

Laws requiring nighttime executions were first enacted in midwestern states in the late nineteenth century. In 1885, Ohio became the first jurisdiction to pass legislation requiring executions "before the hour of sunrise." The Ohio law required executions to take place "within the walls of the Ohio penitentiary," but allowed "a reporter for each one of the two leading [county] newspapers of opposite politics" to attend them. The bill to require private, nighttime executions passed the state senate by a vote of 19–7, cleared the Ohio House of Representatives by a vote of 55–25, and was signed into law on April 29, 1885. On April 22, 1885, the house had rejected several proposed amendments to the bill. One proposal would have required penitentiary inmates to watch executions "so as to strike terror to their hearts," and another would have allowed county sheriffs to select such local newspaper reporters to attend as he might designate. This latter proposal was "objected to by many members, for the reason that the sheriff could farm out the privileges as he saw fit." Another proposed amendment that was rejected would have required public executions at the "Fair grounds at Columbus, Ohio" and would have mandated that "railroad companies . . . sell tickets at one-half the usual rate, to all persons desiring to attend" these public hangings.[8]

The impetus for Ohio's law, which the *Akron Daily Beacon* described as "a wholesome innovation upon the prevailing mode of execution," was a mob spirit that developed at a previous hanging. The hundreds of dollars "paid for militia to guard the [county] jail" and "the demoralizing influence of the morbid sentimentalism developed, especially among weak minded women," the *Akron Daily Beacon* explained, "were all powerful arguments for private executions behind prison walls which mobs could not tear down." The *Cleveland Plain Dealer* also applauded the passage of the law because there would be "an end to the scandalous scenes that so frequently attend the bungling performance" of county sheriffs at executions. The newspaper added that "[t]he murderer will have no opportunity to go into heroics on the scaffold and make fine speeches before he is swung off, and the whole population of the surrounding country will not be given an opportunity to make the occasion of a murderer's being hanged a cause for a holiday." The 2:40 A.M. execution on July 31, 1885, of Valentine Wagoner—the first man executed at the state's penitentiary—marked the beginning of nighttime executions in Ohio. Prior to that time, executions were scheduled for between 10:00 A.M. and 2:00 P.M.[9]

The governor of Indiana signed into law a bill similar to Ohio's law on March 6, 1889. That bill, introduced by Senator Henry Johnson on January 15, 1889, passed the senate by a vote of 37–13, and cleared the house by a vote of 80–11. Like Ohio's law, the Indiana law required executions to take place "before the hour of sunrise" within an enclosure "higher than the gallows" or "inside the walls of the State Prison." However, unlike Ohio's statute, Indiana's law made no provision for the attendance of newspaper reporters. The *Indianapolis News* endorsed this latter provision, editorializing: "The wide advertising of executions and the prominence given to details by newspapers can have none but a bad moral influence. The way to get rid of this is by making executions secret and keeping flower-strewing sentimentalists out of the way of the doomed men."[10]

Some state legislators, favoring total abolition of capital punishment, only reluctantly supported Senator Johnson's bill. In fact, one legislator, Senator Mark DeMotte, actually proposed striking out all of the language of Senator Johnson's bill and replacing it with the following clause: "The death penalty, as a punishment for crime is hereby abolished." However, Senator DeMotte's motion failed to pass. As the *Indianapolis News* reported: "Several Senators expressed themselves as opposed to capital punishment, but would not vote for [Senator DeMotte's] substitute [language] because it might defeat [Senator Johnson's] bill, which they believed ought to become a law if the death penalty could not be abolished." After his motion lost, DeMotte himself voted for Johnson's bill. When Indiana's new law took effect, executions in Indiana took place shortly after midnight.[11]

Just over a month after Indiana passed its law, Minnesota followed suit, passing the "midnight assassination law," as it was dubbed by local newspapers. That law required executions to take place "before the hour of sunrise" and "within the walls of the jail" or "within an enclosure which shall be higher than the gallows." The prisoner was required to be kept in solitary confinement, and only his immediate family members, the sheriff and his deputies, the prisoner's attorney, and a priest or clergyman could visit the condemned inmate. Execution attendance also was severely restricted. Only the following persons could watch an execution: the sheriff and his assistants, a clergyman or priest, a physician, three persons designated by the prisoner, and "not exceeding six" other persons designated by the sheriff. The law expressly prohibited newspaper reporters from attending executions and provided that "[n]o account of the details" of the execution, "beyond the statement of the fact that such convict was on the day in question duly executed," could be published in any newspaper. Any violation of the law was punishable as a misdemeanor.[12]

The "midnight assassination law" was guided to passage in April 1889 by an abolitionist legislator, John Day Smith, after attempts earlier in the legislative session to abolish capital punishment were rejected. The hanging of the Barrett brothers in Minneapolis on March 22, 1889, for the murder of a streetcar driver had "set the tongues of reformers wagging" about the need to abolish capital punishment and restrict execution publicity. Before that double hanging, the county sheriff had sent out a large number of invitations that read: "The execution of Timothy and Peter Barrett will take place in Hennepin County on Friday, March 22, 1889, at 11 A.M. This will admit you." At the execution itself, prominent citizens and newspaper reporters with telegraphic instruments packed the spectators' platform inside the Hennepin County Jail. "Every inch of space was utilized by the lookers-on," but a photographer, John Bodley, was notably missing. Having expressed his desire to record the Barretts' last scene on the gallows, Bodley had been imprisoned the day before for selling "obscene pictures" that depicted the condemned men in jail. It was just ten days after the Barrett boys were hanged that a bill to outlaw capital punishment was debated on the house floor. Representative John Day Smith, an attorney, championed the bill, emphasizing that innocent men had been "sacrificed to satisfy the law." Another lawyer, Representative Frank E. Searle, who had favored capital punishment only a month earlier, now supported the bill. The "sickening details" of the Barretts' hanging "broadcast over the land" had changed his mind. However, Representative John Day Smith's motion to report the bill favorably narrowly lost by a vote of 31–33.[13]

Although the Minnesota legislature failed to abolish capital punishment in 1889, John Day Smith was "happy" and "pleased" over the passage of the "midnight assassination law," which was his "pet measure." "The law is intended to promote morality," Smith said, and he indicated his intention to proceed against any newspaper that violated the law. "It is degrading to humanity to witness executions the way they are sometimes conducted in the country. The sheriff strings his man up out in an open field and invites the whole country to see him do it. The law will prevent all that." The *Daily Pioneer Press* of St. Paul specifically opined that Smith's law was designed "to rob an execution of much of its horror by strictly limiting the number of witnesses and excluding the representatives of the press." Senator Frank A. Day, publisher of the *Martin County Sentinel,* commented favorably on the passage of the Smith law:

> Thanks to Representative John Day Smith, public execution of criminals will hereafter be largely private and newspaper readers will be spared the horrible and sensational reports of a mode of punishment which is a disgrace to our christian civilization. Every man and woman, whose sense of decency is not morbid and depraved will read H.F. No. 1185 in the law supplements with feelings of satisfaction.[14]

The daily newspapers of Minneapolis and St. Paul, by contrast, did not give the Smith law such rave reviews. The *Minneapolis Tribune* concluded that the provision of the Smith law requiring executions before the hour of sunrise "is principally based upon the hope that an execution in the early morning hours will prevent the appearance of details in the morning papers." In its news coverage, the *Minneapolis Journal* focused on the "most unique feature" of the law: the prohibition on the newspaper publication of execution details. "This is for the purpose of preventing the circumstantial and sensational accounts of executions usually printed," the paper wrote. Noting that a similar provision of New York law had yet to be "tested," the paper called into question the Smith law's constitutionality. "A number of lawyers have expressed the opinion that the newspaper feature of the law won't hold water," the paper reported.[15]

A veteran of the Civil War who fought at Gettysburg, John Day Smith had seen many public executions during his military service. As the official historian of his Maine infantry regiment, Smith wrote that Union men "were ordered out with sickening frequency to witness the execution of men by shooting or hanging." He called these public executions a "relic of barbarism," and specifically questioned their deterrent effect. Smith recalled that within two days after a deserter's public execution, "four soldiers were reported as deserting to the enemy from the same regiment to which the dead deserter belonged." As evidenced by his desire to statutorily mandate private executions and to prohibit newspapers from reporting any details about them, Smith clearly felt that public or well-publicized executions had a demoralizing influence on American society.[16]

Nighttime Executions Proliferate

In the U.S. Supreme Court's ruling in *Holden v. Minnesota,* fully described in Chapter 3, the Court commented favorably on the constitutionality of Minnesota's "midnight assassination law." In that decision of December 8, 1890, the Court ruled:

> Whether a convict, sentenced to death, shall be executed before or after sunrise, or within or without the walls of the jail, or within or outside of some other inclosure, and whether the inclosure within which he is executed shall be higher than the gallows, thus excluding the view of persons outside, are regulations that do not affect his substantial rights.

This dicta, off-handedly written in an opinion about the legality of ex post facto laws, put the High Court's imprimatur on state laws requiring private, nighttime executions.[17]

After the Supreme Court's ruling in *Holden,* several states passed laws requiring nighttime executions. Connecticut passed a law in 1893 requiring executions to "be inflicted within the walls" of the state prison "before the hour of sunrise," and Massachusetts enacted a law in 1898 requiring executions to take place at "an hour between midnight and sunrise." North Dakota passed a law requiring executions "before the hour of sunrise" in 1903, and Wyoming joined the ranks of states requiring executions "before the hour of sunrise" in 1905.[18]

The Connecticut law was passed without opposition, but only after vigorous attempts were made to abolish capital punishment altogether. In the House of Representatives, Representative Walter S. Judd of Litchfield, a staunch abolitionist, had the bill requiring nighttime executions at the Wethersfield state prison tabled until the house could settle the question of whether the death penalty should be abolished. Judd told fellow legislators that the death penalty was not a deterrent, and he "condemned the details of hangings as published in the newspapers." He stated: "Of 163 men executed for murder, it was found that 160 had witnessed executions." Judd believed that "morbid public curiosity" and "busy reporters" would make private executions impractical. However, another representative argued that Judd's "objections arising from the evil effects of the publicity of executions would be avoided" by the bill to move executions into the Wethersfield penitentiary, where executions would be "well guarded from public view." Only after Judd's abolitionist proposal failed on a 125–54 vote did Judd capitulate. Immediately after that vote, the Connecticut House of Representatives quickly passed the bill requiring nighttime executions at the state prison on Judd's own motion, launching a new mode of executions in Connecticut.[19]

After the trap was sprung open on John Cronin at 1:02 A.M. on December 18, 1894, the *Hartford Times* reported that the hour selected for the operation of the gallows "was a new one—at least in the history of Connecticut hangings." The paper remarked: "To hang a man one hour after midnight may not be, to the person chiefly concerned, a highly important difference as compared with the customary daylight hour for such performances. . . . But to the general public the idea of a midnight execution probably adds a little to the horror of the experience." The newspaper added that "[t]here was an intent, evidently, in selecting such an hour—the discouraging of street gatherings in the vicinity of the prison. It works thoroughly to that end."[20]

Some state legislatures did not act so fast. Texas and Alabama did not pass laws requiring executions "before the hour of sunrise" until 1923. South Dakota passed its law requiring executions between 12:01 and 6:00 A.M. in 1939, and Kentucky's law requiring executions "before sunrise" passed in 1944. Louisiana and Delaware enacted their laws requiring executions between midnight and 3:00 A.M. in 1952 and 1994, respectively. The sponsor of the Louisiana law was Representative Algie Brown of Shreveport. "When an execution is held, it throws an entire courthouse into confusion," Brown explained. "There is great objection from women employees." Louisiana executions had traditionally taken place between noon and 3:00 P.M. Executions in New York, Pennsylvania, and Vermont also were moved to times between 11:00 P.M. and 12:30 A.M., even though no law required them to be performed at night.[21]

A few states used to explicitly require that executions occur during daylight hours. Iowa's 1860 criminal code and Arkansas's 1868 penal code required executions to take place "between sunrise and sunset." Texas's 1885 penal code required that death sentences "be carried into effect at any time after eleven o'clock, and before sunset." Many other states and the federal government simply scheduled executions by custom for early morning, noontime, or mid-afternoon. For example, when Captain Henry Wirz—commandant of the barbaric Andersonville prison, which housed Yankee prisoners during the Civil War—was sentenced to die in 1865, President Andrew Johnson ordered that the hanging take place "between the hours of 6 o'clock A.M. and 12 o'clock noon." By contrast, executions carried out during World War II as a result of American courts-martial usually happened at 1:00 A.M.[22]

After passing its new law requiring nighttime executions, Texas authorities wasted no time in implementing it. On February 8, 1924, at 12:09 A.M.—nine minutes after the law took effect—Charles Reynolds entered the room housing the state's new electric chair, "Old Sparky." He was pronounced dead at 12:16 A.M. after three surges of electricity. The deaths of Ewell Morris, George Washington, Mack Matthews, and Melvin Johnson quickly followed, with the last man dying before 2:00 A.M. All five men

The hanging of Captain Henry Wirz on November 10, 1865, in the courtyard of the Old Capitol prison in Washington, D.C. Wirz was the commandant of the Andersonville prison in southwest Georgia, where 13,000 Yankee prisoners died of disease, exposure, or malnutrition. The Old Capitol prison— now the site of the U.S. Supreme Court—was once a temporary location for Congress after the Capitol building was destroyed during the War of 1812. After Congress moved back to its permanent location, the brick building was used as a prison, with high board fences built around it. In the picture, Wirz has just dropped through the trap. (Library of Congress)

were African American. This nighttime "harvest of death," as the *Austin American-Statesman* called it, was in marked contrast to Texas's last public execution. When convicted murderer Roy Mitchell was hung next to the McLennan County Jail in Waco about an hour before noon, thousands of onlookers watched Mitchell's swaying body.[23]

Some states began requiring nighttime executions after the power to conduct executions was taken away from county sheriffs and handed over to state prison authorities. For example, the nighttime execution

An estimated crowd of 10,000 people gather in Paris, Texas, on February 1, 1893, to watch an African American man, Henry Smith, burned to death. In the illegal lynching, Smith was tortured with hot iron brands—applied from his feet to his face—for fifty minutes before his body was set on fire. The unruly mob lynched Smith as a result of the rape and murder of three-year-old Myrtle Vance, who was the daughter of a police officer who once hit Smith with a club in the course of arresting him for drunk and disorderly conduct. After being arrested, Smith had sworn to seek vengeance against the police officer. (Library of Congress)

laws in Wyoming and Texas were enacted as part of legislation that moved executions to the state penitentiary from the county jails around those states. The author of the Texas bill, Senator J. W. Thomas, had run for office on the platform that hangings should be removed from local communities after some brutal lynchings—three persons accused of crimes were burned to death—occurred in 1922 a short distance from his hometown. The legislation itself indicated that "putting to death condemned convicts by hanging . . . in the counties . . . frequently creates great disturbance in the county" and that the bill was needed because of "an imperative public necessity."[24]

Likewise, the Maryland legislature passed a law in 1922 requiring executions to take place at the state penitentiary. The stated intention of the law was to remove convicted felons "from the county or city jail as the law now provides, and to relieve the counties of this State from the curious mobs that frequent hangings taking place in the counties of this State, and who attempt to make public affairs of the same." The first person put to death under Maryland's 1922 law was George Chelton, a black man who had been convicted of assaulting a fourteen-year-old white girl. Chelton was hung at 12:39 A.M., "marking a departure from the usual custom of hanging convicted men at daybreak."[25]

North Dakota's nighttime execution law also was passed in 1903 as part of emergency legislation moving executions to the state penitentiary. The law required the death penalty to be inflicted "within the walls of the North Dakota penitentiary at Bismarck" in an enclosure "constructed as to exclude public view." Only the following persons were allowed to attend an execution: the warden and any necessary guards, county sheriffs, a physician, a clergyman, five persons designated by the prisoner, representatives of the newspapers in the county in which the crime was committed, and one reporter from each newspaper published in Bismarck. On October 17, 1905, at 1:05 A.M., convicted murderer John Rooney became the first person to hang under the auspices of the new law. "I am sorry to entertain you at such a late hour," Rooney told the twenty-eight spectators, "but you all know the circumstances."[26]

Although fifty persons sought invitations to attend Rooney's execution, only those allowed by law were permitted to attend. Warden Boucher believed that the purpose of the law was to rob executions of "the sensationalism common to capital punishment where any and everybody is allowed to see" the condemned man. Prior to the execution, Warden Boucher only told reporters that Rooney would be executed "between the hours of midnight tonight and daylight tomorrow morning" and that "[t]he provisions of the law will be carried out by the letter." As the *Fargo Forum* reported: "In accordance with his interpretation of the law, to keep the glaring details of the execution as secret as possible, the warden declined to make any further statement other than that every courtesy possible would be extended to persons entitled to witness the execution." Warden Boucher even refused to make known the names of Rooney's five invited guests.[27]

Like North Dakota's penitentiary warden, the *Bismarck Daily Tribune* believed that the object of the law was "to remove the executions of criminals from public observation and to avoid the notoriety and publicity too frequently following upon executions held in the jail yard of a county." As that newspaper editorialized, the law "intends to rob the execution of any opportunity for a display of bravado. It intends to permit the presence of no morbidly curious or half-criminal-worshiping spectators. It intends to furnish no unintelligent audience before which the criminal may declaim, in the knowledge that he has some sympathetic hearers." The *Bismarck Daily Tribune* emphasized that discussion and comment by "men, women and children" after an execution "is neither healthful nor desirable."[28]

Other states moved to nighttime executions when the electric chair was substituted for the gallows. Public hangings in Illinois used to occur in the early afternoon to accommodate the large crowds drawn to them, and even after Illinois abolished public executions in 1859, executions still were regularly conducted between 7:00 and 9:00 A.M. With the advent of the electric chair, however, "jail officials decided to get the distasteful job out of the way the sooner the better, and carried out their assignments shortly after midnight on the appointed day." When the first two electrocutions took place in Illinois on February 20, 1929, Warden Edward Fogarty had the electric chair ready at the stroke of midnight. At that "doubleheader," convicted murderers Anthony Grecco and Charles Walz were pronounced dead at 12:03 A.M. and 12:16 A.M., respectively. Alabama and South Dakota also started requiring nighttime executions when laws mandating death by electrocution were implemented. On April 8, 1927, at 12:42 A.M., double murderer Horace De-Vaughn became the first casualty of Alabama's electric chair, and on April 8, 1947, at 12:15 A.M., convicted murderer George Sitts became the first person in South Dakota to die by electrocution.[29]

In South Dakota, the passage of the state's 1939 law requiring private, nighttime executions also coincided with the reinstatement of capital punishment after twenty-four years of abolition. The new death penalty law was necessary, Senator Sioux Grigsby explained, to stop "morons, sex maniacs and gangsters who cross our borders to commit their crimes." After South Dakota's death penalty was abolished in 1915, several attempts to reinstate it failed in one form or another. In the 1927 legislative session, a death penalty bill cleared the house and senate but was vetoed, and in the 1937 session, a death penalty bill passed the senate but was defeated in the house. Another proposal in the 1930s to make kidnapping punishable by death also failed, but only after a bitter fight. Although strongly worded newspaper editorials in the 1930s called for the reinstatement of capital punishment—one 1938 editorial said that "[l]ynching needs to be practiced more as in the days of the frontier building of our country"—it is interesting to note that South Dakota legislators chose not to return to the days of public executions when they reinstated capital punishment in 1939. Perhaps elected officials, feeling political pressure after the hideous kidnapping and sex-slaying of a seventeen-year-old girl from Sioux Falls, feared being thrown out of office if they did not support the death penalty law, but realized that their constituents would no longer tolerate the spectacles created by public executions. In August 1938, the *Pierre Daily Capital-Journal* had urged voters to oust "any constitutional officer or lawmaker candidate who is not favorable to reenactment of capital punishment law in this state."[30]

Some state legislators resisted the passage of laws requiring nighttime executions. A bill was introduced in Massachusetts in 1898 providing for criminals to "be conveyed as secretly as may be" to the state prison for electrocution "at an hour between midnight and sunrise." After the bill's introduction, one legislator moved to amend the bill to require executions "between nine o'clock in the forenoon and three o'clock in the afternoon." That proposed amendment was rejected, however, by a vote of 78–54, and the bill went on to passage. Accordingly, when the law took effect on April 13, 1898, electrocutions in Massachusetts—the current being turned on "by an invisible hand"—began taking place shortly after midnight. In contrast, under the state's prior capital punishment law requiring death by hanging, executions took place during daylight hours. The *Boston Evening Transcript* called Massachusetts' new method of execution "an advance in humanity and civilization."[31]

In some countries, like Mexico and England, executions were usually timed for daybreak or for a time between early morning and midafternoon. The English resisted nighttime executions, although the concept had been proposed in England as early as the 1860s. Testifying before the Royal Commission on Capital Punishment, an ex-sheriff of London, H. N. Nissen, suggested that the public witness executions in the prison yard at 4:00 A.M. Elsewhere, though, executions sometimes were scheduled to take place at night in the hope that it would be too early for crowds to gather. In France, while executions usually took place between dawn and 4:00 P.M., when Jean Louschart was executed in Versailles in 1788, the cart carrying the condemned man—whom many people believed was innocent—made its way to the scaffold at 4:30 A.M. "in hopes that . . . everything could be finished before the population awoke." Likewise, on June 18, 1939, the public execution of Siegfried Eugen Weidmann in front of the Palais de Justice in Versailles was scheduled for 5:00 A.M. However, "[d]espite the rain that fell all night, the population of Versailles was not deterred from gathering on the rue Georges Clemenceau in front of the prison gates, where at about three o'clock in the morning, Monsieur [Henri] Desfourneaux and his aides set up the guillotine." When Weidmann was beheaded just before 5:00 A.M., an unruly mob of men and women were present to watch him die. The spectacle, photographed by newspapers throughout France, produced such an effect that public executions were forbidden one week later. Thereafter, executions in France would take place in the prison yard, to be witnessed by only a select few individuals; after the execution a placard listing the date and hour of death would be affixed to the prison gates.[32]

Today, executions throughout the United States remain shrouded in darkness and secrecy. State laws permit only a few citizens who are handpicked by governmental officials to witness executions, and television cameras are universally prohibited in execution chambers. Because the general public is excluded from execution proceedings, death penalty proponents and foes alike must brave the elements outside prison walls to voice their views. At Jesse Bishop's midnight execution in late October 1979, 120 people endured 26-degree temperatures in Carson City, Nevada, to demonstrate at the prison. Likewise, at Steven Judy's 12:12 A.M. execution in 1981 in Michigan City, Indiana, 200 death penalty opponents were forced to hold a candlelight vigil outside the prison gates, despite subfreezing temperatures.[33]

Without question, the timing and private nature of executions has had a chilling effect on the ability of Americans and media organizations to exercise their First Amendment rights. Because executions frequently occur at night and in remote or rural locations like Starke, Florida, it is difficult for activists to effectively organize pro– or anti–death penalty demonstrations at prisons when executions occur. The timing and inaccessible nature of executions also makes press coverage equally arduous.

Reporters must stay up extremely late to cover executions, sometimes only to find out shortly before midnight that an execution, which they may be excluded from watching anyway, will not go forward because of a last-minute stay or postponement. Although the overall number of nighttime executions will decrease now that Texas requires executions after 6:00 P.M., even the light of day cannot pierce the walls of Huntsville's maximum security prison, where that state's death row inmates are executed. The move to 6:00 P.M. executions in Texas hardly signals a new openness insofar as execution proceedings are concerned; it merely represents the voices of lawyers and judges who do not want to stay up late or be awakened in the middle of the night to decide a convicted murderer's fate. Throughout America, executions remain private affairs, and the public continues to be kept in the dark about the nature of executions.

✒ 5

Minnesota's "Midnight Assassination Law"

The "Midnight Assassination Law" in Operation

Minnesota no longer authorizes capital punishment, but the state once played a pivotal role in influencing how American executions are conducted. In fact, although other states acted first in passing laws requiring private, nighttime executions,[1] Minnesota's "midnight assassination law" is the only American law of its kind ever commented on by the U.S. Supreme Court and attacked as unconstitutional by the press prior to 1976. Accordingly, a thorough examination of the history of Minnesota's law is indispensable to understanding the origins of American laws requiring private, nighttime executions. Dubbed the "midnight assassination law" by local newspapers, Minnesota's 1889 law, as described in prior chapters, required executions to take place in private "before the hour of sunrise" and severely restricted the number of execution spectators. It also prohibited newspaper reporters from attending hangings and forbade newspapers from printing any execution details. Only the minimal fact that the execution occurred could be lawfully printed. Sheriffs or reporters who violated the law could be criminally prosecuted.[2] Authored by Minneapolis legislator John Day Smith, the "midnight assassination law" was also commonly referred to as the "John Day Smith law."

The passage of John Day Smith's "midnight assassination law" in April 1889 was quickly followed by several executions in Minnesota. On

July 19, 1889, in Little Falls, Albert Bulow became the first person to hang under the auspices of the Smith law. Morrison County Sheriff Henry Rasicot "performed his duties faithfully, obeyed the law literally, and won the commendation of everyone by his wise and prudent course." In accordance with the execution warrant, the hanging was performed between 1:00 and 4:00 A.M. within a high board enclosure adjoining the jail. Sheriff Rasicot sprung the trap at 1:47 A.M. One newspaper reported that it was "so dark in the shadows of the enclosure that the features of those who were there could hardly be distinguished." The "morbidly curious," who wanted to catch a glimpse of the scaffold industriously bored holes through the board fence. Those excluded from the enclosure were forced to call at the Harling & Son's morgue, which welcomed hundreds later that day "to see the face of the criminal."[3]

John Day Smith's "midnight assassination law" was severely criticized in the wake of Bulow's hanging. The *Brainerd Journal* called the provision requiring nighttime executions "a relic of barbarism that ought to be repealed at the first opportunity" and described Representative Smith as "undoubtedly insane." "It is very strange that a man like Smith could be elected to the legislature," the paper editorialized, "but still more strange that a bill containing indisputable evidence of having emanated from a madman would run the gauntlet of both branches of the legislature and become a law." The *Little Falls Transcript* was only slightly more charitable: "While there are perhaps some good features of the Smith hanging law, we have failed to learn of anybody who endorses it as it now is. The barbarity of killing a criminal in the night is disgusting to people who are not savages." The paper concluded: "The John Day Smith law was so indefinite that many papers have been unable to learn just what should be done in order to please that narrow minded gentleman." The *Alexandria Post* further complained that newspapers had "confined the announcement of the execution under the John Day Smith law to four columns and editorial comment." The paper added: "It is not right to limit the prerogatives of the exponent of public opinion or the public morals."[4]

The *St. Paul Dispatch* further criticized the John Day Smith law, calling it "An Absurd Law" that "requires the execution to take the form of a midnight assassination." The editorial continued:

The law, we are informed, was fulfilled by the letter. No "newspaper reporter or representative" was admitted, but strangely enough the readers of newspapers are now in possession of every essential detail of the execution, and of many details that are not essential. Of course, as a result, the *Dispatch* and all its contemporaries are misdemeanants.

Why did not Mr. John D. Smith take the precaution to provide for the creation of a press censor when he was framing that law! It is unique as a piece of paternal, sumptuary law-making, but in the nature of things it is incomplete without the addition we suggest. The "morbid" propensity of the reading public is something lamentable: but not nearly so much so as that of many who undertake, in the making of statutes, to dictate to them what they shall and shall not do.

If the people of this state desire to know the particulars of the execution of criminals they have an unquestionable right to be informed. It is their business. They pay for its transaction and they should not be deprived of the right to decide for themselves whether that business is properly or improperly transacted and to know, on unexceptionable authority, whether it has been transacted at all.[5]

The author of the newspaper gag law, Representative John Day Smith, was away in the East during Bulow's hanging. The *Minneapolis Journal* described Smith's reaction on his return: "He is not at all pleased with the way the newspapers have treated him and his new law. He says that allusions made to him were unmannerly. He is even bitter in his abuse of the newspapers for what he terms the slush and filth that they print." When asked if the newspapers that printed reports of the Bulow hanging would be prosecuted, Smith replied that he had "nothing to say." He added, smiling, "I am not the prosecuting attorney, you know." Smith did quickly point out the effect his law had on Bulow's execution. "Before the law was passed Sheriff Rasicot said if the people wanted to see the hanging he would put a rope around the scaffold and hang him in the open air. Was it not better that that man should be slid off in the night away from the sight and view of the crowd than that the execution of the law should be made the occasion of a gala day and a circus?"

Smith added that the "best sentiment of the community favors the law." When a reporter remarked that "the papers all over the country are opposed to it," Smith replied: "No, they are not. The best papers in the state have expressed themselves in favor of it. I don't mean the daily papers in St. Paul and Minneapolis." Smith said newspapers should be "controlled" for the "health and morals of the community," and again trumpeted the legality and wisdom of his law.[6]

Some newspapers, in fact, did defend John Day Smith's "midnight assassination law." The *Martin County Sentinel,* published by Senator Frank A. Day, ran an editorial entitled "Disreputable Journalism" after Bulow's hanging that accused the daily newspapers of St. Paul and Minneapolis of bringing "reproach" on "the profession of journalism" by printing execution details. The paper praised the Smith law as "a good one," stating:

> The hanging of the Barretts in Minneapolis had ripened public sentiment for this reform. The sheriff who had the execution of those murderers in charge issued public invitations to hundreds, the same as would be issued to a wedding, a reception or a banquet. People flocked from all parts of the state to see the poor depraved wretches drop from the scaffold, swing by their necks, and dangle in the air until the last breath of life had left their mortal bodies. At the close of the execution the hangman's rope and the scaffold were cut into pieces and distributed among the executioner's guests as mementos of the great event. In satisfying the demands of justice the morbid and depraved taste of a great multitude had been satiated. And then came the newspapers with every minute detail of the horrifying affair, and enlarged, elaborated, exaggerated and sensationalized. To every refined and sensitive nature these accounts were revolting. They were of no benefit to law or society. They cultivated in the young a taste for sensational blood-and-thunder literature which could but result in their moral debasement.

The *Martin County Sentinel*'s editorial hoped that "every newspaper that . . . openly and wantonly violated" the Smith law would be "unsparingly prosecuted." Despite Senator Day's call for the offending newspapers to be brought to justice, no prosecutions were commenced.[7]

On September 20, 1889, Thomas Brown became the second person to hang under the auspices of the "midnight assassination law." He was hung in Moorhead at 4:30 A.M. for the murder of a policeman, Peter Poull. Clay County Sheriff Jorgen Jensen "faithfully followed" the Smith law, and took "extra care" to ensure that no newspaper reporters attended the execution. The local newspaper also provided very few execution details, stating only that "no mishap or hitch of any kind" occurred and that "Brown's neck was broken and he died without a struggle." While the *Moorhead Daily News* was "cognizant" of many details of the execution, it would "refrain from publishing them" to comply with the Smith law. Instead, the paper published a history of Brown's crime and a summary of the events leading up to the execution. Smith's law, proclaimed the paper, did not prohibit the newspaper publication of these kind of details. In contrast, most newspapers—like the *St. Paul Dispatch*—continued to describe the most minute execution details.[8]

In the next two years, three more men were hung in Minnesota under the auspices of the "midnight assassination law." One of the condemned men, William Rose, was "swung into eternity" in Redwood Falls on October 16, 1891, for killing a neighboring farmer, Moses Lufkin. A large crowd gathered for the hanging, including several drunken men, but musket-carrying guards protected the ramshackle execution enclosure. Only Sheriff C. W. Mead's "friends" and "cronies" and one local newspaper editor were allowed into the enclosure—a "small, unpainted shanty, with the light shining through cracks and knotholes," more resembling a "slaughterhouse, where the lives of cattle are taken," than a place where a human being should be hung. Only when the guards deserted their posts to watch the execution through "the nearest crevice" were reporters—who later fully described the execution—able to look through knotholes to obtain a complete account of what transpired inside.[9]

When the trap was swung open at 4:56 A.M., Rose's 190-pound body broke the rope. Sheriff Mead whispered "Pick him up," and Rose's unconscious body was quickly carried back up the scaffold. A second noose was placed around his neck, and the trap was sprung again at exactly 5:00 A.M. This time the rope held, and Rose was soon pronounced dead.

However, Rose was not "the only sufferer"—as the *St. Paul Pioneer Press* put it—of the October 16 hanging. The *St. Paul Globe,* which on the morning of the execution published a story entitled "Dropped to Death," soon became its second victim. The *Globe's* story, advertised as a "Special to the Globe," reported that Rose was hanged "in the early dawn." It did not publish the hour and minute of death but confidently proclaimed that "[t]here were no sensational features, no terrible details" to Rose's hanging. This latter statement was obviously false and did not go unnoticed by the *Globe's* competitors, who accused the *Globe* of committing the "very old and very cheap trick" of making up facts to scoop the other newspapers. The *St. Paul Pioneer Press* said those who ran the *Globe* used "journalistic enterprise" to "evolve facts out of their inner consciousness." An editorial in the *Minneapolis Tribune* was even more sarcastic: "It costs a little more and requires time and trouble to secure the news, but it pays better in the long run. Newspapers, like politicians, may fool part of the people part of the time, but they cannot fool all of the people all of the time." The *Globe's* only defense was that its reporter had dashed to the telegraph office right after "the sounds of the falling weights told him that the deed was done." It emphasized the "[p]eculiar difficulties" surrounding execution news coverage "because the existing statutes forbid the presence of reporters at the execution." Reporters have to "depend on information they can obtain from others, who attend it not to tell, but to act."[10]

The three executions in Minnesota from 1890 to 1891 all prompted renewed press criticism of the John Day Smith law. After the 3:30 A.M. hanging of William Brooker in Pine City on June 27, 1890, the *Pine County Pioneer* declared: "If John Day Smith . . . thought he was doing a wonderful thing toward relieving the tragedy of some of its horrors, he was mistaken. . . . The act is but the aimless product of a crank's mind, and should be repealed by the next legislature. If the state is so ashamed of its laws that it compels its officers to fulfill them at the dark hour of midnight, and hidden from the investigation of the world by the exclusion of reporters, it is a good evidence that the law should be repealed."[11]

The Rose hanging produced an equally virulent response. "The execution of Rose fully demonstrated both the injustice and absurdity of the John Day Smith law," wrote the *St. Paul Pioneer Press.* The absurdity of the law was that "as full an account of the closing scenes as the morning papers could use" had to be on the telegraph wires "within twenty minutes after the drop fell." "The injustice of the law was equally well shown by the indignities heaped upon the reporters of the daily papers, and the partiality shown to local newspaper men. Among the witnesses of the execution, of which there were about twenty-five, was a representative of the *Sleepy Eye Herald,* who was allowed a position inside the slaughter pen, while the reporters of the dailies were steadfastly refused admission."[12]

In the wake of Adelbert Goheen's 12:15 A.M. execution in Fergus Falls on October 23, 1891, the press continued its attack on the Smith law. The *Minneapolis Tribune* declared that "[i]t is becoming painfully evident that the John Day Smith execution law has failed to accomplish the purposes for which it was passed." Its editorial opined that the law was enacted "to squelch if possible that unhealthful and morbid public interest which is always aroused by the public execution of a criminal." Although it was "very reasonably supposed that the private execution of a justly convicted criminal would beget fewer flowers and female tears," the newspaper concluded that "this well meant law has proven altogether futile." The paper emphasized that "[m]ore sentimental twaddle has been written about the last days of William Rose than ever appeared in print in any case prior to the passage of this law," and that felon Adelbert Goheen "is more talked about today than any ten living and virtuous people in the state." In its opinion, John Day Smith's law had failed because of "the attempted exclusion of representatives of the press from the scene of execution" and "an overwhelming human curiosity which nothing can eradicate." When reporters "have been unable to gain admission," the paper asserted, "their accounts of executions have been more harrowing than had they been present upon the spot."

The *Minneapolis Tribune* concluded that "[a]t least one competent and trustworthy representative of the press should be present to give a brief and unsensational account of the execution." "An execution is a state function and the people of the state should know whether the machinery which they have provided for capital punishment is efficient or otherwise," the paper wrote. In addition, the *St. Paul Pioneer Press* called for repeal of the provision of the Smith law "relative to publication of details of executions."[13] Despite these calls for reform, legislative efforts to repeal or amend the Smith law were unsuccessful. The Minnesota

House of Representatives passed a bill in 1897 by a vote of 65–18 to allow four press representatives to attend executions, but that proposal died in the Senate Judiciary Committee.[14]

Noncompliance, Nonenforcement

Despite the U.S. Supreme Court's 1890 pronouncement in *Holden v. Minnesota* upholding the constitutionality of John Day Smith's "midnight assassination law," the provision of the Smith law restricting execution attendance was frequently ignored. For example, on October 19, 1894, two teenagers, Charles Ermisch and Otto Wonigkeit, were hanged on a double gallows in St. Paul for the murder of a bartender. Before the execution took place, some fifteen thousand people viewed the gallows, and in spite of the Smith law, fifty or sixty men packed the enclosure for the 5:00 A.M. hanging. Many were friends of the sheriff, and others were newspaper reporters. Flasks of whisky were passed among the spectators inside the enclosure on the plea that a "bracer" was needed. The spectators were later accused of coming only "to get a few minutes of doubtful entertainment" and of "making an orgy of a solemn act of justice."[15]

In 1895, John Day Smith himself witnessed an execution that was attended by more than the number of witnesses allowed by law. At that execution, one newspaper reported that over one hundred persons were present and "the newspapers were represented by all kinds of persons except (happily) by the person who gives the woman's view." The condemned man, Harry Hayward, had been sentenced to death in March 1895—after a trial in which he was represented by John Day Smith—for the murder for hire of his would-be bride, Catherine Ging.[16] After Hayward's conviction, John Day Smith—who suffered a "nervous breakdown" in 1911 as an overworked district court judge—continued representing Hayward, mounting a strenuous effort to get Hayward's sentence commuted. A group of physicians filed a petition questioning Hayward's sanity, and a second petition, containing 156 names, was dropped off at the governor's mansion by Smith himself. Smith later penned a personal letter to Governor David Clough, emphasizing a simple message: "The state cannot afford to hang a lunatic." But Governor Clough refused to commute Hayward's sentence, and the execution date was set for December 11, 1895. The execution warrant referenced John Day Smith's law and specifically commanded that the hanging occur "before the hour of sunrise." By fixing the execution date for a Wednesday, Governor Clough broke a superstitious tradition of conducting executions on Fridays.[17]

Prior to execution day, Hayward requested that the gallows be painted red, and this request was honored. With no prospect for clemency for Hayward, Hennepin County Sheriff John E. Holmberg was deluged with requests for "tickets" to the hanging. Some people even offered to "pay handsomely" for the privilege of attending. Indeed, a continuous string of people came to Minneapolis from all over Minnesota, Iowa, and Wisconsin seeking passes, "as if they had not read that the law only allowed a limited number of persons to be present." Sheriff Holmberg "turned them away with the best grace possible," but many "were inclined to be angry that they were not taken care of."

By December 10, the jail office became so crowded with visitors that the outer door to the jail had to be locked. Even so, curiosity seekers gathered outside the jail all day long, with large numbers arriving at around 6:00 P.M. The noisy crowd became so dense at one point that deputies refused to open the jail door, even to those with passes, for fear that the surging masses would enter the jail. The "many prominent citizens" in the crowd were "treated as roughly as any."[18] At around midnight, Hayward was visited by John Day Smith, a devout Christian, who made Hayward promise that he would declare his trust in Christ on the scaffold. After Smith's visit, deputies clothed Hayward in a black robe and cap, and he was led to the gallows by Sheriff Holmberg. When asked for a final statement, Hayward rambled on for quite some time. Eventually, out of "great respect" for his attorney, Hayward kept his promise to Smith. "[H]e is a religious man, as well as an attorney," he said, "and I told him I would pledge him what he asked of me to say. I pledged it to him, although if I honestly believed it, I would say it, and satisfy myself, and it was this: 'Oh, God, for Christ's sake, forgive me for my sins.'"

The trap was swung open at 2:05 A.M. after Hayward uttered his last words, and Hayward was pronounced dead a few minutes later. Although one newspaper later reported that "upward of a hundred persons" were present at the execution, other sources reported that only about two dozen people witnessed the hanging. "A half dozen women, evidently from Sheriff Holmberg's household, attempted to get in, but the sheriff ordered them back." After his body was cut down, cranial measurements were taken and the autopsy determined that Hayward had an "abnormal" brain and an "unusually thick" skull. The red gallows was later sold to the Palace Museum, which had already obtained a phonographic recording of Hayward's voice. Sheriff Holmberg was paid $250 for his services. After Hayward's hanging, the *St. Paul Pioneer Press* expressed its high regard for private executions. "It is a wise provision of our modern laws that these horrible spectacles are no longer ghastly public shows for the entertainment of crowds of brutal men and women, but are secluded as far as possible from the public gaze."[19]

From 1896 to 1905, ten more men swung from the gallows in Minnesota. Although newspaper reporters were usually permitted to attend these executions, they were sometimes excluded. For example, when convicted murderer C. D. Crawford was hung at 1:48 A.M. on December 5, 1905, in an enclosure in Elk River, only thirty-five to forty men—most of them visiting sheriffs—witnessed the hanging. Several reporters made "vigorous efforts to get in," but Sherburne County Sheriff E. L. Ward obeyed the John Day Smith law "to the letter." Sheriff Ward's literal compliance was most likely the result of a personal letter from newly elected Governor John A. Johnson, a popular Democratic politician in a traditionally Republican state. A former newspaper editor, Governor Johnson called Sheriff Ward's attention to the provisions of the Smith law in his letter. In a "pleasant, but at the same time unmistakable manner," Johnson suggested that Sheriff Ward had a duty to enforce the law. After Crawford's execution, one newspaper actually accused Sheriff Ward of refusing to admit Crawford's three invited friends because Ward suspected that they were newspaper men. Ward denied the charge, but his suspected actions sparked unsuccessful press calls for a gubernatorial investigation. A local paper's demand that executions take place at the state penitentiary in Stillwater also fell on deaf ears. On other occasions, some newspaper reporters "used their ingenuity—one dressed as a priest—so that they could watch and then continue to write their descriptive stories" about executions.[20]

In accordance with John Day Smith's "midnight assassination law," all Minnesota hangings from 1896 to 1905 occurred "before the hour of sunrise."[21] During that time, however, county sheriffs often violated the

spirit of the "midnight assassination law" by inviting more than six witnesses to attend executions. This was done by deputizing men as execution "assistants." Thus, 125 spectators were sworn in as deputy sheriffs by
Sheriff August Gaffke before Theodore Wallert's 1:00 A.M. hanging in
Henderson on March 29, 1901. Approximately 150 people were sworn in
as deputies before the 12:45 A.M. hanging of Andrew Tapper in Chaska
in 1902, and over 400 spectators crowded the execution enclosure when
wife-murderer Joseph Ott was hung in 1898 at 1:27 A.M. in Granite Falls.
According to one account: "[S]heriffs were not averse to sending invitations, some engraved, to several hundred 'select friends' to witness an execution. One sheriff served drinks and refreshments to his guests while
an underling cut the rope used in the hanging into pieces that were distributed as a memento of a social affair."[22]

One man who was sentenced to death in Minnesota cheated the
gallows by committing suicide, but the events surrounding his death
sparked renewed interest in John Day Smith's "midnight assassination
law." After the condemned man, Edward Gottschalk, hanged himself
on July 19, 1905, it was discovered that Ramsey County Sheriff Anton
Miesen had sent out a large number of invitation cards, inviting
friends to attend the hanging. The cards declared: "You have been appointed Deputy Sheriff to assist me at the Execution of Edward
Gottschalk. You will report at County Jail at 1 o'clock A.M. sharp, August 8, 1905." Governor John A. Johnson, who was personally opposed
to capital punishment but who was willing to "execute the law," had
scheduled Gottschalk's execution for that day.[23]

When the existence of the invitation cards was unearthed, the *St.
Paul Pioneer Press* charged Sheriff Miesen with intending to violate the
spirit, if not the letter, of the Smith law. The newspaper opined that the
cards make "the hollow pretense of appointing deputies as if there were
not already more than enough deputies to afford all possible assistance
in the execution." The paper concluded that it was "high time" that
"abuses of this kind, with their purely brutalizing effects, should be
brought to an end." After Gottschalk's suicide, the *St. Paul Pioneer Press*
also declared that a "stop should be put to all possibility of turning an
execution into a public orgy and spectacle." "[T]he only effectual way to
put a stop to this sort of thing, as long as sheriffs ignore the plain intent
of the law is to impose the duty of carrying out death sentences on state

prison authorities," the paper proclaimed. That same year, Sheriff J. W. Dreger of Minneapolis, the president of the Interstate Sheriffs' Association, indicated his agreement. In his annual address to the association, Dreger said he "favored the plan of having all executions held at the state prison." However, the state prison warden opposed the plan because of the negative effect it would have on other prisoners, and the proposal went nowhere.[24]

The Hanging of William Williams

William Williams was the last person executed in Minnesota. He had been convicted of first-degree murder on May 19, 1905, and sentenced to death for killing Johnny Keller, a teenager with whom Williams was suspected of having "a strong and strange attachment to." During jury selection, Ramsey County Attorney Thomas R. Kane had "succeeded in having excluded one or two [jurors] that might otherwise have proved acceptable, on the score of having scruples against the infliction of the death penalty." After the verdict was read, the trial judge told Williams that he would "hang by the neck until dead," and the Minnesota Supreme Court affirmed Williams's conviction and death sentence. One justice dissented, arguing that Williams was entitled to a new trial. Governor John A. Johnson set Williams's execution date for February 13, 1906, and the federal courts refused to interfere with it.[25]

Because Sheriff Miesen had previously invited a large number of his friends to watch Edward Gottschalk's execution, Governor Johnson sent Sheriff Miesen a letter accompanying Williams's death warrant. His letter asked Sheriff Miesen to observe that the John Day Smith law "is very specific as to who may witness executions of this state." His letter continued:

> In view of violations of this law in the past I deem it necessary to charge you with a strict observance of the law. It has been customary in some cases for the sheriff to designate many people as deputy sheriffs for the sole purpose of permitting them to be present and witness the execution.
>
> Persons permitted by you, except those specifically named in the statute, must not exceed six in number. I trust

that the custom that has hitherto obtained will not obtain in
this instance.

It is the duty of this office to hold all officers of the law
to a strict accountability in the performance of their duties
in upholding the majesty of the law and it would become my
duty in case this law is violated to take proper action in the
premises.

Believing that you will do your full duty in this matter
and be governed strictly by the letter and spirit of the law, I
am, sir, yours with great respect.[26]

Sheriff Miesen pledged to faithfully abide by all of the provisions of
the Smith law. Indeed, in response to numerous solicitations for invitations, the sheriff told people that "he did not make the law, and that his
duty is merely to carry out its provisions strictly." Although the law had
never been construed by a Minnesota court, Sheriff Miesen took the
word "assistants" in the statute to mean only those on his staff, not such
persons as the sheriff might deputize for the night. When one invitation
seeker was shown the statute, the person responded: "To hell with the
law. I want to see the execution." It was "foreign to his nature" to refuse
such requests, but Sheriff Miesen was under intense political pressure to
restrict the number of invitations. According to one newspaper report,
"[T]he sheriff, who stands accountable to the governor for obedience to
the requirements of his office, knows that he has the alternative of facing two potent factors in his future career—the authority of the governor of the state to remove him for disobedience, and the political power
wielded by persons who become enemies through his refusal."[27]

On February 13, 1906, Williams was hanged as planned in the sub-
basement of the Ramsey County Jail by Sheriff Miesen, but when the trap
door was swung open at 12:31 A.M., Williams's body immediately hit the
ground. "He's on the floor!" shouted the spectators. Sheriff Miesen, who
attended a dinner party earlier that evening, had miscalculated the length
of the rope. Three deputies, standing on the scaffold, instantly seized the
rope and pulled it up so Williams's feet would not touch the floor. The
deputies had to hold up Williams's body for fourteen and a half minutes
until the coroner pronounced him dead from strangulation.[28]

After the hanging, several newspapers printed detailed accounts of
it. The St. Paul Pioneer Press reported that "the death trap was swung in

the basement of the county jail, and fourteen and a half minutes later William Williams was pronounced dead." Some execution details were described, but the paper did not report that the hanging was botched. "The sheriff pulled the lever, the trap dropped, and with a snap the body hung suspended," the paper blandly reported. Other newspaper reports were more graphic. For example, the *St. Paul Daily News* reported that Williams's "feet touched the ground by reason of the fact that his neck stretched four and one-half inches and the rope nearly eight inches." It added that the three sheriff's deputies—whom the newspaper named— "took turns holding up the body" by pulling on the rope "so that Williams' head was kept up and strangulation could slowly go on." Likewise, the *St. Paul Dispatch* described in great detail the fourteen and a half minutes that the spectators were forced to endure.[29]

In the aftermath of the hanging, the *St. Paul Dispatch* accused Sheriff Miesen of violating the John Day Smith law. "It is safe to say that the feature of a crowded execution was eliminated by Sheriff Miesen," the paper declared, "but, if the number of persons who left the jail at its close are any index of the number who saw it, it is certain that the six persons designated in the law as the number the sheriff may personally invite, was unmercifully stretched." The paper even reported a rumor that Governor Johnson's office was "going to probe the sheriff's office," although it expressed the opinion that Sheriff Miesen had not "committed any offense that calls for gubernatorial review."[30]

In contrast, the *Minneapolis Journal* specifically asked that Governor Johnson "take cognizance of any flagrant infringements" of the John Day Smith law. "If the sheriff of Ramsey county has deliberately defied the law made for his guidance, he should be punished," the newspaper asserted. "Perhaps the deposition of one sheriff would do as much to enlarge respect for the Smith law as anything that could be done. Politicians like to oblige their friends, but they do not like to do it at the risk of losing their jobs." The newspaper conceded that the Smith law had never been strictly enforced, and that "[t]here have always been more persons present at executions than the law allowed." The paper blamed this lack of enforcement on "political sheriffs" who made it "difficult to enforce the law literally." While "not rigorously enforced," the newspaper praised John Day Smith's creation as "a good law." The law had done "a great deal" to curtail "morbid public curiosity about the legal killing of an individual." "There is no sense nor civilization in making the execution of a criminal a public spectacle," the paper explained, "and the world has come a great ways since condemned men were hanged in the public square for the edification of men and women and children."[31]

After Williams's execution, other newspapers urged that executions be conducted at the state penitentiary in Stillwater, rather than by county sheriffs. The *St. Paul Dispatch* wrote that county executions perpetuated a "local morbid element that exists in human nature." "Just so long as a hanging is made in a local jail," the paper opined, "will newspapers that give all the news feel it necessary to give 'the bare details' of the affair." Only if convicts were executed at the remote Stillwater prison would newspapers "give no more value to it as news than could be put in the space of a 'stick' or two of type."[32] Despite repeated calls to move executions to Stillwater, bills aimed at accomplishing this reform always failed to pass the Minnesota legislature.[33]

The Gubernatorial Investigation

On the evening of February 13, 1906, Governor Johnson, a former editor and publisher of the *St. Peter Herald,* announced that an investigation of Williams's hanging would be conducted. "I shall examine into the execution," he proclaimed, "and if there has been the slightest violation of the law, even a technical violation, Sheriff Miesen will have to answer for it." "I meant just exactly what I said when I sent the letter cautioning Miesen," Johnson continued, "and if he has violated the law I shall go after him." Johnson understood from "official circles" that only ten persons were present at the execution. Thus, he was surprised to learn from another source that over twenty-five witnesses may have been present. Also, because two newspaper reporters supposedly attended the hanging—one article was captioned "The Only Newspaper Man Who Witnessed the Execution"—Governor Johnson announced that he would investigate whether reporters were present with the cognizance of Sheriff Miesen or his deputies. If this fact could be proved, Johnson declared, the sheriff's office would be held accountable. "I have laid aside all the accounts in the newspapers and shall examine them carefully tomorrow," Governor Johnson concluded.[34]

The next day, Johnson personally questioned Miesen. "The official reports of the meeting in the governor's private office were that the governor got after the sheriff 'real fierce' and cross-questioned him closely." However, Johnson ultimately accepted every explanation offered by Miesen. For instance, Johnson accepted Miesen's explanation that a newspaper reporter slipped in through an oversight when a door was left unlocked. Likewise, he found satisfactory Sheriff Miesen's explanation that, while thirty-two persons admittedly witnessed the hanging, twenty of them were "deputies."[35]

By February 25, Governor Johnson had completed his investigation of the botched hanging. He found that "the letter of the law" had been carried out by Sheriff Miesen and decided that no further action would be taken against him. The details of Williams's death, though, "grated on the governor's nerves." Consequently, Johnson announced that he would recommend the abolition of capital punishment in his next legislative message. The death penalty is a "survival of the relic of the past," he said, "and the sooner it is done away with the better." "If I as governor personally had to aid in the execution of a condemned man," he told a friend, "I would resign my office in preference to carrying out such a duty." Governor Johnson's willingness to accept Sheriff Miesen's rather feeble explanations led to a charge of political favoritism by the *St. Paul Pioneer Press*. "[A] search of the political calendar suggests that this is the closed season on Democratic sheriffs," wrote the paper. Both Governor Johnson and Sheriff Miesen were Democrats.[36]

Three Newspapers Indicted

On February 15, 1906, representatives of the Law and Order League formally protested the newspaper accounts of Williams's botched hanging, first complaining to Municipal Court Judge John W. Finehout, who promptly referred them to the county attorney's office. Ramsey County Attorney Thomas R. Kane was "most courteous" in hearing their complaint, but he handed them over to the prosecuting city attorney, Emil W. Helmes. Although Helmes was busy, he arranged to meet with Law and Order League members late that afternoon. After lodging these numerous complaints, the Law and Order League was eventually successful in alerting Ramsey County District Court Judge George L. Bunn to the legal violations committed by the newspapers.[37]

On February 19, a Ramsey County grand jury convened before Judge Bunn, who singled out the newspapers' violation of the John Day Smith law. Judge Bunn told the grand jurors:

> There is but one thing I desire to call your attention to at this time, and that is this: I call your attention to the fact that it is the law of this state relating to executions that the newspapers shall publish only a bare statement of the fact that the convict has been executed. I call your attention to the existence of that law on our statute books and the apparent gross violation of that law by all the newspapers of this city, with reference to the execution of Williams lately. Now, there is a matter that in your discretion you may take up and consider.

This was the first time that a Minnesota court had ever taken notice of the Smith law.[38]

On March 2, after a "lively discussion," the twenty-one-member grand jury indicted three St. Paul newspapers—the *St. Paul Pioneer Press,* the *St. Paul Dispatch,* and the *St. Paul Daily News*—of "the crime of Publishing the Details of the Execution of a Convict." One faction of the all-male grand jury who opposed the indictments felt that the portion of the John Day Smith law related to newspapers had been "carried out in the breach rather than in the observance." The other faction "took the view that the law was on the books and if it was a bad law the best way to defeat it would be to obey it to the letter." After several sessions, where the advice of Ramsey County Attorney Kane was frequently sought, a small majority voted in favor of the indictments. The "true bills" were drawn up against the newspapers in their corporate capacities and not against the managers, editors, or reporters. A violation of Smith's "midnight assassination law" was a misdemeanor, punishable by up to a $100 fine or ninety days of imprisonment. However, because only the corporations were indicted, Kane announced that the newspapers, if found guilty, could only be fined. Although Sheriff Miesen was widely believed to have flagrantly violated the law, he was not indicted by the grand jury.[39]

Rumors existed that the three St. Paul newspapers, wishing to test the constitutionality of the Smith law, actually helped to procure the indictments by bringing evidence before the grand jury. An editorial in the *St. Paul Pioneer Press* certainly did not dispel these rumors, perhaps even lending credence to them. The newspaper noted that it had "demurred and will carry the case to the supreme court for a ruling on the validity of the law." Even though "its own ox" had been "gored," the paper could nevertheless find "no fault" with the attempt to enforce the Smith law. "If it is an improper provision either it should be declared so by the courts or it should be repealed by the legislature. And the way to secure repeal by court or legislature is to force the issue. So long as it is on the statute books, it, like other laws, should be enforced."[40]

Although indicted, the *St. Paul Pioneer Press* was "thoroughly in sympathy" with the "spirit and purposes" of the John Day Smith law. "There has been altogether too much sickening pandering to morbid tastes and too much cultivation of those tastes by hyperbolical accounts of the doings of murderers before executions and of the executions themselves," the paper editorialized. The newspaper commented that it "tried to treat the Williams hanging as it treats all other news matters" by attempting "to give an accurate account of an event of public interest, to give essential details, omitting ghastly particulars, without pandering to the demand of the morbid." It had attempted "to give a decent and uncolored story." "[I]n short," it had tried "to avoid the methods of 'yellow journalism,' in which some of the other newspapers delight to revel." "Had all stories of hangings been of the same type" as its news story of Williams's hanging, the *Pioneer Press* wrote, "there would have been no occasion for the John Day Smith law."

Nonetheless, the *Pioneer Press* was indignant about having been indicted under the Smith law "for printing the news." "[W]e do not believe it is a safe or a proper law, so far as it attempts to regulate newspaper accounts," the paper wrote, stressing that "[i]t is questionable whether any law on the subject would be safe." According to the paper:

> Here was a case of atrocious bungling in the execution itself and of flat violation of the law and of the direct orders of the governor. Under the restrictions of the John Day

Smith law the newspapers could make no reference to either the execution or to the presence of witnesses prohibited by the same law or any of the other circumstances
which it was of importance that the public should know.
Evidence of the incompetence of the sheriff so clearly indicated in the details of the hanging and of his utter disregard
of the law would have to pass unnoticed. Under the press
muzzling provisions of this law the worst orgies could be
held and even the cruelest barbarities could be practiced,
and those responsible for them would be protected from
criticism and exposure. Such restrictions are thoroughly
and palpably unsafe.[41]

The *Pioneer Press* emphasized that, ironically, it had actually first
drawn attention to the lack of enforcement of the Smith law. In printing a facsimile of one of Sheriff Miesen's invitations to Edward
Gottschalk's hanging, it had exposed Sheriff Miesen's "plan for a gross
violation of the law." This article had prompted Governor Johnson to
pen his letter to the sheriff to remind him of the law, and only after
"calling attention" to the law's lack of enforcement had the paper "got
itself indicted." The paper quipped: "The alleged publication of the
alleged facts regarding the recent alleged hanging of a reputed convicted murderer seems to be producing more alleged effect than the
alleged exposure of alleged irregularities at the time of the alleged
hanging."[42]

On March 3, the three indicted newspapers were arraigned and
pled not guilty. Judge Bunn presided. Because all three newspapers anticipated filing amended pleas, the newspapers reserved the right to
change their pleas or file demurrers to the indictments. The newspapers wanted four days to accomplish this task, but Judge Bunn allowed
them only two extra days. All three newspapers in fact did withdraw
their not guilty pleas within that time frame. In their place, the newspapers filed demurrers to the indictments on the ground that the publication of execution details did not "constitute a public offense." The
newspapers, represented by separate legal counsel, all decided to attack
the constitutionality of John Day Smith's "midnight assassination
law."[43]

The District Court Ruling

On March 10, 1906, the respective parties appeared before Judge Bunn concerning their demurrers. The attorney for the *St. Paul Dispatch,* N. M. Thygeson, argued that the Smith law violated the newspapers' constitutionally guaranteed right to freedom of the press. "The officers performing the execution should be responsible to an intelligent public opinion for the proper performance of their important duties," he declared. "Cruel and inhuman treatment of the convict might be indulged in, yet no newspaper would have the right to state such facts for the purpose of remedying the wrong," he added. Mr. Thygeson also asserted that the Smith law violated the accused's right to a public trial. "Can it be possible that the accused is entitled to a public trial, where the public can watch and see that he is accorded fair treatment," he asked rhetorically, "but when it comes to the execution of the judgment of that trial then he need not have the protection of publicity?"[44]

The newspapers' lawyers also argued that a county sheriff could carry out an execution "in a brutal manner without the public ever knowing anything about it." "While it might be proper to prohibit gruesome details of the execution, which appeal to the morbid tastes of a part of the community," it was asserted, "a plain uncolored statement of the manner of the carrying out of the mandate of the law is not against the morals of the community." The newspapers' lawyers then argued that the press, "as the medium through which the public is informed of current events," had a right to be present at executions. It was noted that the John Day Smith law did not prohibit the publication of pamphlets or books "containing just the matter which the newspapers are prohibited from publishing." All three newspapers specifically alleged that the Smith law contravened Article 1, Section 3 of the Minnesota Constitution, providing: "The liberty of the press shall forever remain inviolate and all persons may freely speak, write and publish their sentiments on all subjects, being responsible for the abuse of such right."[45]

The papers' lawyers further argued that the public had a right to know a condemned person's last words. The lawyers contended that the John Day Smith law impermissibly prevented the publication of a condemned convict's dying words or an admission of guilt uttered at the execution. In contrast, Ramsey County Attorney Thomas Kane asserted that the Smith law was within the legislature's power to enact. He said the object of the law was to prevent the publication of execution details that appealed to morbid tastes and lowered public morals. At the conclusion of the hearing, Judge Bunn took the matter under advisement.[46]

On April 16, 1906, Judge Bunn upheld the constitutionality of John Day Smith's "midnight assassination law" in open court. His written order stated that the "object and chief purpose of the act was to avoid general publicity." The order continued: "It is quite clear that forbidding the publication of the details tends strongly to accomplish the purpose of the act. . . . The purpose of the act is in a large measure defeated if the morbidly curious public, who are forbidden to see the hanging, may satisfy their curiosity by reading the ghastly details in a newspaper, and feasting their eyes on pictures of the scene." Judge Bunn had "no doubt" that the legislature had the right to enact the law in the interest of public morals. He wrote: "The legislature has said that the publication of the details of an execution is bad for public morals. Its decision should be upheld unless the court can see plainly that it is wrong. I think the decision is right, and the law wise and wholesome." He specifically cited the U.S. Supreme Court's 1890 decision in *Holden v. Minnesota* to support his ruling. Because of the question's importance, however, Judge Bunn agreed to certify the question of the statute's constitutionality to the Minnesota Supreme Court. The case was certified by Judge Bunn on May 8, 1906, at the request of the *St. Paul Pioneer Press's* attorneys, Frederick Ingersoll and Charles Hart. The *St. Paul Dispatch* and the *St. Paul Daily News* agreed to be bound by the result of the *Pioneer Press's* appeal.[47]

The Minnesota Supreme Court Case

On appeal, the *St. Paul Pioneer Press* conceded that the legislature has "the power to restrict the publication of matters which tend to demoralize or degrade the public morals." However, the newspaper contended that the John Day Smith law went too far. According to the newspaper's appellate brief:

> A newspaper performs a public function in that it places before the public, accounts of occurrences in which the public

has a right to be interested and of which there should be a
public criticism. While conceding that the gruesome details
of an execution of a criminal are not necessary subjects of
public information, yet we assert that there are many things
surrounding the manner of an execution which the public
are entitled to know and upon which the public are entitled
to pass criticism.

For example, the paper asserted that the public has a right to know a
condemned man's dying declarations and how sheriffs performed their
duties. Thus, the newspaper believed that the Smith law was overbroad.
"The statute in question prohibits not only those things that are detrimental to the public, and we concede that ghastly accounts of gruesome
details might be harmful in effect," the paper argued, "*but prohibits
everything* save the legal conclusion, that the execution took place."

The *St. Paul Pioneer Press* took the position that sensational articles
should be the subject of "proper censorship." "[I]t is true that cartoons
illustrating such affairs are objectionable," its legal brief declared, "and
that the publication of all degrading or demoralizing particulars should
be forbidden." However, the newspaper vehemently argued that its article was "in no way sensational." The *St. Paul Pioneer Press* asserted that
its article was "remarkably brief, well timed and carefully written. No
cartoons were run, and there was an absence of any attempt to give it
more than ordinary prominence in the paper; it was not made one of the
leading features of that issue and in no important respect violated either
the language or the spirit of the Act."[48]

In its responsive brief, the state of Minnesota defended the Smith
law. The state's brief declared that the Smith law was intended "to do
away with public executions, and to make all future executions secret except so far as certain specified witnesses may be present." "The obvious
purpose of the act is the suppression of details which are nauseating and
horrible and whose dissemination arouses morbidness," the brief concluded. The state mused that the publication of execution details might
even "tend directly to promote crime, while subserving no useful purpose." It argued that the press was not deprived of its right to print the
news because the law "expressly authorizes the publication of the fact
that the criminal was executed." Publication of execution details "tends

only to gratify a debased morbid curiosity or sensualism which is demoralizing to the public good." The state contended that the Smith law
did not "prevent the newspapers from discussing the advisability of capital punishment . . . or giving their sentiments on the subject as a public question."[49]

On February 21, 1907, the Minnesota Supreme Court upheld the
constitutionality of the Smith law, ruling that the "evident purpose of
the act was to surround the execution of criminals with as much secrecy
as possible, in order to avoid exciting an unwholesome effect on the
public mind." To accomplish this objective, the court believed that executions "must take place before dawn, while the masses are at rest, and
within an inclosure, so as to debar the morbidly curious." The court also
upheld the statutory provisions that forbade newspaper reporters from
attending executions and that prohibited the publication of execution
details. This was necessary "to give further effect" to the law's "purpose
of avoiding publicity." "Publication of the facts in a newspaper would
tend to offset all the benefits of secrecy provided for," the court ruled.
The court noted that the *St. Paul Pioneer Press* article was "moderate"
and did not "resort to any unusual language, or exhibit cartoons for the
purpose of emphasizing the horrors of executing the death penalty."
However, the court stressed that "if, in the opinion of the Legislature, it
is detrimental to public morals to publish anything more than the mere
fact that the execution has taken place, then, under the authorities and
upon principle, the appellant was not deprived of any constitutional
right in being so limited."[50]

As a result of the ruling, the *St. Paul Pioneer Press*'s case was remanded back to the district court to be tried on the merits. On March
17, 1908, a twelve-person jury was impaneled, but the *Pioneer Press* refused to enter a plea, forcing the court to enter a plea of not guilty for
the newspaper. The next day, the jury returned a verdict of "guilty as
charged in the indictment." Consequently, on March 19, the court imposed a $25 fine against the *Pioneer Press*. Having agreed to be bound by
the outcome of the *Pioneer Press*'s trial, the *St. Paul Dispatch* and the *St.
Paul Daily News* were also fined $25 each.[51]

In an editorial, the *St. Paul Pioneer Press* denounced the Minnesota
Supreme Court's ruling against it. The paper said that it was "in full
sympathy" with any law that suppressed "purely unimportant and un-

wholesome details of an execution." However, it declared that the John Day Smith law "is not so entirely wise as its intent is worthy." The hanging of William Williams "showed that except for publication in newspapers of something more than a bare mention there was no way in which to inform the public whether a hanging was properly or even legally conducted." The editorial concluded by asking that executions be moved to the state prison, "where the warden is more responsible and less subject to political pressure than the average prison sheriff, where there would be less danger of bungling, and where there would be no morbid crowd hovering about trying to catch a glimpse of the proceedings." Again, though, legislative proposals to move executions to the Stillwater state prison always failed.[52]

Abolitionist Efforts in Minnesota

Toward the end of the nineteenth century, numerous efforts were made in the Minnesota legislature to abolish capital punishment. Members of the Minnesota House of Representatives introduced bills to abolish capital punishment in 1891, 1893, 1895, and 1897, but each time the bills failed to pass. Although the 1893 bill, which sought to substitute life imprisonment as the punishment for murder, cleared the house by a 67–26 vote, it never reached a vote on the senate floor. The debate on these bills was often intense. For instance, in 1895, Representative J. D. Jones, a death penalty supporter, stated that "the skeleton hands of the murdered victims are stretching up from their graves through their thin covering of earth beckoning to us for vengeance." In 1897, the author of a bill to abolish capital punishment, Representative Sylvanus A. Stockwell, called "for the breaking of one more link in the chain that binds us to our savage ancestry," insisting that capital punishment "is a developer of crime."[53]

After the turn of the century, abolitionist efforts continued. In 1901, Representative Peder M. Hendricks, a farmer from Otter Tail County, introduced an abolitionist bill, which the House of Representatives later tabled. Likewise, in 1905, two more abolitionist bills were introduced in the Minnesota legislature. The first bill was introduced in the senate by Senator John T. Alley, a Republican lawyer from Wright County. That bill set life imprisonment as the punishment for first-degree murder unless the jury prescribed the punishment of death. A second bill was introduced in the house by Representative John G. Lund. "It is a simple affair of two lines, and only says that the penalty for murder in the first degree shall be imprisonment for life," the *Minneapolis Journal* reported. Representative Lund's bill was "strongly advocated by the author and a number of friends of the idea." However, when his bill failed to get reported out of the Committee on Crimes and Punishment, Representative Lund moved that Senator Alley's bill be substituted for his bill and that consideration of his own bill be "indefinitely postponed." That motion prevailed, but Senator Alley's bill—which passed the senate by a vote of 44–4—never reached a house vote.[54]

In 1907, abolitionists renewed their legislative efforts. Representative Frederick B. Phillips, a thirty-two-year-old lawyer from White Bear, introduced a bill seeking to require that executions take place before sunrise at the Stillwater state prison. Representative Phillips was particularly concerned about "the evil effect upon the community of having hangings" at county jails. He emphasized how at the hanging of William Williams in St. Paul "men, women and children came in groups around the county jail to get a glimpse of the prisoner." Representative Phillips believed that if executions took place at the state prison, these "hanging parties" would be put to a stop. Representative Phillips's bill retained the provision of the Smith law against admitting newspaper reporters to executions and against newspapers printing execution details. After its introduction, the *St. Paul Pioneer Press* called Representative Phillips's bill "a sensible, wholesome measure," but the house voted to indefinitely postpone consideration of the bill by a tally of 39–28.[55]

Another abolitionist bill was introduced in the Minnesota House of Representatives in 1907 by Representative Fred B. Wright, a Republican lawyer from Minneapolis. His bill also sought to move executions to the state prison at Stillwater, but additionally sought to substitute the electric chair for hanging as the method of execution. Electrocution was "the coming process," he said. State Prison Warden Henry Wolfer agreed that "the present method is not what it ought to be and there should be a central place where executions could be performed methodically and uniformly and away from the usual notoriety." However, Wolfer did not want to oversee executions at the state prison. "I feel that placing this duty on the head of that institution is hardly in keeping with the spirit of the general purpose of the institution," he said, "not because of the effect upon the warden but because of the effect upon the inmates. The state has a duty to those inmates and the duty of reforming them is hardly compatible with the duty of performing executions." Wolfer suggested that the state execute people in a building "on an island perhaps away from where people congregate," instead of executing them at the state prison. After Representative Wright's bill was referred to the House Committee on Crimes and Punishment, which reported it back without recommendation, no further action was ever taken on the bill.[56]

A third bill in 1907 was introduced by Representatives Phillips and Wright, the authors of the two previous death penalty bills. The Phillips-Wright bill sought to substitute life imprisonment for death as the punishment for first-degree murder and prohibited the pardoning of convicted murderers unless indisputable evidence of innocence was established. In debating the Phillips-Wright bill, Representative Clarence B. Miller, a lawyer from Duluth, said that statistics showed that capital punishment has no deterrent effect. "Passing over the right of the state to take human life," he asserted, "I do not think that as a matter of practical utility it ever did a bit of good. The abolition of capital punishment will facilitate verdicts. Juries will not hesitate when the evidence is clear unless they know that their verdict will send the man to the gallows." In contrast, Representative Burdett Thayer of Spring Valley argued that "[y]ou can get statistics on either side." Ultimately, the house voted 47–34 to table the Phillips-Wright bill.[57]

In 1909, Representative C. M. Bendixen, a farmer from Redwood County, introduced another bill to abolish capital punishment. The House Committee on Crimes and Punishment recommended passage of Representative Bendixen's bill, but the full house voted down the bill by a vote of 31–9. Despite its failure, Representative Bendixen's bill was debated for nearly an hour on the house floor. Aside from Representative Bendixen, Representative George A. MacKenzie, a Republican lawyer from Gaylord, was practically the only person who spoke in support of the measure. In what the St. Paul Pioneer Press called an "eloquent plea," Representative MacKenzie urged that the state abandon its "barbaric" power of taking human life. As the Sibley County Attorney, MacKenzie had prosecuted Theodore Wallert in 1901 for murder and had turned against capital punishment after watching Wallert hanged and witnessing other "vigilante hangings" out West and the hanging of an innocent man. "The law is inconsistent," Representative MacKenzie argued, in that "it makes it unlawful for a man to take his own life, yet lets the state take life." He added that the infliction of the death penalty only "nourishes the spirit of revenge, demoralizes the community, lessens the sacredness of human life, [and] largely prevents the prosecution and punishment of crime." "If the death penalty deters others from murder," he asked rhetorically, "why not have executions public?"[58]

The Minnesota legislature, which normally met every other year, did not convene in 1910. However, in December of that year, Ramsey County Attorney Richard D. O'Brien called for the abolition of capital punishment. In a newspaper article, O'Brien was quoted as saying:

> I wish somebody would start agitating for the abolition of capital punishment in this state. . . . The law allowing the imposition of the death sentence upon conviction of murder makes it practically impossible for the state to obtain the right sort of jury, and after the jury is secured the chances of conviction, even with the strongest evidence, are at a minimum. There are many men, otherwise competent to serve as jurymen, who honestly have conscientious scruples against taking a life into their hands. There are many more men of high character who, deliberately or otherwise, seize upon the death penalty as an excuse from serving. I am convinced that should the death penalty be stricken from the statutes the state would be in much better position to secure convictions.[59]

The thirty-seventh session of the Minnesota legislature convened on January 3, 1911, almost five years after the botched hanging of William Williams. A day later, in his inaugural message delivered to a joint legislative session, Governor Adolph O. Eberhart called for the abolition of capital punishment.

> The experience of this and other states, as well as the verdict of most criminologists, agrees on the question of abolishing capital punishment, and I am firmly convinced that there would be more convictions for murder in the first degree if

either capital punishment were abolished, or imposed only in extreme cases, and then only upon the order of the court or the unanimous recommendation of the jury. The old argument against its abolition on the ground that the board of pardons would frequently reduce the life sentence is amply refuted by the records of the present state board of pardons, and the question is before this legislature entirely upon its merits. I believe the interests of justice and humanity demand the repeal of the law and I am convinced that the state would secure more convictions in capital cases and that consequently crime in general would be reduced by the abolition of this antiquated practice in criminal procedure.[60]

On January 5, Representative George MacKenzie introduced yet another bill in the House of Representatives to abolish capital punishment. That bill was referred to the House Committee on Crimes and Punishment, which recommended its passage on February 2. One person who spoke in favor of abolition before that committee was Stillwater state prison warden Henry Wolfer. "I have never favored capital punishment," he said, "and the more I study methods of dealing with the criminal classes the more convinced I am that the death penalty should not be invoked." He emphasized that the death penalty does not deter crime. "Experience shows and penologists are quite agreed that as a deterring influence this form of punishment is without effect."[61]

On February 28, the house passed Representative MacKenzie's bill by an overwhelming vote of 95–19. This represented a "personal triumph" for Representative MacKenzie, who had worked for the bill's passage for six years. Representative MacKenzie "made one of the most eloquent and impressive speeches in behalf of the measure that has been made in the House chamber." He implored fellow legislators: "Let us bar this thing of Vengeance and the Furies from the confines of our great State; Let not this harlot of judicial murder smear the pages of our history with her bloody fingers, or trail her crimson robes through our Halls of Justice, and let never again the Great Seal of the Great State of Minnesota be affixed upon a warrant to take a human life." Representative MacKenzie further described witnessing the death penalty being inflicted and argued that the state does not have the right to kill. When

Representative MacKenzie concluded, the members of the house warmly applauded his remarks.[62]

Only a few voices were raised in defense of capital punishment. One farmer from Swift Falls, Representative Knute Knutson, said "he was as sympathetic as any member in the House, but his sympathies went out to the friends of the victim of the murderer rather than to the criminal." Others raised objections to Representative MacKenzie's bill, fearing that convicted murderers could be paroled by the State Board of Pardons. This latter concern was alleviated, however, by the house's passage of a bill authored by Representative Joseph R. Keefe on the same day that Representative MacKenzie's bill passed the house. Representative Keefe's bill, passed by a vote of 95–4, took away the Board of Pardons' right to pardon convicted first-degree murderers unless their innocence could be established beyond a reasonable doubt.[63]

After clearing the house, advocates of the MacKenzie bill admitted that it would have "a harder row to hoe in the Senate than it had in the House." However, in the closing hours of the legislative session, the senate passed Representative MacKenzie's bill with "no fight" by a vote of 35–19. No debate on the measure occurred on the senate floor because "[c]areful polls previously made showed that at least thirty-five senators favored it." Governor Eberhart signed Representative MacKenzie's bill on April 22, proclaiming that the abolition of capital punishment entitled the members of the legislature "to a large measure of credit."[64]

A front-page cartoon in the *Minneapolis Journal* marked the culmination of abolitionist efforts. The cartoon, which had two panels, was captioned "Spring Fashions for Minnesota." The first panel depicted a noose and contained the inscription "This necktie will not be worn in Minnesota hereafter." The next panel, depicting a stripped prison uniform with a patch on it labeled "Life Sentence," stated simply: "While this suit will be worn a little longer." After many hard-fought legislative battles, the abolitionists had triumphed; no longer would people be put to death in Minnesota.[65]

The Lessons of Minnesota's "Midnight Assassination Law"

As shown in Chapters 2 and 3, public or semipublic executions were once common on the Minnesota frontier. Yet, over time, Minnesota's

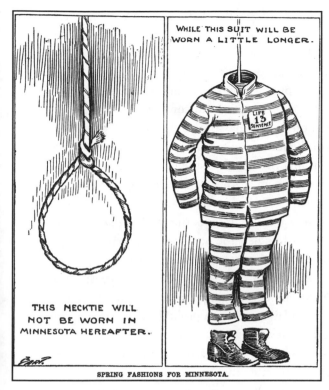

WHILE THIS SUIT WILL BE WORN A LITTLE LONGER.

LIFE 13 SENTENCE

THIS NECKTIE WILL NOT BE WORN IN MINNESOTA HEREAFTER.

SPRING FASHIONS FOR MINNESOTA.

A cartoon published in the *Minneapolis Journal* right after the Minnesota Legislature abolished capital punishment in 1911. (Minnesota Historical Society)

civic leaders came to abhor such spectacles. It became evident to them that execution day crowds were not coming to hangings to honor the sanctity of life. They were coming out of morbid curiosity or, worse yet, to be entertained. Community leaders found it particularly troubling that execution spectators were drinking alcohol, and that women—whom nineteenth-century newspapermen labeled "the tender sex"—were exposed to hangings. Some public officials even feared the possibility of rioting because of the unruly execution day crowds. Because public executions came to be viewed by community leaders as uncivilized, tremendous pressure was put on county sheriffs to privatize executions.[66]

Prior to 1889, many executions in Minnesota in fact were conducted by county sheriffs in a semiprivate fashion. These law enforcement officials generally constructed the gallows within the county jail or the confines of board enclosures, some up to eighteen feet high. They usually invited sheriffs, friends, ministers, and newspaper reporters to attend these private affairs, but generally excluded the public from attending executions. Women and children were rarely able to witness the gallows in operation, and Minnesotans had to rely on newspaper accounts of executions to get information about them. The public's ability to get information about executions was further eroded in 1889 when Representative John Day Smith successfully spearheaded a legislative effort—resulting in the passage of the "midnight assassination law"—to ensure that no public executions would ever occur in Minnesota again.

Many newspapers ignored the provision of the "midnight assassination law" that prohibited the publication of execution details, but others altered their news coverage of executions to comply with that provision. After the 1889 execution of Thomas Brown, the second person to hang under the auspices of the John Day Smith law, the *Moorhead Daily News* refrained from publishing the details of the hanging, even though it was "cognizant" of many of them. Other newspapers made accounts of executions less sensational, even if it meant inaccurate news reporting. When William Williams was hung in 1906, the *St. Paul Pioneer Press* did not report that the sheriff bungled the hanging. It merely reported that it took Williams fourteen and a half minutes to die, without explaining why. Regardless of editorial decisions, though, all newspapers were hindered in reporting about hangings because county sheriffs sometimes enforced the Smith law's provision prohibiting newspaper reporters from attending executions.[67]

Ironically, the newspapers that exposed the gruesome details of Williams's death in direct violation of the "midnight assassination law" made it Minnesota's last hanging. Only after these newspapers printed a full account of Williams's death did Governor John A. Johnson announce that he would recommend the abolition of capital punishment in Minnesota. The details of Williams's hanging reportedly "grated on the governor's nerves," and while capital punishment was not abolished until 1911, the newspapers' exposure of Williams's botched hanging certainly gave momentum to the abolitionist movement. Indeed, all death sentences after Williams's death were commuted by Minnesota governors.[68] If newspapers had not violated John Day Smith's "midnight assassination law" and printed the details of Williams's execution, Minnesota might have retained capital punishment, or the death penalty might not have been abolished as quickly.

The history of Minnesota's "midnight assassination law" holds two important lessons. First, press coverage of executions can affect public opinion. By reporting about William Williams's execution, the newspapers' exposure of that botched hanging eventually led to the abolition of capital punishment in Minnesota. In other instances, exposure of execution details led to calls for moving executions to the Stillwater state prison or for substituting electrocution, widely believed to be a more humane form of punishment at that time, for hanging. Second, and perhaps more important, restrictions on press access to executions, as shown by the history of the Smith law, are rooted in paternalism and secrecy. This historical fact—that laws requiring private, nighttime executions were intended to shield ordinary citizens from the workings of government—is particularly troublesome because openness in government is the hallmark of America's democracy. After all, if ordinary citizens are unfit to monitor executions because politicians believe the public at large would find them too disgusting or gruesome to watch, one must seriously question whether politicians should be authorizing capital punishment in the first place.

⚘ 6

Politicizing Death

Politicians, Public Opinion, and the Courts

The latest public opinion polls show that roughly 70 percent of Americans favor capital punishment. One poll conducted by ABC News and the *Washington Post* asked, "Do you favor or oppose the death penalty for persons convicted of murder?" Seventy-five percent of respondents favored the death penalty, while only 19 percent were opposed to it. Five percent said "it depends," with 1 percent expressing no opinion. A similar poll conducted in 1992 by NBC News and the *Wall Street Journal* also asked, "Do you favor or oppose the death penalty?" Sixty-nine percent of respondents favored the death penalty, while 24 percent said they were opposed to it. Seven percent said they were not sure. In some parts of the country, poll results are even more dramatic. A recent poll taken by the *Atlanta Constitution* showed that nearly all southerners support the death penalty, and another poll found that nine out of ten Texans hold pro–death penalty views.[1]

With this kind of polling data, it is no surprise that politicians are attempting to capitalize on the pro–death penalty public sentiment. After the Oklahoma City bombing, for instance, President Clinton immediately called for the bombing perpetrators to be executed, and the U.S. Senate voted unanimously, 97–0, that a jury should have the right to impose the death penalty for that crime. Likewise, in unseating former New York Governor Mario Cuomo, Governor George Pataki made his pro–death penalty views a central theme of his gubernatorial campaign, and it was "a critical issue in the election." Other politicians have even resorted to publicity stunts to publicize their pro–death penalty views. One state senator from Nebraska set up a toll-free number in 1991 so voters could voice support for one convicted felon's execution, and an Alabama gubernatorial candidate printed bumper stickers stating, "Fry them, 'til their eyes pop out."[2]

Even longtime opponents of capital punishment are abandoning their anti–death penalty positions. For instance, former California Assembly Speaker Willie Brown—now the mayor of San Francisco—renounced his opposition to capital punishment just hours after California executed David Mason in 1993. Brown told reporters: "You've got to come to the reality that there are some people who are bad people—real bad people." Similarly, former Virginia Governor Douglas Wilder and former Atlanta Mayor Andrew Young—once anti–death penalty advocates—switched sides to favor capital punishment during their gubernatorial campaigns. Mario Cuomo, who vetoed twelve death penalty bills as New York's governor, even softened his hard-line stance against capital punishment when locked in his tight race with George Pataki. Cuomo offered to let the voters decide via referendum among three choices: capital punishment, life imprisonment without parole, or life imprisonment with parole.[3]

While capital punishment now enjoys unprecedented popularity, the death penalty was not always so fashionable. A 1966 Gallup poll reveals that a plurality of Americans once opposed capital punishment. That poll found that 47 percent of Americans opposed the death penalty, while only 42 percent supported it. Eleven percent expressed no opinion. These 1966 poll results marked a six-year decline in public support for capital punishment and actually translated into a nine-year hiatus on executions, or de facto abolition, in the United States beginning in June 1967. The number of executions had fallen from a high of 199 in 1935 to 1 in 1966. The first person executed in America after 1967, Gary Gilmore, did not die by firing squad until January 1977. It was in this political climate that the U.S. Supreme Court handed down its decision in *Furman v. Georgia* in 1972. In that case, the Court struck down state death penalty statutes as unconstitutional, thereby invalidating the death sentences of all 558 persons on death row at that time.[4]

Prior to *Furman,* legal scholars had fiercely debated the constitutionality of capital punishment under the U.S. Constitution's Eighth Amendment. That amendment, applicable to the states under the Due Process Clause of the Fourteenth Amendment, provides: "Excessive bail shall not be required, nor excessive fines imposed, *nor cruel and unusual punishments inflicted.*" The debate among scholars was particularly intense because of the lack of evidence of the Framers' original intent regarding this clause. Only in two of the state ratifying conventions do legislators even discuss "cruel" punishments, and the eighteenth-century debates of the First Congress of the Bill of Rights provide less guidance still on the intended meaning of the Eighth Amendment. In fact, all that appears regarding the concept of "cruel and unusual punishments" in the legislative record of the First Congress is two comments. One legislator from South Carolina objected to the words as being too "indefinite" in their meaning. Another legislator believed the words expressed "a great deal of humanity," but thought the clause unnecessary because "it seems to have no meaning in it." This legislator feared aloud that the clause might be used in the future to prevent the infliction of common punishments such as hanging, whipping, or ear cropping. "[A]re we in the future to be prevented from inflicting these punishments because they are cruel?" he asked rhetorically.[5]

The U.S. Supreme Court has long rejected a strictly historical interpretation of the Eighth Amendment because following that course would have forever permitted punishments such as whipping and ear cropping, and the Eighth Amendment "would have been effectively read out of the Bill of Rights." Instead, the Supreme Court has consistently held that the Eighth Amendment "must draw its meaning from the evolving standards of decency that mark the progress of a maturing society." Thus, "a penalty that was permissible at one time in our Nation is not necessarily permissible today." To determine to what extent society's standards have evolved, the Justices look not to their "own conceptions of decency, but to those of modern American society as a whole." "Eighth Amendment judgments should not be, or appear to be, merely the subjective views of individual Justices; judgment should be informed by objective factors to the maximum extent possible," the Court has ruled. Laws passed by elected officials are the most important of the "'objective indicia that reflect the public attitude toward a given sanction,'" the Court has found. Other salient factors are jury verdicts and international opinion, although the Court has declined to use public opinion polls in the Eighth Amendment context.[6]

In *Furman,* the Supreme Court ruled that death penalty statutes were so arbitrary in application as to violate the Eighth Amendment's prohibition against cruel and unusual punishments. Members of the 5–4 majority in *Furman* compared the death penalty to a "lottery system" or "being struck by lightning" because of the infinitesimal number of people put to death each year. Supreme Court Justice William Brennan emphasized that "[w]hen a country of over 200 million people inflicts an unusually severe punishment no more than 50 times a year, the inference is strong that the punishment is not being regularly and fairly applied." Justice Byron White also focused on the great infrequency with which the death penalty is imposed, concluding that "there is no meaningful basis for distinguishing the few cases in which it is imposed from the many cases in which it is not." Although five Justices in *Furman* voted to strike down state death penalty laws, only two Justices, Brennan and Thurgood Marshall, believed that the Eighth Amendment prohibited capital punishment under all circumstances. Thus, *Furman* left open the possibility that states could reenact new death penalty statutes that would provide greater guidance to judges and juries in imposing death sentences.[7]

The public backlash to *Furman,* perceived as an anti-majoritarian ruling and an unwarranted federal intrusion on states' rights, was pronounced. Thirty-five states immediately reenacted new death penalty laws, and the Supreme Court was compelled to address the constitutionality of death penalty statutes once again in 1976. In that year, in *Gregg v. Georgia,* the Court upheld the constitutionality of Georgia's new death penalty law, which mandated that at least one of ten "aggravating circumstances" be found before a convicted murderer could be sentenced to death. The Court ruled that "the concerns expressed in *Furman* that the penalty of death not be imposed in an arbitrary or capricious manner can be met by a carefully drafted statute that ensures that the sentencing authority is given adequate information and guidance." In particular, the Court held that Georgia's statute, by requiring the jury to find "at least one statutory aggravating factor before it may impose a penalty of death," effectively "channeled" the jury's discretion. "No longer can a jury wantonly and freakishly impose the death sentence; it is always circumscribed by the legislative guidelines." Finally, the Court ruled that the swift passage of new death penalty laws had undercut the premise of *Furman.* "It is now evident that a large proportion of American society continues to regard [capital punishment] as an appropriate and necessary criminal sanction," the Court proclaimed.[8]

Justice Marshall dissented. He insisted that "the American people, [if] fully informed as to the purposes of the death penalty and its liabilities, [would] reject it as morally unacceptable." Writing that the death penalty's constitutionality turns "on the opinion of an *informed* citizenry," Marshall opined that "even the enactment of new death statutes cannot be viewed as conclusive." In *Furman,* Marshall had spurned reliance on public opinion polls, which had shown "great fluctuation," in concluding that capital punishment violates the Eighth Amendment. Whether or not a punishment is cruel and unusual depends "not on whether its mere mention 'shocks the conscience and sense of justice of the people,'" he wrote, "but on whether people who were fully informed as to the purposes of the penalty and its liabilities would find the penalty shocking, unjust, and unacceptable." For Marshall, this premise undercut the argument that "since the legislature is the voice of the people, its retention of capital punishment must represent the will of the people." He declared: "So few people have been executed in the past decade that capital punishment is a subject only rarely brought to the attention of the average American. Lack of exposure to the problem is likely to lead to indifference, and indifference and ignorance result in preservation of the status quo, whether or not that is desirable, or desired."[9]

Since *Gregg,* the U.S. Supreme Court has stopped wrestling with the constitutionality of capital punishment and has abandoned its once preeminent role in reviewing death penalty cases. For example, today's Court uses the "Great Writ" of habeas corpus—once termed "the greatest of the safeguards of personal liberty"—only infrequently to protect federal constitutional rights. Commonly filed by death row inmates, petitions for writs of habeas corpus, if granted, permit prisoners to be released from custody if the prisoner's constitutional rights were violated at trial. Instead, the Court has erected numerous procedural barriers—many of them insurmountable—for death row inmates to overcome before the Court will review their constitutional claims, with the Court now largely deferring to *state* courts to enforce *federal* constitutional rights. In *Barefoot v. Estelle,* the Court held that the role of federal habeas proceedings is "limited" and that "[f]ederal courts are not forums in which to relitigate state trials." In *Teague v. Lane,* the Court held that "new" constitutional rights found by the Court would not be applied retroactively to invalidate final state convictions on federal habeas review. In other cases, the Court has used the procedural default and abuse of the writ doctrines to avoid reaching the merits of constitutional claims. These procedural devices preclude federal courts from hearing claims not previously raised in state court or in prior habeas corpus petitions, and effectively preclude a prisoner from arguing that his conviction was unconstitutional based solely on his attorney's failure to raise the claims earlier. In *Coleman v. Thompson,* the Court held that a death row inmate's constitutional claims were barred by his lawyer's failure to follow state procedural rules. The lawyer had missed Virginia's deadline for filing his client's notice of appeal by three days.[10]

Beginning in the 1980s, the U.S. Supreme Court actually made itself "a less important institution in the regulation of capital punishment," according to death penalty expert Franklin Zimring. In that decade, in the name of states' rights, the Court upheld the death sentence of an African American man despite powerful statistical evidence of racial discrimination in Georgia's capital sentencing proceedings. In that 1987 case, *McCleskey v. Kemp,* the Court rejected reliance on statistics that showed that death sentences "correlate with race," holding instead that racial "disparities in sentencing are an inevitable part of our criminal justice system." The Court also sanctioned the execution of mentally retarded defendants in *Penry v. Lynaugh,* decided in 1989. Law professor Welsh White concludes that, since 1983, the Supreme Court "has become increasingly concerned with promoting expeditious executions."

This assessment is fact, not fiction. In the early 1980s, an exasperated Chief Justice William Rehnquist, calling for an end to delays in the carrying out of death sentences, once said, "Let's get on with it." While the U.S. Supreme Court granted stays of execution in 29 percent of stay decisions in the mid- and late 1980s, the Supreme Court has granted only 17 percent of stay requests since 1989. The Court's entry of its unprecedented order forbidding lower courts from further interfering with

Robert Alton Harris's 1992 execution in California also shows that the Court desperately wants to expedite executions. The Supreme Court's pronouncements have had a profound ripple effect on lower federal court decisions. From 1981 to 1987, the Fifth and Eleventh Circuit courts, governing Alabama, Florida, Georgia, Louisiana, Mississippi, and Texas, granted 38 percent of all stay requests. Since 1987, however, only 12 percent of all stay requests in those two circuit courts have been granted.

Today's U.S. Supreme Court even defers to state governors to decide whether death row inmates have cognizable claims of innocence. In *Herrera v. Collins,* the Court ruled that postconviction claims of actual innocence should be resolved in pleas for executive clemency made to state governors, not by the Court, except in extraordinary circumstances. Chief Justice Rehnquist, calling persistent appeals a "mockery" of the criminal justice system, has become particularly impatient with prolonged death penalty litigation, leading habeas corpus reform efforts since 1977. The Court's newfound reluctance to review (much less overturn) death sentences has prompted one scholar to call the writ of habeas corpus the "No-Longer Great Writ." On five separate occasions since 1985, death row inmates have actually succeeded in garnering the four votes necessary to have their cases reviewed by the U.S. Supreme Court, only to fail to obtain stays of execution to provide time for their cases to be heard. The Supreme Court's rules require only four votes to grant review, or certiorari, but a stay application needs five votes to be granted.[11]

Inmates' rights to file habeas corpus petitions were curtailed even further with the passage of the Anti-Terrorism and Effective Death Penalty Act of 1996, signed into law by President Clinton. Under that act, federal courts cannot grant habeas corpus relief unless a state court ruling was "contrary to, or involved an unreasonable application of, clearly established Federal law." The act also gives prisoners only one year from the date on which their convictions and sentences are final to file federal petitions. To file a second or successive habeas corpus petition, which raises claims not raised in a prior petition, the inmate must get permission from a three-judge appellate panel and show evidence of innocence by "clear and convincing" evidence, an onerous burden of proof. The panel's denial of the right to file a successive petition is not even appealable to the Supreme Court. The Supreme Court has already upheld the constitutionality of title I of the act, which puts severe re-strictions on prisoners' ability to file successive petitions.[12]

The Politics of Death

Surging pro–death penalty sentiment, as expressed in many public opinion polls, has changed the face of national, state, and local elections. A 1991 Gallup poll found that 65 percent of Americans believe that a candidate's death penalty stance is important when selecting a party's candidate for president, and a 1992 Gallup poll found that the same per-centage of Americans would be more likely to vote for a candidate who backs a mandatory death penalty for murder. Accordingly, it is not sur-prising that George Bush made support for capital punishment a major theme of his 1988 presidential bid, promising to "bring back the death penalty and make sure it's used." In that campaign, Democratic chal-lenger Michael Dukakis reportedly "stumbled badly" when he was asked during a Los Angeles debate with Bush "how he would react if his wife were raped and murdered." Dukakis stoically replied, "I don't see any ev-idence [the death penalty] is a deterrent. There are better and more ef-fective ways to deal with violent crime." Dukakis's answer was "so un-emotional and academic, given the nature of the question," the *Los Angeles Times* later reported, "that it was said to have been one of the is-sues that contributed to his defeat at the hands of Bush." An ABC exit poll showed that 27 percent of voters in the 1988 race called the death penalty an important issue, and Bush beat Dukakis 3 to 1 with those vot-ers. Bush's infamous Willie Horton ad further exploited voters' fears that Dukakis might be soft on crime.[13]

In the 1992 presidential election, Democrats responded by nomi-nating a death penalty proponent, Bill Clinton. Clinton had overseen executions as Arkansas's governor and even flew back to Arkansas dur-ing the crucial New Hampshire primary to preside over the execution of death row inmate Rickey Ray Rector. A forty-year-old black man, Rec-tor had killed a white police officer, then shot himself in the head, in-flicting severe brain damage. So mentally impaired was Rector that, only an hour before the execution, Rector saw a television newscast about Clinton's alleged affair with Gennifer Flowers and said that he might vote for him. After Rector's execution, guards on death row found the slice of pecan pie from Rector's final meal untouched on a saucer in his cell. While incarcerated, Rector always saved his dessert until bedtime. His lawyers said that Rector left the pie because he believed he would return to his cell and did not know he was about to die. Clinton won the 1992 election and went on to make the expansion of capital crimes a centerpiece of his 1994 federal crime bill. During Clinton's administration, Attorney General Janet Reno has already approved forty-nine capital prosecutions.[14]

Clinton's experience in Arkansas explains his staunch pro–death penalty views. In his first term as Arkansas governor, Clinton "was widely viewed as opposed to capital punishment for declining to set execution dates for two dozen death-row inmates." In that term, Clinton commuted life-without-parole sentences of forty-four convicted murderers and twenty-two other criminals, but then lost a 1980 reelection bid. In his next gubernatorial bid in 1982, the "Comeback Kid" promised "not to commute so many sentences if . . . given another chance." He won. After that victory, Clinton moved swiftly to set execution dates, commuted only seven life-without-parole sentences, and never granted clemency to stay an execution. During the 1996 presidential campaign, Clinton returned to his successful 1992 strategy, running television ads declaring his support for capital punishment. Meanwhile, Clinton's opponent, Senator Bob Dole, actually toured California's death chamber at San Quentin, where he pledged to push for laws to speed up executions.[15]

The public sentiment favoring capital punishment also has influenced Congress, which brought back the federal death penalty in 1988 and passed President Clinton's federal crime bill in 1994. That legislation, signed into law on September 13, 1994, makes over fifty new offenses—many of them more symbolic than likely to occur (for example, killing a federal poultry inspector)—death-eligible. Representative Newt Gingrich's statement in support of the bill was typical. "Let us get tough with an effective, believable, and timely death penalty for violent criminals," he said. In 1995, members of Congress also cancelled federal funding for the nation's death penalty resource centers after they came under attack by the National Association of Attorneys General. That attack was led by South Carolina's newly elected attorney general, who once pledged to replace the state's electric chair with an electric sofa so more people could be executed at one time. These resource centers were created by Congress in 1988 in response to the federal judiciary's concerns over the inadequate pool of qualified lawyers willing to represent death row inmates in postconviction proceedings. Even the U.S. Senate's confirmation process has been affected by pro–death penalty sentiment. "Senate Republicans have given notice that they will challenge any of President Clinton's judicial nominees they consider insufficiently committed to the death penalty," reported the *New York Times* in 1993. The *New York Times* noted that "[k]ey Republican staff members" said that "the death penalty is a politically potent issue and worth raising." During Justice Stephen Breyer's confirmation hearings, Breyer was "pressed by Senators before satisfying them of his acceptance of the constitutionality of executions."[16]

At the state level, politicians are equally eager to capitalize on the public's perceived zest for the death penalty. A recent survey of New York legislators found that 42 percent of them believed that a vote against the death penalty would "definitely hurt" their reelection chances, and some New York politicians in 1990 even opposed a life-without-parole bill because its passage might make the death penalty "less of a campaign issue." Capital punishment was recently reinstated in Kansas and New York, and Ohio voters approved a measure put on the ballot by elected officials in 1994 to accelerate death penalty appeals by eliminating one level of appellate review. Former Kansas Governor Joan Finney allowed the bill reinstating capital punishment in Kansas to become law in 1994 without her signature. A death penalty opponent, Finney cited public support for the death penalty in explaining why she did not veto the legislation. After New York reinstated the death penalty in 1995, the *New York Times* reported that New York Governor George Pataki got a "political boost" by restoring it. In 1992, a Mississippi Supreme Court Justice, James Robertson, also was voted out of office following aggressive campaigning against him. An advertisement urged citizens to "vote against Robertson because he's opposed to the death penalty and he wants to let all these people go." One of the decisions Robertson's opponent attacked him for was a concurring opinion expressing the view that the U.S. Constitution did not permit the death penalty for rape. Robertson's opponent exploited this opinion even though the U.S. Supreme Court had specifically ruled ten years earlier that the Constitution did not permit rapists to be executed where there was no loss of life associated with the rape.[17]

State court judges are subject to tremendous political pressure when deciding capital cases. Of the thirty-eight death penalty states, thirty-two states subject judges to elections or retention votes at one time or another, and eight of them even require judges to run for elective office under party affiliations. This latter practice makes judges particularly susceptible to partisan attacks. For instance, in the 1994 elections, Texas Republicans swept into state judicial offices as part of the party's general success in those elections. Republicans won every slot they sought on the Texas Court of Criminal Appeals and swept all but one of the forty-two contested races for judgeships in Harris County, which includes Houston. In all, nineteen Democratic judges were defeated, leading the dean of a Texas law school to remark, "If Bozo the Clown had been running as a Republican against any Democrat, he would have had a chance." One of the Republicans elected to the Texas Court of Criminal Appeals that year was Stephen Mansfield, whose campaign pledges included the death penalty for murderers and sanctions for attorneys who file "frivolous appeals especially in death penalty cases." Mansfield won despite having been a member of the Texas bar for only two years and admitting before the election that he had lied to voters about his birthplace—it was Massachusetts, not Texas.[18]

The Canons of Judicial Ethics provide that judges "should be unswayed by partisan interests, public clamor, or fear of criticism," but elected state court judges are greatly affected by pro–death penalty sentiment. In the last five years, the California Supreme Court—fully cognizant of the fact that voters once threw out Chief Justice Rose Bird and two of her colleagues for their anti–death penalty votes—has affirmed nearly 97 percent of the capital cases it has reviewed. In contrast, nonelected, life-tenured federal judges find reversible constitutional errors in over 40 percent of the capital cases that they review. One statistical study even showed that dissents favoring defendants in capital cases were reduced among state supreme court justices "who otherwise tended to support defendants' claims in criminal cases if the justices . . . were nearing a reelection contest."[19]

The political pressure faced by state court judges is readily apparent in the four death penalty states—Alabama, Delaware, Florida, and

Indiana—that give judges the power to override jury verdicts, a practice sanctioned by the U.S. Supreme Court. In 1984, Ernest Dobbert became the first person since executions resumed in the United States in 1977 to be executed as a result of a jury override. Dobbert's jury had decided by a vote of 10–2 that Dobbert should live, but trial judge R. Hudson Oliff imposed a death sentence anyway. As of mid-1983, Judge Oliff had sentenced four defendants to death; in all four cases, he overrode the jury's recommendation of life imprisonment. That Judge Oliff is no aberration is reinforced by the fact that nearly 25 percent of all death sentences in Florida and over 30 percent of death sentences in Alabama were imposed due to jury overrides. Between 1972 and 1992, Florida trial judges imposed death sentences despite jury recommendations of life imprisonment in 134 cases, approximately 3.6 times as often as judges made death-to-life overrides. In Alabama, state trial judges in four separate cases have overridden unanimous jury recommendations that a defendant's life be spared and imposed death sentences. A 1995 study confirmed that, where elected judges are permitted to override jury verdicts, "judges override jury sentences of life imprisonment and impose death far more often than they override death sentences and impose life imprisonment."[20]

Because of the popularity of capital punishment, judges sometimes even invite publicity when imposing death sentences. In 1992, a Houston judge, Charles J. Hearn, created a stir when he signed Robert Drew's death warrant with a "happy face." He gave the frail excuse that he had signed all of his correspondence with this cartoon for years. Drew's lawyer, the late William Kunstler, accused Judge Hearn of "callous mockery." Likewise, Judge William Harmon, a former prosecutor, told a defendant during a 1991 capital trial in Texas that he was doing "God's work" to see that the defendant was executed. In that case, Judge Harmon taped a photograph of the "hanging saloon" of Texas Judge Roy Bean to the bench with his own name superimposed over Judge Bean's. In another instance, when someone suggested transporting death row inmates to court, Judge Harmon stated, "Could we arrange for a van to blow up the bus on the way down here?" These are hardly the words of an apolitical, unbiased factfinder.[21]

The decline of executive clemency in capital cases further illustrates the highly politicized nature of capital punishment. Prior to the

Supreme Court's 1972 ruling in *Furman v. Georgia,* governors frequently commuted death sentences. Florida governors commuted over
30 percent of all death sentences in pre-*Furman* cases, but have commuted less than 10 percent of death sentences in the post-*Furman* period. The national clemency rate also has fallen dramatically. From 1961
to 1970, there were 1,155 death sentences handed out and 182 commutations, or one commutation for every 6.3 death sentences. However,
from 1979 to 1988, there were 2,535 death sentences handed out and
only 63 commutations, or one commutation for every 40.2 death sentences. Only one death sentence was commuted in 1994, and no death
row inmates were granted clemency in 1995. These figures demonstrate
that today's governors are afraid of being labeled soft on crime if they
commute death sentences.[22]

Governors who seek reelection do face tough political odds if they
commute death sentences. Political pundits widely believe that Ohio's
former Governor Michael DiSalle lost his 1962 reelection bid because he
granted clemency in six death penalty cases. In the current political climate, upcoming elections can easily affect clemency decisions. In the
1984 Hunt-Helms U.S. Senate race in North Carolina, a clemency request for fifty-two-year-old grandmother and convicted murderer Velma
Barfield became a politically charged campaign issue when a trial judge
set Barfield's execution date just four days before the general election.
Governor James Hunt, locked in a tight race with conservative opponent Jesse Helms, denied clemency to avoid being labeled soft on crime.
In his statement denying clemency, Governor Hunt passed the buck,
saying: "I cannot in good conscience justify making an exception to the
law as enacted by our State Legislature, or overruling those 12 jurors
who, after hearing the evidence, concluded that Mrs. Barfield should
pay the maximum penalty for her brutal actions." In all likelihood,
Barfield became the first woman executed in America since 1962 because
Hunt feared political backlash if he granted her clemency request.
"Wariness of political repercussions," notes clemency expert Daniel
Kobil, explains "why the number of commutations has declined since
1982, even as the number of persons slated for execution has increased."[23]

Typically, governors control the clemency power—what former California Governor Pat Brown called the "awesome, ultimate power over

the lives of others" and what Chief Justice Rehnquist has described as the "fail safe" in our criminal justice system. Some states have advisory panels that make nonbinding recommendations, but twenty-nine states place the clemency power in the governor's hands alone. In sixteen states, clemency decisions are shared by the governor and an administrative body, and only in five states do administrative panels have the authority to make clemency decisions. Even though some pardon boards can make nonbinding recommendations of mercy, governors frequently refuse to abide by them. In 1990, Louisiana Governor Buddy Roemer denied clemency to Dalton Prejean, despite the pardon board's politically unpopular clemency recommendation. A convicted murderer, Prejean was only seventeen years old when the crime was committed and had brain damage caused by physical abuse. Prejean was killed in the electric chair on May 18, 1990.[24]

No matter what their power, most state pardon boards do not depoliticize clemency decisions. "Theoretically," *Dead Man Walking* author Sister Helen Prejean writes, "pardon boards are supposed to have wide latitude to dispense mercy." "But," she continues, "being appointees of the governor (and subject to removal at his discretion), they can hardly ignore the wishes of their patron." Howard Marsellus, a former member of Louisiana's pardon board, emphasizes the loyalty that board members owe to the governor and the need to be a "team player." Marsellus specifically recalls one conversation he had with Governor Edwin Edwards's chief legal counsel, Bill Roberts. In that instance, Marsellus felt he had a "clear case for mercy" in death row inmate Tim Baldwin's clemency petition before the board. However, Roberts told Marsellus that "the governor did not like to be confronted with these cases and wanted us to handle it." Roberts added: "Why do you think we appointed you, Howard? This is why you're chair of this committee. If you can't hack it, we'll just have to replace you with someone who can." After the telephone conversation with Roberts, the pardon board voted to uphold Baldwin's death sentence.[25]

Although modern-day death sentences are rarely commuted for mercy's sake alone, there are instances where they have been commuted to score political points or by lame duck governors who no longer need to worry about public approval ratings. The death sentences of women who killed abusive husbands have been commuted by state governors in

Maryland and Ohio to curry favor with women's rights groups. Likewise, in 1986, New Mexico's outgoing governor Toney Anaya made national news by commuting several death sentences before leaving office.
One of Anaya's more vivid memories about death penalty politics was of
a candidates' forum, sponsored by religious leaders during his 1982 gubernatorial campaign, where a question was asked about crime and capital punishment. Anaya recalls how the seven candidates preceding him
tried to "outdo each other" in terms of being tough on criminals and in
inflicting the death penalty. After all seven candidates declared their support for capital punishment, the crowd applauded. When Anaya spoke,
arguing against capital punishment and in favor of crime prevention
programs, boos and hisses engulfed the church building. Although
Anaya was eventually elected, he described capital punishment as "a false
god that is worshipped by too many—politicians and voters alike," and
derided politicians who use "kill the killers" as their sole crime-fighting
approach.

In 1986, New Mexico's constitution precluded Anaya from seeking
another term. However, capital punishment was fiercely debated during
that year's gubernatorial race. "It seemed at times that the candidates for
Governor felt that imposing the death penalty was the solution not only
to rising crime but also to all the other ills of society, including education, housing, health care, and jobs," Anaya wrote. Ultimately, voters
elected a strong death penalty proponent who made public statements
prior to taking office that he would "sign an execution warrant" and put
inmates to death on his first day in office. In a private meeting with
Anaya, he warned Anaya that he did not want any death sentences commuted before Anaya left office. He told Anaya that the death row inmates were "his." However, Anaya commuted the death sentences of all
five inmates on New Mexico's death row shortly before leaving office,
prompting outrage from death penalty advocates.[26]

At the local level, elected prosecutors also frequently use the death
penalty for political gain. Johnny B. Holmes Jr., the prosecutor for Harris County, Texas, prosecuted eighteen capital trials in 1993 alone, and almost one-third of Texas's death row inmates are from Harris County.
Holmes is not particularly concerned about statistical arguments about
the deterrent effect of capital punishment. "How the f—— do I know
how it affects people?" he drawls. "Executions are something mankind

has thought was appropriate since the days of Jesus Christ." And by no stretch of the imagination are these bloodthirsty prosecutors all macho, law-and-order Republicans from southern states. "The D.A. most zealous in pursuit of the death penalty," reported the *New York Times Magazine* in 1995, is "a) a Democrat, b) a woman, c) not from Texas." She is Lynne Abraham, Philadelphia's chief prosecutor, and her office "seeks death virtually as often as the law will allow." Consequently, Philadelphia County's death row population of 105 is the third largest of any county in America. Often using their offices as political stepping stones, elected prosecutors sometimes go to great lengths to obtain death sentences. At the trial of death row inmate Mumia Abu-Jamal, the prosecutor's closing argument emphasized that Abu-Jamal would get multiple appeals and that the jury was not being "asked to kill anybody."[27]

Prosecutors who ask for the death penalty too little, like Louisiana district attorney Marion Farmer, are often defeated at the polls. Farmer was severely criticized for not seeking the death penalty in certain cases, and despite subsequent capital prosecutions, he was defeated for reelection in 1984. Prosecutors who refuse to bring capital prosecutions actually risk being taken off their cases. On March 21, 1996, New York Governor George Pataki removed Bronx District Attorney Robert Johnson from a murder case against an ex-convict accused of killing a police officer because Johnson opposes the death penalty. Pataki replaced Johnson with Attorney General Dennis Vacco, who has been described as a "capital-punishment enthusiast." Johnson, a Democrat, was overwhelmingly elected after publicly declaring his opposition to the death penalty. In explaining his unprecedented action, Pataki told reporters, "We cannot have different standards and different laws in different parts of the state."[28]

No Responsibility, No Accountability

Although the American public is not allowed to watch executions, politicians have not kept their increasingly pro–death penalty views in the closet. On the contrary, politicians now frequently brag about how many executions they have overseen. When Florida Governor Bob Martinez ran for reelection in 1990, he aired a television commercial in which he proclaimed, "I have now signed some 90 death warrants in the

State of Florida." The advertisement ended by freezing on a frame depicting convicted serial killer Ted Bundy smiling slightly. In another 1990 race, former Texas Governor Mark White ran a television commercial in his bid for the Democratic gubernatorial nomination. The ad declared: "These hardened criminals will never again murder, rape or deal drugs. As governor, I made sure they received the ultimate punishment—death." His opponent, Jim Mattox, also emphasized his pro–death penalty credentials as the attorney general of Texas. "Mark White carried out the death penalty one time," his television commercial stated, "I carried it out 32 times."

That same year, California Attorney General John Van de Kamp aired a similar advertisement in his quest for that state's Democratic gubernatorial nomination. "As District Attorney and Attorney General," the ad boasted, "he's put or kept 277 murderers on death row." However, Van de Kamp was defeated by former San Francisco Mayor Dianne Feinstein, who came from behind to obtain a nineteen-point advantage over Van de Kamp after a $500,000 ad blitz stressed her support for capital punishment. Feinstein, a prior death penalty opponent, used a pro–death penalty slogan—"The only Democrat for the death penalty"—in the primary to defeat Van de Kamp, who was personally opposed to capital punishment but willing to enforce it. In her winning 1992 U.S. Senate race, Feinstein even ran television ads showing Democratic activists booing her during a speech in which she expressed support for capital punishment.[29]

While politicians publicly tout their pro–death penalty views, prison wardens and guards, many of whom believe that executions are unnecessary or morally wrong, are forced to carry out the resulting executions while politicians slumber. For example, after overseeing two executions as the warden of the Mississippi State Penitentiary in Parchman, Donald Cabana, once convinced of the need for capital punishment, no longer had the stomach for it. He is now a staunch abolitionist who believes that the solution to violent crime lies not with the death penalty but with "fighting poverty, child abuse, drugs, and a host of other scourges." In 1924, Captain R. F. Coleman, the longtime warden of the Huntsville, Texas, prison, actually resigned one day before the state's first electrocutions were to take place. Coleman told reporters that he was "severing his connection with the prison system" that he

had served continuously since 1888 because of "the new State law placing on the warden of Huntsville the duty of executing condemned
men." Coleman explained: "A Warden can't be a warden and a killer
too. The penitentiary is a place to reform a man, not to kill him." Some
states, like Utah, have stress inoculation programs in place to prevent
prison staff members from suffering from posttraumatic stress disorder
after an execution.[30]

Moreover, despite the public rhetoric of politicians, the private nature of executions makes politicians largely unaccountable for their
death penalty views. Legislators are free to pass death penalty laws,
knowing full well that the public will never see the resulting executions.
Elected prosecutors can seek death sentences with impunity, knowing
that their constituents will never see condemned inmates in the throes
of death. Governors and elected state court judges, by withholding
clemency or imposing or affirming death sentences, have little reason
to fear either by letting executions take place. The condemned inmates
will be executed behind prison walls in the dead of night, beyond the
reach of television cameras that might engender public sympathy for
them. Ironically, despite their increasingly rabid pro–death penalty
rhetoric, many politicians skip the executions themselves, probably because executions are seen as "dirty work." Instead, professional executioners are paid money out of state coffers to perform that function. For
example, Mississippi pays executioners $500 per execution. As Sister
Helen Prejean observes: "After politicians have made speeches and
passed laws to legalize state executions, they're nowhere around when
the Don Cabanas go to work in the middle of the night to kill a man
or woman." Of politicians who "boast of their zeal for the death
penalty," Sister Prejean raises some interesting questions: "Where are
they when the prisoners are killed? Why don't they come in the darkness of midnight to throw the switch or do the injecting themselves
rather than be asleep in their beds?"[31]

The entire criminal justice system, in fact, presently creates a "shell
game of moral responsibility" for executions. Legislators who pass death
penalty statutes just authorize capital punishment; it is prosecutors who
seek death sentences, and judges and juries who impose them. Conversely, prosecutors, judges, and juries just carry out death penalty
statutes as enacted by legislators. Personal responsibility for executions is

particularly hard to pinpoint because elected officials, judges, and jurors are not required to pull the lever that actuates an execution. Indeed, each actor in the criminal justice system usually points to another actor as the most responsible agent for executions. For example, the Houston area's chief prosecutor, Johnny Holmes Jr., refuses to accept personal responsibility for executions, placing ultimate responsibility for death verdicts with jurors. Holmes has remarked: "I take no great pride in the fact that we are No. 1 in death penalty cases. I don't like being called a killer. But I have a job to do. Everyone who got death out of Harris County has gotten it from a jury." Trial court judges and jurors are also aware that all death sentences will be reviewed by several appellate courts, further diffusing personal responsibility. The Capital Jury Project, an ongoing fourteen-state study of how jurors make life and death sentencing decisions, actually found that over 30 percent of jurors in capital cases described "the law" as the most responsible agent for the defendant's punishment. In contrast, only 6.4 percent of jurors believed that they were the most responsible agent for the punishment, and only 8.8 percent believed that the jury as a body was the most responsible agent. The study found that three-fourths of jurors "saw themselves as sharing responsibility with the judicial authorities, because their decision may be overturned, because it will be reviewed, or because it is only the first step in a process that will determine the defendant's punishment."

Some prosecutors even try to lessen jurors' sense of personal responsibility in capital sentencing proceedings. In a recent case from Alabama, where juries make nonbinding sentencing recommendations to trial judges in capital cases, the prosecutor's opening remarks at the penalty phase of the trial began as follows: "Again, let me, please, make sure you understand it's a recommendation. Don't let anybody getting up here [be] giving you the idea that you're sending someone to their death, that you're killing anybody. You're not. Don't let anybody try to put a guilt trip on you or anything like that." The prosecutor drove home this theme again in his rebuttal argument. He stated: "Ladies and gentleman, you're not going to kill anybody. Nobody is asking you to do that. Nobody is walking up and saying, 'Here's the switch, pull it.' Nothing like that." Although the U.S. Supreme Court held in *Caldwell v. Mississippi* in 1985 that "it is constitutionally impermissible to rest a death sentence on a determination made by a sentencer who has been led to believe that the responsibility for determining the appropriateness of the defendant's death rests elsewhere," the Alabama Supreme Court ruled that the prosecutor's remarks were not unlawful and affirmed the death sentence that was unanimously recommended by the jury and imposed by the trial judge.[32]

Even governors who refuse to grant clemency requests can sidestep responsibility for executions by taking the position that they are simply deferring to judicial determinations. For instance, before Patrick Sonnier's execution in 1987, Louisiana Governor Edwin Edwards adamantly refused to interfere in the execution process. He asked those pleading for clemency to understand: "I'm the governor and represent the state and must carry out the laws and must submerge my own personal views to carry out the expressed will of the people." A year later, Governor Edwards transferred the responsibility for signing death warrants from himself to the sentencing judge to further distance himself from the death machinery. In the past, judges themselves have downplayed governors' personal responsibility for executions. In 1913, the Oklahoma Court of Criminal Appeals tried to convince the state's governor to reverse his long-standing policy of commuting death sentences because of his opposition to capital punishment. "There is no provision of law in Oklahoma which requires the Governor to approve a verdict assessing the death penalty before it can be executed. His duty with reference to such verdicts is negative and not affirmative," the court wrote. It added: "It is not true that when a defendant is executed according to law the Governor is in any wise responsible therefor. The execution takes place in obedience to law and not because the Governor orders it."[33]

Executioners themselves are oftentimes absolved from personal responsibility for executions. A blank is put in one of the firing squad guns, an unknown executioner stands behind a one-way mirror, or only one of two buttons—pushed by different individuals—activates the lethal injection machine. At Gary Gilmore's execution in Utah in 1977, it was an anonymous five-member firing squad concealed behind a gray sailcloth partition that fired four .30 caliber bullets into Gilmore's heart. One rifle was loaded with a blank so that the executioners would not know who fired the fatal shot. Likewise, two executioners, paid $300 each, presided over William Andrews's 1:46 A.M. execution in Utah in 1992. One of them released a deadly mixture of chemicals and the other released a harmless solution so that neither of them knew who actually caused Andrews's death. Even the head of the Louisiana Department of Corrections, C. Paul Phelps, maintains that executioners "don't have to take any personal responsibility for what they are doing." "It's their job," he says. "They are told to do it. They are told how to do it. They are told how long it's going to take and what you do when you do it. It's like a drill, like an exercise, so they have no personal responsibility." In the 1890s and early twentieth century, prison wardens in Colorado, Connecticut, and Wyoming actually developed and used "automatic gallows" to further distance themselves from the execution process. These hydraulic devices, activated by the condemned man's own weight, allowed the prisoner to be hanged "without a single person touching the apparatus."[34]

Indeed, executioners frequently remain anonymous, wear black hoods, or get paid in cash for their services to protect their identities. For example, anonymous, black-hooded executioners paid $150 for their work throw the switch at Florida electrocutions. When Charles Campbell was hanged in Walla Walla, Washington, in 1994, the executioner's identity was masked by blinds that allowed official witnesses to see only his silhouette. Executioners, who have worn masks or hoods for centuries to prevent their recognition, have been universally despised throughout history. Daughters of executioners were forbidden to marry men outside the profession, and communities sometimes decreed that executioners' houses had to be painted red. Merchants frequently refused to sell goods to executioners, fearing that other customers would be frightened away. Even an executioner's donkey was cropped and marked so people would know that it belonged to the hangman. The dishonoring status of executioners was evident in Maryland in 1684, when a man condemned to death was pardoned but only on the condition that he perform for life the role of common hangman. In England, the lowly status of executioners was judicially recognized when a court awarded damages for slander to a gentleman who, after being mistakenly identified as a hangman, was thrown into a pond. Rejecting the defendant's argument that it is "no more a libel to describe a man as an Executioner than to say that he is a Judge" because they are both "necessary to the security of the State," the court held that the hangman label was intended to bring its target "hatred, ridicule and contempt." That executioners throughout history have been compensated for their services itself indicates the undesirable and loathsome nature of executioners' work.[35]

The identity of executioners is even protected by statute in many states, including Florida, Illinois, Montana, New Jersey, and New York. For instance, the Illinois statute provides:

> The identity of executioners and other persons who partici-
> pate or perform ancillary functions in an execution and in-
> formation contained in records that would identify those
> persons shall remain confidential, shall not be subject to dis-
> closure, and shall not be admissible as evidence or be dis-
> coverable in any action of any kind in any court or before
> any tribunal, board, agency, or person. In order to protect
> the confidentiality of persons participating in an execution,
> the Director of Corrections may direct that the Department
> make payments in cash for such services.

State officials become uneasy when executioners reveal their identities. After Louisiana's executioner (alias "Sam Jones") started giving television interviews and was profiled in the *Angolite,* a Louisiana State Penitentiary magazine, correctional authorities announced that the services of "Sam Jones" would no longer be needed.[36]

The condemned prisoners themselves are often hooded or masked right before executions take place to spare spectators the sight of the condemned person's distorted or disfigured features resulting from the executions. One English executioner, Albert Pierrepoint, specifically noted that a white cap was originally used in British executions "to mask the contortions of slow strangulation, which were considered too horrible even for the ghoulish British public to witness, although the logic that public executions were a public deterrent against crime might strictly have been followed by exposing the ultimate horror in order to achieve the maximum deterrence." "Later," Pierrepoint added, "the cap was still retained, partly for the sake of official witnesses, since the varying drop did not always take a man's head below the scaffold floor." New York's executioner, Robert Elliott, who oversaw 387 electrocutions, also stated that black leather masks served the purpose of "shielding the face." The now widespread use of lethal injection also can be seen as an attempt to sanitize the death penalty by eliminating any visible, bodily disfiguring that often accompanies hangings or electrocutions.[37]

To restore accountability to America's criminal justice system, no longer can anonymous, black-hooded executioners be permitted to perform executions. Instead, elected prosecutors who seek death sentences and judges and jurors who hand them out must be required to pull the switches and levers that activate execution mechanisms. This reform would make criminal justice actors accept more personal responsibility for their actions. Another intriguing possibility would be to make legislators who vote for the death penalty or governors who refuse to commute death sentences pull the triggering switch. A legislator could be selected at random to perform this task, which is necessary, after all, to carry out a state legislature's deadly directive. Moreover, no longer should jurors who oppose the death penalty be excluded automatically from jury service, a practice currently sanctioned by the U.S. Supreme Court. Jury panels in capital cases should not be stacked against criminal defendants.

At the very least, the judge and jurors who preside over a capital trial should be required to attend executions, as they were in New York in the 1840s. According to former U.S. Attorney Jeremy Epstein: "Requiring the presence of judge and jury at all executions would have many beneficial consequences. It would focus the attention of those imposing the punishment on the gravity of their act. Jurors could not simply depart from the courtroom and leave the state with the unpleasant task of disposing of the defendant." Epstein adds that "a judge and jury's involvement in the actual execution might also remove from public debate some of the detachment with which the death penalty is beginning to be viewed." Epstein concludes: "One of the purposes of any penal system is to teach that acts have consequences: crime, in short, leads to punishment. It is no less fitting that judge and jury understand that their acts, taken in the isolation of the courtroom, have consequences that reverberate far beyond it." New York executioner Robert Elliott, who came to oppose capital punishment, concurred in his book *Agent of Death*. "So long as capital punishment exists," Elliott wrote, "it would be wholly congruous to require any citizen to be present in the death chamber at the always awful moment when the spark of life is crushed from a man or a woman whom the state has doomed. . . . Thus would the repugnant horror of, and his responsibility in, legal slaying be impressed upon the average person."[38]

The Electorate and Death Penalty Myths

In the 1972 *Furman v. Georgia* decision, Justice Thurgood Marshall remarked on how frequently it is noted "that American citizens know almost nothing about capital punishment." In light of that belief, Marshall stated in *Furman* that "[i]t is imperative for constitutional purposes to attempt to discern the probable opinion of an *informed electorate*." "[T]he question with which we must deal is not whether a substantial proportion of American citizens would today, if polled, opine that capital punishment is barbarously cruel," Marshall wrote, "but whether they would find it to be so in light of all information presently available." Marshall predicted that, given full information about capital punishment, "the great mass of citizens would conclude . . . that the death penalty is immoral and therefore unconstitutional."[39] However, in 1976, Justice Marshall's reasoning was flatly rejected in *Gregg v. Georgia,* in which the Supreme Court upheld the constitutionality of Georgia's new death penalty law. The Court emphasized that the reenactment of death penalty laws in thirty-five states following *Furman* had completely "undercut" the rationale of *Furman*.

Although Justice Marshall's conclusion in *Furman* that the death penalty is unconstitutional was rejected in *Gregg,* Marshall's contention in *Furman* that Americans know little about capital punishment is accurate. A 1991 study found that, on average, test subjects answered only 52 percent of true/false questions about the death penalty correctly, with many test subjects undoubtedly only guessing the right answer. Test subjects were particularly misinformed about certain capital punishment "knowledge items." For instance, less than 30 percent of test subjects correctly knew or guessed that the death penalty costs taxpayers more money than life imprisonment. More important, the study reached the "disturbing finding" that a large number of test subjects "believed they were accurately informed about the death penalty and its effects, when, in fact, they were not." This finding is not academic. Social science studies show that increased knowledge about capital punishment correlates with greater opposition to it.[40]

At present, over 70 percent of Americans say in polls that they "favor" capital punishment. Such poll results, in fact, are highly misleading. In answer to the simple question "Do you favor or oppose the death penalty?" over 70 percent of Americans admittedly express approval of it. However, other polls indicate that pro–death penalty sentiment drops to as low as 41 percent when life imprisonment without the possibility of parole is offered as an alternative.[41] In addition, other polls show that pro–death penalty sentiment drops precipitously for several categories of offenders. Sixty-one percent of Americans oppose the death penalty for the mentally retarded, and 54 percent of Americans oppose capital punishment for those under twenty-one years of age. Pro–death penalty support also falls dramatically when less abstract questions are asked. For example, only a minority of respondents favor capital punishment if forced to take an active part in an execution by convicting in a capital trial or pulling the switch that causes death. These latter polls—which have received little media attention and which show that support for the death penalty is quite shallow—suggest that what the public really wants is *protection* from criminals, not the *killing* of criminals.[42]

Analyses of public opinion data by death penalty expert William Bowers confirms that "[t]he recent political stampede on execution could be the product of pollsters failing to ask the right questions or misreading the results." In 1993 and 1994 studies, Bowers concludes that oversimplified favor/oppose poll results showing that over 70 percent of Americans "favor" capital punishment have been misinterpreted "as solid public support for capital punishment by the pollsters, the news media, and the politicians." Although Bowers admits that these polls show *acceptance* of capital punishment, he persuasively argues that these polls do not indicate *preference* for the death penalty over alternative punishments. Bowers cites poll results from several states—among them Arkansas, California, Florida, Georgia, Indiana, Kansas, Massachusetts, Nebraska, and New York—showing that a majority of those states' residents actually prefer life imprisonment without the possibility of parole over the death penalty, if offenders are also required to work in prison for money that would go to their victims' families. When presented with the life-without-parole-plus-restitution alternative, support for capital punishment often plummets by 40 percentage points or more. For example, whereas one poll showed that 79.5 percent of Californians favor capital punishment, when offered the life-without-parole-plus-restitu-tion alternative only 26 percent of respondents preferred the death penalty. Sixty-seven percent of respondents preferred the life-without-parole alternative.

These latter poll results prompted Bowers to hypothesize that the death penalty is accepted by American jurors only "because it is viewed as better than the presently available alternative in their states." Bowers was already aware of data showing "that jurors, like the public at large, imagine"—in many cases quite erroneously—"that murderers not sen-tenced to death will be paroled or released relatively soon." In light of this fact, Bowers further hypothesized that "if people are more likely to favor the death penalty when they think the alternative option is too le-nient, [it] suggests that as jurors they might be more willing to impose a death sentence." Surveys of capital jurors in California, Florida, and South Carolina bore out Bowers's theory. His data found that, in these three states, "believing that convicted first-degree murderers not sen-tenced to death would get out sooner is associated with voting for death." Moreover, Bowers's data revealed that "the relationship between belief in early release and voting for death is more pronounced as fewer jurors in the state appear to know what the mandatory minimum sen-tence is." These findings lead Bowers to conclude that "[p]eople will ac-cept the death penalty unless or until they can have an alternative they want more."[43]

Laws requiring private, nighttime executions have, undoubtedly, greatly contributed to keeping the American public in the dark about the facts about capital punishment. First, many Americans erroneously believe that innocent people are never executed. In fact, in their 1992 book, *In Spite of Innocence,* authors Michael Radelet, Hugo Adam Bedau, and Constance Putnam catalogue 23 instances where innocent people were executed in the United States between 1900 and 1992. That book and a related study published in the *Stanford Law Review* also doc-umented 416 cases where the death row inmate's guilt was seriously in doubt and spotlighted 22 "close calls" where executions of innocent peo-ple were averted with only a day or two, or in some cases only a few hours, to spare. For example, in 1915 and 1942, two innocent men, Charles Stielow and William Wellman, were already strapped into the electric chair when the governor's rescuing reprieve arrived.

Today, innocent people continue to be wrongfully sentenced to death. In 1994, Joe Burrows was released from prison after spending five years on Illinois's death row. He had been sentenced to death for the murder of an eighty-eight-year-old man, a crime that Burrows did not commit. Likewise, after spending fourteen years on death row, Joseph Green Brown was released from a Florida prison in 1987 after it was discovered that the prosecution knowingly relied on false testimony to obtain his conviction. Brown had once come within fifteen hours of being executed. Walter McMillian was released from prison too in 1993 after spending nearly six years on death row. The Alabama Court of Criminal Appeals reversed his conviction because the state had suppressed evidence that could have demonstrated his innocence at trial. Since 1970, at least fifty-nine death row inmates have been released from prison based on evidence of innocence. These statistics illustrate that, as Charles Dickens once wrote, the death penalty is "an irrevocable punishment" administered by people of "fallible" judgment.[44]

Second, many people believe—with little reason—that the death penalty deters crime. A 1991 Gallup poll found that 51 percent of Americans believe that the death penalty has a deterrent effect, and a 1994 poll found that 57 percent of New York State registered voters believe that the death penalty deters murder. However, FBI statistics reveal that in states with large numbers of executions, murder rates are often well above the national average. The homicide rate in Texas, which executes more people than any other state, is 15.3 per 100,000, compared to a national average of 9.8 per 100,000. Likewise, in 1993, over 20 people were murdered per 100,000 state residents in Louisiana, where executions frequently occur. By contrast, in Canada, which abolished capital punishment in 1977, the homicide rate is far lower than it is in the United States. In 1991, Canada had only 2.8 homicides per 100,000 people. Many American prosecutors even concede that deterrence is no longer a legitimate rationale for capital punishment. "I don't think anybody argues the death penalty is a deterrence anymore," says Georgia Attorney General Michael Bowers. "It's viewed as straight punishment. You did this horrible crime and this is the penalty."[45]

Despite the growing number of American executions, the death penalty has done nothing to stop violent crime. The U.S. prison population continues to spiral out of control. In 1980, roughly 500,000 people were behind bars; by 1996, that number had risen to over 1.6 million—the highest incarceration rate in the world. In some states, like Louisiana, prison populations have literally exploded. Between 1975 and 1991, Louisiana built nine new prisons and increased its prison population by 249 percent. The annual cost to Louisiana taxpayers is $15,000 per inmate, not including prison construction costs, which run about $50,000 for each prison bed. From 1979 to 1990, Census Bureau figures show that state government spending on prison construction nationwide increased a staggering 612 percent. If parole and probation systems are included, roughly 1 of every 43 American adults is in the criminal justice system at an annual cost of $20 billion. To the extent that politicians claim that the death penalty is the answer to America's crime problem, they simply mislead the American public.[46]

Third, a myth persists among Americans that convicted murderers are often quickly paroled. In a 1993 poll conducted by the Democratic polling firm Greenberg/Lake and the Republican Tarrance Group, only 4 percent of survey respondents believed that defendants sentenced to life imprisonment for first-degree murder would be imprisoned for the rest of their lives. Respondents predicted that these convicted criminals would only serve 15.6 years. Even when asked how long someone with a sentence calling for life without parole would serve, only 11 percent of respondents believed such a person would never be released. This perception used to be accurate. Bureau of Justice statistics show that in 1986 the average amount of time served on a life sentence in the United States was only six years, nine months. Today, however, the District of Columbia, the federal government, and thirty-three states have statutes guaranteeing that murderers sentenced to life without parole will never be eligible for release. Most of the remaining states forbid considering parole for murderers for at least twenty-five years. As William Bowers explains: "No doubt, the public's exaggerated sense that convicted murderers will be back on the streets so soon is the product of selective media reporting of crime by previously incarcerated inmates."

According to a 1993 report, jurors serving in capital cases "are equally in the dark, frequently assuming that their choice is between a meaningless life sentence and death." Noting that judges "often are forbidden by law from explaining to the jury that inmates must now serve 25, 35 or more years before even becoming eligible for parole," the report

concludes that "the death penalty rides a wave of misinformation with
no basis in current sentencing law." Data from the Capital Jury Project
found that "three-fourths of those jurors who sentenced a defendant to
death believed that the defendant would spend less than twenty years in
prison if not condemned to die." One juror interviewed stated, "No one
wanted to be responsible for imposing [the] death penalty, but in the
end, [we] didn't want him on the street and [the death penalty] was [the]
only choice that guaranteed that." The juror feared that the defendant
"could be paroled in [a] relatively short time." When asked how much
time he thought the defendant would serve if given a life sentence, the
juror responded "two to three years," and "probably not more than ten"
years if the sentence was life imprisonment without the possibility of parole. Only in 1994 did the U.S. Supreme Court rule that the Constitution requires jurors to be informed of a defendant's ineligibility for parole where the state urges that a defendant's future dangerousness
warrants a death sentence.[47]

Fourth, many Americans erroneously believe that death row inmates receive fair trials and get adequate legal representation. However,
low-quality representation is pervasive in southern "Death Belt" states.
Twenty-five percent of all Kentucky death row inmates in 1989 were represented at trial by lawyers who were later suspended, disbarred, or imprisoned. Spending caps on capital trials also has led to low-quality representation. In rural parts of Texas, lawyers receive no more than $800
to handle a capital case, and Alabama law limits compensation for out-
of-court preparation to $20 per hour, with a $2,000 cap. In Mississippi,
where that state's supreme court recently upheld Mississippi's $1,000
compensation limit, one lawyer who logged 779.2 hours in a capital case
got paid only $1.28 an hour. Some death row inmates were prosecuted
at trial by "private prosecutors"—private lawyers hired and paid for by
murder victims' relatives to prosecute the accused, raising serious con-
flict-of-interest issues—and judges frequently appoint newly admitted
lawyers to the bar, political cronies, or lawyers who have never tried a
single case to defend capital prosecutions. Judges in Houston have repeatedly appointed an attorney who falls asleep in court, hurries
through capital proceedings like "greased lightning," and makes few objections at trial. Not surprisingly, ten of his clients have gotten death
sentences. In postconviction proceedings, many death row inmates are

actually *unrepresented.* Some sixty-five to seventy Texas death row inmates do not even have lawyers, prompting a Texas bar report to label the shortage of counsel "overwhelming and of grave consequence." In Missouri, one inmate was recently executed after nobody could be found to take his case. Dismal lawyer attitudes are also prevalent. In four Georgia cases in which the death penalty was imposed, defense attorneys referred to their clients as "niggers," and in a Texas case, defense counsel referred to a Mexican client as a "wetback" in front of an all-white jury. Since capital punishment resumed in the United States in 1977, approximately 2,000 of the 5,000 death sentences imposed have been overturned, many because of ineffective assistance of counsel. The American Bar Association itself voted 280–119 in 1997 to put a moratorium on executions, asserting that the death penalty is administered through "a haphazard maze of unfair practices."[48]

Fifth, many people believe that the death penalty is handed out by jurors chosen from an impartial pool of jurors. However, capital juries are frequently not reflective of the population as a whole because prosecutors use their allotted peremptory strikes in a racially discriminatory fashion. In one Georgia location, 90 percent of the district attorney's peremptory strikes were used to exclude African Americans from the jury in cases where black defendants were charged with capital crimes. The U.S. Supreme Court also permits "death-qualified" juries, even though this makes the resulting juries more conviction-prone. Although juries normally are supposed to represent a "fair cross-section of the community," the Court held in *Witherspoon v. Illinois* that a prosecutor can remove from a capital case all potential jurors who would "invariably" or "automatically" vote against the death penalty. Ironically, one "objective" factor by which the Supreme Court analyzes the "evolving standards of decency that mark the progress of a maturing society"—as part of the Court's Eighth Amendment jurisprudence to determine if a punishment is cruel and unusual—is how often juries hand down death verdicts. As the Court stated in *Witherspoon:* "[O]ne of the most important functions any jury can perform . . . is to maintain a link between contemporary community values and the penal system— a link without which the determination of punishment could hardly reflect 'the evolving standards of decency that mark the progress of a maturing society.'" In allowing death-qualified juries—especially since some states require unanimity in juries' decisions to impose the death penalty—executions are taking place across America even though a random sample of Americans might not approve of them. Indeed, in skewing the number of death verdicts by death-qualifying juries, the Supreme Court has hindered its own ability to assess the constitutionality of capital punishment in the future. This is so because jury verdicts are an important objective factor that the Court looks to, as part of its own Eighth Amendment jurisprudence, to assess the American public's "evolving standards of decency."[49]

Sixth, many people mistakenly believe that the death penalty is reserved for the most heinous murderers. However, as the Director of the Southern Center for Human Rights, Stephen Bright, aptly notes, "It is not the facts of the crime, but the quality of legal representation, that distinguishes [cases] where the death penalty was imposed, from many similar cases, where it was not." Bright concludes, "Those facing the death penalty are generally poor, often members of racial minorities, [and] often afflicted with substantial mental impairments." Statistics readily support Bright's findings, which were published in 1994 in the *Yale Law Journal.* Bureau of Justice and NAACP statistics show that between 1930 and 1990, 4,016 people were executed in the United States, of which 2,129, or 53 percent, were black. Between 1930 and 1976, 90 percent of people executed for rape were black, even though African Americans comprised only 12 percent of the U.S. population during that time period. Death sentences are, in fact, 4.3 times more likely to be imposed on convicted murderers whose victims were white than on those whose victims were black. Likewise, a study of 15 death row inmates found that all 15 "had histories of severe head injury, five had major neurological impairment, and seven others had other, less serious neurological problems (*e.g.,* blackouts, soft signs)."[50]

Historically, the death penalty has never been inflicted on only those who commit the most heinous crimes. The Hammurabi Code in ancient Babylonia made selling beer illegally a capital crime; the early Hebrews killed anyone who cursed a parent; and the Romans executed women who stole the keys to their husbands' wine cellars. In the Massachusetts Bay Colony, witchcraft, adultery, and sodomy warranted the death penalty. Today, although approximately 22,000 murders are committed each year, only about 250 death sentences are handed out annually. Because the death penalty is imposed in such an arbitrary fashion, U.S. Supreme Court Justice Harry Blackmun, a death penalty supporter on the Court for twenty years, announced in 1994 that he would "no longer . . . tinker with the machinery of death." "It seems," Blackmun wrote in his dissent in *Callins v. Collins,* "that the decision whether a human being should live or die is so inherently subjective— rife with all of life's understandings, experiences, prejudices and passions—that it inevitably defies the rationality and consistency required by the Constitution."[51]

Finally, Americans hold the false impression that the death penalty costs less to administer than life imprisonment without the possibility of parole. Many people are simply unaware of the enormous cost of capital trials, and the expensive forensic and mental health experts that are needed for them. In Florida, each death sentence costs an estimated $3.18 million, compared to $516,000 for a life sentence of forty years. In Texas, a death penalty case costs an average of $2.3 million, approximately three times the cost of imprisoning someone in a single cell at the highest security level for forty years. Capital litigation is so expensive because of the high stakes—life versus death—and because of the complicated nature of capital proceedings. Jury selection in capital cases takes 5.3 times longer than in other criminal cases, and capital trials average 3.5 times longer than noncapital trials. In addition, capital cases drain the time and financial resources of the judiciary. For example, the California and Florida Supreme Courts spend approximately 50 percent of their time reviewing capital cases. People forget that "lawyers cost more than prison guards."[52]

If these myths about capital punishment were dispelled, it is difficult to predict how America's death penalty debate would be affected. Would Americans decide to retain death penalty laws and continue executing people, even if they knew the death penalty did not deter crime? Would Americans start questioning the propriety of capital punishment for specific categories of offenders like teenagers or the mentally retarded? Would Americans press for fewer capital trials and midnight executions, which cost taxpayers large sums of money, and call for more crime-prevention programs like "midnight basketball" leagues? Or, would Americans lobby state legislators for the total abolition of capital punishment and ask that convicted murderers be locked away for life with no possibility of parole? No matter what the American people decide, however, one thing is crystal clear: For the public to make an informed choice, the press must do a better job of educating Americans about capital punishment and the alternatives to it and must stop printing misleading public opinion data. If adequate information about the death penalty is not made readily available, the American public and jurors in capital cases will continue to decide matters of life and death in the dark, as they do now.

7

Televised Executions?

Cameras Prohibited Here

Since executions were privatized in the United States, only two photographs of truly private executions in America have ever appeared in print. The first picture sparked an uproar when it appeared on the front page of the *New York Daily News* on January 13, 1928. The photographer, Tom Howard, went to Sing Sing to record the electrocution of Ruth Synder, a Queens housewife who had been convicted of strangling her husband. Because of the small size of the execution chamber, Howard was one of only twenty journalists permitted to watch the execution, even though 125 newspapers and news services had sought permission to attend. By strapping a camera to his leg and concealing it in some baggy trousers, Howard was able to shoot a picture from ankle level. The blurry picture is undeniably eerie. This incident led to searches of official witnesses at subsequent New York executions.

The second photograph was taken at the execution of James "Mad Dog" Morelli and printed in the *Chicago Herald-American* on November 26, 1949. To get the picture, photographer Joe Migon hid a tiny Minox camera in the hollowed-out heel of his shoe and twice passed through an X-ray machine in the jail that failed to pick up the camera because it was so close to the floor. When Morelli was strapped into the electric chair shortly after midnight, Migon slipped the camera out of his shoe and fellow reporter Basil "Gus" Talbott, a former boxer, feigned

ality of prison regulations that barred the press from conducting interviews with *specific* prisoners. The Court ruled that "newsmen have no constitutional right of access to prisons or their inmates beyond that afforded the general public." The Court concluded that the Constitution did not impose "upon government the affirmative duty to make available to journalists sources of information not available to members of the public generally." In rejecting Garrett's First Amendment claim, the Fifth Circuit likewise held that "the first amendment does not accompany the press where the public may not go."

In addition, the Fifth Circuit rejected Garrett's equal protection claim that he, unlike print journalists, was unconstitutionally denied the use of his usual reporting tools. The Fifth Circuit ruled: "The Texas media regulation denies Garrett use of his camera, and it also denies the print reporter use of his camera, and the radio reporter use of his tape recorder. Garrett is free to make his report by means of anchor desk or stand-up delivery on the TV screen, or even by simulation. There is no denial of equal protection. . . . Despite the unavailability of film of the actual execution the public can be fully informed." The Fifth Circuit added that "the free flow of ideas need not be inhibited." The U.S. Supreme Court declined to review Garrett's case on July 3, 1978.[5]

Many other media representatives have sought but failed to get permission to film executions. One documentary producer, Brian Halquist, sued Washington's Department of Corrections in 1989, claiming a right to attend and videotape an execution. The department admitted that executions are newsworthy events and further acknowledged that twelve media representatives would be allowed to witness any execution. However, the department denied Halquist's videotaping request because of security and privacy concerns. Halquist agreed that the department had "legitimate concerns for the security of the penitentiary and the confidentiality of those persons who will carry out the execution." Accordingly, Halquist agreed to respect the privacy of the staff and allow the final videotape to be reviewed to assure confidentiality, to submit himself and his equipment to a pre-execution search, and not to film anything without the condemned inmate's consent. Despite these stipulations, the department still refused to allow Halquist to film an execution. In addressing Halquist's legal claims, the Supreme Court of Washington conceded that "a videotape of an execution is information that is qualitatively different from a mere verbal report about an execution." However, the court nevertheless refused to find a constitutional right for Halquist to attend or videotape an execution. Because the court identified no theoretical basis for Halquist's lawsuit in the Washington Constitution, Halquist's claims were dismissed on October 31, 1989.[6]

Gary Gilmore's Vanishing Act

In 1977, a federal judge in Utah also rejected attempts by the press to attend the execution of Gary Gilmore, the convicted killer of a motel clerk. Gilmore was the first person executed in the United States since 1967, and the final months of Gilmore's life were later detailed in Norman Mailer's Pulitzer Prize–winning book, *The Executioner's Song*. The controversy began when Utah prison officials, relying on a state law that made no provision for press attendance at executions, announced that the press would be barred from attending Gilmore's execution, even though the press had attended all of Utah's forty-four prior executions. Warden Samual Smith predicted that press attendance at the execution would only create a "spectacle." This announcement prompted the *Salt Lake Tribune* and a local television station, KUTV, to sue the Utah Board of Corrections. At a hearing on January 12, 1977, the *Salt Lake Tribune* and KUTV argued that Utah's law violated their First Amendment right to gather news. The *Salt Lake Tribune* had already previously challenged a corrections department policy that prohibited interviews with Gilmore, who was scheduled to die before sunrise.[7]

The lawsuit seeking access to Gilmore's execution was resolved in a two-page order written by U.S. District Court Judge Aldon Anderson. Judge Anderson ruled that Utah's law did not lack a rational basis under the First Amendment, and that the press could be barred because Utah's law sought to avoid "sensationalizing" executions. While Anderson's opinion was bereft of legal citations to support this conclusion, Gilmore's execution was undeniably sensational. It was America's first execution in nearly ten years, and Gilmore, who refused to appeal, wanted to die. A motion picture producer, Lawrence Schiller, had even bought the rights to Gilmore's life story for $100,000.[8]

These unique circumstances brought hundreds of reporters to Utah from around the world and throughout the United States. Because of the enormous media attention, plans were made for an indoor execution, but prison officials soon realized that the shed under consideration was used to slaughter livestock. When the shed was dropped as a potential site, reporters and cameramen reserved every helicopter in the state for the morning of the execution in the event that it took place outdoors. Although Warden Smith refused to specify an execution site, the Federal Aviation Administration took the unusual step of banning all aircraft from the area just in case the execution took place outdoors.[9]

After intense legal maneuvering, Gilmore was eventually executed at 8:07 A.M. on January 17, 1977, but only after a prior court order was modified so that the execution could occur after the original sunrise deadline. A prison warehouse, cleared of paint drums and aluminum ladders, served as the execution site. Gilmore uttered his last words, "Let's do it," just before a black corduroy hood was drawn over his head and an anonymous five-man firing squad fired four .30-caliber bullets into Gilmore's heart. One rifle had been loaded with a blank so that the executioners would not know who fired the fatal shot or feel any personal guilt. The firing squad foreman received $125 for his services, and the other gunmen were paid $100 each.[10]

The 250 media representatives first learned of Gilmore's execution from Ken Schulman, a Utah prison aide. After hanging up a beige telephone, Schulman bluntly announced, "Gary Mark Gilmore is dead." Before reporters were ushered to the execution site, the scene was reportedly "cleaned up a bit." Gravel was spread around the execution platform to cover blood stains, and the black leather armchair was wiped clean. The four bullet holes in the back of the chair and a drying trickle of blood on a plywood board were the only remaining evidence of Gilmore's execution. In a few short minutes, Gary Gilmore had vanished.[11]

Executions on Talk Shows? Pay-per-View?

In 1994, Phil Donahue, with a weekly television talk show audience of 20 million people, sought to televise North Carolina's execution of convicted killer David Lawson. "I would be pleased to have an execution on the 'Donahue Show,'" he announced. "What's wrong with it? Let's see future bad guys watch these people fry right here on television."

Donahue's remarks were not made flippantly. On April 13, 1994, Lawson wrote to Gary Dixon, the warden of Raleigh's Central Prison, asking that Donahue and an Emmy-award winning cameraman, James Arnold, be allowed to attend and videotape Lawson's execution. Donahue sent a separate letter to Dixon simultaneously requesting the right to film Lawson's execution, stressing that "we intend to do this program tastefully, in a responsible way, without sensationalism and with no discredit to your institution."[12]

Approximately two weeks later, Warden Dixon denied the videotaping requests, citing the "interests of the orderly operation and security of this institution." Lawson, Donahue, and Arnold then sued Warden Dixon in North Carolina state court, alleging violations of their First Amendment rights. A superior court judge ordered Dixon to show cause why the videotaping should not occur, but the North Carolina Supreme Court, at Warden Dixon's request, took immediate jurisdiction of the case by granting Dixon's motion to bypass the lower state courts. After granting Dixon's highly unusual request, the state's highest court found that no constitutional right exists to videotape executions. In its decision of May 17, 1994, the court held that Warden Dixon could not be forced to accommodate any videotaping request.

Finding no relief in state court, Lawson, Donahue, and Arnold then filed a lawsuit in federal court on June 1, 1994. Six days later, however, a federal trial judge dismissed their suit, again finding that no constitutional right exists to videotape executions. The three plaintiffs then appealed to the U.S. Court of Appeals for the Fourth Circuit, which refused to even address the merits of their appeal. The Fourth Circuit ruled instead that the North Carolina Supreme Court's prior ruling procedurally barred the plaintiff's federal lawsuit, even though the lawsuit alleged violations of federal law.[13]

In their certiorari petition to the U.S. Supreme Court, Donahue's attorneys asked that Warden Dixon be ordered "to permit and to take all steps necessary to facilitate the videotaping" of Lawson's execution. They argued that the tape could be held under seal until the Supreme Court could properly consider the constitutional arguments against laws forbidding the filming of executions. However, the U.S. Supreme Court, without comment or dissent, declined to review the Fourth Circuit's decision, and no cameras were present at Lawson's execution. After Lawson's death, Donahue vowed to pursue the legal right to put executions on television "even though I'm going to have to petition my own corporation in order to sue." Donahue noted that no advertiser would touch such a broadcast.[14]

In the wake of Donahue's lawsuit, two lawyers, Mark Sandground and Michael Shapiro, actually proposed a whole series of pay-per-view televised executions. Sandground said the "Death Watch" program "would educate people about the death penalty and be a deterrent to violent crime." Contemplating the creation of a million-dollar fund to start the program and renew Donahue's lost legal battle, Sandground said the pay-per-view television program would feature "the execution of the month." Shapiro, a leading Los Angeles entertainment lawyer, announced that part of the profits would go into a special fund for victims. However, Sandground and Shapiro failed to locate financial sponsors for the venture.[15]

Live from Death Row

Like journalists, death row inmates have sought televised executions. For instance, in 1990, a Virginia judge refused a request by death row inmate Joseph Savino to televise his execution. "I deny such a request," Bedford Circuit Judge William Sweeney told Savino without discussion. Sentenced to death for killing his gay lover, Savino had written Judge Sweeney a letter asking for a televised execution. Savino wanted his execution publicized because he thought it should be "if it's to be a deterrence to anyone else." Likewise, in 1984 and 1994, prison officials in Florida and Maryland denied respective requests for televised executions by death row inmates Arthur Frederick Goode and John Thanos. In another instance, in 1982, the Florida Supreme Court denied a similar request by death row inmate John Ferguson. Relying on procedural grounds, the Florida Supreme Court refused to even address the merits of Ferguson's claim that he had a First Amendment right to have his execution televised.[16]

Convicted murderer James Autry's request that his execution be filmed also was denied by Texas officials in 1984. Confined on Texas's death row, Autry sought a televised execution because he believed that if Americans are "serious about using the death penalty as a deterrent, they should let the public see it." Fellow death row inmate Billy Hughes agreed. "If they think it acts as a deterrent, then why do they want to hide it?" Hughes asked rhetorically. Texas Attorney General Jim Mattox did not oppose Autry's request. "If executions serve as a deterrent," he said, "then there's a very logical argument that they should be done publicly." Mattox stressed that with "today's media techniques, in which television plays such an important role," it was appropriate to allow "one camera into the death chamber to witness and record an execution." However, Texas Governor Mark White disagreed. "Executions used to be public," he said, "but you had to go down to the courthouse to see it." "Today," he emphasized, "TV is in the home, business, just about everywhere. Televising executions would be invading the home atmosphere." He added, "Frankly, there are a lot of programs on television today that I don't want my family to be watching . . . and this would fall into the same characterization."

On March 12, 1984, the Texas Board of Corrections denied Autry's request for a televised execution by a vote of 8–0. "I have many concerns about this," said Board Chairman Robert Gunn, "[n]ot just the propriety and decency of it, but the potential that it could have an effect on the death penalty itself." "An individual's death should be private," Gunn said, "and I will vote against any exploitation or sensationalism of such a situation." Board member Pete Cortez agreed. Having watched Charlie Brooks's execution in 1982, Cortez declared that "after witnessing that execution, I'm not at all ready to favor putting it on television."[17]

Legislative Initiatives

In the last fifteen years, several legislative efforts have similarly failed to get executions on television. At the federal level, Republican Senator Ted Stevens of Alaska unsuccessfully proposed a bill in 1985 to televise the firing squad executions of spies for treasonous espionage. Six years later, U.S. Senator Mark Hatfield of Oregon also introduced a bill to require that federally imposed death sentences be carried out in public. The bill provided that the official "charged with supervising an execution shall cause the execution to be carried out at a place that is convenient for members of the public to view the execution in person and for the communications media to broadcast the execution, and at a time of day when most members of the public who desire to view the execution will be able to do so." A longtime capital punishment opponent, Hatfield said that the public would turn against capital punishment if executions were televised. The bill was referred to the Senate Judiciary Committee on May 23, 1991, but no further action was ever taken.[18]

Several unsuccessful efforts also have been launched in state legislatures to mandate televised executions. Since 1984, a Georgia legislator, Tyrone Brooks, has repeatedly proposed requiring the state's public television station to televise executions. "Call it shock treatment," he says. "If we're ever going to convince people that capital punishment is inhumane, cruel and absolutely atrocious, we're going to have to show them what public executions are." However, the Georgia legislature has consistently failed to adopt such legislation. In 1981, Seattle legislator George Fleming's proposal to televise executions in Washington was defeated on a voice vote. Ten years later, the Florida legislature also refused to pass a bill mandating televised executions.[19]

In Arkansas, a bill to require live broadcasts of executions was proposed in 1983. The bill's sponsor, Representative Grover Richardson, asked the members of the House Judiciary Committee, "Do we really believe that [the death penalty] is a deterrent to crime?" "I'm affording us an opportunity to make it work," the Little Rock legislator said. "If you say it is effective, why not televise it?" Another Little Rock legislator, Representative Henry Osterloh, also supported the legislative initiative. He called it "the most progressive" bill since a plan several years earlier that tried to stage executions at War Memorial Stadium in Little Rock. Despite these legislators' pleas, the House Judiciary Committee rejected Richardson's proposal on a voice vote, having earlier voted down a proposal by Richardson to abolish capital punishment altogether. Representatives John Ward and Bobby Glover both voted against the bill to televise executions. Ward said it would hurt the families of death row inmates, and Glover favored televised executions only on closed-circuit television inside prisons, stating that broadcasts of executions shown outside of prisons would only make a "public circus" of them.[20]

A bill to require televised executions with the condemned person's consent was actually defeated twice in the California Assembly in 1991.

The legislative sponsor, San Francisco Democrat John Burton, said he did not know what his bill would do "except give people the right to view these executions." A death penalty opponent, Burton was surprised by the reaction of some legislators to his proposal. Two Democrats opposed it because they feared it might encourage more executions. Many Republicans also voiced opposition, worrying that televised executions might make viewers too sympathetic to the condemned inmate unless crime re-creations were broadcast. Burton's bill passed the California Assembly's Ways and Means Committee with little debate by a vote of 13–8. When the bill reached the assembly floor in May 1991, though, it was rejected by a vote of 37–24. A second vote on the measure, taken in September, also fell 13 votes shy of the 41 votes needed for passage. The tally was 28–40.

Each vote prompted spirited debate. As the bill's author, Burton defended the measure on the basis that "people have the right" to see executions. Burton had "no idea" how the issue would cut, but he speculated that televised executions might deter crime. Another Democratic proponent of the measure, Assemblyman Richard Katz, agreed. "There is no better way to make deterrence real than to give people an opportunity to see the consequences of their actions," he said. In contrast, Republican Assemblyman Stan Statham opposed the bill. "There is a hidden agenda to this bill," he said, "and that is to eliminate capital punishment in California." Only if reenactments of the crime were shown would he support the measure. "If we're not forced to see the crime," he argued, "we shouldn't be forced to see the execution." Republican Assemblyman Tom McClintock concurred. "This bill takes morbid curiosity one step too far," he said. "This bill is designed to create sympathy for the condemned." Another opponent, Democrat Richard Floyd, suggested facetiously that the state sell tickets on execution day in the open air Los Angeles Coliseum. "The hell with doing it on free TV," he added. "Let's make some bucks out of it."[21]

Opposition in California to televised executions dates back to 1977, when legislative leaders first expressed reservations to such broadcasts. Then Senate Republican leader George Deukmejian, who led the ballot initiative drive that restored capital punishment in California, said that putting executions on television would only create "a spectacle, circus-like atmosphere." The California Assembly Speaker, Leo T. McCarthy, expressed similar sentiments. "I think we have enough violence on tele-vision now," he said. "That's all we need is some nut watching it who then goes out and knocks somebody off because of the stimulus."[22]

In Minnesota, one state legislator also proposed putting executions on television if capital punishment were reinstated in that state. In that instance, in 1995, Representative Hilda Bettermann had offered an amendment to a judiciary finance bill in the Minnesota House of Rep-resentatives seeking to bring back capital punishment to Minnesota. Her proposed amendment would have required executions to take place at a maximum security prison "enclosed from public view," and would have permitted only twelve citizens and six media representatives to attend them. When it was debated on the house floor, Representative Dee Long offered what she termed a "friendly amendment" to Representative Bet-termann's amendment, proposing that executions be televised and occur in prime time between 7:00 and 9:00 P.M. Representative Long believed those legislators who supported capital punishment—she pointed out that she did not—"ought to be willing to let the public," who some leg-islators maintained were crying for executions, "observe those executions and see what the result of their desires in this matter are."

However, Representative Bettermann refused to accept Representa-tive Long's amendment as friendly, stating that executions "would be portrayed as violence" and that she wanted to "take violence off televi-sion." Another death penalty proponent, Representative Ron Abrams, added that executions ought to be conducted in private. Surprised by Representative Bettermann's refusal to accept her friendly amendment, Representative Long voluntarily withdrew it. Although Representative Bettermann's proposed amendment was soundly defeated on May 2, 1995, by a vote of 37–96, her proposal was not taken lightly by death penalty foes because Minnesota Governor Arne Carlson had publicly stated only a few months earlier that he was willing to rethink his long-time opposition to capital punishment.[23]

On February 4, 1994, twenty delegates of the Maryland House of Delegates, led by Delegate Gilbert Genn, also introduced legislation to permit televised executions. House Bill 1149 would have required execu-tions to be carried out at "a suitable and efficient room or place [that is] in full public view and is located at the Maryland Penitentiary." In ad-dition, the bill would have allowed the Maryland Public Broadcasting

Commission and private newscasts to provide live or taped coverage of executions, although filming could only take place with the condemned person's consent. Baltimore lawyer H. Mark Stichel testified in favor of the bill before the House Judiciary Committee. "There is great public interest in capital punishment and the public has the right to the best possible information about it," Stichel testified, adding, "If the deterrence theory does have any validity, broadcasting executions will make what is now a closed and remote event a very real and much more effective deterrent." Genn's bill died in the House Judiciary Committee.

Despite the failure of such legislative initiatives, many prominent public officials have expressed an interest in putting executions on television. For instance, Illinois Senate President James "Pate" Philip, in previewing his conservative Republican agenda, announced that he wanted to broaden the death penalty in Illinois to cover nearly all murder cases. He said he was open to the prospect of televised executions, declaring that, "[i]f you look back in history, back in the wild, wild West, we had public hangings. And people would bring their family and come into town and bring their lunch and watch a hanging to teach their family and their young people how bad a hanging is and what happens when you violate the law." Proposals to put executions on television have even spilled over into political campaigns. Joan Wollin, a self-styled "alternative" candidate for Florida governor, proposed a referendum in 1986 on whether convicted murderer Ted Bundy should be executed on television. "I don't want to force it down the throats of the people," Wollin said. "I'd ask the people of Florida, do you want to see Bundy die on television. If they say yes, it should be public. If they say no, then it shouldn't."[24]

May It Please the Court

Only two judges in American history have ordered televised executions. U.S. District Court Judge William Taylor in Texas was the first, but the Fifth Circuit reversed his ruling in 1977. The second was ordered by Ohio District Court Judge Anthony Calabrese in November 1994. In sentencing Tyson Dixon to death, Judge Calabrese decreed: "Since we have everything else on TV, let this be shown so the public can see there is swift and certain punishment." Even though Dixon's execution was not imminent, Judge Calabrese's ruling was quickly attacked from all corners, including by the county prosecutor, Stephanie Jones. Having secured two death sentences herself in three years, Jones said that the death penalty "should not be something that is held up for the world to see." Joe Andrews, a spokesman for the Ohio Department of Rehabilitation and Correction, concurred. The department's policy is "no cameras or mechanical recording devices, to preserve the dignity of the event," he said. Even the official newspaper of the Vatican, *L'Osservatore Romana,* criticized the ruling of Judge Calabrese, a devout Roman Catholic. Theologian Gino Concetti called the idea "horrendous and offensive." He said that televised executions would "hold life up to mockery." Dixon's execution has not yet taken place and will most likely not occur any time soon because of the lengthy appeals process. If history is any guide, Ohio officials are sure to challenge Calabrese's order calling for a televised execution before Dixon is executed.[25]

Other American judges have ordered executions to be filmed but not for the purpose of being broadcast on television. In 1992, on the afternoon before Timothy Bunch's execution in Virginia, U.S. District Court Judge Robert R. Merhige Jr. ordered that Bunch's death be videotaped. Merhige ordered the taping in response to a lawsuit by death row inmate Syvasky Poyner on behalf of himself and all others similarly situated alleging that death by electrocution is a cruel and unusual punishment. The suit also argued that Virginia's execution procedures, calling for inmates to wear diapers and face masks, are designed to hide the inmate's suffering at death. Merhige ordered that "the execution be performed with the condemned prisoner's face visible" during the execution, so long as Bunch consented, which he did. Bunch said he wanted execution witnesses "to look [him] in the face" when he died. Execution experts predicted that Bunch's facial contortions while being electrocuted would be truly horrific. After holding a conference call, however, a three-judge panel of the Fourth Circuit overturned Merhige's order, ruling that a videotaping order should not be made in "undue haste in this matter of grave importance."[26]

In 1993, death row inmate Donald Thomas similarly petitioned to have John Thanos's execution in Maryland filmed, making the further request that Thanos's brain waves be monitored by an electroencephalograph (EEG). These acts were necessary, Thomas argued, to preserve "unique evidence" critical to his Eighth Amendment challenge to the constitutionality of death by lethal gas. Thanos had no objection to these requests, even signing a written statement to that effect. Thomas's lawyer, H. Mark Stichel, told U.S. District Court Judge Marvin Garbis that Thomas's requests, if approved, "would provide a visual impression of a Maryland gas execution and hard, scientific evidence" directly relevant to whether lethal gas executions are cruel and unusual punishments. The state Division of Corrections objected to the videotaping request based on "the lack of relevance of any of this information to the question of constitutionality, the interference with the warden's discretion in the conduct of executions and the practical problems in acceding to these requests." The Maryland Penitentiary warden argued that because "unobstructed access is required for the safe operation of the chamber," the chamber area could not be "encumbered by a video camera with or without a video camera operator."

After hearing oral arguments, Judge Garbis granted Thomas's requests. Garbis specifically rejected the state's argument that Thomas's filming request would infringe on the confidentiality surrounding executions. Noting that Maryland is the only state that still uses lethal gas as its sole means of carrying out death sentences, Garbis found that Thomas's "right of access for the purpose of collecting and preserving critical discovery" outweighs any asserted confidentiality right. Garbis emphasized that Thomas did not seek permission to televise Thanos's execution "or in any way make a public spectacle of it." Alluding to a provision of Maryland law that requires prison officials to keep secret the specific time of an inmate's execution, Garbis added that "the confidentiality of the time of execution need not be threatened by the granting of the Petition." Garbis noted that "[a]dvance planning [will] prevent the general public from being informed contrary to the statutory mandate."

After the videotape and EEG were made, Garbis ordered that the results be "delivered to the Clerk of this Court, without prior viewing or copying." No "disclosure of any videotape or EEG results to anyone except as may be permitted by further Order of this Court" was authorized. When asked whether anyone outside the Thomas case would be allowed to view the videotape, Judge Garbis said he would answer that question when faced with it. Judge Garbis's ruling, however, prompted

Maryland's General Assembly to pass an "emergency bill" supported by three-fifths of each house authorizing lethal injection as an alternative to the gas chamber. The state's governor quickly signed this bill on March 25, 1994, and Thanos opted to die by lethal injection, thereby mooting Thomas's videotaping request. Consequently, Thanos's execution was never filmed.[27]

In 1994, the Indiana chapter of the American Civil Liberties Union also unsuccessfully fought to have death row inmate Gregory Resnover's execution filmed. Like Syvasky Poyner's lawsuit, the ACLU was trying to prove that electrocution was a cruel and unusual punishment violative of the Eighth Amendment. A lower court judge initially ruled that the execution could be videotaped and that Resnover did not have to wear the traditional black fabric hood. However, the Indiana Supreme Court overturned those rulings seventy minutes before Resnover's execution. Accordingly, at 12:13 A.M. on December 8, 1994, Resnover died without cameras present after 2,300 volts of electricity surged through his body for ten seconds, followed by 500 volts for twenty seconds. "I didn't see much movement, but a lot of sparks flew out of his head," reported Eric McCauley, an execution witness. A similar attempt to videotape an electrocution in Georgia also was denied by a federal district judge in 1996. That judge expressed the belief that, although public hangings on the courthouse square were commonplace during the last century, such displays "would be unacceptable today."[28]

In 1993, in an attempt to prove that hanging was a cruel and unusual punishment, death row inmate Charles Campbell had similarly applied to film Washington's scheduled 12:01 A.M. hanging of Westley Allan Dodd. The trial judge, though, denied Campbell's request, finding that the evidentiary value of a videotape was doubtful and unnecessary for an informed ruling on whether hanging violates the Eighth Amendment. The judge also held that videotaping the execution might infringe on Dodd's privacy rights "because there could be no guarantee against the intentional or inadvertent release of the recording to the public." Dodd had never formally consented to have his execution videotaped.

The U.S. Court of Appeals for the Ninth Circuit affirmed the trial judge's ruling, refusing to create a permanent audiovisual record of an execution, "the most serious of all state legal proceedings against its citizens." The Ninth Circuit held that Campbell had failed "to identify what it is that would be learned by watching Dodd's execution or how it would shed any light on whether hanging violates the Eighth Amendment." According to the court: "The proposed videotape would not show the impact of the physical instrument (the rope) as it affects the body, because of the hood worn by the condemned extending over the face, neck and chest; nor would it show the location of the physical injuries, as they are either internal or hidden behind the hood. . . . We are left to conclude that Campbell desires the evidence for its sheer emotional impact." The Ninth Circuit also credited the trial court's reliance on protecting Dodd's privacy concerns. "[W]e simply cannot guarantee that no duplicate will be made or that this tape will not appear on CNN someday," the court held.

Ninth Circuit Judge Stephen Reinhardt dissented, calling the district court's order denying Campbell "the opportunity to preserve crucial evidence to a fair adjudication of his eighth amendment claim . . . a violation of Campbell's right to due process of law." Campbell only asks that "the events of the hanging be preserved on videotape and deposited with the court," Reinhardt noted, pointing out that "[t]he state has already given permission for a substantial number of persons—media representatives, the prosecutor, the sentencing judge, and the victims' families—to witness the execution and to describe the event graphically in the press and on television." "Dodd's privacy is already invaded to a substantial extent by that act of the state," Reinhardt reasoned, stating further: "If Campbell's proposed order is granted, the number of persons who will ultimately see the execution will only increase by the number of persons present at a federal court hearing, plus the cameraman. Under these circumstances, the minimal incremental infringement on Dodd's privacy is far outweighed by the importance of the evidence that Campbell seeks to preserve." Reinhardt concluded his dissent by reminding his fellow judges: "A videotape of a state-conducted hanging is obviously the *best possible evidence* of whether or not hanging constitutes cruel and unusual punishment. . . . Videotape is not perfect, but . . . it can dramatically diminish the margin for miscommunication and misperception."[29]

The Power of Television

Television was introduced into American households in the 1940s. From the minute television sets hit retail outlets, the new medium was a blockbuster success. In 1946, there were only 10,000 television sets in use. By 1950, that number rose to 10.5 million, and by 1960 the number of television sets in use had skyrocketed to 54 million. By the end of the 1980s, television sets were in more than 98 percent of all American households. Even more remarkably, by that time Americans were spending roughly seven hours a day in front of the tube. In 1993, almost 63 percent of American households subscribed to cable television, and two-thirds of all households owned VCR equipment.[30]

On average, today's American adults spend over 40 percent of their leisure time, or more than thirty hours each week, watching television. Children are avid television watchers too. By the time a student graduates from high school, the average teenager has spent more hours watching television than in the classroom. Television plays a particularly prominent role in the dissemination of news, with 69 percent of adults acquiring most of their news from television. In contrast, only half of Americans buy daily newspapers, and only 5 to 7 percent of Americans rely on magazines for news. While television news reaches over 200 million viewers in the United States, the combined circulation of the three major news magazines—*Newsweek, Time,* and *U.S. News and World Report*—is less than 10 million. Moreover, 13 percent of Americans are either illiterate or functionally illiterate, and only 2 percent of Americans derive their news from sources exclusive of television.[31]

Americans regard television as the most complete and unbiased source of news. This fact is hardly surprising. Television produces unfiltered images, while newspapers and magazines provide only secondhand accounts of newsworthy events. In addition, television news reaches viewers more quickly. While newspapers and magazines disseminate news the next day or the following week or month, television coverage is often live. When people want up-to-date news on breaking events like the Oklahoma City bombing, they no longer rush to the newsstand. Instead, they reach for their remote controls and tune into CNN Headline News with its twenty-four-hour programming. The proliferation of cable television stations like C-SPAN and Court TV, and other round-the-clock news channels, has made television even more attractive to news consumers.[32]

Television is so powerful in American society that it can create media icons like Madonna overnight or reshape the images of pop superstars like Michael Jackson. It can sell Coke, cars, or toothpaste in astronomical quantities, and it can turn little-known billionaires like Ross Perot into serious presidential contenders. Television broadcasts can literally shape human events. Would the Los Angeles riots have happened if not for a single videotape depicting Rodney King being brutally beaten by a throng of cops? Probably not. And would the issue of sexual harassment be so openly discussed if not for Anita Hill's televised testimony before the all-male Senate Judiciary Committee? Almost certainly not. If television had never been invented, the names Rodney King and Anita Hill would likely be totally unrecognizable to most Americans.

The Debate

The question of whether to televise executions has sparked fierce debate in the media throughout the United States. KQED's lawsuit against San Quentin Warden Daniel Vasquez, discussed in Chapter 1, prompted a *Nightline* episode, and the issue has even caught the attention of Hollywood. In a recent made-for-TV movie, Sean Young played an executive with Tycom, a company that specializes in pay-per-view events. Young's character, Jessica Traynor, wanted to put executions on television. The issue also has been explored in an *L.A. Law* episode and a movie, *Somebody Has to Shoot the Picture*. That movie stars Roy Scheider, who plays a photographer hired by the condemned man to take his picture at the moment of his execution.[33]

The debate among politicians about whether to put executions on television has cut across party lines, pitting Democrats against Democrats and Republicans against Republicans. Even those with strongly held views about capital punishment, both pro and con, have been unable to reach a consensus on whether executions should be televised. Some death penalty proponents want executions televised to reap their potential deterrent value, while other death penalty advocates believe these broadcasts would only brutalize society. Likewise, death penalty opponents are split on whether televised executions would lead to the abolition of capital punishment or only make executions more attractive to voters. The divisive nature of the debate is evidenced by the fact that the American Bar Association, the American Civil Liberties Union, and the National Coalition to Abolish the Death Penalty are sharply divided by the issue.[34]

Those favoring televised executions fall into three categories. The first group hopes that "the spectacle will so disgust the public that it will turn against capital punishment." Anti–death penalty advocates like Sister Helen Prejean who seek to educate the public about capital punishment fall into this category. Sister Prejean hopes that the power of television will be able to reinvigorate the abolitionist movement. In her book *Dead Man Walking,* she writes: "I have no doubt that we will one day abolish the death penalty in America. It will come sooner if people like me who know the truth about executions do our work well and educate the public. . . . I am convinced that if executions were made public, the torture and violence would be unmasked, and we would be shamed into abolishing executions." Other actors in the criminal justice system also have condemned the private nature of executions. After Louisiana's 12:15 A.M. execution of Pat Sonnier, defense lawyer Millard Farmer remarked: "Look how shamefully secret this whole thing is. A few select witnesses brought deep inside this prison in the dead of night to watch a man be killed. If most people in Louisiana would see what the state did tonight, they would throw up."[35]

History holds conflicting evidence about whether televised executions might be necessary to revitalize the abolitionist movement. It is true that public executions once helped fuel the anti–death penalty movement in some states. For example, when John McCaffary was publicly hung in Kenosha, Wisconsin, on August 21, 1851, two to three thousand people watched in horror as McCaffary struggled at the end of the rope for five minutes. As historian Philip Mackey explains, "Hangings had been rare in Wisconsin, and many citizens were appalled to learn what they were like." Anti–death penalty sentiment created by McCaffary's execution led to the acquittal of a man widely believed to be guilty of murder by a Milwaukee jury in 1852, and the next year the Wisconsin legislature abolished capital punishment. The bill was pushed through by "an odd coalition of persons angered by the botched hanging and others concerned about acquittals of the guilty." In the 1880s, a similar outcry in New York over a series of publicized, bungled hangings did not lead to the abolition of capital punishment but to the adoption of a new, more "humane" method of execution: the electric chair. It is also true, however, that executions became much less common in the United States between 1940 and the mid-1960s, even though no public executions took place during that period. To be sure, though, some abolitionists believe that it is only the private nature of executions that has allowed capital punishment to flourish in the post-*Furman* era, and that televised executions are necessary to expose the hypocrisy of secretive, midnight executions.[36]

The second group favoring televised executions opposes government censorship. They believe the press has the First Amendment right to air execution film footage, and that the public has the right to watch them. After David Lawson's gas chamber death, Phil Donahue said that he would have broadcast the execution despite its gruesome and lengthy nature. "From what I hear and read, it was awful," Donahue said, alluding to the thirteen minutes it took Lawson to die. "But so was the killing of John F. Kennedy and executions in Sarajevo and I'm going to continue to make a First Amendment effort not to sanitize the reality, make it convenient for viewers." On CNN's *Crossfire* program, Donahue argued that television broadcasts would spark a "robust, informed, good old American free speech debate" about capital punishment. "I believe that if you give people light they will find their own way," he explained. "That's the Scripps Howard motto and I subscribe to it." California public television station KQED's lawyer, William Bennett Turner, has acknowledged that televised executions "would be degrading in some way for all." Nevertheless, he believes that executions should not be hidden from public view. He wants to expose what executions are like because in his view the evil is the death penalty itself. "The only thing worse than having executions and watching them," Turner says, "is having executions and having our government prohibit us from watching them."[37]

A third group that favors televised executions seeks to harness their potential deterrent value. New Orleans District Attorney Harry Connick Sr. and former California U.S. Attorney Joseph Russoniello, both death penalty proponents, have publicly said that putting executions on television would enhance their deterrent effect. Likewise, Vernon Harvey, a murder victim's father, wants to "fry the bastards on prime-time TV [to]

see if that doesn't give second thoughts to anybody thinking of murder."
The mayor of Columbus, Dana Rinehart, agrees, proposing televised executions as "one way to stop the spiraling murder rate in Columbus." "I
think you'd have an overnight reduction in homicides if we had capital
punishment. Let the first person who is in the electric chair be on television. Let people watch that," Rinehart said. This view is bolstered by the
belief of sociologist Steven Stack, who has studied the effects of well-publicized executions. "Media publicity regarding executions is a necessary
condition for deterrence because if the public is unaware of executions,
they can have very little impact on homicide," Stack writes.[38]

Modern-day executions do get very little media coverage. Of the
ninety-three executions between 1977 and 1987, only thirty-three of
them received coverage by one or more of the three major networks.
And of thirty-three South Carolina executions between 1950 and 1963,
nine received no coverage at all in the *Charleston News and Courier,* the
newspaper of South Carolina's second largest city. Only four of the
thirty-three executions made the newspaper's front page. Print coverage
declines even further as executions become commonplace. The first executions since executions resumed in the United States in 1977 made the
front page of the *New York Times,* but by 1984, executions were usually
reported in inside pages. In fact, although the *New York Times* reported
on all executions between 1977 and 1983, it then began a policy of increasingly selective coverage. Today, only high-profile executions draw
much media attention. While reporters still descend en masse when a
notorious killer like John Wayne Gacy is executed, a run-of-the-mill execution is more likely to end up as a two-line blurb in the *Washington
Post*'s "Addenda" section. Even when television news coverage is provided, live film footage from outside the prison often goes unwatched
because many Americans are already sound asleep.[39]

Social scientists disagree as to whether televised executions would
deter crime. Some studies, like one conducted by William Bowers and
Glenn Pierce, find that the effect of well-publicized executions is brutalization, not deterrence. The study done by Bowers and Pierce found that
in New York from 1907 to 1963 there were, on average, two more murders in the month following an execution. As Bowers concludes:
"[P]ublicizing executions, even without allowing people to witness them,
may cause some people—perhaps those on the fringe of sanity—to be-

come fascinated or obsessed with the condemned person's crime, even to the point of imitating it." Indeed, the American Psychological Association's Commission on Violence and Youth concluded in 1993 "that higher levels of viewing violence on television are correlated with increased acceptance of aggressive attitudes and increased aggressive behavior."[40]

Other studies find that well-publicized executions might reduce the homicide rate. Sociologist David Phillips, studying executions in England between 1858 and 1921, found that well-publicized stories about executions reduced the homicide rate in the week of and the week after the executions by 32.8 percent. Phillips claimed to show that "the more publicity given to the execution, the more homicides drop."[41] Likewise, a study conducted by Steven Stack found that "months with publicized execution stories have fewer homicides than months lacking such stories." Stack's 1987 study of over seven hundred executions found that a well-publicized execution story is associated with a drop of thirty homicides in the month of the story. "Nonpublicized executions had no impact on the monthly incidence of homicide," Stack reported. These latter studies provide ammunition for those who argue that televised executions will deter violent crime. Still other social scientists find that execution publicity will neither deter nor promote killings.[42]

Significantly, Phillips's study, which claimed to provide "the first compelling statistical evidence" that executions deter homicides, has been discredited, and Stack's research has been criticized as flawed. In replicating and extending Phillips's study, William Bowers collected homicide data for *ten weeks* on either side of the executions studied by Phillips. After analyzing this data, Bowers discovered that the limited time frame of Phillips's study created "the illusion of a short-term deterrent effect and masked the evidence of brutalization." The data for the ten weeks on either side of the twenty-two executions of notorious murderers originally studied by Phillips showed that there were actually more homicides after than before each execution. While there were 271 homicides in the ten-week pre-execution period, there were 324 homicides in the ten-week post-execution period. Bowers's brutalization findings were statistically significant, as confirmed by regression analysis. "The *net* result of executions is more, not fewer, killings," Bowers concluded. Moreover, Bowers found that "[t]he brutalizing effect appears to be a direct linear function of publicity." In the ten-week periods on either side of the executions,

Bowers found there were "36 more homicides after than before the 11 most highly publicized cases, but only 17 more homicides after than before the 11 less publicized cases." Bowers concluded that, "for every 200 inches of newspaper coverage in the *Times* of London, there was one additional homicide within 10 weeks." While Bowers found that Phillips's study did not "rule out the possibility that some homicides are deterred by executions," Bowers's study showed that "the brutalizing effect tends to be longer in duration and stronger in impact than any deterrent effect that may occur—that the *net* effect is brutalization rather than deterrence." It is completely possible, of course, that well-publicized executions both deter and cause violent crime. As Bowers explains: "Strictly speaking, deterrent and brutalizing effects are not mutually exclusive; the same execution could dissuade some potential murderers and provoke others to kill." When coding errors were corrected in Stack's analysis, sociologists William Bailey and Ruth Peterson found a chance-only association between execution publicity and homicide rates.[43]

Opponents of televised executions also have advanced different reasons for their stance. Some commentators, like George Will, believe televised executions will only "further coarsen American life." Author Thomas Sowell echoes Will's concern. "The public has no more desire to see executions than to see abdominal surgery. Nor is there any reason why they should be presented with either on the 6 o'clock news, as they sit down to dinner," Sowell writes. Columnist Anthony Lewis further worries that television will only "trivialize executions—reduce them to the level of entertainment, to be clicked on and off." He is concerned that people will "invite friends over for beer, pretzels and death." Ernest van den Haag, an outspoken proponent of capital punishment, also opposes televised executions because they "should not serve as public entertainment" wedged in "between game shows, situation comedies and the like."[44]

Other opponents of televised executions are concerned about rampant television violence and worry that executions on television will only exacerbate the problem. Television violence is widespread. A 1990 study conducted by the University of Pennsylvania's Annenberg School of Communications found that prime-time television programs average five or six violent acts each hour, and that Saturday morning children's programs average twenty-six violent acts per hour. The National Coalition on Television Violence reports that, by age eighteen, an average child will have seen 200,000 violent acts on television, including approximately 40,000 murders. And the Center for Media and Public Affairs identified 1,846 violent scenes broadcast between 6 A.M. and midnight on one day alone in Washington, D.C. Television news is no exception. The Rocky Mountain Media Watch in Denver analyzed the tapes of one hundred local news programs in fifty-eight cities on a single night and found that the typical half-hour program offered about twelve minutes of news, more than 40 percent of it depicting violent crimes or disasters. Of the one hundred news programs, thirty-seven stations led off the news with stories about crime.[45]

Those who are concerned about television violence particularly worry that children, who watch an average of twenty-seven hours of television per week, and those who have already shown a propensity toward violence will watch televised executions. The concern that children will watch executions is already expressed in the existing laws of eleven states, which prohibit minors from witnessing executions. For example, in California, Louisiana, and Utah, those under the age of eighteen cannot attend executions, and in Missouri and Nevada, only those older than twenty years of age may attend them. Three states—Alabama, Ohio, and Texas—also expressly forbid convicts from witnessing executions. The fear that watching executions may actually incite violence dates back to the nineteenth century, when skull-measuring phrenologists believed that public executions only stimulated "the desire to kill in those in whom the propensity is naturally strong." Modern-day studies also have concluded that higher levels of television violence can contribute to violent attitudes.[46]

Other persons oppose putting executions on television because, in the words of Ernest van den Haag, such broadcasts would emphasize the "physical aspects of the punishment" instead of the "nature of the crime and the suffering of the victim." Victims' rights advocates worry that, just as Nicole Brown and Ronald Goldman were sometimes forgotten at O. J. Simpson's murder trial (which focused largely on Simpson himself), too much emphasis will be placed on the death row inmate, to the exclusion of information about the crime itself. "Far from communicating the moral significance of the execution," van den Haag writes, television "would shift the focus to the pitiable fear of the murderer." Some members of this group, like the California legislators who opposed a bill in 1991 that would have required televised executions, might support television executions if crime reenactments were broadcast before execution film footage was aired.[47]

Still other opponents of televised executions want to protect the solemnity of death. Former Attorney General Edwin Meese has opposed public executions at least in part on this basis. "I think that [with] the way television portrays most things," Meese stated, "it would tend to open the opportunity for distortion and could easily transform a serious event into something of a circus type situation." Some condemned prisoners, in fact, have specifically asked for private executions. In 1986, death row inmates Michael Evan and Richard Andrade both opposed letting people watch their executions in Texas. Andrade's reaction was particularly severe when he learned that five reporters would witness his execution. "He cried and cried and cried—he sobbed," said prison spokesman Charles Brown.[48]

Finally, prison wardens frequently mention security concerns as a reason for keeping executions off television. They assert that putting executions on television might cause prison riots if viewed by inmates or jeopardize prison personnel or their families by identifying staff members participating in the execution. For example, in KQED's lawsuit against San Quentin Warden Daniel Vasquez, the state of California asserted that execution broadcasts could create a "ripple effect" of anger and violence throughout the prison. Warden Vasquez even testified that a camera operator might hurl a camera against the gas chamber's windows to try and stop an execution. Thus, prison wardens, whose security concerns sometimes border on the paranoid, want to keep television cameras out of execution chambers at all costs.[49]

Restoring Accountability

Americans are ambivalent about the idea of televised executions. A Harris poll taken at the time of Gary Gilmore's execution in 1977 found that 86 percent of respondents opposed viewing his execution on television. A random sample of 600 lawyers done in the mid-1980s revealed that 68 percent of attorneys believe that the public should be excluded from executions, and a poll conducted for CNN in 1991 found that 71 percent of the television-viewing public opposed televised executions. In 1991, an unscientific call-in poll with 1,301 respondents also found that 722 people opposed televised executions, with only 579 respondents favoring the idea. However, on February 13, 1994, after NBC aired the movie *Witness to the Execution,* which dealt with a pay-per-view televised execution, an unscientific poll conducted afterward found that 77 percent of respondents favored televising executions. Also, after Ohio judge Anthony Calabrese ordered that a murderer's execution be televised in November 1994, public support for televised executions was reported to be over 80 percent. But poll results are just poll results, and the question remains: *Should* executions be televised?[50]

Today, only a handful of official witnesses handpicked by prison wardens or state bureaucrats actually watch executions. Quite undeniably, this fact has changed the nature of America's death penalty debate. Because death row inmates are executed behind prison walls and cameras are forbidden in execution chambers, citizens are no longer able to assess for themselves the appropriateness or morality of capital punishment. Instead, they must rely on secondhand accounts of executions in newspapers and magazines to form an opinion about the propriety of this punishment. Information about executions is limited further because the number of media representatives who can attend executions is severely restricted by private execution laws. The lack of information about executions is only compounded by the fact that executions frequently take place in the middle of the night when most Americans are asleep.[51]

Laws requiring private, nighttime executions are, almost by definition, flagrantly antidemocratic. By prohibiting Americans from witnessing executions, citizens are unable to monitor their own government's actions, and politicians are not held accountable to their constituents for their death penalty stances. In sanitizing the news, these paternalistic laws—which were admittedly intended, in the words of one state supreme court, to protect "the masses" and to reduce execution "publicity"—have blinded Americans to the reality of what happens behind prison walls. Instead of executing people openly in public squares at high noon, as they did a century ago, Americans now execute people in prisons under cover of darkness. These covert executions more resemble justice meted out by England's fifteenth-century Star Chamber than America's democratic tradition with its Sunshine Laws, open-meeting laws, and Freedom of Information Act.

The lack of publicity surrounding executions, along with the unaccountability of politicians for them, has led to calls for televised executions. These calls should be heeded. In the nineteenth century, Americans got the vast majority of their news from newspapers. In this century, however, television has usurped much of the power that the print media once monopolized. Thus, televised executions are necessary to restore accountability to America's death penalty debate. By putting executions on television, no longer will politicians be able to advocate the use of capital punishment as a crime-fighting measure without having to live with the real life-and-death consequences of their get-tough-on-crime rhetoric. The public would watch as brain-damaged or mentally retarded inmates are executed. They would look on as young men are executed for crimes they committed as teenagers. And they would watch men catch fire in the electric chair. Obviously, this is not to suggest that executions must now take place in Central Park or downtown Dallas, creating traffic jams and crowd-control problems. Using modern-day technology, broadcast journalists can act as surrogates for the public, filming executions in prisons and transmitting the footage into American households via television or videotape.[52]

After Americans watch executions firsthand, they might adhere to pro–death penalty views. On the other hand, they might very well clamor for the abolition of the death penalty or its narrower enforcement. For example, the public may decide that juveniles and the mentally retarded should not be executed. In fact, a recent study done by three social scientists at the University of the Pacific in California suggests that televised executions might reduce support for capital punishment. In that study, 291 registered California voters filled out a capital punishment questionnaire before being divided up into two groups. The first group watched a seven-minute color segment from a graphic videotape, *Faces of Death*, containing an electrocution and a gas chamber death, while the second group watched a nature film of similar length. The study participants then immediately responded to another death penalty questionnaire. The researchers found that "more people who viewed an execution videotape decreased their support of capital punishment than did people who viewed a nature videotape." Whereas 27 percent of the participants in the execution-videotape group became more supportive of capital punishment, 57 percent of the participants in that group became less supportive of capital punishment. Sixteen percent of participants' views were unchanged.[53]

Televised executions might also lead to what some people view as more humane forms of capital punishment like lethal injection. For example, Arizona changed its method of execution from hanging to lethal gas in 1933 as a result of the botched hanging of Eva Dugan in 1930. Dugan weighed 250 pounds, and the tremendous force of the drop tore off her head. According to historian David Abney, "The headless corpse naturally disgusted the spectators and encouraged the legislature to consider a method less susceptible to that sort of bloody error." By watching executions, Americans will be able to decide, with the best possible information, what method of capital punishment is least cruel. Of course, after watching executions, Americans may conclude that all execution methods are inhumane and decide that capital punishment should not be retained at all.[54]

Putting executions on television will let the American people decide for themselves whether capital punishment is morally justified. Will television executions be gruesome to watch? Yes. In fact, many people oppose televised executions on this basis alone. A 1994 study by three Stanford psychiatrists of the media eyewitnesses to Robert Alton Harris's execution found that the eyewitnesses suffered from posttraumatic stress and "experienced a high prevalence of dissociative symptoms . . . similar to that of people who endured a natural disaster." "We found that killing is killing, whether socially sanctioned or not," concluded Dr. David Spiegel, one of the researchers. Because of the psychological impact of executions, Spiegel was "very leery of televised executions." "The kind of people who would be upset by it have empathy, and murderers don't," Spiegel stated. However, there is a larger question here. Instead of asking whether televised executions will be repulsive to watch, Americans must ask whether the public has the right to watch executions. The answer to this question is harder, but it is, in fact, yes: Americans must have the right to watch state-sanctioned killings.[55]

If state governments are allowed to hide executions from public scrutiny, what does that say about the strength of America's democracy? And where does one draw the line? If execution film footage can be censored because of its graphic nature, how about film clips of the Vietnam war? Some people may forget that it was an NBC broadcast of a South Vietnamese general casually shooting a bound Viet Cong prisoner in the head that helped fuel America's antiwar movement. And how about film footage of a local bank robbery or of executions that occur in foreign lands? Can that film footage be censored? In the last fifteen years, public executions have taken place in at least twenty-two countries, and many of these executions—including ones in Iraq, Saudi Arabia, and Vietnam—have been shown on U.S. news programs. For example, American television stations broadcast the firing squad execution of Romania's former dictator, Nicolae Ceausescu.[56]

If Americans can watch executions in totalitarian countries, shouldn't Americans be permitted to watch executions in their own country? After all, America traditionally has had a more open form of government than some countries, where executions are conducted without any public notification whatsoever. In Nigeria, neither the time nor the fact of execution is made public. Death sentences are not publicly recorded and are not reported to anyone except the immediate family of the accused. In Japan, the only way to find out if an execution has taken place is to check the family register in the condemned person's hometown. When the condemned person's name is struck out, the execution has taken place. No public announcement of the execution is made, and neither the condemned prisoner nor his family members are told of the specific execution date. Only after the execution has taken place are the condemned prisoner's relatives notified so that they can pick up the body. Until recently, the Japanese Ministry of Justice even declined to give out information on the number of persons executed in Japan.[57]

The arguments against televised executions are unpersuasive. First, the contentions that television broadcasts of executions will only mock human life, tempt inmates to act for television cameras, or be too gruesome or shocking for the public to watch are irrelevant because of the overriding censorship issues at stake. Undoubtedly, some community members will gather in their homes and at bars to watch executions for entertainment or sport, much like they watch heavyweight prize fights on television. However, the only alternative is to have executions hidden from public view, which is completely unacceptable in a democracy like America that values free and open debate. Thus, it does not matter whether televised executions will "coarsen American life" or even "trivialize" death. The only salient inquiry is whether Americans should be allowed to monitor what their own government does to human beings in the dark of night, and whether politicians and bureaucrats should be permitted to sanitize the news. After all, it is not television that makes executions gruesome and repulsive. Television cameras only objectively record what takes place behind prison walls.[58]

While it is understandable that most Americans would fear having their children watch executions on television, one must view this issue in the larger context of what is newsworthy. State-sanctioned killings are certainly newsworthy, and because the Constitution guarantees the freedom of the press, journalists must be allowed to fully report about them. There is no legitimate reason why the public shouldn't be able to hear firsthand a condemned inmate's dying words, be they penitent or merely said in jest for television cameras. Even the U.S. Supreme Court has recognized that "the government may not 'reduce the adult population . . . to [seeing] only what is fit for children.'" The argument that executions are too violent for television also presupposes that we should ban television broadcasts of other violent acts. But do we really want to censor film footage of the Oklahoma City bombing or of John F. Kennedy's assassination? Obviously not. The general public must be informed on matters of such importance. Instead of banning cameras from execution chambers, parents must monitor—as many do now—what their children watch on television. Perhaps if Americans are too afraid that their children will watch executions, Americans should not be executing people at all.[59]

Similarly, American states must permit executions to be televised irrespective of whether such broadcasts would deter crime or only brutalize society. It is simply unacceptable for the government to conduct executions, while at the same time forbidding the press from fully publicizing them. First, if televised executions purportedly brutalize society, it is logical to conclude that it is executions themselves, not the presence of inanimate television cameras at executions, that brutalize society. Because television cameras only objectively record what transpires in execution chambers, if people find the idea of televised executions revolting, maybe it is the actual taking of human life that they really find disturbing. In short, if politicians worry that the sight of executions will cause, rather than deter, crime, maybe politicians need to reconsider whether they should be authorizing capital punishment in the first place. Second, if politicians were allowed to bar television cameras in execution chambers over fears that television publicity would be brutaliz-

ing, politicians might soon be passing laws—as they did a century ago—
banning newspaper coverage of executions. However, under modern-
day First Amendment principles, such laws would be quickly declared
unconstitutional, even though newspaper coverage of executions is pre-
sumably only less brutalizing in degree than television coverage of executions. Instead of banning television coverage of executions, perhaps
politicians need to consider that by supposedly fighting crime with
state-sanctioned violence, they are sending the wrong message to America's crime-ridden society by promoting the notion that violence is a socially acceptable problem-solving technique.

The contention that televised executions will spark prison riots or
threaten prison personnel by revealing their identities is pure speculation. What are the chances, as Judge Schnacke suggested in KQED's
lawsuit, that a "suicidal cameraman" will throw a camera against the gas
chamber glass to try and stop an execution? Factually speaking, as two
scholars have recently concluded, there is simply "no evidence that dangers would result to witnesses, that the sight of fellow prisoners dying
would cause inmates to riot, or that a camera would ever be thrown at a
gas chamber." Indeed, prison inmates are usually confined to their cells
during executions, and well-settled U.S. Supreme Court precedent establishes that only where the danger is "likely" or "imminent" can restrictions on free speech withstand constitutional scrutiny.[60] Obviously,
the remote possibility that televised executions will cause prison riots or
endanger prison personnel is not anywhere near likely or imminent. If
such speculative possibilities were legitimate reasons for the government
to keep violent programming off television, popular shows like *N.Y.P.D.
Blue* would be forced off the air, and even portions of public television
specials depicting violent animal behavior might end up on the cutting
room floor. In a society that gives the media the First Amendment right
to show all forms of violence on television, the press must certainly be
allowed to show executions on television lest *state-sanctioned killing* be
made the only exception to that constitutional guarantee.

That the specter of prison riots is a ruse for restricting cameras in
execution chambers is reinforced by the fact that many of the reasons advanced for excluding television cameras from California's gas chamber at
KQED's 1991 trial against Warden Vasquez had nothing to do with
prison security. In that case, witnesses gave the following reasons for

wanting to exclude television cameras: "dignity," "don't want this turned into a circus," "thought it was not an appropriate item for public viewing," and "wouldn't be in good taste." Some public officials, in fact, have proposed broadcasting execution film footage into prisons as a deterrent to criminals. Charles Condon, a death penalty proponent, proposed legislation in 1985 to require South Carolina prisons to show televised electrocutions to all eight thousand of the state's inmates. The legislation would have affected all twenty-eight of that state's prisons and youth facilities. "Let them watch it," Condon said, "I think if they see what happens to them, or could happen to them, they'll think twice." "The death penalty can be a powerful, powerful deterrent if the right people see it," he concluded.[61]

The argument that printed sources can convey the same information as television also is misplaced. A qualitative difference exists between printed material and film, as illustrated by the degree to which some printed accounts vary depending on the writer's perspective. After Aaron Mitchell's execution in California in 1967, the conservative *San Francisco Examiner* said Mitchell went to his death "screaming and groaning to the end." In contrast, the *Oakland Tribune* described Mitchell primarily as a victim, saying he was "forcibly carried into the San Quentin gas chamber." Newspaper accounts of Mitchell's execution even fail to agree on his last words. One reporter had him insanely shouting, "I am Jesus Christ," while another had him resignedly muttering, "Oh, my Jesus Christ." Another eyewitness, a prison official, remembered no last words at all. When Marshall McLuhan wrote that "[t]he medium is the message," he was right.[62]

Barring television cameras from execution chambers could actually forever banish serious discussion of the propriety of capital punishment to the back burner of American politics. This is so because television, like it or not, sets the American agenda. If an issue is not publicized on the nightly news, that issue is very unlikely to catch the attention of Americans, who are constantly bombarded with powerful television images. For instance, in 1995, Ted Koppel did a *Nightline* program in Texas about an execution, although he was not allowed to televise the prisoner's lethal injection. During that program, Koppel persuasively argued, "If what society wants is the death penalty, then let us at least have the decency to be fully conscious of what we are doing and why." Almost certainly, if Koppel had been allowed to film the execution, Americans—forced to look into the eyes of the condemned man—would have had to grapple more seriously with the issue of capital punishment. Putting executions on television would also enable voters to make more informed choices at the ballot box when voting on candidates and death penalty referenda.[63]

More importantly, televised executions would change America's political culture. No longer would legislators be able to pass death penalty laws without full public awareness of the real human consequences of such legislation. This fact is particularly important because it is frequently legislators—not the public via referenda—who authorize the death penalty. Two well-known scholars, Franklin Zimring and Gordon Hawkins, have concluded that it is "political culture rather than public opinion [that] determines the passage of death penalty legislation and the occurrence of executions." They point out that two-thirds of the populations in Great Britain, Canada, and Germany actually opposed abolition when legislators abolished capital punishment in those countries. Only after abolition did support for capital punishment, as expressed in public opinion polls, gradually diminish. Today, of course, Canada and all European countries do not permit capital punishment, apparently the result of political leadership rather than popular demand. As Zimring and Hawkins explain of the European and Canadian experiences, it is only after "time passes after abolition and increases in violent crime do not materialize [that] the felt necessity for the capital sanction diminishes gradually."[64]

A First Amendment Right

The U.S. Supreme Court has never squarely addressed the constitutionality of laws barring television cameras from execution chambers. In *Holden v. Minnesota*, decided in 1890, the Supreme Court dealt with whether Minnesota's "midnight assassination law" constituted an unlawful ex post facto law. Only in dicta did the Court opine that the law's provisions requiring private, nighttime executions were ones "which the Legislature, in its wisdom, and for the public good, could legally prescribe." Because *Holden* focused on the constitutionality of an alleged ex post facto law, rather than on the constitutionality of private execution laws, the Court's dicta cannot be considered dispositive. The *Holden* Court simply failed to consider all of the arguments for and against the constitutionality of private execution laws.[65]

Over the years, the U.S. Supreme Court has sent conflicting signals about whether executions should be conducted publicly or privately. In *Wilkerson v. Utah,* decided in 1879, the Supreme Court unanimously upheld a trial judge's order that a convicted murderer be publicly shot between "the hours of ten o'clock in the forenoon and three o'clock in the afternoon." However, in a concurring opinion in *Furman v. Georgia,* Justice William Brennan—who voiced the opinion throughout his Court tenure that capital punishment is an unconstitutionally cruel and unusual punishment—expressed disdain for public executions. In that 1972 case, Justice Brennan commented in dicta: "[I]f the deliberate extinguishment of human life has any effect at all, it more likely tends to lower our respect for life and brutalize our values. That, after all, is why we no longer carry out public executions." He similarly remarked: "No longer does our society countenance the spectacle of public executions, once thought desirable as a deterrent to criminal behavior by others. Today we reject public executions as debasing and brutalizing to us all." Even Justice Brennan, however, in his dissent in *Glass v. Louisiana,* seemed to lament that the public did not have more information about executions. In that opinion, in which Brennan argued that death by electrocution is a cruel and unusual punishment, he commented that the "[d]etails concerning the actual process of electrocution are not widely known, primarily because 'executions are carried out in private; there are few witnesses; pictures are not allowed; and newspaper accounts are, because of family newspaper requirements of taste, sparing in detail.'"[66]

Because the Supreme Court's sporadic dicta over the past one hundred years sheds little light on the constitutionality of laws banning television cameras from execution chambers, legal academics across America have vigorously debated whether these laws are constitutionally permissible. Some scholars, including eminent constitutional lawyer and Harvard Law School Professor Laurence Tribe, believe journalists should have the right to televise executions. These scholars variously contend that laws banning television cameras from execution chambers infringe on the press's First Amendment rights or the public's right to know about execution proceedings. Conversely, other scholars vigorously defend private execution laws as a legitimate exercise of state power. They assert that these laws are necessary to prevent prison riots and to protect prison guards' and death row inmates' privacy rights. The only thing both sets of scholars seem to agree on is that a First Amendment analysis is required to determine the constitutionality of laws barring television cameras in execution chambers.[67]

The First Amendment states, in unequivocal terms, that "Congress shall make no law . . . abridging the freedom of speech, or of the press." In interpreting that clause, the U.S. Supreme Court has held that all laws regulating the *content* of speech are subject to "strict scrutiny." Content-based restrictions include laws that prohibit the publication of confidential information or that outlaw the display of swastikas in certain communities. Content-neutral restrictions, by contrast, are subject to less strenuous judicial review. These laws restrict communication without regard to the content or communicative impact of the message conveyed. Laws that ban billboards in residential neighborhoods or prohibit noisy speech near hospitals are examples of content-neutral regulations.[68]

In *Police Department of Chicago v. Mosley,* the U.S. Supreme Court forcefully emphasized the importance of forbidding government censorship and content control in order to permit "the continued building of our politics and culture, and to assure self-fulfillment for each individual." The Court held that "above all else, the First Amendment means that government has no power to restrict expression because of its message, its ideas, its subject matter, or its content. . . . Any restriction on expressive activity because of its content would completely undercut the 'profound national commitment to the principle that debate on public issues should be uninhibited, robust, and wide-open.'"[69]

Even shocking or offensive speech cannot be censored by governmental authorities. For example, in *Cohen v. California,* the U.S. Supreme Court found that the phrase "Fuck the Draft," publicly displayed, might shock or offend some people. However, the Court held that the statement was protected speech. Likewise, in *Texas v. Johnson,* the Supreme Court upheld the right of citizens to burn the American flag, the very symbol of our nation's democracy. The Court ruled: "[A] principal 'function of free speech under our system of government is to invite dispute. It may indeed best serve its high purpose when it induces a condition of unrest, creates dissatisfaction with conditions as they are, or even stirs people to anger.' . . . If there is a bedrock principle underlying the First Amendment, it is that the government may not prohibit the expression of an idea simply because society finds the idea itself offensive or disagreeable."[70]

In construing the language of the First Amendment, the Supreme Court has expressed some ambivalence about whether members of the press enjoy more rights than the public at large to gather news and information. In *Pell v. Procunier* and *Saxbe v. Washington Post Co.*, the Court ruled that media representatives have "no constitutional right of access to prisons or their inmates beyond that afforded the general public." However, in *Branzburg v. Hayes,* the Court seemed to recognize that the First Amendment gives the press a limited right of access to gather news and information. In that case, the Court held that "without some protection for seeking out the news, freedom of the press could be eviscerated."[71]

The U.S. Constitution itself, in a separate clause of the First Amendment, states that "Congress shall make no law . . . abridging the freedom of speech, *or of the press.*" This clause provides special protection for the press, the only private institution to get such protection. "That the First Amendment speaks separately of freedom of speech and freedom of the press is no constitutional accident, but an acknowledgment of the critical role played by the press in American society," Justice Potter Stewart wrote, adding that "[i]f the Free Press guarantee meant no more than freedom of expression, it would be a constitutional redundancy." Justice Stewart aptly wrote that "[t]he primary purpose of the constitutional guarantee of a free press was . . . to create a fourth institution outside the Government as an additional check on the three official branches." Stewart used the metaphor of the "Fourth Estate," a reference to what Thomas Carlyle wrote about the British political system a century earlier: "Burke said there were Three Estates in Parliament; but, in the Reporters' Gallery yonder, there sat a Fourth Estate more important far than they all. It is not a figure of speech or witty saying; it is a literal fact—very momentous to us in these times." Elsewhere, Justice Stewart expounded on the vital role that the press plays in American life:

"Enlightened choice by an informed citizenry is the basic ideal upon which an open society is premised. . . ." Our society depends heavily on the press for that enlightenment. Though not without its lapses, the press "has been a mighty catalyst in awakening public interest in governmental affairs, exposing corruption among public officers and employees and generally informing the citizenry of public events and occurrences. . . ."[72]

As a factual matter, constitutional historian Leonard Levy has determined that, when the Bill of Rights was ratified, American newspapers already played a "watchdog function as the Fourth Estate." In his book *The Emergence of a Free Press,* Levy writes: "Freedom of the press . . . meant that the press had achieved a special status as an unofficial fourth branch of government, 'the Fourth Estate', whose function was to check the three official branches by exposing misdeeds and policies contrary to the public interest." Levy convincingly cites several pieces of evidence for this conclusion, including a 1789 letter from John Adams to U.S. Supreme Court Justice William Cushing, referencing "[o]ur chief magistrates and Senators." Adams asked, "How are their characters and conduct to be known to their constituents but by the press?" Likewise, Levy refers to a 1790 Virginia newspaper that identifies the press as the source from which people "learn the circumstances of our country, its various interests, and relations." The newspaper article continues: "Here too public men and measures are scrutinized. Should any man or body of men dare to form a system against our interests, by this means it will be unfolded to the great body of the people, and the alarm instantly spread through every part of the continent. In this way only, can we know how far our public servants perform the duties of their respective stations."[73]

When analyzed, private execution laws are blatantly unconstitutional under the First Amendment. For example, the present-day Arkansas law that prohibits newspapers from printing any execution details is clearly violative of the press's First Amendment rights. By singling out executions as the one area of public affairs that newspapers are not free to lawfully write about, the Arkansas law impermissibly regulates the content of speech. It is hard to imagine a more content-based restriction on speech than a state law that prohibits journalists from printing any details about an important governmental proceeding like an execution. Laws forbidding television cameras in execution chambers are also impermissible content-based restrictions. As KQED's lawyers William Bennett Turner and Beth Brinkmann have persuasively argued, "The warden's alleged concerns about the impact of the broadcast on viewers (inducing them to harm witnesses or officers, or to riot) meant that he justified the policy based on the broadcast's *content.*" "Further," Turner and Brinkmann convincingly note, "the restrictions on news coverage apply only to *executions.* Television coverage of other events at San Quentin is permitted, including parole and clemency hearings in capital cases. The no-pictures policy only applies to the 'subject matter' of executions."[74]

Because execution film footage conveys information and content that the print media is incapable of conveying, laws prohibiting cameras in execution chambers must be struck down as unconstitutional. Jurists themselves already recognize the qualitative difference between print and television news coverage. In a 1977 Supreme Court opinion, Justice Lewis Powell wrote that the public is the "loser" when news coverage is limited to "watered-down verbal reporting, perhaps with an occasional still picture." "This is hardly the kind of news reportage that the First Amendment is meant to foster," he opined. Likewise, in 1981, a federal judge in Georgia described the unique qualities of television news: "[V]isual impressions can and sometimes do add a material dimension to one's impression of particular news events. Television film coverage of the news provides a comprehensive visual element and an immediacy, or simultaneous aspect, not found in print media."[75]

The right-to-privacy argument is somewhat more persuasive, although convicted killers obviously forfeit many rights by committing their crimes. However, a convincing argument can be made that even convicted murderers should possess the right to die in private if that is their last dying wish. Former U.S. Supreme Court Justice William Brennan, who has expressed a distaste for public executions, would probably agree. "Dying is personal. And it is profound," Justice Brennan wrote in 1990. "For many, the thought of an ignoble end . . . is abhorrent. A quiet, proud death . . . is a matter of extreme consequence," Brennan concluded. While state legislatures should be able to balance a death row inmate's right-to-privacy concerns against the public's right to know, one thing is clear: legislators should not be able to bar cameras in the execution chamber where the condemned inmate consents to the presence of cameras. If the condemned inmate consents to television cameras in the execution chamber, no interest whatsoever justifies the exclusion of cameras. Only the condemned inmate should have standing to raise a right-to-privacy claim, although even then legislators should have the power to trump that right-to-privacy claim and allow any execution to be televised based on the public's right to know how and when the state takes a human life.[76]

In concluding that laws banning television cameras from execution chambers are unconstitutional, one does not even need to reach the issue of whether the press has greater rights than the public to gather news and information. Readers will recall that in *Pell v. Procunier* and *Saxbe v. Washington Post Co.,* the U.S. Supreme Court held that members of the press have "no constitutional right of access to prisons or their inmates beyond that afforded the general public." In the context of executions, however, the decisions of *Pell* and *Saxbe* are irrelevant because some members of the public already possess the right to attend executions as official witnesses. As outlined in Chapter 3, most private executions laws allow from six to twelve "respectable" or "reputable" citizens to attend executions, and these official witnesses attend executions as representatives of the public at large. When New York abolished public executions in 1835, a contemporaneous legislative report urging private hangings specifically contemplated that the statutorily prescribed "respectable citizens . . . would attend . . . execution[s] not as private spectators but as public witnesses." Because the public already possesses the right to attend executions through these official witnesses, the press must be allowed equal access to execution proceedings.[77]

Under existing legal precedents, the press already enjoys a constitutional right of access to attend some governmental proceedings. For instance, in 1980, the U.S. Supreme Court held in *Richmond Newspapers v. Virginia* that the press has a constitutional right to attend criminal trials. In that landmark ruling, the Supreme Court repeatedly emphasized the Anglo-American tradition of open trials dating back to "the days before the Norman Conquest." Chief Justice Warren Burger's plurality opinion explicitly held that "the right to attend criminal trials is implicit in the guarantees of the First Amendment," with Burger stating that "[t]he crucial prophylactic aspects of the administration of justice cannot function in the dark; no community catharsis can occur if justice is 'done in a corner [or] in any covert manner.'" "People in an open society do not demand infallibility from their institutions," Burger wrote, "but it is difficult for them to accept what they are prohibited from observing."[78]

Justice Brennan's concurring opinion in *Richmond Newspapers* also stressed that "public access to court proceedings is one of the numerous 'checks and balances'" of the criminal justice system and "an effective restraint on possible abuse of judicial power." "[T]he First Amendment embodies more than a commitment to free expression and communicative interchange for their own sake," Justice Brennan opined; "it has a *structural* role to play in securing and fostering our republican system of self-government." "Implicit in this structural role," Brennan concluded, "is not only 'the principle that debate on public issues should be uninhibited, robust, and wide open,' but also the antecedent assumption that valuable public debate—as well as other civic behavior—must be informed."[79]

The Supreme Court has not yet decided whether the press enjoys a constitutional right to televise trials, but it has made clear that cameras are certainly not always forbidden in courtrooms across America. In *Chandler v. Florida,* a 1981 decision, the Court held that televising a criminal trial was not a per se violation of a defendant's due process rights. With the exception of the federal courts, television cameras are actually fast becoming courtroom fixtures, with forty-seven states now allowing cameras in the courtroom in various circumstances. In September 1994, the U.S. Judicial Conference, a twenty-seven-member policymaking body headed by Chief Justice William Rehnquist, voted to discontinue a three-year experiment that permitted cameras in the federal courts. However, as Steve Haworth, CNN's vice president of public relations, noted, that decision ran "counter to the trend in American society to open institutions to more rather than less public scrutiny." The Judicial Conference's decision also was criticized by Brian Lamb, C-SPAN's chief executive. "One-third of our federal government will remain inaccessible to American citizens," Lamb said.[80]

New cable channels like Court TV have made court proceedings even more publicly accessible. No longer are the number of courtroom observers limited by the number of courtroom seats, and the public no longer has to rely on artist sketches or day-old newspaper accounts of trials to get information about them. People's living room couches have been transformed into courtroom seats. Although O. J. Simpson's high-profile trial left some commentators asking whether criminal trials should be televised, television coverage of trials clearly benefits the public. The public learns about the judicial process and gets incalculable information about criminal justice issues. Court TV's live coverage of William Kennedy Smith's trial brought to the forefront the issue of rape, and other televised trials have highlighted important issues like child abuse and battered woman's syndrome. Even O. J. Simpson's murder trial, a one-of-a-kind spectacle, has sparked increased awareness of domestic violence and the use of DNA evidence.[81]

If the press is permitted to televise trials, the press should certainly be allowed to televise executions. In fact, the only reason courts sometimes refuse to allow television cameras at criminal trials is over concerns about defendants' due process rights related to the potential impact of television cameras on witnesses and jurors. For example, in *Estes v. Texas,* decided in 1965, the U.S. Supreme Court held that a defendant's due process rights were violated by the presence of television cameras at trial because large cameras might have unduly disrupted the trial. Obviously, the argument that the presence of television cameras at an execution will infringe on an inmate's due process rights is nonsensical. The inmate, after all, will be dead at the conclusion of the proceeding. Again, so long as the condemned inmate consents to the presence of television cameras in the execution chamber, no legitimate reason exists to exclude cameras from recording the event. The Supreme Court has specifically held that "the people in our democracy are entrusted with the responsibility for judging and evaluating the relative merits of conflicting arguments . . . [and] if there be any danger that the people cannot evaluate the information and arguments . . . it is a danger contemplated by the Framers of the First Amendment."[82]

In America, television news directors, not state bureaucrats, must decide whether executions should be televised. Some television stations will not broadcast execution film footage, as evidenced by the fact that, in 1984, twenty-six stations participating in a Texas survey said that they would not show an execution on television even if allowed to film it.

Other television stations, though, will show executions live or as part of a news program, like the twelve stations in that survey that indicated that they would broadcast execution film footage.[83] Some media organizations may even attempt to put executions on pay-per-view television or sensationalize them, as shows like *A Current Affair* and *Hard Copy* frequently do with almost every news story they cover. However, because America is a democratic country, broadcast journalists must have the right to televise executions so that the public can be kept fully informed about capital punishment.

That televised executions will help educate Americans about capital punishment is beyond question. In Europe, television is already being used to educate Europeans about controversial social issues like physician-assisted suicide. For example, in 1994, Dutch TV produced an hour-long documentary on euthanasia that depicted a mercy killing. The documentary showed a doctor giving a lethal injection to a sixty-three-year-old man with Lou Gehrig's disease, an incurable neurological disorder.[84] In America, televised executions will help eradicate the many misconceptions and factual myths about capital punishment that now exist and will allow Americans to debate the propriety of capital punishment with full access to information about it. Televised executions, above all else, will let Americans decide for themselves whether the death penalty is right or wrong.

ᥫ᭡ CONCLUSION

Executions in America are hidden from public view. Private execution laws severely restrict the number of execution witnesses, and television cameras are strictly forbidden in execution chambers. Throughout the United States, these laws effectively ensure that the vast majority of Americans will never watch an execution. Only official witnesses, hand-picked by governmental officials, will ever witness the ultimate act of the state. Many state laws also require that death row inmates be executed at night. From 1977 to 1995, over 82 percent of executions occurred between 11:00 P.M. and 7:30 A.M.[1] These laws further inhibit the public's access to information about state-sanctioned killings because local television news programs are already over by the time many executions take place.

As Americans debate whether executions should be televised, the transition from public, daytime executions to private, nighttime executions must not be forgotten. By privatizing executions, nineteenth-century legislators, worried that executions might only incite criminal activity, sought to eliminate the spectacle of public executions. In those days, it was common knowledge that execution day crowds were often mischievous, with alcohol consumption and pickpockets regularly associated with public hangings. Rioting at public hangings also was not unknown. The "scientific" findings by skull-measuring phrenologists that public executions did not deter crime but actually caused more of it lent credence to the movement to privatize executions. The fear that well-publicized executions might only cause crime certainly helps explain why many states passed laws prohibiting the publication of execution details.[2]

By moving executions into prisons, paternalistic legislators and civic leaders also sought to protect society's sensibilities. Embarrassed by the

206

spectacle of public hangings, and the drinking and rabble-rousing that occurred at them, legislators passed laws requiring executions to take place within the confines of prisons beginning in the 1830s. Over the next one hundred years, hangings before large, boisterous crowds gradually ebbed, as civic leaders came to view public executions as corrupting of public morals and as incongruous with the occasion's solemnity. Women and children were seen as particularly unfit execution spectators, with some private execution laws excluding these groups from executions altogether. As in England, where even newspaper publicity of executions was thought to have a demoralizing influence on the community, especially children, American legislators tried to shroud executions with secrecy to prevent what they viewed as the unhealthy effects of public executions.[3]

Finally, private execution laws were sometimes passed to appease abolitionists after abolitionists made strong legislative efforts to abolish capital punishment. Many death penalty opponents, believing public executions would be instrumental in abolishing capital punishment, initially resisted the passage of such laws. However, abolitionists eventually relented and either acquiesced in the passage of these laws or pushed for their enactment. For instance, Minneapolis legislator John Day Smith, an ardent abolitionist, actually authored the law that privatized executions in Minnesota. He probably believed, like many other abolitionists of his time, that death penalty proponents would be deprived of their most powerful argument (that capital punishment deters crime) once executions were privatized. Ironically, the passage of private execution laws only removed the issue of capital punishment from public consciousness and made Americans apathetic toward executions.

In attempting to civilize society, private execution laws had the perverse effect of degrading America's democracy. Not only did these laws limit the number of execution spectators and restrict the public's access to information about capital punishment, but they often attempted to suppress public debate of the death penalty itself. In several states, laws were passed that prohibited newspaper reporters from attending executions or forbade newspapers from publishing any execution details. Only the bare fact that the prisoner was executed could be printed. Newspaper reporters who violated these laws could be criminally prosecuted as happened in the case of Minnesota and New York newspapers.

By sanitizing the news, these private execution laws did not civilize America, but made America rather *un*-American—for lack of a better word—and more resembling of a totalitarian regime that frequently censors the news.

Laws requiring nighttime executions also were enacted with paternalistic and publicity-squelching zeal. In upholding the constitutionality of the "midnight assassination law," the Minnesota Supreme Court specifically found: "The evident purpose of the act was to surround the execution of criminals with as much secrecy as possible, in order to avoid exciting an unwholesome effect on the public mind. For that reason it must take place before dawn, while the masses are at rest, and within an inclosure, so as to debar the morbidly curious." In requiring after-dark executions, these laws only further denigrated America's democracy by suggesting that Americans have something to hide or fear carrying out their chosen public policy in broad daylight. That nighttime executions are blatantly at odds with America's democratic tradition is amply illustrated by the fact that, under federal law, the "universal custom" is to display the American flag "only from sunrise to sunset."[4]

Today, laws requiring private, nighttime executions continue to stifle execution publicity and keep the public in the dark about the facts surrounding capital punishment. The public believes capital punishment deters crime, when in fact overwhelming evidence shows that capital punishment has no deterrent effect. The public believes all criminal defendants get adequate legal representation and fair trials, when in fact many of them do not. And at least some members of the public believe that the death penalty is not administered in an arbitrary or racially discriminatory manner, when in fact just the opposite is true. By cloaking executions in secrecy, these laws leave the public uninformed about capital punishment and unable to judge for themselves the morality of the death penalty. In addition, these laws leave politicians free to cry out for the use of capital punishment without having to live with the real life-and-death consequences of their get-tough-on-crime rhetoric. As Sister Helen Prejean aptly observes: "Beyond the rhetoric of all the legislators who score their political points for being tough on crime, what it all boils down to is that a handful of people are hired to kill a guy in the middle of the night."[5]

To restore accountability to America's death penalty debate, several remedial steps must be taken. First, judges or jurors who sentence criminal defendants to death (or governors who refuse to exercise their clemency powers) must be required to pull the triggering switch at executions, and all of those individuals must be required to attend them. This will inject some much-needed accountability and personal responsibility into capital sentencing and clemency decisions. Even Alex Kozinski, a conservative judge on the U.S. Court of Appeals for the Ninth Circuit and a death penalty supporter, has wondered aloud whether judges "who make life-and-death decisions on a regular basis should not be required to watch as the machinery of death grinds up a human being." Kozinski writes: "I ponder what it says about me that I can, with cool precision, cast votes and write opinions that seal another human being's fate but lack the courage to witness the consequences of my actions."

Second, no longer can jurors who oppose the death penalty be excluded from jury service. The death penalty is the most severe sanction that any society can impose, so the notion of excluding potential jurors from service solely because they oppose its use is like stacking a deck of cards before playing a game of poker when the ante is a human being's life. The blatant discrimination against jurors who oppose the death penalty, as presently sanctioned by the U.S. Supreme Court, is intolerable. Juries should reflect a fair cross-section of community views on this issue.

Third, the practice of allowing politically sensitive, elected state court judges to override jury verdicts of life imprisonment and impose death sentences must be outlawed via legislation. Only juries, which reflect a better sampling of a community's conscience, must be allowed to make life-and-death decisions. As Justice Stevens opined in his 1995 dissent in *Harris v. Alabama,* "the men and women of the jury may be regarded as a microcosm of the community, who will reflect the changing attitudes of society as a whole to the infliction of capital punishment." In Alabama, 99 percent of all trial judges are white males earning approximately $72,000 per year. By contrast, 52 percent of Alabama citizens are female, 75 percent of the population is black, and the average yearly income is $13,700. When recommendations of mercy are overridden in places like Alabama, the death sentences that are imposed by trial judges hardly reflect the community's collective conscience.

Fourth, the few remaining death penalty states that do not authorize the punishment of life imprisonment without the possibility of parole for murder must do so at once, and jurors in capital cases must always be made aware of that sentencing option. It is simply unconscionable that some sentencing juries continue to be faced with the Hobson's choice of voting for death, which they might find undesirable, or returning verdicts that they fear would let violent criminals walk the streets again. Judges and jurors must have the option of putting convicted murderers behind bars for the rest of their lives, and states must pass truth-in-sentencing laws so that jurors can be told, without reservation, that life without parole *means* life without parole.

Fifth, in light of the recent public opinion data showing that a majority of Americans actually prefer life imprisonment without parole over the death penalty, journalists must stop misleading the public and politicians into believing that the death penalty is so popular by printing, without qualification, oversimplified favor/oppose public opinion polls. Instead, journalists must better educate the public about capital punishment and the alternatives to it by writing hard-hitting news stories exposing the myths about the death penalty that politicians regularly perpetuate. Only after the American public has all the facts about capital punishment and its alternatives will they be able to decide whether the death penalty is an appropriate or just punishment for society to impose.

Finally, executions must be televised. Americans must acknowledge the critical role that television plays in our society and admit that printed accounts of executions are a woefully inadequate substitute for television news coverage of them. Concurrently, broadcast journalists must recognize their ethical obligation to keep the public fully informed about capital punishment issues and redouble their efforts to put executions on television so that the news is no longer sanitized. The executions-are-too-gruesome-for-television argument must be rejected. The public has a right to know when and how the state takes a human life, and both advocates and opponents of capital punishment should be able to agree that news reporting in America should not be censored by the government. If Americans want executions, they should have nothing to hide. As columnist Anna Quindlen has remarked about capital punishment, "Having it on television makes it no worse. It simply makes the reality inescapable, and our role undeniable. If we want it, we should be able to look at it. If we can't bear to look at it, maybe it's time to rethink our desires."[6] Televised executions are necessary to let the public fully scrutinize the propriety of capital punishment. Without televised executions, Americans will always lack complete information as they debate the morality of the death penalty.

Recalling the paternalistic intent of American laws requiring private, nighttime executions probably will not help Americans decide whether capital punishment is right or wrong. However, the history of such laws serves as a stern warning about the dangers of regulating press access to executions and the impact such governmental interference can have on the democratic process. In America, the press is a vital organ of the public. It keeps the public informed about newsworthy events and exposes governmental abuses, fulfilling its role as the "Fourth Estate" by serving as a check and balance on the three official branches of government. The First Amendment, which guarantees the freedom of the press, was adopted to protect that role, and it becomes nothing more than a hollow promise if the press is denied full access to important governmental proceedings like executions.

When the freedom of the press is curtailed, as it has been by private execution laws, the public is left uninformed about newsworthy events, and democracy is threatened. Indeed, it is a tragic commentary on America's democracy when governmental policies—especially those involving life and death—are carried out behind thick prison walls in the middle of the night. As James Madison warned, "A popular Government, without popular information, or the means of acquiring it, is but a Prologue to a Farce or a Tragedy; or perhaps both. Knowledge will forever govern ignorance; And a people who mean to be their own Governors, must arm themselves with the power which knowledge gives."[7] Because an informed citizenry is essential to America's democracy, Americans can no longer afford to tolerate death in the dark. The press must be allowed to put executions on television, lest Americans relinquish to their government "the power which knowledge gives"—something that should happen only in a George Orwell novel, not in America.

 **APPENDIX**

Executions in the United States, 1977–1995[*]

Name of Defendant	Date of Execution	Time of Execution[**]	Site of Execution
1. Jerry White	12-04-95	12:19 P.M.	Starke, Florida[1]
2. Daniel Thomas	04-15-86	12:19 P.M.	Starke, Florida[2]
3. Darrell Devier	05-17-95	1:28 P.M.	Jackson, Georgia[3]
4. David Funchess	04-22-86	5:11 P.M.	Starke, Florida[4]
5. Ronald Straight	05-20-86	5:12 P.M.	Starke, Florida[5]
6. Jeffrey Daugherty	11-07-88	5:16 P.M.	Starke, Florida[6]
7. Jimmie Jeffers	09-13-95	6:07 P.M.	Florence, Arizona[7]
8. Esquel Banda	12-11-95	6:21 P.M.	Huntsville, Texas[8]
9. Hai Hai Vuong	12-07-95	6:22 P.M.	Huntsville, Texas[9]
10. Harold J. Lane	10-04-95	6:28 P.M.	Huntsville, Texas[10]
11. Bernard Amos	12-06-95	6:31 P.M.	Huntsville, Texas[11]
12. James Briddle	12-12-95	6:35 P.M.	Huntsville, Texas[12]
13. Anthony Bertolotti	07-27-90	7:07 P.M.	Starke, Florida[13]
14. Hoyt Clines	08-03-94	7:11 P.M.	Varner, Arkansas[14]
15. Billy Mitchell	09-01-87	7:21 P.M.	Jackson, Georgia[15]
16. Timothy McCorquodale	09-21-87	7:23 P.M.	Jackson, Georgia[16]
17. James Messer Jr.	07-28-88	7:23 P.M.	Jackson, Georgia[17]
18. Joseph Mulligan	05-15-87	7:25 P.M.	Jackson, Georgia[18]
19. William Boyd Tucker	05-29-87	7:29 P.M.	Jackson, Georgia[19]
20. Darryl Richley	08-03-94	7:59 P.M.	Varner, Arkansas[20]
21. Jonas Whitmore	05-11-94	8:08 P.M.	Varner, Arkansas[21]
22. John Evans	04-22-83	8:44 P.M.	Atmore, Alabama[22]
23. John Edward Swindler	06-18-90	9:05 P.M.	Varner, Arkansas[23]
24. Willie Lloyd Turner	05-26-95	9:07 P.M.	Jarratt, Virginia[24]
25. Edward C. Pickens	05-11-94	9:08 P.M.	Varner, Arkansas[25]
26. Dennis Stockton	09-27-95	9:09 P.M.	Jarratt, Virginia[26]
27. Steven Hill	05-07-92	9:10 P.M.	Varner, Arkansas[27]
28. Barry Lee Fairchild	08-31-95	9:11 P.M.	Varner, Arkansas[28]
29. Dana Ray Edmonds	01-24-95	9:14 P.M.	Jarratt, Virginia[29]
30. Nicholas Ingram	04-07-95	9:15 P.M.	Jackson, Georgia[30]
31. Richard Snell	04-19-95	9:16 P.M.	Varner, Arkansas[31]
32. R. Gene Simmons	06-25-90	9:19 P.M.	Varner, Arkansas[32]

[*]The names of the death row inmates and the dates of the executions in this chart were obtained from *Death Row, U.S.A.* (Winter 1995), published by the NAACP Legal Defense and Educational Fund, Inc. The information regarding execution times and sites was gathered from original research.

[**]"Time of Execution" indicates when the death row inmate was pronounced dead.

Name of Defendant	Date of Execution	Time of Execution	Site of Execution
33. James Holmes	08-03-94	9:24 P.M.	Varner, Arkansas[33]
34. Ricky Lee Grubbs	10-21-92	9:35 P.M.	Potosi, Missouri[34]
35. Winford Stokes	05-11-90	9:39 P.M.	Potosi, Missouri[35]
36. Mickey Davidson	10-19-95	9:41 P.M.	Jarratt, Virginia[36]
37. Christopher Burger	12-07-93	9:51 P.M.	Jackson, Georgia[37]
38. Larry Joe Johnson	05-09-93	10:07 P.M.	Starke, Florida[38]
39. Rickey Ray Rector	01-24-92	10:09 P.M.	Varner, Arkansas[39]
40. William H. Hance	03-31-94	10:10 P.M.	Jackson, Georgia[40]
41. Herman Barnes	11-13-95	10:11 P.M.	Jarratt, Virginia[41]
42. Keith Zettlemoyer	05-02-95	10:25 P.M.	Rockview, Pennsylvania[42]
43. Linwood Briley	10-12-84	11:05 P.M.	Richmond, Virginia[43]
44. Alton Waye	08-30-89	11:05 P.M.	Richmond, Virginia[44]
45. Buddy Earl Justus	12-13-90	11:06 P.M.	Richmond, Virginia[45]
46. James Briley	04-18-85	11:07 P.M.	Richmond, Virginia[46]
47. Morris Mason	06-25-85	11:07 P.M.	Richmond, Virginia[47]
48. Richard Lee Whitley	07-06-87	11:07 P.M.	Richmond, Virginia[48]
49. Earl Clanton Jr.	04-14-88	11:07 P.M.	Richmond, Virginia[49]
50. Richard T. Boggs	07-19-90	11:07 P.M.	Richmond, Virginia[50]
51. Albert Clozza	07-24-91	11:07 P.M.	Jarratt, Virginia[51]
52. Andrew Chabrol	06-17-93	11:07 P.M.	Jarratt, Virginia[52]
53. Willie Leroy Jones	09-15-92	11:08 P.M.	Jarratt, Virginia[53]
54. Wilbert Lee Evans	10-17-90	11:09 P.M.	Richmond, Virginia[54]
55. David Pruett	12-16-93	11:11 P.M.	Jarratt, Virginia[55]
56. Johnny Watkins	03-03-94	11:11 P.M.	Jarratt, Virginia[56]
57. Edward Fitzgerald	07-23-92	11:12 P.M.	Jarratt, Virginia[57]
58. Derick Lynn Peterson	08-22-91	11:13 P.M.	Jarratt, Virginia[58]
59. Syvasky Poyner	03-18-93	11:13 P.M.	Jarratt, Virginia[59]
60. Timothy Spencer	04-27-94	11:13 P.M.	Jarratt, Virginia[60]
61. Charles Stamper	01-19-93	11:15 P.M.	Jarratt, Virginia[61]
62. Thomas Dean Stevens	06-29-93	11:15 P.M.	Jackson, Georgia[62]
63. Henry Willis	05-18-89	11:20 P.M.	Jackson, Georgia[63]
64. Timothy Bunch	12-10-92	11:20 P.M.	Jarratt, Virginia[64]
65. Frank Coppola	08-10-82	11:27 P.M.	Richmond, Virginia[65]
66. Roger Coleman	05-20-92	11:38 P.M.	Jarratt, Virginia[66]
67. Michael Smith	07-31-86	11:42 P.M.	Richmond, Virginia[67]
68. Leon Moser	08-15-95	11:47 P.M.	Rockview, Pennsylvania[68]
69. Willie Clisby	04-28-95	12:01 A.M.	Atmore, Alabama[69]
70. James D. Clark	04-14-93	12:07 A.M.	Florence, Arizona[70]
71. Anthony R. Murray	07-26-95	12:07 A.M.	Potosi, Missouri[71]
72. Frank Guinan	10-06-93	12:08 A.M.	Potosi, Missouri[72]
73. George "Tiny" Mercer	01-06-89	12:09 A.M.	Jefferson City, Missouri[73]
74. Gerald Smith	01-18-90	12:09 A.M.	Potosi, Missouri[74]
75. Leonard Laws	05-17-90	12:09 A.M.	Potosi, Missouri[75]
76. Westley A. Dodd	01-05-93	12:09 A.M.	Walla Walla, Washington[76]
77. Martsay Bolder	01-27-93	12:09 A.M.	Potosi, Missouri[77]
78. Robert Sawyer	03-05-93	12:09 A.M.	Angola, Louisiana[78]

(continued)

Name of Defendant	Date of Execution	Time of Execution	Site of Execution
79. Varnall Weeks	05-12-95	12:09 A.M.	Atmore, Alabama[79]
80. Michael Lindsey	05-26-89	12:10 A.M.	Atmore, Alabama[80]
81. George C. Gilmore	08-31-90	12:10 A.M.	Potosi, Missouri[81]
82. Andrew Lee Jones	07-22-91	12:10 A.M.	Angola, Louisiana[82]
83. Frederick Lashley	07-28-93	12:11 A.M.	Potosi, Missouri[83]
84. Steven Judy	03-09-81	12:12 A.M.	Michigan City, Indiana[84]
85. John Brogdon	07-30-87	12:12 A.M.	Angola, Louisiana[85]
86. Edward Byrne Jr.	06-14-88	12:12 A.M.	Angola, Louisiana[86]
87. Charles Walker	09-12-90	12:12 A.M.	Joliet, Illinois[87]
88. Thomas Lee Ward	05-16-95	12:12 A.M.	Angola, Louisiana[88]
89. Anthony LaRette	11-29-95	12:12 A.M.	Potosi, Missouri[89]
90. Timothy Baldwin	09-10-84	12:13 A.M.	Angola, Louisiana[90]
91. Alvin Moore	06-09-87	12:13 A.M.	Angola, Louisiana[91]
92. Maurice Oscar Byrd	08-23-91	12:13 A.M.	Potosi, Missouri[92]
93. Greg Resnover	12-07-94	12:13 A.M.	Michigan City, Indiana[93]
94. Elmo Sonnier	04-05-84	12:14 A.M.	Angola, Louisiana[94]
95. Jimmy Glass	06-12-87	12:14 A.M.	Angola, Louisiana[95]
96. Wayne Felde	03-15-88	12:14 A.M.	Angola, Louisiana[96]
97. Herbert Lee Richardson	08-18-89	12:14 A.M.	Atmore, Alabama[97]
98. Charles Campbell	05-27-94	12:14 A.M.	Walla Walla, Washington[98]
99. Robert Lee Willie	12-28-84	12:15 A.M.	Angola, Louisiana[99]
100. Arthur Lee Jones Jr.	03-21-86	12:15 A.M.	Atmore, Alabama[100]
101. Leo Edwards Jr.	06-21-89	12:15 A.M.	Parchman, Mississippi[101]
102. Anthony Cook	11-10-93	12:15 A.M.	Huntsville, Texas[102]
103. John Taylor	02-29-84	12:16 A.M.	Angola, Louisiana[103]
104. David Martin	01-04-85	12:16 A.M.	Angola, Louisiana[104]
105. Benjamin Berry	06-07-87	12:16 A.M.	Angola, Louisiana[105]
106. Sterling Rault	08-24-87	12:16 A.M.	Angola, Louisiana[106]
107. Arthur Bishop	06-10-88	12:16 A.M.	Point of the Mountain, Utah[107]
108. Curtis Lee Johnson	08-11-92	12:16 A.M.	Huntsville, Texas[108]
109. Markham Duff-Smith	06-29-93	12:16 A.M.	Huntsville, Texas[109]
110. David Holland	08-12-93	12:16 A.M.	Huntsville, Texas[110]
111. Richard Wilkerson	08-31-93	12:16 A.M.	Huntsville, Texas[111]
112. Ernest Knighton	10-30-84	12:17 A.M.	Angola, Louisiana[112]
113. Jesse de la Rosa	05-15-85	12:17 A.M.	Huntsville, Texas[113]
114. Jimmy Wingo	06-16-87	12:17 A.M.	Angola, Louisiana[114]
115. James "Skip" Paster	09-20-89	12:17 A.M.	Huntsville, Texas[115]
116. Mikel Derrick	07-18-90	12:17 A.M.	Huntsville, Texas[116]
117. G. W. Green	11-12-91	12:17 A.M.	Huntsville, Texas[117]
118. Jeffery Lee Griffin	11-19-92	12:17 A.M.	Huntsville, Texas[118]
119. Johnny James	09-03-93	12:17 A.M.	Huntsville, Texas[119]
120. Jimmy Lee Gray	09-02-83	12:18 A.M.	Parchman, Mississippi[120]
121. Kenneth Brock	06-19-86	12:18 A.M.	Huntsville, Texas[121]
122. Wayne Ritter	08-28-87	12:18 A.M.	Atmore, Alabama[122]
123. Ignacio Cuevas	05-23-91	12:18 A.M.	Huntsville, Texas[123]

(continued)

Name of Defendant	Date of Execution	Time of Execution	Site of Execution
124. Joe Angel Cordova	01-22-92	12:18 A.M.	Huntsville, Texas[124]
125. Johnny Frank Garrett	02-11-92	12:18 A.M.	Huntsville, Texas[125]
126. Justin Lee May	05-07-92	12:18 A.M.	Huntsville, Texas[126]
127. Kavin Lincecum	12-10-92	12:18 A.M.	Huntsville, Texas[127]
128. John Brewer	03-03-93	12:18 A.M.	Florence, Arizona[128]
129. Ramon Montoya	03-25-93	12:18 A.M.	Huntsville, Texas[129]
130. Danny Harris	07-30-93	12:18 A.M.	Huntsville, Texas[130]
131. Elisio Moreno	03-04-87	12:19 A.M.	Huntsville, Texas[131]
132. Wallace Norrell Thomas	07-13-90	12:19 A.M.	Atmore, Alabama[132]
133. George Lott	09-20-94	12:19 A.M.	Huntsville, Texas[133]
134. Jesse D. Jacobs	01-04-95	12:19 A.M.	Huntsville, Texas[134]
135. William Vandiver	10-16-85	12:20 A.M.	Michigan City, Indiana[135]
136. Chester Lee Wicker	08-26-86	12:20 A.M.	Huntsville, Texas[136]
137. John R. Thompson	07-08-87	12:20 A.M.	Huntsville, Texas[137]
138. Robert Black	05-22-92	12:20 A.M.	Huntsville, Texas[138]
139. Cornelius Singleton	11-20-92	12:20 A.M.	Atmore, Alabama[139]
140. Freddie Webb Sr.	03-31-94	12:20 A.M.	Huntsville, Texas[140]
141. Paul Rougeau	05-03-94	12:20 A.M.	Huntsville, Texas[141]
142. Jessie Gutierrez	09-16-94	12:20 A.M.	Huntsville, Texas[142]
143. Jeffrey D. Motley	02-07-95	12:20 A.M.	Huntsville, Texas[143]
144. Jesse Bishop	10-22-79	12:21 A.M.	Carson City, Nevada[144]
145. Charles William Bass	03-12-86	12:21 A.M.	Huntsville, Texas[145]
146. Rudy Ramos Esquivel	06-09-86	12:21 A.M.	Huntsville, Texas[146]
147. Michael Wayne Evans	12-04-86	12:21 A.M.	Huntsville, Texas[147]
148. Edward Earl Johnson	05-20-87	12:21 A.M.	Parchman, Mississippi[148]
149. Arthur James Julius	11-17-89	12:21 A.M.	Atmore, Alabama[149]
150. Lawrence Lee Buxton	02-26-91	12:21 A.M.	Huntsville, Texas[150]
151. Jerry Joe Bird	06-18-91	12:21 A.M.	Huntsville, Texas[151]
152. Walter Williams	10-05-94	12:21 A.M.	Huntsville, Texas[152]
153. Mario S. Marquez	01-17-95	12:21 A.M.	Huntsville, Texas[153]
154. Samuel Hawkins	02-21-95	12:21 A.M.	Huntsville, Texas[154]
155. Jeffrey Allen Barney	04-16-86	12:22 A.M.	Huntsville, Texas[155]
156. Anthony Williams	05-28-87	12:22 A.M.	Huntsville, Texas[156]
157. Connie Ray Evans	07-08-87	12:22 A.M.	Parchman, Mississippi[157]
158. James Demouchette	09-22-92	12:22 A.M.	Huntsville, Texas[158]
159. Carl Kelly	08-20-93	12:22 A.M.	Huntsville, Texas[159]
160. Ruben Cantu	08-24-93	12:22 A.M.	Huntsville, Texas[160]
161. Denton Alan Crank	06-14-94	12:22 A.M.	Huntsville, Texas[161]
162. Robert Drew Sr.	08-02-94	12:22 A.M.	Huntsville, Texas[162]
163. Billy Gardner	02-16-95	12:22 A.M.	Huntsville, Texas[163]
164. Thomas Grasso	03-20-95	12:22 A.M.	McAlester, Oklahoma[164]
165. John Fearance Jr.	06-20-95	12:22 A.M.	Huntsville, Texas[165]
166. Doyle Skillern	01-16-85	12:23 A.M.	Huntsville, Texas[166]
167. Randy Woolls	08-20-86	12:23 A.M.	Huntsville, Texas[167]
168. John Sawyers	05-18-93	12:23 A.M.	Huntsville, Texas[168]

(continued)

Name of Defendant	Date of Execution	Time of Execution	Site of Execution
169. David Mason	08-24-93	12:23 A.M.	San Quentin Village, California[169]
170. Karl Hammond	06-21-95	12:23 A.M.	Huntsville, Texas[170]
171. Ivon Stanley	07-12-84	12:24 A.M.	Jackson, Georgia[171]
172. Thomas Barefoot	10-30-84	12:24 A.M.	Huntsville, Texas[172]
173. Larry Smith	08-22-86	12:24 A.M.	Huntsville, Texas[173]
174. Carlos DeLuna	12-07-89	12:24 A.M.	Huntsville, Texas[174]
175. Carl Johnson Jr.	09-19-95	12:24 A.M.	Huntsville, Texas[175]
176. Charles Albanese	09-20-95	12:24 A.M.	Joliet, Illinois[176]
177. Jay Pinkerton	05-15-86	12:25 A.M.	Huntsville, Texas[177]
178. Leslie Lowenfield	04-13-88	12:25 A.M.	Angola, Louisiana[178]
179. Stephen McCoy	05-24-89	12:25 A.M.	Huntsville, Texas[179]
180. Darryl Stewart	05-04-93	12:25 A.M.	Huntsville, Texas[180]
181. Warren Bridge	11-22-94	12:25 A.M.	Huntsville, Texas[181]
182. Vernon Sattiewhite	08-15-95	12:25 A.M.	Huntsville, Texas[182]
183. John Young	03-20-85	12:26 A.M.	Jackson, Georgia[183]
184. Jerome Butler	04-21-90	12:26 A.M.	Huntsville, Texas[184]
185. Van R. Solomon	02-20-85	12:27 A.M.	Jackson, Georgia[185]
186. Charles Rumbaugh	09-11-85	12:27 A.M.	Huntsville, Texas[186]
187. Willie Celestine	07-20-87	12:27 A.M.	Angola, Louisiana[187]
188. Leon Rutherford King	03-22-89	12:27 A.M.	Huntsville, Texas[188]
189. Horace Dunkins Jr.	07-14-89	12:27 A.M.	Atmore, Alabama[189]
190. Larry Heath	03-20-92	12:27 A.M.	Atmore, Alabama[190]
191. Curtis Paul Harris	07-01-93	12:27 A.M.	Huntsville, Texas[191]
192. Harold Barnard	02-02-94	12:27 A.M.	Huntsville, Texas[192]
193. Roosevelt Green	01-09-85	12:28 A.M.	Jackson, Georgia[193]
194. Antonio Bonham	09-28-93	12:28 A.M.	Huntsville, Texas[194]
195. Herman Clark	12-06-94	12:28 A.M.	Huntsville, Texas[195]
196. Girvies Davis	05-17-95	12:28 A.M.	Joliet, Illinois[196]
197. Donald E. Harding	04-06-92	12:29 A.M.	Florence, Arizona[197]
198. Richard Lee Beavers	04-04-94	12:29 A.M.	Huntsville, Texas[198]
199. Clifton C. Russell	01-31-95	12:29 A.M.	Huntsville, Texas[199]
200. Joseph Starvaggi	09-10-87	12:30 A.M.	Huntsville, Texas[200]
201. Donald Gene Franklin	11-03-88	12:30 A.M.	Huntsville, Texas[201]
202. Johnny Ray Anderson	05-17-90	12:30 A.M.	Huntsville, Texas[202]
203. Stephen Nethery	05-27-94	12:30 A.M.	Huntsville, Texas[203]
204. Roger Stafford	07-01-95	12:30 A.M.	McAlester, Oklahoma[204]
205. George Del Vecchio	11-22-95	12:30 A.M.	Joliet, Illinois[205]
206. Henry Martinez Porter	07-09-85	12:31 A.M.	Huntsville, Texas[206]
207. James Smith	06-26-90	12:31 A.M.	Huntsville, Texas[207]
208. Joseph P. Jernigan	08-05-93	12:31 A.M.	Huntsville, Texas[208]
209. Richard Andrade	12-18-86	12:32 A.M.	Huntsville, Texas[209]
210. Harold Lamont Otey	09-02-94	12:33 A.M.	Lincoln, Nebraska[210]
211. Emmitt Foster	05-03-95	12:33 A.M.	Potosi, Missouri[211]
212. Nelson Shelton	03-17-95	12:34 A.M.	Smyrna, Delaware[212]

(continued)

Name of Defendant	Date of Execution	Time of Execution	Site of Execution
213. Charles Troy Coleman	09-10-90	12:35 A.M.	McAlester, Oklahoma[213]
214. Mark Hopkinson	01-22-92	12:35 A.M.	Rawlins, Wyoming[214]
215. Andre Deputy	06-23-94	12:35 A.M.	Smyrna, Delaware[215]
216. Robert Sidebottom	11-15-95	12:35 A.M.	Potosi, Missouri[216]
217. Alpha Otis Stephens	12-12-84	12:36 A.M.	Jackson, Georgia[217]
218. Ronald K. Allridge	06-08-95	12:38 A.M.	Huntsville, Texas[218]
219. James Autry	03-14-84	12:40 A.M.	Huntsville, Texas[219]
220. Robyn Leroy Parks	03-10-92	12:40 A.M.	McAlester, Oklahoma[220]
221. Larry Anderson	04-26-94	12:42 A.M.	Huntsville, Texas[221]
222. James Free	03-22-95	12:42 A.M.	Joliet, Illinois[222]
223. Raymond Landry	12-13-88	12:45 A.M.	Huntsville, Texas[223]
224. Ronald O'Bryan	03-31-84	12:48 A.M.	Huntsville, Texas[224]
225. Keith Eugene Wells	01-06-94	12:50 A.M.	Boise, Idaho[225]
226. Clifford Phillips	12-14-93	12:53 A.M.	Huntsville, Texas[226]
227. Stephen Peter Morin	03-13-85	12:55 A.M.	Huntsville, Texas[227]
228. Elliot Johnson	06-24-87	12:55 A.M.	Huntsville, Texas[228]
229. William W. White	04-23-92	12:58 A.M.	Huntsville, Texas[229]
230. John Wayne Gacy	05-10-94	12:58 A.M.	Joliet, Illinois[230]
231. Donald Gaskins	09-06-91	1:10 A.M.	Columbia, South Carolina[231]
232. John Thanos	05-17-94	1:10 A.M.	Baltimore, Maryland[232]
233. Sylvester Adams	08-18-95	1:10 A.M.	Columbia, South Carolina[233]
234. Dale Selby Pierre	08-28-87	1:12 A.M.	Point of the Mountain, Utah[234]
235. Ronald Woomer	04-27-90	1:12 A.M.	Columbia, South Carolina[235]
236. Ramon Hernandez	01-30-87	1:13 A.M.	Huntsville, Texas[236]
237. Robert Wayne Williams	12-14-83	1:15 A.M.	Angola, Louisiana[237]
238. Charlie Brooks	12-07-82	1:16 A.M.	Huntsville, Texas[238]
239. Robert O'Neal	12-06-95	1:17 A.M.	Potosi, Missouri[239]
240. James Russell	09-19-91	1:20 A.M.	Huntsville, Texas[240]
241. Fletcher T. Mann	06-01-95	1:20 A.M.	Huntsville, Texas[241]
242. Dalton Prejean	05-18-90	1:21 A.M.	Angola, Louisiana[242]
243. Charles Milton	06-25-85	1:33 A.M.	Huntsville, Texas[243]
244. Walter Blair	07-21-93	1:35 A.M.	Potosi, Missouri[244]
245. David Michael Clark	02-28-92	1:38 A.M.	Huntsville, Texas[245]
246. Jesus Romero	05-20-92	1:40 A.M.	Huntsville, Texas[246]
247. Noble D. Mays	04-06-95	1:42 A.M.	Huntsville, Texas[247]
248. Hernando Williams	03-22-95	1:45 A.M.	Joliet, Illinois[248]
249. William Andrews	07-30-92	1:46 A.M.	Point of the Mountain, Utah[249]
250. Robert Brecheen	08-11-95	1:55 A.M.	McAlester, Oklahoma[250]
251. Willie Ray Williams	01-31-95	1:57 A.M.	Huntsville, Texas[251]
252. Willie Watson	07-24-87	2:09 A.M.	Angola, Louisiana[252]
253. William Paul Thompson	06-19-89	2:09 A.M.	Carson City, Nevada[253]

(continued)

Name of Defendant	Date of Execution	Time of Execution	Site of Execution
254. Sean Patrick Flannagan	06-23-89	2:09 A.M.	Carson City, Nevada[254]
255. Carroll Cole	12-06-85	2:10 A.M.	Carson City, Nevada[255]
256. John Rook	09-19-86	2:11 A.M.	Raleigh, North Carolina[256]
257. Kermit Smith Jr.	01-24-95	2:12 A.M.	Raleigh, North Carolina[257]
258. Phillip Ingle	09-22-95	2:14 A.M.	Raleigh, North Carolina[258]
259. Velma Barfield	11-02-84	2:15 A.M.	Raleigh, North Carolina[259]
260. John Gardner	10-23-92	2:15 A.M.	Raleigh, North Carolina[260]
261. James Hutchins	03-16-84	2:18 A.M.	Raleigh, North Carolina[261]
262. David Lawson	06-15-94	2:18 A.M.	Raleigh, North Carolina[262]
263. Michael McDougall	10-18-91	2:20 A.M.	Raleigh, North Carolina[263]
264. Duncan McKenzie	05-10-95	2:22 A.M.	Deer Lodge, Montana[264]
265. Larry Griffin	06-21-95	2:47 A.M.	Potosi, Missouri[265]
266. Carlos Santana	03-23-93	2:54 A.M.	Huntsville, Texas[266]
267. Warren McCleskey	09-25-91	3:13 A.M.	Jackson, Georgia[267]
268. Robert Streetman	01-07-88	3:26 A.M.	Huntsville, Texas[268]
269. Edward Ellis	03-03-92	3:44 A.M.	Huntsville, Texas[269]
270. Leonel Herrera	05-12-93	4:49 A.M.	Huntsville, Texas[270]
271. Joseph Carl Shaw	01-11-85	5:16 A.M.	Columbia, South Carolina[271]
272. James Terry Roach	01-10-86	5:16 A.M.	Columbia, South Carolina[272]
273. Raymond Carl Kinnamon	12-11-94	5:56 A.M.	Huntsville, Texas[273]
274. Robert Alton Harris	04-21-92	6:21 A.M.	San Quentin Village, California[274]
275. Olan Randle Robison	03-13-92	6:29 A.M.	McAlester, Oklahoma[275]
276. Roy Allen Harich	04-24-91	7:06 A.M.	Starke, Florida[276]
277. Raymond Robert Clark	11-19-90	7:07 A.M.	Starke, Florida[277]
278. Bobby Marion Francis	06-25-91	7:07 A.M.	Starke, Florida[278]
279. Edward D. Kennedy	07-21-92	7:07 A.M.	Starke, Florida[279]
280. Anthony Antone	01-26-84	7:08 A.M.	Starke, Florida[280]
281. Arthur Goode	04-05-84	7:09 A.M.	Starke, Florida[281]
282. David Washington	07-13-84	7:09 A.M.	Starke, Florida[282]
283. James Dupree Henry	09-20-84	7:09 A.M.	Starke, Florida[283]
284. Aubrey Adams Jr.	05-04-89	7:09 A.M.	Starke, Florida[284]
285. John Paul Witt	03-06-85	7:10 A.M.	Starke, Florida[285]
286. Robert Dale Henderson	04-21-93	7:10 A.M.	Starke, Florida[286]
287. James Adams	05-10-84	7:11 A.M.	Starke, Florida[287]
288. James Raulerson	01-30-85	7:11 A.M.	Starke, Florida[288]

(continued)

Name of Defendant	Date of Execution	Time of Execution	Site of Execution
289. Beauford White	08-28-87	7:11 A.M.	Starke, Florida[289]
290. Roy Allen Stewart	04-22-94	7:11 A.M.	Starke, Florida[290]
291. Carl Shriner	06-20-84	7:12 A.M.	Starke, Florida[291]
292. Willie Darden	03-15-88	7:12 A.M.	Starke, Florida[292]
293. James William Hamblen	09-21-90	7:12 A.M.	Starke, Florida[293]
294. Jessie Joseph Tafero	05-04-90	7:13 A.M.	Starke, Florida[294]
295. Nollie Lee Martin	05-12-92	7:13 A.M.	Starke, Florida[295]
296. Thomas Baal	06-03-90	7:14 A.M.	Carson City, Nevada[296]
297. Theodore Bundy	01-24-89	7:16 A.M.	Starke, Florida[297]
298. Michael Durocher	08-25-93	7:16 A.M.	Starke, Florida[298]
299. Marvin Francois	05-29-85	7:18 A.M.	Starke, Florida[299]
300. Richard Tucker Jr.	05-22-87	7:23 A.M.	Jackson, Georgia[300]
301. Gary Gilmore	01-17-77	8:07 A.M.	Point of the Mountain, Utah[301]
302. John Eldon Smith	12-15-83	8:17 A.M.	Jackson, Georgia[302]
303. Steven Brian Pennell	03-14-92	9:01 A.M.	Smyrna, Delaware[303]
304. Kenneth DeShields	08-31-93	9:17 A.M.	Smyrna, Delaware[304]
305. Timothy Palmes	11-08-84	10:07 A.M.	Starke, Florida[305]
306. Ernest Dobbert	09-07-84	10:09 A.M.	Starke, Florida[306]
307. Jerome Bowden	06-24-86	10:13 A.M.	Jackson, Georgia[307]
308. Robert Sullivan	11-30-83	10:16 A.M.	Starke, Florida[308]
309. Phillip Atkins	12-05-95	10:17 A.M.	Starke, Florida[309]
310. John Spenkelink	05-25-79	10:18 A.M.	Starke, Florida[310]
311. Bernard Bolender	07-18-95	10:19 A.M.	Starke, Florida[311]
312. James Allen Red Dog	03-03-93	10:28 A.M.	Smyrna, Delaware[312]
313. Joe Louis Wise	09-14-93	11:12 A.M.	Jarratt, Virginia[313]

NOTES

Introduction

1. *Death Row, U.S.A.,* NAACP Legal Defense and Educational Fund, Inc. (Winter 1995) (listing the names of persons executed in the United States since 1976).

2. DEL. CODE ANN. tit. 11, § 4209(f) (Supp. 1994); KY. REV. STAT. ANN. § 431.240(1) (Michie/Bobbs-Merrill Supp. 1992) (requiring executions to take place "before sunrise"); IND. CODE ANN. § 35-38-6-1(b) (West 1986) (requiring executions "before the hour of sunrise"); LA. REV. STAT. ANN. § 15:569.1 (West 1992); S.D. CODIFIED LAWS ANN. § 23A-27A-17 (1988) (requiring executions between the hours of 12:01 and 6:00 A.M.); WYO. STAT. § 7-13-905(a) (1987) (requiring executions "before the hour of sunrise").

3. John D. Bessler, *Televised Executions and the Constitution: Recognizing a First Amendment Right of Access to State Executions,* 45 FED. COMM. L.J. 355, 367–68 (1993) (containing citations); *Donahue Asks to Videotape Execution for His Program,* MINNEAPOLIS STAR-TRIB., May 6, 1994, at 20A, col. 1.

4. LOUIS P. MASUR, RITES OF EXECUTION: CAPITAL PUNISHMENT AND THE TRANSFORMATION OF AMERICAN CULTURE, 1776–1865, at 59 (1989); *see* Chapters 2 & 3.

5. *See* Appendix.

6. George F. Will, *Capital Punishment and Public Theater,* WASH. POST, May 12, 1991, at C7.

7. James Brooke, *Utah Debates Firing Squads in Clash of Past and Present,* N.Y. TIMES, Jan. 14, 1996, at 10, col. 5; *Death Row, U.S.A.,* NAACP Legal Defense and Educational Fund, Inc. (Winter 1995); *Executions Reached 38-Year High in '95,* MINNEAPOLIS STAR-TRIB., Dec. 5, 1996, at A4.

Chapter One

1. Bob Baker & Paul Feldman, *Unlikely Allies Join Execution Foes at Prison,* L.A. TIMES (Wash. ed.), Apr. 21, 1992, at A1, col. 5, & A7, col. 6; Dan Morain, *Witness to the Execution: A Macabre, Surreal Event,* L.A. TIMES (Wash. ed.), Apr. 22, 1992, at A1, cols. 5–6; Katherine Bishop, *Foes of Execution Fear California May Set Tone,* N.Y. TIMES, Apr. 21, 1992, at A14, cols. 1–2; Daniel Weintraub, *Wilson View on Clemency Forged Out of a Conflict in Beliefs,* L.A. TIMES, Apr. 18, 1992, at A16; Dan Morain, *Video Plea Made to Save Harris,* L.A. TIMES, Mar. 31, 1992, at A3; Douglas Shuit, *Death Penalty Draws Little Debate During This Political Season,* L.A. TIMES,

Apr. 15, 1992, at B2; *Execution: Harris Somber as Lawyers Appeal,* L.A. TIMES, Apr. 21, 1992, at A7.

2.   Baker & Feldman, *supra* note 1, at A1, col. 5, & A7, col. 6; Pat Morrison, *Final Legal War Troubling to Both Sides,* L.A. TIMES (Wash. ed.), Apr. 22, 1992, at A3, col. 3; L.A. TIMES, Apr. 22, 1992, at A10 (picture); Andrew Freinkel, Cheryl Koopman, & David Spiegel, *Dissociative Symptoms in Media Eyewitnesses of an Execution,* 151 AM. J. PSYCHIATRY 1335–36 (1994).

3.   Baker & Feldman, *supra* note 1, at A1, col. 5, & A7, col. 6; Peter H. King, *What a Son Should Know About This,* L.A. TIMES (Wash. ed.), Apr. 22, 1992, at A3, col. 1; L.A. TIMES, Apr. 22, 1992, at A10 (picture).

4.   *The Final Hours,* L.A. TIMES, Apr. 22, 1992, at A10; Judge Stephen Reinhardt, *The Supreme Court, the Death Penalty, and the* Harris *Case,* 102 YALE L.J. 205, 209–14 (1992); Evan Caminker & Erwin Chemerinsky, *The Lawless Execution of Robert Alton Harris,* 102 YALE L.J. 225, 227–30 (1992); Gomez v. United States District Court, 503 U.S. 653 (1992); *Execution: Justices End Delays, Harris Dies,* L.A. TIMES, Apr. 22, 1992, at A10, col. 2; John T. Noonan Jr., *Horses of the Night:* Harris v. Vasquez, 45 STAN. L. REV. 1011, 1020 (1993).

5.   Morrison, *supra* note 2, at A3, cols. 2–3, & A16, cols. 3–6; Dan Morain & Tom Gorman, *Harris Dies After Judicial Duel: 4 Stays Quashed; "I'm Sorry," Murderer Says,* L.A. TIMES (Wash. ed.), Apr. 22, 1992, at A1, cols. 5–6, & A10, cols. 2–4. The Harris execution has been a hot subject for legal commentators. *E.g.,* Reinhardt, *supra* note 4, at 205; Caminker & Chemerinsky, *supra* note 4, at 225; Steven G. Calabresi & Gary Lawson, *Equity and Hierarchy: Reflections on the Harris Execution,* 102 YALE L.J. 255 (1992); Daniel E. Lungren & Mark C. Krotoski, *Public Policy Lessons from the Robert Alton Harris Case,* 40 UCLA L. REV. 295 (1992); Charles M. Sevilla & Michael Laurence, *Thoughts on the Cause of the Present Discontents: The Death Penalty Case of Robert Alton Harris,* 40 UCLA L. REV. 345 (1992); *Courts Battle Over Harris Execution,* A.B.A. J., July 1992, at 26.

6.   *Execution: Justices End Delays, Harris Dies, supra* note 4, at A10, col. 2; WENDY LESSER, PICTURES AT AN EXECUTION 250 (1993); Bill Stall, *Wilson Escalates Tough Talk on Crime, Enforcing Death Penalty,* L.A. TIMES, Feb. 7, 1991, at A3; Shuit, *supra* note 1, at B2; Weintraub, *supra* note 1, at A16; Robert P. Davidow, *Federal Habeas Corpus: The Effect of Holding State Collateral Proceedings Before a Judge Running for Re-Election,* 8 NOTRE DAME J.L., ETHICS & PUB. POL'Y 317, 325 (1994); John T. Wold & John H. Culver, *The Defeat of the California Justices: The Campaign, the Electorate, and the Issue of Judicial Accountability,* 70 JUDICATURE 348, 349 (1987); Conference, *The Death Penalty in the Twenty-First Century,* 45 AM. U. L. REV. 239, 283 & nn.136–37 (1995); George Skelton, *Wilson Denounces "Macabre Circus" of Execution,* L.A. TIMES, Apr. 23, 1992, at A36; Caminker & Chemerinsky, *supra* note 4, at 229; Dan Morain & Daniel Weintraub, *Wilson Rejects Plea of Mercy for Harris,* L.A. TIMES, Apr. 17, 1992, at A1.

7.   *Condemned Killer: "No Problem" with Televised Execution,* Associated Press, June 14, 1991 (PM cycle) (LEXIS).

8. LESSER, *supra* note 6, at 28–29, 149–50, 165, 259; Plaintiff's Post-Trial Brief at 21–22, KQED, Inc. v. Vasquez, 18 Media L. Rep. (BNA) 2323 (N.D. Cal. 1991) (No. C90-1383RHS).

9. Plaintiff's Trial Brief at 2 & Plaintiff's Post-Trial Brief at 13, 22, KQED, Inc. v. Vasquez, 18 Media L. Rep. (BNA) 2323 (N.D. Cal. 1991) (No. C90-1383RHS); Steve Keeva, *Watching a Killer Die: A California TV Station Sues to Televise Execution,* 76 A.B.A. J. 24 (1990) (suit filed against Daniel B. Vasquez and Governor George Deukmejian on May 19, 1990).

10. Philip Hager, *Trial Ordered Over Right to Televise Executions,* L.A. TIMES, Nov. 10, 1990, at A26; Lance Williams, *Trial to Open on Executions on TV,* S.F. EXAMINER, Mar. 24, 1991, at A1; LESSER, *supra* note 6, at 30.

11. Williams, *supra* note 10, at A1; Seth Rosenfeld, *Judge Frowns on TV Deaths,* S.F. EXAMINER, Mar. 26, 1991, at A2; Seth Rosenfeld, *Warden Afraid of Revenge on Guards if Executions on TV,* S.F. EXAMINER, Mar. 28, 1991, at A5, col. 5; LESSER, *supra* note 6, at 29.

12. Rosenfeld, *Judge Frowns on TV Deaths, supra* note 11, at A2; LESSER, *supra* note 6, at 35, 136–37, 139.

13. Rosenfeld, *Judge Frowns on TV Deaths, supra* note 11, at A2; LESSER, *supra* note 6, at 41, 103; JOHN BARTLETT, FAMILIAR QUOTATIONS 772 (15th ed. 1980).

14. Seth Rosenfeld, *Ex-state Prison Head Backs Using Cameras at Executions,* S.F. EXAMINER, Mar. 27, 1991, at A7; LESSER, *supra* note 6, at 33–34.

15. Rosenfeld, *Warden Afraid of Revenge on Guards if Executions on TV, supra* note 11, at A5.

16. Philip Hager, *U.S. Judge Upholds Ban on TV Cameras at Executions,* L.A. TIMES, June 8, 1991, at A1; Rick DelVecchio, *Judge Upholds Ban on Cameras at Executions,* S.F. CHRONICLE, June 8, 1991, at A1; KQED, Inc. v. Vasquez, 18 Media L. Rep. (BNA) 2323, 2326–27 (N.D. Cal. 1991). In an unrelated lawsuit, the *San Francisco Examiner,* as the region's major afternoon newspaper, brought a lawsuit in the Superior Court of Marin County seeking access to Harris's execution. The San Quentin prison is located in Marin County. Judge Beverly Savitt ruled for the *Examiner,* permitting its reporter Larry Hatfield to attend the execution. LESSER, *supra* note 6, at 259; Tipton C. Kindel, *Planning Is the Key to Handling Media Interest in an Execution,* CORRECTIONS TODAY, July 1993, at 69.

17. Katherine Bishop, *Judge Upholds Ban on Videotaping of Executions at San Quentin,* N.Y. TIMES, June 8, 1991, at 9; Hager, *supra* note 16, at A1.

18. *TV Bill Killed,* NAT'L L.J., Sept. 16, 1991, at 6; Amy Singer, *Station Seeks to Televise Executions,* AM. LAW., Mar. 1991, at 23; LESSER, *supra* note 6, at 94.

19. Katherine Bishop, *After Night of Court Battles, a California Execution,* N.Y. TIMES, Apr. 22, 1992, at A1, cols. 2–5, & A22, cols. 1–5; Philip Hager, *Should Tape of Harris Execution Be Released?,* L.A. TIMES, May 10, 1992, at A3, col. 5; *Video May Be Key in Cruelty Suit ACLU Fighting to Ban Gas Chamber,* SACRAMENTO BEE, Apr. 22, 1992, at A16; Tony Perry, *Harris' Treatment After Death Could Spur Anti-Death Forces,* L.A. TIMES, May 1, 1992, at B1, col. 2; Memorandum and Order at 2–4, Declaration of H. Mark

Stichel at 2, Memorandum in Support of Motion to Obtain Access to Videotape, Opposition to Motions to Intervene and to Obtain Access to Videotape of Robert Alton Harris Execution, Memorandum in Support of Motion to Compel Defendants to Preserve Critical Evidence of Robert Harris's Impending Execution at 1–3 (exhibits contain Robert Alton Harris's permission for his execution to be filmed), Fierro v. Gomez, 865 F. Supp. 1387 (N.D. Cal. 1994) (No. C-92-1482-MHP).

20. Seth Rosenfeld, *Execution in Gas Chamber Banned,* S.F. EXAMINER, Oct. 5, 1994, at A1; Campbell v. Wood, 18 F.3d 662, 680–87 (en banc), *reh'g and reh'g en banc denied,* 20 F.3d 1050 (9th Cir. 1994); Fierro v. Gomez, 865 F. Supp. 1387, 1389, 1409 & n.24 (N.D. Cal. 1994) (citing cases approving of shooting and electrocution as methods of execution).

21. *Fierro,* 865 F. Supp. at 1389; *Campbell,* 18 F.3d at 681; Seth Rosenfeld, *Rat Trials May Show Gas Chamber Painless,* SUNDAY S.F. EXAMINER & CHRONICLE, Oct. 24, 1993, at A1; Reply to Opposition to Petition for Discovery, *In re* Thomas, 155 F.R.D. 124 (D. Md. 1994) (Misc. No. 93–95).

22. *Fierro,* 865 F. Supp. at 1393–1403.

23. *Killing Me Cruelly?,* NEWSWEEK, Nov. 8, 1993, at 73; *Videotape of Execution Destroyed by Court,* S.F. CHRONICLE, Feb. 19, 1994, at A28; *California Gas Chamber Ordered Shut,* Facts on File World News Digest, Oct. 27, 1992, at 800 (LEXIS); *Patel Outlaws Gas Chamber in California,* THE RECORDER, Oct. 5, 1994, at 1 (LEXIS); Rosenfeld, *supra* note 20, at A1; *Videotape of a California Execution Is Destroyed,* N.Y. TIMES, Feb. 13, 1994, at 35; *Videotape of Harris Execution Destroyed,* L.A. TIMES, Feb. 11, 1994, at A37, col. 1.

24. *Judge Voids California Executions by Gas,* NAT'L L.J., Oct. 17, 1994, at A10, cols. 1–2; *Fierro,* 865 F. Supp. at 1404, 1413.

25. *Fierro,* 865 F. Supp. at 1409; RONALD DWORKIN, LIFE'S DOMINION: AN ARGUMENT ABOUT ABORTION, EUTHANASIA, AND INDIVIDUAL FREEDOM 119 (1994).

26. *Fierro,* 865 F. Supp. at 1406 n.19, 1414–15, *aff'd,* 77 F.3d 301, 309 (9th Cir. 1996). In a four-line order, the U.S. Supreme Court vacated the Ninth Circuit's order outlawing gas chamber executions as unconstitutionally "cruel and unusual." The U.S. Supreme Court remanded the case back to the Ninth Circuit "for further consideration in light of Cal. Penal Code Section 3604." Gomez v. Fierro, 117 S. Ct. 285 (1996); *see also* Frank J. Murray, *High Court Refuses to Bar Gas Chamber,* WASH. TIMES, Oct. 16, 1996, at A13 (describing the U.S. Supreme Court's ruling). Section 3604, which was amended in 1992, establishes the procedure for determining whether a California death row inmate is executed by lethal injection or lethal gas. CAL. PENAL CODE § 3604 (West Supp. 1997).

27. *Judge Voids California Executions by Gas, supra* note 24, at A10, cols. 1–2; *U.S. Judge Rules Gas Chamber in California Is Unconstitutional,* N.Y. TIMES, Oct. 6, 1994, at A10, cols. 1–2; *Videotape of a California Execution Is Destroyed, supra* note 23, at 35; *Fierro,* 77 F.3d at 303; Rosenfeld, *supra* note 20, at A1.

28. Mark Gladstone, *Brown Ties Death Penalty Stance to Upbringing, Faith,* L.A. TIMES, June 22, 1994, at A1; Mark Gladstone, *Gas Chamber Issue Enters Campaign,* L.A. TIMES, Oct. 6, 1994, at A3.

29. *Executions Reached 38-Year High in '95,* MINNEAPOLIS STAR-TRIB., Dec. 5, 1996, at A4.

Chapter Two

1. NATHAN STRONG, THE REASONS AND DESIGN OF PUBLIC PUNISHMENTS (1777); Michael Madow, *Forbidden Spectacle: Executions, the Public and the Press in Nineteenth Century New York,* 43 BUFF. L. REV. 461, 478 n.54 (1995); LOUIS MASUR, RITES OF EXECUTION: CAPITAL PUNISHMENT AND THE TRANSFORMATION OF AMERICAN CULTURE, 1776–1865, at 33, 96 (1989); NEGLEY K. TEETERS & JACK H. HEDBLOM, ". . . HANG BY THE NECK . . ." 34, 39, 44–45 (1967); NEGLEY K. TEETERS, SCAFFOLD AND CHAIR: A COMPILATION OF THEIR USE IN PENNSYLVANIA 1862- 1962, Part 1, at 9–16, 21, 24–25, 28, 34 n.3, 41 n.78, Part 2, at 2 (1963). Although public hangings were abolished in Pennsylvania in 1834, Moran's hanging occurred in Philadelphia three years later because he was convicted under a federal law for piracy that was not subject to Pennsylvania law.

2. TEETERS & HEDBLOM, *supra* note 1, at 44–45; TEETERS, *supra* note 1, at Part 1, at 9–16, 21, 24–25, 28; FREEBORN COUNTY STANDARD (Albert Lea, Minn.), Mar. 2, 1861; PIONEER & DEMOCRAT, Mar. 8, 1861, at 1, col. 2; WALTER TRENERRY, MURDER IN MINNESOTA: A COLLECTION OF TRUE CASES 219 (1985).

3. JAMES W. MARQUART, SHELDON EKLAND-OLSON, & JONATHAN R. SORENSEN, THE ROPE, THE CHAIR, AND THE NEEDLE: CAPITAL PUNISHMENT IN TEXAS, 1923–1990, at 12 (1994); EDWARD BAUMANN, MAY GOD HAVE MERCY ON YOUR SOUL: THE STORY OF THE ROPE AND THE THUNDERBOLT 20–22 (1993); TEETERS & HEDBLOM, *supra* note 1, at 40.

4. TEETERS & HEDBLOM, *supra* note 1, at 40; *The Sioux War,* MANKATO REC., Dec. 20, 1862, at 2, cols. 1–2; *Execution of 39 Sioux,* MANKATO WEEKLY REC. SUPP., Dec. 26, 1862, at 1, cols. 3–5; THEODORE BLEGEN, MINNESOTA: A HISTORY OF THE STATE 279–80 (1989); 2 WILLIAM FOLWELL, A HISTORY OF MINNESOTA 187, 210 (1969); KENNETH CARLEY, THE SIOUX UPRISING OF 1862, at 65–66 (1961); The Dakota Conflict (videotape produced by KTCA St. Paul/Minneapolis) (1992).

5. CARLEY, *supra* note 4, at 66–67; *Execution of 39 Sioux, supra* note 4, at 2, col. 6; The Dakota Conflict, *supra* note 4 (3,000 onlookers).

6. Madow, *supra* note 1, at 477–78; TEETERS, *supra* note 1, at Part 1, at 10–11, Part 2, at 21.

7. MASUR, *supra* note 1, at 27.

8. *Id.* at 27–28, 42, 44.

9. *Id.* at 34–35, 41.

10. *Id.* at 25–26.

11. Madow, *supra* note 1, at 469–72.

12. BAUMANN, *supra* note 3, at 17–19.

13. TEETERS & HEDBLOM, *supra* note 1, at 40–41; MASUR, *supra* note 1, at 95; MARVIN H. BOVEE, REASONS FOR ABOLISHING CAPITAL PUNISHMENT 164–65, 170 (1878); Mark Curriden, *Would Public Executions Curb Crime?,* ATLANTA CONST., July 31, 1994, at R3.

14. BOVEE, *supra* note 13, at 164–65, 170; GEORGE COMBE, THOUGHTS ON CAPITAL PUNISHMENT 13–14 (1847); Chapter 3 (describing the popularity of phrenology in the nineteenth century).

15. Madow, *supra* note 1, at 483–84 n.78.

16. TEETERS & HEDBLOM, *supra* note 1, at 39; TEETERS, *supra* note 1, at Part 1, at 25; MASUR, *supra* note 1, at 95–96.

17. DAILY MINN. PIONEER, Jan. 3, 1855, at 2, col. 2; BLEGEN, *supra* note 4, at 171; DAILY MINN. PIONEER, Dec. 30, 1854, at 2, col. 2; MINN. REPUBLICAN, Jan. 4, 1855, at 2, col. 6.

18. *"Hanging the Indian,"* DAILY MINNESOTIAN, Dec. 30, 1854, at 2, col. 1; DAILY MINNESOTIAN, Jan. 3, 1855, at 2, col. 2; Merle Potter, *Major Fridley's Kingdom,* J. MAG., Sept. 4, 1932 (available in the Minnesota Historical Society's biographical file on Abram M. Fridley).

19. *"Hanging the Indian,"* *supra* note 18, at 2, col. 1; DAILY MINNESOTIAN, Jan. 3, 1855, at 2, col. 2; Potter, *supra* note 18, at 4; *The Approaching Execution,* ST. PAUL PIONEER, Nov. 11, 1865, at 1, col. 1 (describing the execution of U-ha-zy as a "beastly affair").

20. *"Hanging the Indian,"* *supra* note 18, at 2, col. 1; DAILY MINNESOTIAN, Jan. 3, 1855, at 2, col. 2; DAILY MINN. PIONEER, Dec. 30, 1854, at 2, col. 2; MINN. REPUBLICAN, Jan. 4, 1855, at 2, col. 6; DAILY MINN. PIONEER, Jan. 1, 1855, at 2, col. 2; *The Penalty of Death,* DAILY MINNESOTIAN, Jan. 13, 1855, at 2, col. 4; *The Penalty of Death—Is It Expedient?,* DAILY MINNESOTIAN, Jan. 15, 1855, at 2, col. 3; DAILY MINNESOTIAN, Jan. 1, 1855, at 2, col. 1; *see also* Chapter 3.

21. *1500 at Galena, Mo., See Murderer Hanged,* ST. LOUIS POST-DISPATCH, May 21, 1937, at 1A, col. 6; THE DEATH PENALTY IN AMERICA 13 (Hugo Adam Bedau ed., 3d ed. 1982); *Cities Fight Over Last Public Hanging,* HERALD-TIMES (Bloomington, Ind.) (undated) (copy on file with author).

22. *10,000 See Hanging of Kentucky Negro,* N.Y. TIMES, Aug. 15, 1936, at 30; THE DEATH PENALTY IN AMERICA, *supra* note 21, at 13; Leonce Gaiter, *Tragic American Mantra: "Blame the Black Man,"* MINNEAPOLIS STAR-TRIB., Nov. 18, 1994, at 25A (containing picture of crowd at Rainey Bethea's execution); Note, Dane A. Drobny, *Death TV: Media Access to Executions Under the First Amendment,* 70 WASH. U. L.Q. 1179, 1187–88 (1992); George C. Wright, *Executions of Afro-Americans in Kentucky, 1870–1940,* 1 GA. J. S. LEGAL HIST. 321, 336–39 (1991).

23. DAVID D. COOPER, THE LESSON OF THE SCAFFOLD: THE PUBLIC EXECUTION CONTROVERSY IN VICTORIAN ENGLAND 11, 45–47, 50–51, 68–69, 80–87, 90–94, 96, 106–7, 109–13, 120–21, 123–29, 131–34, 143–46, 148–51, 157–58, 161–65, 169–70, 174–77 (1974); ELIZABETH ORMAN TUTTLE, THE CRUSADE AGAINST CAPITAL PUNISHMENT IN GREAT BRITAIN 16–20 (1961); HENRY V. MORTON, IN SEARCH OF LONDON 65, 81–82 (1951); E. H. CARKEET-JAMES, HIS MAJESTY'S TOWER OF LONDON 66–67 (1950); RUSSELL CHAMBERLIN, THE TOWER OF LONDON: AN ILLUSTRATED HISTORY 78–79, 85, 117 (1989); JOHN LAURENCE, A HISTORY OF CAPITAL PUNISHMENT 8–9, 169, 178, 183, 195, 211 (1960); E. ROY CALVERT, CAPITAL PUNISHMENT IN THE TWENTIETH CENTURY 93–94 (1930); EXECUTIONS AND THE BRITISH EXPERIENCE FROM THE 17TH TO THE 20TH CENTURY: A

COLLECTION OF ESSAYS 82–83, 87, 94–95, 108, 139–42, 149–57, 159, 161–63 (William B. Thesing ed., 1990); Betty B. Fletcher, *The Death Penalty in America: Can Justice Be Done?,* 70 N.Y.U. L. REV. 811, 814 (1995); Cyril Greenland, *The Last Public Execution in Canada: Eight Skeletons in the Closet of the Canadian Justice System,* 29 CRIM. L.Q. 415, 416 (1987); Report of the Capital Punishment Commission 84, 384–85, 393, 554–57, 1636, 1640–41, 1973–74 (1866). Sir George Grey's growing distaste for public executions was also evidenced by the fact that he moved executions at the Newgate prison from Monday to Wednesday. He told the House of Commons that Sunday gave people the chance to collect all day and night, and he hoped the change would reduce the size of the crowds. COOPER, *supra,* at 132.

   24. GEOFFRY ABBOTT, LORDS OF THE SCAFFOLD: A HISTORY OF THE EXECUTIONER 146 (1991); FRANKLIN ZIMRING & GORDON HAWKINS, CAPITAL PUNISHMENT AND THE AMERICAN AGENDA 5 (1986); ALBERT PIERREPOINT, EXECUTIONER: PIERREPOINT 66–72 (1974) (book contains copy of the bond, in the amount of £50, that Albert Pierrepoint was required to sign); Gerald D. Robin, *The Executioner: His Place in English Society,* 15 BRITISH J. SOC. 234, 251, & n.85 (1965); CALVERT, *supra* note 23, at 95–96; COOPER, *supra* note 23, at 155, 174; TUTTLE, *supra* note 23, at 32, 34–35.

Chapter Three

   1. 3 BIOGRAPHY OF THE SIGNERS OF THE DECLARATION OF INDEPENDENCE 25–26 (John Sanderson ed., 1828); DAVID FREEMAN HAWKE, BENJAMIN RUSH: REVOLUTIONARY GADFLY 363–66 (1971); Furman v. Georgia, 408 U.S. 238, 338 (1972) (Marshall, J., concurring) ("Dr. Benjamin Rush soon drafted America's first reasoned argument against capital punishment, entitled An Enquiry into the Effects of Public Punishments upon Criminals and Society.") (*citing* Louis Filler, *Movements to Abolish the Death Penalty in the United States,* 284 ANNALS AM. ACAD. POL. & SOC. SCI. 124 (1952)); MARVIN H. BOVEE, REASONS FOR ABOLISHING CAPITAL PUNISHMENT 60–61, 77 (1878); PUNISHMENT AND THE DEATH PENALTY: THE CURRENT DEBATE 104, 114 (Robert M. Baird & Stuart E. Rosenbaum eds., 1995); NEGLEY K. TEETERS, SCAFFOLD AND CHAIR: A COMPILATION OF THEIR USE IN PENNSYLVANIA 1862–1962, Part 1, at 29 (1963).

   2. LOUIS MASUR, RITES OF EXECUTION: CAPITAL PUNISHMENT AND THE TRANSFORMATION OF AMERICAN CULTURE, 1776–1865, at 96, 115–16, 189–90 (1989) (*citing* Jacob Cassat, Journal of the Thirty-fourth House of Representatives of the Commonwealth of Pennsylvania (Harrisburg: John Weistling, 1823–24), at 577, and *quoting* Senate Document No. 79 in Documents of the Senate of the State of New York, Fifty-eighth Session, 1835 (Albany: E. Croswell, 1835), Vol. 2, at 4, 8–10); Albert Post, *Early Efforts to Abolish Capital Punishment in Pennsylvania,* PA. MAG. HIST. & BIO. 68 (Jan. 1944); Chapter 2 (describing John Lechler's hanging); TEETERS, *supra* note 1, at Part 1, at 30; PHILIP MACKEY, HANGING IN THE BALANCE: THE ANTI-CAPITAL PUNISHMENT MOVEMENT IN NEW YORK STATE, 1776–1861, at 113–18 (1982) (citations omitted); Michael Madow, *Forbidden Spectacle: Executions, the Public and the Press in Nineteenth Century New York,* 43 BUFF. L. REV. 461, 510 n.212 (1995) (*citing* Act of June 5, 1830, ch. 1, § 147, 1830 Conn. Pub. Acts 284).

3. Act of Apr. 10, 1834, Pub. Act. No. 127, 1833–1834 Pa. Laws 234; Mass. Rev. Stat. ch. 169, § 13 (1835); Act of Mar. 5, 1835, 1834–1835 N.J. Laws 170; Act of May 9, 1835, ch. 258, 1835 N.Y. Laws 299; Act of Jan. 13, 1837, ch. 273, § 5, 1829–1840 N.H. Laws 240; Masur, *supra* note 2, at 94; Mackey, *supra* note 2, at 118 n.40 (*citing* Teeters, *supra* note 1, at 31, 42; John Bach McMaster, A History of the People of the United States (New York, 1888–1913)); A Hangman's Diary: Being the Journal of Master Franz Schmidt Public Executioner of Nuremberg, 1573–1617, at 49–50, 52 (Albrecht Keller ed., 1928); Raymond T. Bye, Capital Punishment in the United States 3 (1919).

4. Mackey, *supra* note 2, at 113–18 (citations omitted); Masur, *supra* note 2, at 115–16, 189–90 (*quoting* Senate Document No. 79 in Documents of the Senate of the State of New York, Fifty-eighth Session, 1835 (Albany: E. Croswell, 1835), Vol. 2, at 4, 8–10); Madow, *supra* note 2, at 503–4, 507–10. The first attempt to abolish capital punishment came in 1832, when Silas Stilwell, a young New York City assemblyman, advocated abolishing the gallows. Stilwell's bill, however, never reached a vote. The second attempt came two years later, when a Quaker lawyer, Assemblyman Samuel Bowne, introduced another abolitionist bill. That measure was narrowly defeated by a vote of 49–37 just one month before Emmons introduced his bill to abolish public executions. Mackey, *supra* note 2, at 113–18.

5. Capital Punishment: Nineteenth-Century Arguments 16–18, 69–73, 101–3 (1974).

6. Report of Committee to the Legislature of Maine (1835); Report on the Subject of Capital Punishment to the New York Assembly (Apr. 14, 1841) (citing the Maine legislative report).

7. Act of Feb. 15, 1839, ch. 66, act 1, tit. 2, § 25, 1839 Miss. Laws 102, 110; Me. Rev. Stat. ch. 168, § 10 (1840); Act of Oct. 31, 1844, Pub. L. No. 27, § 3, 1844 Vt. Acts 23, 24; Del. Rev. Laws ch. 133, § 30 (1852); Act of Mar. 12, 1844, 1843 Ohio Laws 71; Mich. Rev. Stat. ch. 168, § 11 (1846); 2 Ind. Rev. Stat. pt. 3, § 134 (1852); Act of Feb. 18, 1859, 1859 Ill. Laws 17; Code of Crim. Proc., ch. 27, § 244, 1859 Kan. Sess. Laws 217; Iowa Rev. Stat. § 4894 (1860); William Bennett Turner & Beth S. Brinkmann, *Televising Executions: The First Amendment Issues,* 32 Santa Clara L. Rev. 1135, 1141 (1992); Act of Apr. 21, 1858, Gen. Laws of Cal. 1850–1864, para. 2686; Kan. Laws, ch. 32, § 244 (1862); Ind. Stat., art. XII, sec. CXXXIV (1862); Penal Code, ch. 8, § 3, 1840–1841 Ala. Acts 103, 150; Act of Feb. 20, 1856, ch. 43, 1855–1856 Va. Acts 36; Act of Dec. 15, 1859, Pub. Act No. 83, 1859 Ga. Laws 62; Ga. Code, at 842 (1873); Act of Dec. 3, 1878, Pub. L. No. 37, 1878–1879 Ala. Acts 45; Act of Apr. 2, 1879, ch. 119, 1878–1879 Va. Acts 380; Act of Dec. 18, 1893, Pub. L. No. 285, 1893 Ga. Laws 41.

8. Filler, *supra* note 1, at 124, 129–30; Albert Post, *The Anti-Gallows Movement in Ohio,* 54 Ohio State Archaeological & Hist. Q. 104–12 (Apr./June 1945); David Brion Davis, *The Movement to Abolish Capital Punishment in America, 1787–1861,* Am. Hist. Rev. 23, 32–45 (Oct. 1957); William J. Bowers, Legal Homicide: Death as Punishment in America, 1864–1982, at 8–9 (1984); Mackey, *supra* note 2, at 112–20; Madow, *supra* note 2, at 117–19.

9. CAPITAL PUNISHMENT: NINETEENTH-CENTURY ARGUMENTS 18 (1974); Report on the Subject of Capital Punishment to the New York Assembly (Apr. 14, 1841).

10. BOVEE, *supra* note 1, at 270–79; Elwood R. McIntyre, *A Farmer Halts the Hangman: The Story of Marvin Bovee*, WIS. MAG. HIST., Autumn 1958, at 3, 5–7, 9; EDWARD BAUMANN, MAY GOD HAVE MERCY ON YOUR SOUL: THE STORY OF THE ROPE AND THE THUNDERBOLT 26–30 (1993) (describing the first execution after the passage of the Illinois law banning public executions).

11. THE CIVIL WAR: AN ILLUSTRATED HISTORY xix, 380–81 (1991); ROBERT I. ALOTTA, CIVIL WAR JUSTICE: UNION ARMY EXECUTIONS UNDER LINCOLN 37–44 (1989); Davis, *supra* note 8, at 45–46; BOVEE, *supra* note 1, at vii–viii; MARVIN H. BOVEE, CHRIST AND THE GALLOWS, OR, REASONS FOR THE ABOLITION OF CAPITAL PUNISHMENT (1869); McIntyre, *supra* note 10, at 8, 10; John F. Galliher, Gregory Ray, & Brent Cook, *Abolition and Reinstatement of Capital Punishment During the Progressive Era and Early 20th Century*, 83 J. CRIM. L. & CRIMINOLOGY 538 (1992).

12. Act of Aug. 1, 1868, ch. 1637, ch. 13 §§ 27–28, 1868 Fla. Gen. Laws 61, 110–11; Act of Aug. 15, 1868, ch. 21, 1868 N.C. Sess. Laws 34 (July Sess.); Criminal Practice Act, § 377, 1871 Mont. Laws 189, 246; CAL. PENAL CODE § 1229 (1872); CRIM. CODE, § 547, NEB. GEN. STAT. ch. 58, § 547 (1873); Act of Oct. 28, 1874, 1874 Or. Laws 115; Act of Feb. 9, 1875, ch. 10, 1875 Nev. Stat. 53; Act of Mar. 1, 1878, Pub. L. No. 362, 1877 S.C. Acts 381; CODE CRIM. PROC. § 356, 1878 Utah Laws 60, 136; TEX. REV. STAT., CODE CRIM. PROC. arts. 828 & 833 (1879); Act of May 3, 1882, ch. 403, 1882 Md. Laws 630; DAK. TERR. REV. STAT., CODE CRIM. PROC. § 468 (1883); Act of Mar. 20, 1883, ch. 112, 1883 Tenn. Pub. Acts 139; Act of July 10, 1884, Pub. L. No. 79, 1884 La. Acts 102; ARIZ. REV. STAT. § 1849 (1887); WYO. STAT. § 3335 (1887); Act of Mar. 1, 1887, Pub. L. No. 24, §§ 1, 2, 1887 Ark. Acts 29; Act of Mar. 19, 1887, 1887 Mo. Laws 169; N.J. P.L. 1879, at 18 (*cited in* Gen. Stat. of N.J., at 1145 (1896)); Gen. Stat. of Ky., ch. 29, § 22, at 402 (1887) (*citing* Act of Mar. 30, 1880); Tenn. Acts, ch. 54 (1889).

13. Madow, *supra* note 2, at 512–14. At private executions in Pennsylvania, tickets were also sold to spectators desiring a view of the proceedings inside. For example, at the execution of William Williams in Dauphin County on May 21, 1858, seats on the top of a stable were sold for $1 each. TEETERS, *supra* note 1, at Part 2, at 2.

14. Madow, *supra* note 2, at 533–36, 539.

15. *Id.* at 514–15, 538–39, 541.

16. *Id.* at 538–39, 541.

17. N.Y. Laws, ch. 489 (1888); Madow, *supra* note 2, at 519, 537.

18. BOVEE, *supra* note 1, at 166; McIntyre, *supra* note 10, at 3; Madow, *supra* note 2, at 542–43.

19. Madow, *supra* note 2, at 537, 543–44; John G. Leyden, *Death in the Hot Seat: A Century of Electrocutions*, WASH. POST, Aug. 5, 1990, at D5; *see also* Tom Mahoney, *The First Electrocution*, REAL DETECTIVE, May 1935, at 26–27, 60, 62; Deborah W. Denno, *Is Electrocution an Unconstitutional Method of Execution? The Engineering of Death Over the Century*, 35 WM. & MARY L. REV. 551, 603 (1994).

20. Madow, *supra* note 2, at 544–45.

21. *Id.* at 546–47 & nn.377–78.

22. *Id.* at 547–51.

23. *Id.* at 551–52.

24. *Id.* at 553–55; Denno, *supra* note 19, at 605.

25. Act of Apr. 19, 1889 Colo. Sess. Laws 118, 119; *Passing the Bills*, PUEBLO CHIEFTON, Mar. 8, 1889, at 1, col. 3; ROCKY MT. NEWS, Mar. 29, 1889, at 4, col. 1.

26. U.S. Supreme Court proceedings, Transcript of Record at 3, *In re* Medley, 134 U.S. 160 (1890).

27. State of Colorado's Brief at 7–8 (citing court's opinion), *In re* Medley, 134 U.S. 160 (1890).

28. *Id.* at 14.

29. *Id.* at 21.

30. *In re* Medley, 134 U.S. at 166–67, 171, 173, 176; *In re* Savage, 134 U.S. 176 (1890).

31. *The Hanging of Griego*, PUEBLO CHIEFTON, Nov. 7, 1890, at 7, col. 2; *Hung for Murder*, PUEBLO CHIEFTON, Nov. 9, 1890, at 1, cols. 1–2; ROCKY MT. NEWS, Nov. 9, 1890, at 1, col. 1; *Is Griego Living?*, ROCKY MT. NEWS, Nov. 8, 1890, at 1, col. 5.

32. Act of Apr. 24, 1889, ch. 20, § 5, 1889 Minn. Laws 66. Several Minnesota newspapers reported that this 1889 law was known as the "midnight assassination law." *The Smith Execution Law*, MINNEAPOLIS J., Feb. 14, 1906, at 4, col. 3; *Sheriff's Tea Party*, ST. PAUL DISPATCH, Feb. 14, 1906, at 10, col. 2; *Last Hours of Life*, MINNEAPOLIS TRIB., Oct. 19, 1894, at 1, col. 6; *see also Hanged in Private*, ST. PAUL DISPATCH, July 19, 1889, at 1, cols. 1–2.

33. Holden v. Minnesota, 137 U.S. 483 (1890); U.S. Supreme Court proceedings, Transcript of Record at 1–2, 7, 8, Holden v. Minnesota, *supra*.

34. Holden v. Minnesota, 137 U.S. 483 (1890); *How About Clift Holden?*, ST. PAUL PIONEER PRESS, July 3, 1890, at 5, col. 3; *In re* Medley, 134 U.S. 160 (1890); *In re* Savage, 134 U.S. 176 (1890).

35. U.S. Supreme Court proceedings, Transcript of Record, at 11–12, 17, Holden v. Minnesota, 137 U.S. 483 (1890).

36. U.S. Supreme Court proceedings, Brief of Holden, at 4, 13, 15, 20, Holden v. Minnesota, 137 U.S. 483 (1890).

37. U.S. Supreme Court proceedings, Brief of the State of Minnesota, at 2, 3, 18, Holden v. Minnesota, 137 U.S. 483 (1890).

38. *The Holden Case*, MINNEAPOLIS TRIB., Nov. 21, 1890, at 3, col. 3; *Clifton Holden's Case*, ST. PAUL PIONEER PRESS, Nov. 22, 1890, at 5, col. 3; *Holden Must Hang*, ST. PAUL PIONEER PRESS, Dec. 9, 1890, at 4, col. 5; *To Stretch Hemp*, MINNEAPOLIS TRIB., Dec. 9, 1890, at 1, col. 6; Holden v. Minnesota, 137 U.S. 483, 491 (1890).

39. 1893 Conn. Laws 59–60; 1898 Mass. Acts 265–267; Act of Feb. 18, 1899, ch. 2, § 9, 1899 W. Va. Acts 12; Act of Feb. 23, 1899 Idaho Sess. Laws 481, 484; Act of Mar. 8, 1901, ch. 63, 1901 Wash. Laws 100; Act of Mar. 17, 1903, ch. 76, 1903 N.M. Laws 141; Hugo A. Bedau, *Capital Punishment in Oregon, 1903–64*, 45 OR. L. REV. 1, 5 & n.5, 37 (1965); Robert H. Dann, *Abolition and Restoration of the Death Penalty in Ore-*

gon, reprinted in THE DEATH PENALTY IN AMERICA 343–44 (Hugo Adam Bedau ed., 2d ed. 1968).

40. *See* Chapter 5 (describing the criminal prosecution of the St. Paul newspapers in detail).

41. Va. Laws, ch. 398, §§ 1, 10 (1908); *Gallows Gone From Virginia,* RICHMOND TIMES-DISPATCH, Mar. 6, 1908, at 1, 3; *Some Times-Dispatch Victories,* RICHMOND TIMES-DISPATCH, Mar. 6, 1908, at 6, col. 2; Wash. Laws, ch. 249, § 209 (1909); Wash. Laws, ch. 184, § 11 (1982); WASH. REV. CODE § 9.68.020 (West 1988) (*citing* Wash. Laws 1982, ch. 184, § 11, eff. Apr. 1, 1982); Norman S. Hayner & John R. Cranor, *The Death Penalty in Washington State,* 284 ANNALS AM. ACAD. POL. & SOC. SCI. 101–4 (1952).

42. *Senate,* RICHMOND TIMES-DISPATCH, Mar. 6, 1908, at 3, col. 5; *Death by Electricity,* RICHMOND TIMES-DISPATCH, Oct. 14, 1908, at 6, col. 1.

43. BIRMINGHAM NEWS (Ala.), Oct. 13, 1908; NEWS (Galveston), Aug. 16, 1908; *Attempt to Lynch,* JOURNAL (Atlanta), Aug. 15, 1908, at 4, col. 4; *Death Sudden in Electric Chair,* RICHMOND TIMES-DISPATCH, Oct. 14, 1908, at 12, col. 4; *Smith to Die in Electric Chair,* RICHMOND TIMES-DISPATCH, Oct. 13, 1908, at 12, col. 2; RICHMOND TIMES-DISPATCH, Sept. 29, 1908; *Henry Smith Dies in Chair To-Morrow,* RICHMOND NEWS LEADER, Oct. 12, 1908, at 1, col. 7; *Death Chair Ready,* RICHMOND TIMES-DISPATCH, Oct. 11, 1908, at 9, col. 7; *Negroes First to Try Death Chair,* RICHMOND TIMES-DISPATCH, Oct. 8, 1908, at 12, col. 4; *Secret Chair,* RICHMOND EVENING J., Oct. 12, 1908, at 1, col. 5; *Swift Death in Chair,* RICHMOND EVENING J., Oct. 13, 1908, at 1, 7; *Negro Dies in Electric Chair,* RICHMOND NEWS LEADER, Oct. 13, 1908, at 1–2; *see also Winston Green Dies in Chair,* RICHMOND NEWS LEADER, Oct. 30, 1908, at 1, 9 (after Green, an African American youth, was executed on October 30, 1908, the newspaper reported that "[u]nder the law no details of the electrocution are given out for publication").

44. *The Secret Death,* RICHMOND NEWS LEADER, Oct. 13, 1908, at 4, col. 1.

45. Ark. Acts, Act 55 (1913); *Electrocution Bill Passes,* ARK. GAZ., Feb. 12, 1913, at 3, col. 6; *Primary Election Favored by House,* ARK. GAZ., Jan. 17, 1913, at 3; ARK. GAZ., Jan. 16, 1913, at 7, col. 6; *Electric Chair Measure Passed House Today,* ARK. DEMOCRAT, Feb. 7, 1913, at 4, col. 4; *Electrocution Is Favored by House,* ARK. GAZ., Feb. 7, 1913, at 3, col. 5; *Electric Chair Measure Passed House Thursday,* ARK. DEMOCRAT, Feb. 7, 1913, at 4, cols. 4–5; *see also Committee Favors an Electric Chair,* ARK. GAZ., Jan. 25, 1913, at 4, col. 5; *Judiciary Committee of House Organized,* ARK. DEMOCRAT, Sept. 24, 1913, at 4, col. 1; *Judiciary Committee Favors Electrocution,* ARK. DEMOCRAT, Jan. 25, 1913, at 1, cols. 1, 4; *Provisions of Bill for Electric Chair,* ARK. DEMOCRAT, Feb. 7, 1913, at 14, cols. 1–3; *The Senate,* ARK. DEMOCRAT, Feb. 12, 1913, at 2, cols. 2–3; ARK. DEMOCRAT, Feb. 14, 1913, at 10, col. 2; *Governor Signs Bill Abolishing Legal Hangings,* ARK. DEMOCRAT, Feb. 15, 1913, at 1, col. 1; *Review Week's Work With the Legislaturemen,* ARK. DEMOCRAT, Feb. 15, 1913, at 1, col. 4.

46. JONESBORO EVENING SUN (Ark.), Sept. 5, 1913; ARK. GAZ., Aug. 5, 1913; ARK. GAZ., Aug. 3, 1913; BOWERS, *supra* note 8, at 403; *Lee Simms Dies in Electric Chair,* ARK. GAZ., Sept. 6, 1913, at 12, col. 3; *Simms Dies Today in Electric Chair,* ARK. GAZ., Sept. 5,

1913, at 1, col. 5; *Negro First to Die in the Electric Chair,* ARK. DEMOCRAT, Sept. 5, 1913, at 1, 12.

47. *Gagging the Press,* MINNEAPOLIS J., May 3, 1889, at 5, col. 5; Md. House Bill No. 124 (introduced on Feb. 4, 1916) (copy on file with author); Note from Mike Miller, Maryland State Law Library, dated Feb. 1, 1996 (copy on file with author).

48. WALTER TRENERRY, MURDER IN MINNESOTA: A COLLECTION OF TRUE CASES 219–20 (1985); *Execution!,* ST. PAUL DISPATCH, Mar. 6, 1868, at 1, cols. 2–3; *The Execution of Roesch,* ST. PETER TRIB. (Minn.), Feb. 19, 1868, at 3, col. 1; ST. PETER TRIB. (Minn.), Feb. 26, 1868, at 3, col. 3; *The Execution of Andreas Roesch,* ST. PETER TRIB. (Minn.), Mar. 4, 1868, at 3, col. 1; *The Gallows!,* ST. PAUL DAILY PIONEER, Mar. 7, 1868, at 4, cols. 1–6; THEODORE BLEGEN, MINNESOTA: A HISTORY OF THE STATE 217, 288–89 (1989); *Expiated by the Rope,* DAILY PIONEER PRESS (St. Paul), Aug. 29, 1885, at 2, col. 3; *Execution!,* ST. PAUL DISPATCH, Mar. 6, 1868, at 1, cols. 2–5; *Murderer to Be Executed at St. Peter,* ST. PAUL DAILY PIONEER, Jan. 26, 1868, at 1, col. 3; *"The Poor Murderer,"* ST. PETER TRIB. (Minn.), Jan. 29, 1868, at 3, col. 3; *The Death Penalty in Nicollet County,* ST. PETER TRIB. (Minn.), Jan. 29, 1868, at 2, col. 3; *The St. Peter Murderer,* ST. PAUL DAILY PIONEER, Jan. 30, 1868, at 1, col. 2; *The Execution of Roesch Postponed,* ST. PETER TRIB. (Minn.), Feb. 5, 1868, at 2, col. 3; ST. PETER TRIB. (Minn.), Feb. 12, 1868, at 3, col. 1; ST. PAUL DAILY PIONEER, Feb. 14, 1868, at 1, col. 2.

49. ST. PAUL DISPATCH, Mar. 6, 1868, at 1, col. 1; *The Gallows!, supra* note 48, at 4, cols. 1–6; *Execution!, supra* note 48, at 1, col. 4. The local newspaper later said that it was a "compliment to the character of the citizens of St. Peter" that "but very few of them were present." *The Execution,* ST. PETER TRIB. (Minn.), Mar. 11, 1868, at 3, col. 2.

50. DAILY PIONEER & DEMOCRAT (St. Paul), Mar. 9, 1860, at 2, cols. 3–4; *Escape of Mrs. Bilansky,* DAILY PIONEER & DEMOCRAT (St. Paul), July 27, 1859, at 3, cols. 1–2; *The Bilansky Murder,* DAILY PIONEER & DEMOCRAT (St. Paul), Mar. 24, 1860, at 3, cols. 1–6; DAILY PIONEER & DEMOCRAT (St. Paul), Mar. 24, 1860, at 2, col. 2; *Expiated by the Rope, supra* note 48, at 2, col. 3 (Sheriff Aaron W. Tullis); *see also Mrs. Bilansky,* DAILY PIONEER & DEMOCRAT (St. Paul), Jan. 18, 1860, at 3, col. 2 (urging Governor Ramsey to "exercise his discretion as to make the execution as private as executions usually are in States where public executions are prohibited").

51. *The Bilansky Murder, supra* note 50, at 3, cols. 1–6.

52. *Execution of Mrs. Bilansky,* DAILY PIONEER & DEMOCRAT (St. Paul), Mar. 24, 1860, at 2, col. 2; *The Bilansky Murder, supra* note 50, at 3, cols. 1–6; DAILY PIONEER & DEMOCRAT (St. Paul), Mar. 25, 1860, at 3, col. 1; TRENERRY, *supra* note 48, at 219.

53. G. Mark Mamantov, Note, *The Executioner's Song: Is There a Right to Listen?,* 69 VA. L. REV. 373, 375–76 (1983); 1882 Md. Laws, ch. 403; AUGUST MENCKEN, BY THE NECK: A BOOK OF HANGINGS 33–35 (1942); Louise Barry, *Legal Hangings in Kansas,* 18 KAN. HIST. Q. 279, 280, 287–88, 294–95 (1950); Madow, *supra* note 2, at 512; TEETERS, *supra* note 1, at 28.

54. RAYMOND PATERNOSTER, CAPITAL PUNISHMENT IN AMERICA 7 (1991); BOWERS, *supra* note 8, at 13–14, 43, 513; Chapter 6 (Gary Gilmore, the first person executed after 1967, was not put to death until January 1977). These statutes, which were passed

beginning in the 1840s, required county sheriffs to transfer prisoners to state penitentiaries for execution. ME. REV. STAT. ch. 168, § 10 (1840); Act of Oct. 31, 1844, Pub. L.
No. 27, § 4, 1844 Vt. Acts 23, 24; MICH. REV. STAT. ch. 168, § 11 (1846); N.H. GEN.
STAT. ch. 244, § 6 (1867); Act of Apr. 29, 1885, 1885 Ohio Laws 169; Act of June 4, 1888,
ch. 489, 1888 N.Y. Laws 778; Act of Mar. 31, 1891, ch. 191, § 9, 1891 Cal. Stat. 272; Act
of May 25, 1893, ch. 137, 1893 Conn. Pub. Acts 282; Act of Apr. 24, 1894, ch. 92, 1894
Iowa Acts 92; Act of Apr. 13, 1898, ch. 326, § 4, 1898 Mass. Acts 265, 266; Act of Mar.
6, 1889, ch. 94, 1889 Ind. Acts 192; Act of Apr. 19, 1889, 1889 Colo. Sess. Laws 118;
UTAH REV. STAT. § 4940 (1898); Act of Feb. 18, 1899, ch. 2, 1899 W. Va. Acts 12; Act
of Mar. 8, 1901, ch. 63, 1901 Wash. Laws 100; Act of Mar. 13, 1901, ch. 52, 1901 Nev.
Stat. 66; Act of Mar. 29, 1901, ch. 105, 1901 Neb. Laws 506; Act of Feb. 16, 1903, 1903
Or. Laws 66; Act of Mar. 9, 1903, ch. 99, 1903 N.D. Sess. Laws 119; Act of Feb. 7, 1905,
ch. 11, 1905 Wyo. Sess. Laws 9; Act of Apr. 4, 1906, ch. 79, § 2, 1906 N.J. Laws 112;
Act of Mar. 16, 1908, ch. 398, 1908 Va. Acts 684; Act of May 1, 1909, ch. 500, 1909
Tenn. Pub. Acts 1810; Act of Mar. 21, 1910, ch. 38, § 134, 1910 Ky. Acts 111; ARIZ. REV.
STAT. § 1149 (1913); Act of Feb. 15, 1913, Pub. L. No. 55, 1913 Ark. Acts 171; Act of June
19, 1913, Pub. L. No. 338, 1913 Pa. Laws 528; Act of Feb. 17, 1912, Pub. L. No. 402, 1912
S.C. Acts 702; Act of Apr. 13, 1922, ch. 465, § 2, 1922 Md. Laws 1023; Act of May 7,
1923, ch. 9169, 1923 Fla. Gen. Laws 175; Act of June 4, 1923, ch. 51, 1923 Tex. Gen. Laws
111 (2d Called Sess.); Act of Sept. 29, 1923, Pub. L. No. 587, 1923 Ala. Acts 759; Act of
Aug. 16, 1924, Pub. L. No. 475, 1924 Ga. Laws 195; Act of July 6, 1927, 1927 Ill. Laws
400; Act of Mar. 11, 1929, ch. 69, 1929 N.M. Laws 99; Act of Mar. 11, 1935, ch. 155, 1935
Kan. Sess. Laws 234; Act of June 4, 1937, 1937 Mo. Laws 221; Act of Jan. 27, 1939, ch.
135, 1939 S.D. Sess. Laws 166, 168; Act of Sept. 28, 1954, ch. 33, 1954 Miss. Laws 43
(Ext. Sess.); Act of Sept. 11, 1956, Pub. L. No. 18, 1956 La. Acts 30 (Ext. Sess.). The
hanging of Sandy Kavanagh at the Vermont State Prison on January 20, 1864, was the
first execution performed under state rather than local authority. BOWERS, *supra* note
8, at 13–14, 43, 513.

    55. Act of Apr. 29, 1885, § 1, 1885 Ohio Laws 169, 170; Act of May 25, 1893, ch. 137,
§ 3, 1893 Conn. Pub. Acts 282, 1893 Conn. Laws 59–60; Act of Mar. 21, 1910, ch. 38, §
4, 1910 Ky. Acts 111, 112; Act of June 19, 1913, Pub. L. No. 338, § 5, 1913 Pa. Laws 528, 529;
Act of Jan. 27, 1939, ch. 135, § 11, 1939 S.D. Sess. Laws 166; Act of June 12, 1939, Pub. L.
No. 559, § 272, 1939 Fla. Gen. Laws 1300, 1374; Act of May 1, 1951, ch. 17a, 1951 Okla.
Sess. Laws 64; Act of Mar. 24, 1954, ch. 220, § 2, 1954 Miss. Laws 246; Act of Mar. 17,
1903, ch. 76, 1903 N.M. Laws 141; Act of Sept. 29, 1923, Pub. L. No. 587, § 7, 1923 Ala.
Laws 759–60; Act of Feb. 18, 1899, W. Va. Acts, ch. 2, § 10 (1899); John D. Bessler, *The
"Midnight Assassination Law" and Minnesota's Anti-Death Penalty Movement, 1849–1911,*
22 WM. MITCHELL L. REV. 577 (1996); *John Day Smith—Part II,* ECCO NEWS, Sept.
1979, at 11 (available at the Minneapolis Public Library).

    56. Madow, *supra* note 2, at 519–21; Turner & Brinkmann, *supra* note 7, at 1141–43;
Gen. Stat. of N.J., at 1145, 1147 (1896).

    57. Mamantov, *supra* note 53, at 375; MASUR, *supra* note 2, at 8, 96, 98–100, 109;
Madow, *supra* note 2, at 502–3.

58. Mo. Laws 1937, at 221; *Missouri Lethal Gas Executions Voted by House,* St. Louis Post-Dispatch, May 19, 1937, at 12A, col. 1; *The House Outlaws Legal Hangings,* St. Louis Post-Dispatch, May 20, 1937, at 2C, col. 3; *Will Missouri Be Next?,* St. Louis Post-Dispatch, May 15, 1937, at 4A, col. 2; *1500 at Galena, Mo., See Murderer Hanged,* St. Louis Post-Dispatch, May 21, 1937, at 1A, col. 6; *Missouri to End Public Hangings,* N.Y. Times, May 30, 1937, at 10E, cols. 1–2; Negley K. Teeters & Jack H. Hedblom, ". . . Hang by the Neck . . ." 8 (1967); Chapter 2; George C. Wright, *Executions of Afro-Americans in Kentucky,* 1 Ga. J. S. Legal Hist. 321, 336 (1991).

59. Stat. of Okla., ch. 72, art. 15, § 42 (1891); Gen. Laws of the State of Kan., ch. 32, § 244 (1862); Stat. of Ind., at 422 (1862); 1893 Conn. Laws 59–60; Masur, *supra* note 2, at 112; Madow, *supra* note 2, at 516–18 & n.251; James W. Marquart, Sheldon Ekland-Olson & Jonathan R. Sorensen, The Rope, the Chair, and the Needle: Capital Punishment in Texas, 1923–1990, at 19, 34, 201–2 (1994); Robert Elliott, Agent of Death: The Memoirs of an Executioner 236 (1940).

60. *The Bilansky Murder, supra* note 50, at 3, cols. 1–6; *Execution of Mrs. Bilansky, supra* note 52, at 2, col. 2; Masur, *supra* note 2, at 111.

61. Madow, *supra* note 2, at 501; N.C. Acts, ch. 21, §§ 1, 2 (1868); Wright, *supra* note 58, at 327; Masur, *supra* note 2, at 100–102; Bye, *supra* note 3, at 39–40. One legislator similarly declared that "the loss of time and money, the interruption of business, and the almost total disorganization of almost all pursuits in the immediate neighborhood of the scene [of public executions], are serious evils." *Id.*

62. Masur, *supra* note 2, at 59, 98–100. American newspapers frequently publicized phrenological lectures in articles or by publishing advertisements. *E.g.,* Minneapolis J., Mar. 29, 1889, at 4, col. 4 (publicizing "Free Phrenological Lectures"); *Phrenology Free,* Minneapolis J., Apr. 27, 1889, at 5, col. 3 (same); *Scientific Phrenology,* Minneapolis J., May 15, 1889, at 2, col. 1 ("[O]ther evidences of the correctness of the observations of the phrenologists are cited, and it appears as if the science which has always been regarded as extremely unscientific might be able to sustain itself in this practical age through scientific research.").

63. Mamantov, *supra* note 53, at 375; Masur, *supra* note 2, at 117–18; Galliher, Ray, & Cook, *supra* note 11, at 538. By the end of the 1930s, eight of these states had reinstated capital punishment. *Id.* at 538. Scholars attribute the relatively quick reinstatement of capital punishment in these eight states to America's "changing mood" arising from its entry into World War I, "economic recession and depression," and threats of lynchings. *Id.* at 538–39; David Lawrence Abney, *Capital Punishment in Arizona (1863–1963),* Master's Thesis, Arizona State University (Aug. 1988), at 45–46, 109; Franklin Zimring & Gordon Hawkins, Capital Punishment and the American Agenda 28–29 (1986).

64. Abney, *supra* note 63, at 45, 228, 232.

65. Ark. Code Ann. § 16-90-502(d) (Michie 1987) ("No execution of any person convicted in this state of a capital offense shall be public; but it shall be private."); Conn. Stat. Ann. § 54-100 (1985) ("[P]unishment shall be inflicted only within the walls of said institution in Somers, within an enclosure to be prepared for that purpose. . . ."); Ind. Code Ann. § 35-38-6-5 (Burns 1986) ("The execution must take place

inside the walls of the state prison in a room arranged for that purpose."); MD. ANN. CODE. §§ 72–73 (1992) ("Punishment of death must be inflicted within the walls of the building [of the Maryland Penitentiary]."); MASS. ANN. LAWS ch. 279, § 60 (Law. Co-op. 1992) ("The sentence shall be executed within an enclosure or building for that purpose at the state prison and the company which furnishes the electric power or light to the state prison shall provide all necessary electricity for executions by electrocution at such times as the superintendent orders."); MISS. CODE ANN. § 99-19-55 (Supp. 1992) ("[S]uch punishment shall be inflicted . . . on the premises of the Mississippi State Penitentiary at Parchman, Mississippi."); MO. ANN. STAT. §§ 546.720 & 546.730 (Vernon Supp. 1992) (executions must take place "enclosed from public view, within the walls of a correctional facility"); MONT. CODE ANN. § 46-19-103(5) (1991) ("The warden of the Montana state prison shall provide a suitable and efficient room or place in which executions will be carried out, enclosed from public view, within the walls of the state prison. . . ."); NEB. REV. STAT. § 29-2533 (1989) (executions must take place "within the walls of the Department of Correctional Services adult correctional facility, or within the yard or enclosure adjacent thereto"); NEV. REV. STAT. § 176.355(3) (1991) ("The execution must take place at the state prison."); N.H. REV. STAT. ANN. § 630:6 (1986) ("The punishment of death shall be inflicted within the walls or yard of the state prison."); N.J. STAT. ANN. § 2C:49-4 (West Supp. 1992); N.M. STAT. ANN. § 31-14-15 (Michie 1984) ("A judgment of death must be executed within the walls of the state penitentiary at Santa Fe. . . ."); N.C. GEN. STAT. § 15-190 (1983); OKLA. STAT. ANN. tit. 22, § 1015 (West 1986) ("A judgment of death must be executed within the walls of the state prison at McAlester, Oklahoma. . . ."); PA. STAT. ANN. tit. 61, § 2125 (Supp. 1992); S.C. CODE ANN. § 24-3-550 (Law. Co-op. Supp. 1992); S.D. CODIFIED LAWS ANN. § 23A-27A-32 (1988) ("The punishment of death shall be inflicted within the walls of some building at the state penitentiary or within the yard or enclosure adjoining thereto."); TENN. CODE ANN. § 40-23-116(a) (Michie 1990) ("[T]he warden of the state penitentiary in which the death chamber is located shall cause such death sentence to be carried out within an enclosure to be prepared for that purpose in strict seclusion and privacy."); TEX. CODE CRIM. PROC. art. 43.19 (West Supp. 1992) ("The execution shall take place at a location designated by the Texas Department of Corrections in a room arranged for that purpose."); UTAH CODE ANN. § 77-19-10 (1990) (the execution must be carried out at a "secure correctional facility"); VA. CODE ANN. § 53.1-233 (Michie 1991) ("The Director is hereby authorized and directed to provide and maintain a permanent death chamber within the confines of a state correctional facility."); WASH. REV. CODE § 10.95.180 (1990) ("All executions . . . shall be carried out within the walls of the state penitentiary."); WYO. STAT. § 7-13-905(a) (1987) ("A sentence of death shall be executed within the walls of the state penitentiary. . . ."). Some statutes do not cap the number of witnesses but imply that only a small number of observers should attend. Thus, Arizona, Missouri, and New Mexico all require the attendance of "at least twelve reputable citizens." ARIZ. REV. STAT. ANN. § 13-705 (1989); MO. ANN. STAT. § 546.740 (Vernon 1987 & Supp. 1992); N.M. STAT. ANN. § 31-14-15 (Michie 1984).

66.   ILL. ANN. STAT. ch. 38, para. 119-5(d) (Smith-Hurd 1990 & Supp. 1992) (the execution shall be conducted in the presence of "6 other witnesses who shall certify the execution of the sentence"); LA. REV. STAT. ANN. § 15:570 (West 1992) ("not less than five nor more than seven other witnesses"); MASS. ANN. LAWS ch. 279, § 65 (Law. Co-op. 1992) ("with the approval of the superintendent, not more than three other persons"); MONT. CODE ANN. § 46-19-103(5) (1987) ("[t]he warden must allow the execution to be observed by 12 witnesses"); NEB. REV. STAT. § 29-2534 (1989) ("such other persons, not exceeding six in number, as the warden may designate"); VA. CODE ANN. § 53.1-234 (Michie 1991) ("[a]t the execution there shall be present . . . at least six citizens who shall not be employees of the Department"); ARIZ. REV. STAT. ANN. § 13-705 (1989); ARK. CODE ANN. § 16-90-502 (Michie 1987); COLO. REV. STAT. § 16-11-404 (1990); MO. ANN. STAT. § 546.740 (Vernon 1987 & Supp. 1992); NEV. REV. STAT. § 176.355 (1991); N.M. STAT. ANN. § 31-14-15 (Michie 1984); PA. STAT. ANN. tit. 61, § 2125 (Supp. 1992); S.C. CODE ANN. § 24-3-550 (Law. Co-op. Supp. 1992); TENN. CODE ANN. § 40-23-116(b) (Michie 1990); Tenn. Acts 1909, ch. 500, § 1, Acts 1985 (1st E.S.), ch. 5, § 16. In New Hampshire, the county sheriff where the death sentence was imposed hands out execution invitations. N.H. REV. STAT. ANN. § 31-14-15 (Michie 1984). Other state laws fail to delegate the witness selection task to anyone. ARK. CODE ANN. § 16-90-502(d)(2) (Michie 1987); ILL. ANN. STAT. ch. 38, para. 119-5(d) (Smith-Hurd 1990 & Supp. 1992); LA. REV. STAT. ANN. § 15:570 (West 1992); MD. ANN. CODE art. 27, § 73 (1992); MONT. CODE ANN. § 46-19-103(5) (1987); N.C. GEN. STAT. § 15-190 (1983); VA. CODE ANN. § 53.1-234 (Michie 1991).

67.   ALA. CODE § 15-18-83(a)(4) (1982); ARIZ. REV. STAT. ANN. § 13-705 (1989); ARK. CODE ANN. § 16-90-502(d)(2) (Michie 1987); CAL. PENAL CODE § 3605 (West Supp. 1993); CONN. GEN. STAT. ANN. § 54-100 (West 1985); FLA. STAT. ANN. § 922:11(2) (West 1985); GA. CODE ANN. § 17- 10-41 (1990); IND. CODE ANN. § 35-38-6-6 (Burns 1986); KY. REV. STAT. ANN. § 16-431.250 (Michie/Bobbs-Merrill Supp. 1992); LA. REV. STAT. ANN. § 15:570 (West 1992); MD. ANN. CODE art. 27, § 73 (1992); MASS. ANN. LAWS ch. 279, § 65 (Law. Co-op. 1992); MISS. CODE ANN. § 99-19-55(2) (Supp. 1992); MO. ANN. STAT. § 546.740 (Vernon Supp. 1992); NEB. REV. STAT. § 29-2534 (1989); N.H. REV. STAT. ANN. § 630:6 (1986); N.M. STAT. ANN. § 31-14-15 (Michie 1984); N.C. GEN. STAT. § 15-190 (1983); OHIO REV. CODE ANN. § 2949.25(E) (Baldwin 1992); OHIO ADMIN. CODE § 5120-9-54(A)(5) (1989); OKLA. STAT. ANN. tit. 22, § 1015 (West 1986); PA. STAT. ANN. tit. 61, § 2125 (Supp. 1992); S.C. CODE ANN. § 24-3-550 (Law. Co-op. Supp. 1992); S.D. CODIFIED LAWS ANN. § 23A-27A-35 (1988); TENN. CODE ANN. § 40-23-116(b)(3) (1982); TEX. CRIM. PROC. CODE ANN. § 43.20 (West 1979); UTAH CODE ANN. § 77-19-11(2)(d) (1990); VA. CODE ANN. § 53.1-234 (Michie 1991); WYO. STAT. § 7-13-908 (Supp. 1992).

68.   ALA. CODE § 15-18-83(a)(7) (1982) ("[a]ny of the relatives or friends of the condemned person that he may request, not exceeding five in number"); ARIZ. REV. STAT. ANN. § 13-705 (1989) ("superintendent shall . . . permit . . . any persons, relatives or friends, not to exceed five, to be present at the execution"); CAL. PENAL CODE § 3605 (West 1993) ("any persons, relatives or friends, not to exceed five"); CONN. GEN. STAT. ANN. § 54-100 (West 1985) ("such other adults, as the prisoner may designate, not ex-

ceeding three in number"); GA. CODE ANN. § 17-10-41 (1990) ("the convicted person may request the presence of . . . a reasonable number of relatives and friends, provided that the total number of witnesses appearing at the request of the convicted person shall be determined by the commissioner of corrections"); KY. REV. STAT. ANN. § 16-431.250 (Michie/Bobbs-Merrill Supp. 1992) ("three (3) other persons selected by the condemned"); MASS. ANN. LAWS ch. 279, § 65 (Law. Co-op. 1992) ("the immediate members of the family of the prisoner" can be present); MISS. CODE ANN. § 99-19-55(2) (Supp. 1992) ("the commissioner may permit two (2) members of the condemned person's immediate family as witnesses, if they so request"); MO. ANN. STAT. § 546.740 (Vernon 1992) ("any person, relatives or friends, not to exceed five, to be present at the execution"); MONT. CODE ANN. § 46-19-103(5) (1987) (three witnesses "may be designated by the person to be executed"); NEB. REV. STAT. § 29-2534 (1989) ("such other persons, not exceeding three in number as the prisoner may designate"); N.M. STAT. ANN. § 31-14-15 (Michie 1984) ("any person, relatives or friends, not to exceed five"); N.C. GEN. STAT. § 15-190 (1983) ("any relatives of such person, convict or felon"); OHIO REV. CODE ANN. § 2949.25(E) (Baldwin 1992) ("not more than three other persons, to be designated by such prisoner"); OHIO ADMIN. CODE § 5120-9-54(A)(6) (1989) ("[t]hree persons designated by the prisoner who are not confined in any state institution"); OKLA. STAT. ANN. tit. 22, § 1015 (West 1986) ("any persons, relatives or friends, not to exceed five, as the defendant may name"); S.D. CODIFIED LAWS ANN. § 23A-27A-35 (1988) ("any relatives or friends requested by the defendant not exceeding five"); TEX. CRIM. PROC. CODE ANN. § 43.20 (West 1979) ("any of the relatives or friends of the condemned person that he may request, not exceeding five in number"); UTAH CODE ANN. § 77-19-11(2)(d) (1990) (friends or relatives "designated by the defendant, not exceeding a total of five persons").

69. IND. CODE ANN. § 35-38-6-6 (Burns 1985); WYO. STAT. § 7-13-908 (1987 & Supp. 1992); N.J. STAT. ANN. § 2C:49-7(d) (West Supp. 1992).

70. ARK. CODE ANN. § 16-502(d)(2) (Michie 1987); FLA. STAT. ANN. § 922:11(2) (West 1985); GA. CODE ANN. § 17-10-41 (1990); MD. ANN. CODE art. 27, § 73 (1992); N.C. GEN. STAT. § 15-190 (1983); S.C. CODE ANN. § 24-3-550 (Law. Co-op. Supp. 1991); VA. CODE ANN. § 53.1-234 (Michie 1991); *see also* N.H. REV. STAT. ANN. § 630:6 (1986) (sheriff has the discretion to admit the condemned prisoner's counsel); Joan Cheever, *An Appointment in the Death House*, NAT'L L.J., Nov. 14, 1994, at A16 & A24.

71. George Gordon, *Is This the First Step Back to Public Execution*, Associated Newspapers Ltd (Daily Mail), June 16, 1994 (LEXIS); Leyla Kokmen & Janan Hanna, *Executions Become More Public*, CHI. TRIB., Nov. 21, 1995, § 2, at 1, 4; *Texas Board: Family Can View Executions*, COM. APP. (Memphis), Sept. 16, 1995; Barbara Hoberock, *Victims' Families Seek Closure by Watching Execution*, TULSA WORLD, July 15, 1996, at A11.

72. John D. Bessler, *Televised Executions and the Constitution: Recognizing a First Amendment Right of Access to State Executions*, 45 FED. COMM. L.J. 355, 369-70, 377 & nn.69, 111 (1993) (citing California's policy of admitting up to twenty-five media representatives); MISS. CODE ANN. § 99-19-55(2) (Supp. 1992) ("bona fide members of the press, not to exceed eight (8) in number"); S.C. CODE ANN. § 24-3-550 (Law. Co-op.

Supp. 1992) ("a group of not more than five representatives of the South Carolina media"); *Death Row, U.S.A.*, NAACP Legal Defense and Educational Fund, Inc. (Summer 1994); S.D. CODIFIED LAWS ANN. § 23A-27A-34 (1988); UTAH CODE ANN. § 77-19-11(4) (1990); N.J. STAT. ANN. § 2C:49-7(c) (West Supp. 1992) ("Immediately following the execution, the eight representatives of the news media may hold a press conference for the purpose of giving other news representatives an account of the execution."); CONN. GEN. STAT. ANN. § 54-100 (West 1985) ("representatives of not more than five newspapers in the county where the crime was committed, and one reporter for each of the daily newspapers published in the city of Hartford"); PA. STAT. ANN. tit. 61, § 2125 (Supp. 1992); ARK. CODE ANN. § 16-90-504 (Michie 1987); Ark. Acts, ch. 55, § 10 (1913).

73. OHIO REV. CODE ANN. § 2949.25(F) (Baldwin 1992) ("[r]epresentatives of not exceeding three newspapers in the county where the crime was committed, one reporter for each of the daily newspapers published in the city of Columbus, and such other representatives of the news media as the director of rehabilitation and corrections authorizes"); OHIO ADMIN. CODE § 5120-9-54 (1989); OKLA. STAT. ANN. tit. 22, § 1015 (West 1986) ("newspapermen from recognized newspapers, press, and wire services, and radio reporters"); UTAH CODE ANN. § 77-19-11(4) (1990) (permitting attendance of "broadcast news media" representatives); FLA. ADMIN. CODE ANN. ch. 33.15.002 (1990); KY. REV. STAT. ANN. § 16-431.250 (Michie/Bobbs-Merrill Supp. 1992); MISS. CODE ANN. § 99-19-55(2) (Supp. 1992); OHIO ADMIN. CODE § 5120-9-54(B) (1989); S.C. CODE ANN. § 24-3-550 (Law. Co-op. Supp. 1992); Texas Department of Corrections, Policy No. 1-82 (1982) (*cited in* Mamantov, *supra* note 53, at 380 n.37); UTAH CODE ANN. § 77-19-11(5)(a) (1990); N.J. STAT. ANN. § 2C:49-6 (West Supp. 1992); PA. STAT. ANN. tit. 61, § 2124 (Supp. 1992); S.D. CODIFIED LAWS § 23A-27A-16 (1988); WYO. STAT. § 7-13-907(a) (1987); FLA. ADMIN. CODE ANN., Vol. 13, § 33-15.003; N.J. STAT. § 2C:49-6(b.) (West Supp. 1992).

74. S.C. CODE ANN. § 24-3-550 (Supp. 1991); S.D. CODIFIED LAWS ANN. § 23A-27A-34 (1988); Plaintiff's Post-Trial Brief at 21, KQED, Inc. v. Vasquez, 18 Media L. Rep. (BNA) 2323 (N.D. Cal. 1991) (No. C90-1383RHS); Marty Trillhause, *Wells Executed; Death Penalty Resumes After 36-Year Gap*, IDAHO FALLS POST REG., Jan. 6, 1994, at A1; *see also* Chapter 1.

75. Graham Stewart, *Domestic News*, Reuters Ltd., March 9, 1981 (PM cycle) (LEXIS); Thomas Slaughter, *Domestic News*, Associated Press, May 26, 1979 (BC cycle) (LEXIS); Rich Chapman, *Witnesses Describe Killer's "Macabre" Final Minutes*, CHI. SUN-TIMES, May 11, 1994, at 5; Mike Regan, *57 Minutes to Execute Serial Killer*, Daily Rec. (Scottish Daily Rec. & Sunday Mail Ltd. 1994) (WESTLAW); *Amnesty International Seeks Review of Landry Death*, United Press International, Dec. 15, 1988 (BC cycle) (LEXIS); *Tube Springs Leak*, CHI. TRIB., Dec. 14, 1988, at C18; *Murderer Executed After a Leaky Lethal Injection*, N.Y. TIMES, Dec. 14, 1988, at A29, col. 1; Kathy Walt, *After 100 Executions, Interest Seems to Have Waned*, SAN DIEGO UNION-TRIB., Oct. 8, 1995, at A33.

76. Susan Blaustein, *Witness to Another Execution*, HARPER'S MAG., May 1994, at 54; Richard Price, *California Execution Draws Little Interest*, USA TODAY, Aug. 24, 1993, at

2A; *Mexican National's Execution Draws Angry Remarks, Protests,* HOUSTON CHRON., Mar. 26, 1993, at A34.

77. Michael Dougan & Tanya Schevitz Wills, *This Time, Fewer Rally Against the Execution,* S.F. EXAMINER, Aug. 24, 1993, at A8; Sandra Gonzales & E. A. Torriero, *The Execution of David Edwin Mason,* SAN JOSE MERCURY NEWS, Aug. 24, 1993, at 1A; Price, *supra* note 76, at 2A; Walt, *supra* note 75, at A33.

78. *See* Chapters 4 & 7, Appendix.

79. Jonathan Freedland, *Crowds Celebrate Execution of U.S. Serial Killer,* GUARDIAN, May 11, 1994, at 11 (LEXIS); Glen Creno, *Guards Face Discipline Over Execution T-Shirts,* PHOENIX GAZ., Mar. 4, 1993, at B4.

80. *Betting on Hanging,* ST. PAUL PIONEER PRESS, Dec. 7, 1905; *Probe Tale of Execution Orgy at Jersey Jail,* HOUSTON POST, May 7, 1923, at 1–2; *In Jail to See Hanging,* NATRONA COUNTY TRIB., May 29, 1912, at 12, col. 4.

81. Charles Howe, *Arizona Killer Dies in Gas Chamber,* S.F. CHRON., Apr. 7, 1992, at A2; *More Multiple Executions Mulled,* BOSTON GLOBE, May 13, 1994, at 16; *Arkansas Says Double Execution Saves Time, Money and Staffing,* STATE (Columbia), May 15, 1994, at D9; *Three Murderers Die in Triple Execution,* COLUMBIAN, Aug. 4, 1994, at C2; *Arkansas Plans to Execute 3 on Same Night,* N.Y. TIMES, Dec. 1, 1996, at 16.

82. Michael Radelet, *Post-Furman Botched Executions,* LIFELINES, No. 50 (1990), at 7; Glass v. Louisiana, 471 U.S. 1080, 1087–88 (1985) (Brennan, J., dissenting); Peter Applebome, *2 Electric Jolts in Alabama Execution,* N.Y. TIMES, July 15, 1989, at 6, cols. 1–3; Transcript, "All Things Considered," National Public Radio, Sept. 27, 1994. When former drug user Stephen Morin was executed in 1985, it took technicians more than forty minutes to locate his vein to insert the lethal needle. *Murderer of Three Women Is Executed in Texas,* N.Y. TIMES, Mar. 14, 1985, at A22, cols. 1–6.

83. Madow, *supra* note 2, at 557; MACKEY, *supra* note 2, at 119 & n.41; Davis, *supra* note 8, at 45–46; Galliher, Ray, & Cook, *supra* note 11, at 538; BOWERS, *supra* note 8, at 10.

84. MASUR, *supra* note 2, at 113, 117; Madow, *supra* note 2, at 520–21.

Chapter Four

1. Appendix (listing times when death row inmates were executed); HERBERT H. HOWARD, MICHAEL S. KIEVMAN, & BARBARA A. MOORE, RADIO, TV, AND CABLE PROGRAMMING 182, 187–88 (1994).

2. TEX. CODE CRIM. PROC. 43.14 (Vernon Supp. 1996).

3. LA. REV. STAT. ANN. § 569.1 (West 1992); DEL. CODE ANN. tit. 11, § 4209(f) (West Supp. 1994); S.D. CODIFIED LAWS ANN. § 23A-27A-17 (1988); 18 U.S.C.A. § 3596 (West Supp. 1995); TEX. CODE CRIM. PROC. art. 43.14 (Vernon 1994); IND. CODE ANN. § 35-38-6-1(b) (Burns 1986); KY. REV. STAT. ANN. § 431.240(1) (Michie/Bobbs-Merrill Supp. 1992); WYO. STAT. § 7-13-905(a) (1987); Bruce Tomaso, *100th Inmate Executed,* DALLAS MORNING NEWS, Oct. 5, 1995, at 27A; *Texas Murderer Dies by Lethal Injection,* BALT. SUN, Oct. 5, 1995, at 6A; Jesse Katz, *Executions in Texas: No Big Deal,* L.A. TIMES, May 20, 1997, at A1; Mark Hansen, *From Death's Door,* A.B.A. J., June 1996, at 59; *see also* Appendix (listing times when death row inmates were executed).

4. Criminal Executions in Maryland 1923–1961, at 6 (unpublished listing of Maryland executions on file with author); Capital Punishment (unpublished report of Warden Vernon L. Pepersack dated August 24, 1954, on file with author); John C. Ahlers, *Death Hit After Hangman's Noose Was Idle 4 Years, 16 Days,* EVENING SUN, June 2, 1954; Letter from Warden Pepersack to Maryland Governor Theodor McKeldin dated June 14, 1957 (copy on file with author); James P. Connolly, *The Gas . . . Coughing . . . 13 Minutes . . . Dead,* NEWS POST, June 29, 1957; Appendix. In Utah and New Jersey, correctional officials are allowed to set the hour of execution. N.J. STAT. ANN. § 2C:49-5(c) (West Supp. 1992); UTAH CODE ANN. § 77-19-10(5) (1990).

5. Teresa Allen & Brad Breithaupt, *San Quentin Prepares to Resume Executions,* Gannett News Service, March 8, 1990 (LEXIS); Frank Green, *Inmate Executed for Killing 2 People,* RICHMOND TIMES-DISPATCH, Nov. 14, 1995 (WESTLAW); Donald Cabana, *The Executioner's Perspective, in* THE MACHINERY OF DEATH 169 (1995); DONALD CABANA, DEATH AT MIDNIGHT: THE CONFESSION OF AN EXECUTIONER 183 (1996).

6. S.D. CODIFIED LAWS ANN. §§ 23A-27A-15, 23A-27A-17 & 23A-27A-37 (1988); COLO. REV. STAT. § 16-11-404 (1990); MASS. ANN. LAWS ch. 279, § 59 (Law. Co-op. 1992); *In re* Storti, 60 N.E. 210 (Mass. 1901); WILLIAM J. BOWERS, LEGAL HOMICIDE: DEATH AS PUNISHMENT IN AMERICA, 1864- 1982, at 12 (1984); *see also* Robert Sech, *Hang 'Em High: A Proposal for Thoroughly Evaluating the Constitutionality of Execution Methods,* 30 VAL. U. L. REV. 381, 393, & n.68 (1995) ("The original plan was to isolate the prisoner in a special cell and to admit lethal gas to this cell while the prisoner was asleep.").

7. MD. ANN. CODE art. 27, § 75(e) (1992); 1951 Md. Laws, ch. 285, § 2; Dennis Cauchon, *Killer of Three Teens Executed in Maryland,* U.S.A. TODAY, May 17, 1994, at 3A; Paul Valentine, *Execution of Thanos Went "Like Clockwork,"* WASH. POST, May 18, 1994, at D1; Tom Stuckey, *Maryland Couldn't Keep Secret, Media Flocked to Execution,* TIMES-PICAYUNE (New Orleans), May 18, 1994, at A7; *see* Appendix (listing the time that John Thanos was executed).

8. OHIO SEN. J., at 376 (1885); OHIO HOUSE J., at 783–84 (1885); Ohio Laws 169–70 (1885); *At the State Capital,* CLEVE. PLAIN DEALER, Apr. 23, 1885, at 4, col. 5.

9. AKRON DAILY BEACON, Apr. 22, 1885, at 2, cols. 1–2; *Hangings in the Penitentiary,* CLEVE. PLAIN DEALER, Apr. 23, 1885, at 4, cols. 2–3; *Myers Tries It Again,* OHIO ST. J., Mar. 26, 1885, at 2, col. 4; H. M. FOGLE, THE PALACE OF DEATH 16–17 (1909); *Sealed,* OHIO ST. J., July 9, 1885, at 2, col. 4; *Victim No. 1,* MORROW COUNTY SENTINEL, Aug. 6, 1885, at 1.

10. 1889 Ind. Acts 192–195; *Executions Shall Be Secret,* INDIANAPOLIS NEWS, Mar. 5, 1889, at 3, col. 5; IND. SEN. J., at 93, 191, 320, 938, 1276 (1889); IND. HOUSE J., at 905–6, 987, 1064 (1889); 1 A BIOGRAPHICAL DIRECTORY OF THE INDIANA GENERAL ASSEMBLY 207 (1980) (Senator Henry Johnson); INDIANAPOLIS NEWS, Feb. 7, 1889, at 2, col. 1.

11. *Execution of the Death Penalty,* INDIANAPOLIS NEWS, Feb. 7, 1889, at 1, col. 8; IND. SEN. J., at 474–75, 938 (1889); A BIOGRAPHICAL DIRECTORY OF THE INDIANA GENERAL ASSEMBLY, *supra* note 10, at 98 (Senator Mark DeMotte); *James E. Stone Executed,* INDIANAPOLIS NEWS, Feb. 16, 1894, at 1, cols. 3–4.

12. Minn. Laws 1889, ch. 20; *The Smith Execution Law,* MINNEAPOLIS J., Feb. 14, 1906, at 4, col. 3; *Sheriff's Tea Party,* ST. PAUL DISPATCH, Feb. 14, 1906, at 10, col. 2; *Last Hours of Life,* MINNEAPOLIS TRIB., Oct. 19, 1894, at 1, col. 6; *Hanged in Private,* ST. PAUL DISPATCH, July 19, 1889, at 1, cols. 1–2. Prior to the passage of the Smith law, execution warrants in Minnesota required executions to take place during the day. For example, the death warrant for Nels Olsom Holong's 1888 execution required the execution to take place "between the hours of 9 A.M. and 5 o'clock P.M." at such place as Sheriff Brandenburg might select. Holong was led to the scaffold at 2:00 P.M. *No Hope for Holong,* FERGUS FALLS WEEKLY J. (Minn.), Apr. 12, 1888, at 5, col. 6; *All Is Over,* FERGUS FALLS WEEKLY J. (Minn.), Apr. 19, 1888, at 1–2; THEODORE BLEGEN, MINNESOTA: A HISTORY OF THE STATE 386 (1989) (Governor Andrew R. McGill); *Through a Trap,* ST. PAUL GLOBE, Oct. 23, 1891, at 1, col. 6 (describing Holong's crime); WALTER TRENERRY, MURDER IN MINNESOTA: A COLLECTION OF TRUE CASES 221 (1985) (same). Likewise, the 1885 death warrant for John Waisenen mandated that the execution take place between 9:00 A.M. and 5:00 P.M. *The Hanging at Duluth,* WEEKLY PIONEER PRESS (St. Paul), Sept. 3, 1885, at 4, col. 4; *Owned His Guilt,* MINNEAPOLIS J., Aug. 28, 1885, at 1, cols. 1–2; *Meets His Doom To-Day,* ST. PAUL PIONEER PRESS, Aug. 28, 1885, at 1, col. 4; *Expiated by the Rope,* DAILY PIONEER PRESS (St. Paul), Aug. 29, 1885, at 1, cols. 4–7, at 2, col. 2; TRENERRY, *supra,* at 220 (*citing* DULUTH NEWS TRIB., Aug. 29, 1885; DAILY PIONEER PRESS (St. Paul), Aug. 29, 1885); LEGISLATIVE MANUAL FOR THE STATE OF MINNESOTA 278 (1883) (S. C. McQuade).

13. ST. PAUL PIONEER PRESS, Mar. 12, 1889, at 6, col. 3; *A Quiet Day,* ST. PAUL PIONEER PRESS, Mar. 19, 1889, at 6, col. 4; *A Fight for Life,* ST. PAUL PIONEER PRESS, Mar. 22, 1889, at 2, cols. 1–2; MINNESOTA LEGISLATIVE MANUAL 295, 631, 637–38 (1889); MINN. HOUSE J. (1889); MINN. SEN. J. (1889); ALEXANDRIA POST (Minn.), Jan. 25, 1889, at 4, col. 4; ST. PAUL PIONEER PRESS, Feb. 22, 1889, at 6, col. 2; ST. PAUL PIONEER PRESS, Mar. 22, 1889, at 1, cols. 6–7; MINNEAPOLIS J., Mar. 22, 1889, at 1, cols. 1–4; *Disreputable Journalism,* MARTIN COUNTY SENTINEL (Minn.), July 26, 1889, at 4, cols. 1–2; *Death's Discount,* ST. PAUL PIONEER PRESS, Mar. 23, 1889, at 1, cols. 2–5; *Down to Death!,* MINNEAPOLIS J., Mar. 22, 1889, at 1, cols. 1–4; *Time Heals All Wounds,* MINNEAPOLIS J., Mar. 23, 1889, at 1, col. 1; *Echoes of the Barrett Execution,* MINNEAPOLIS J., Apr. 4, 1889, at 4, cols. 2–3; *Murderers Must Hang,* MINNEAPOLIS J., Apr. 2, 1889, at 1, col. 3; *Hanging Will Do,* MINNEAPOLIS TRIB., Apr. 3, 1889, at 2, col. 1; *Capital Punishment,* ST. PAUL PIONEER PRESS, Apr. 3, 1889, at 1, col. 5; *The House Decides That Capital Punishment Is Proper and Postpones Mr. Davis' Bill,* ST. PAUL PIONEER PRESS, Mar. 13, 1889, at 1, cols. 5–6; MINNESOTA LEGISLATIVE MANUAL 637–38 (1911).

14. *Will It Work?,* MINNEAPOLIS J., Apr. 24, 1889, at 8, col. 1; *Hard on the Reporters,* DAILY PIONEER PRESS (St. Paul), Apr. 24, 1889, at 3, cols. 1–2; DAILY PIONEER PRESS (St. Paul), Apr. 23, 1889, at 9, col. 2; MARTIN COUNTY SENTINEL (Minn.), May 10, 1889, at 4, col. 1. Interestingly, before the passage of John Day Smith's law, Senator Day's own newspaper printed a detailed account of the hanging of the Barrett brothers. *Two Lives Taken,* MARTIN COUNTY SENTINEL (Minn.), Mar. 29, 1889, at 2, cols. 5–6.

15. *Will It Work?, supra* note 14, at 8, col. 1; *A Change Required,* MINNEAPOLIS TRIB., Oct. 24, 1891, at 4, cols. 1–2; *see* Chapter 3 (containing pertinent text of the New York law).

16. JOHN DAY SMITH, THE HISTORY OF THE NINETEENTH REGIMENT OF MAINE VOLUNTEER INFANTRY 1862–1865, at 86–87, 123–24, 317, 336 (1909).

17. *Full of Horrors,* ST. PAUL PIONEER PRESS, Oct. 16, 1891, at 1, col. 2.

18. 1893 Conn. Laws 59–60; *Paid Penalty,* BOSTON GLOBE, Apr. 14, 1898, at 3 (convicted murderer executed "shortly after midnight" in Connecticut); Wyo. Laws, ch. 11, § 1 (1905); 1898 Mass. Acts 265–67; 1903 N.D. Laws, ch. 99, § 2.

19. *In Favor of Baldwin,* HARTFORD TIMES, Feb. 1, 1893, at 1, col. 1; *Legislation of '93,* HARTFORD TIMES, Feb. 16, 1893, at 2, col. 1; *Legislative Notes,* HARTFORD COURANT, Feb. 17, 1893, at 4, col. 4; *The Legislature,* HARTFORD COURANT, Feb. 17, 1893, at 8, col. 2; *Legislative Notes,* HARTFORD COURANT, Mar. 1, 1893, at 4, col. 4; *The Legislature,* HARTFORD COURANT, Mar. 1, 1893, at 8, col. 2; *The Legislature,* HARTFORD COURANT, Mar. 22, 1893, at 8, col. 1; *Legislation of '93,* HARTFORD TIMES, Feb. 28, 1893, at 1, col. 6; *The Legislature,* HARTFORD COURANT, May 18, 1893, at 8, col. 2; *Legislation of '93,* HARTFORD TIMES, Mar. 16, 1893, at 2, col. 1; *To Abolish the Gallows,* HARTFORD COURANT, Feb. 18, 1893, at 4, col. 4; *The House,* HARTFORD COURANT, Mar. 17, 1893, at 8, col. 1; *Legislative Notes,* HARTFORD COURANT, May 26, 1893, at 4, col. 4; *Murderers Must Hang,* NEW HAVEN REG., Mar. 16, 1893, at 1, cols. 2–3.

20. *Cronin,* HARTFORD TIMES, Dec. 18, 1894, at 6, col. 2; *Paid the Penalty,* HARTFORD TIMES, Dec. 18, 1894, at 1; *The Death Penalty,* HARTFORD TIMES, Dec. 18, 1894, at 6, cols. 3–4; *To Be Hanged at 1 A.M.,* NEW HAVEN REG., Dec. 17, 1894, at 1, cols. 1–2; *Execution of Cronin,* NEW HAVEN REG., Dec. 18, 1894, at 3, col. 2.

21. ROBERT ELLIOTT, AGENT OF DEATH: THE MEMOIRS OF AN EXECUTIONER 102, 104, 123, 128–29, 231, 258 (1940); Tex. Laws, ch. 51, § 1 (1923); 1923 Ala. Laws 759–62; S.D. Laws, ch. 135, § 2 (1939); Ky. Laws, ch. 145, § 1 (1944); La. Acts, ch. 160 (1952); DEL. CODE ANN. tit. 11, § 4209(f) (Supp. 1994); Del. Laws, ch. 206 (1994); *House Changes Execution Hours,* TIMES-PICAYUNE (New Orleans), June 19, 1952, at 16, col. 5; *Girl's Assailant Is Electrocuted,* TIMES-PICAYUNE (New Orleans), Sept. 26, 1952, at 6, col. 3; *Two Executed at Gretna Jail,* TIMES-PICAYUNE (New Orleans), July 12, 1952, at 24, col. 4. Alabama's law gave the prison warden the discretion to admit reporters to executions. 1923 Ala. Laws 759–62.

22. Iowa Stat., ch. 219, § 4890 (1860); ARK. CODE PRAC. CIV. & CRIM. CASES 320 (1869); Iowa Laws, ch. 165, at 151 (1878); TEX. PEN. CODE art. 826 (1885); ALBERT PIERREPOINT, EXECUTIONER: PIERREPOINT 143–44 (1974); AMBROSE SPENCER, A NARRATIVE OF ANDERSONVILLE, DRAWN FROM THE EVIDENCE ELICITED ON THE TRIAL OF HENRY WIRZ, THE JAILER 266–69 (1866); JAMES M. MCPHERSON, BATTLE CRY OF FREEDOM: THE CIVIL WAR ERA 795–802 (1988); *see also* David Lawrence Abney, Capital Punishment in Arizona (1863–1963) 16, 18, 20 (Aug. 1988) (Master's Thesis, Arizona State University); *Dock Driver Is Hanged for the Crime of Murder,* ARK. DEMOCRAT, Jan. 31, 1913, at 14, col. 5 (referencing execution shortly before noon in Arkansas); *Electric Chair Claims Second Victim in State,* ARK. DEMOCRAT, Dec. 12, 1913, at 1, col. 7 (referencing execution in Arkansas shortly before 10:00 A.M.); *Davis Hanged for Murder of Sweetheart,*

ARK. DEMOCRAT, Sept. 11, 1913, at 1, col. 4 (referencing execution in Arkansas at 6:39 A.M.); *Harris Put to Death,* HARTFORD COURANT, May 9, 1893, at 1, col. 5 (referencing execution in New York at 12:40 P.M.); ELLIOTT, *supra* note 21, at 41, 71–72 (New York executions used to take place at 11:40 A.M. and then 6:00 A.M.); *Almy Hanged at Concord,* HARTFORD COURANT, May 17, 1893, at 1, col. 2 (referencing execution in New Hampshire at 10:16 A.M.).

23. JAMES W. MARQUART, SHELDON EKLAND-OLSON, & JONATHAN R. SORENSEN, THE ROPE, THE CHAIR, AND THE NEEDLE: CAPITAL PUNISHMENT IN TEXAS, 1923–1990, at 19–20 (1994); *Last Minute Effort Fails to Save One,* HOUSTON CHRON., Feb. 8, 1924, at 1–2; *Executions Are First Under New State Law,* AUSTIN AM.-STATESMAN, Feb. 8, 1924, at 1–2; H. C. Waters, *How Five Died in Electric Chair,* HOUSTON POST, Feb. 8, 1924, at 1, 16; *Midnight Appeal Causes Pain in Harvest of Death,* AUSTIN AM.-STATESMAN, Feb. 7, 1924; Sharon Herbaugh, *Prison Board Decides Against Televising Executions,* Associated Press, Mar. 12, 1984 (PM cycle) (LEXIS); *Slayer of Eight Last Texas Black to Hang Legally,* TIMES-PICAYUNE (New Orleans), July 31, 1923, at 1, col. 6; *Four Negroes Executed in Death Chair,* AUSTIN AM.-STATESMAN, Feb. 8, 1924, at 1–2.

24. *Bill Providing for Electrocution Passed by Senate,* AUSTIN AM.-STATESMAN, May 10, 1923, at 2, col. 7; Tex. Gen. Laws 1923, ch. 51, § 14 (Sen. Bill No. 63); MARQUART, EKLAND-OLSON, & SORENSEN, *supra* note 23, at 13, 18; *Seng Pays Death Penalty,* NATRONA COUNTY TRIB. (Wyo.), June 19, 1905, at 3, col. 5; *Would Move the School,* CHEYENNE DAILY LEADER, Jan. 22, 1905, at 6, col. 1; *The Senate,* CHEYENNE DAILY LEADER, Jan. 27, 1905, at 6, col. 1; *Seng to Hang May 24th,* NATRONA COUNTY TRIB. (Wyo.), May 29, 1905, at 8, col. 5; *Discuss Importance of Bills,* CHEYENNE DAILY LEADER, Jan. 31, 1905, at 6, col. 2; Wyo. Laws, ch. 11, § 1 (1905).

25. Md. Laws, ch. 465 (1922); *First Hanging Is Held in State Penitentiary,* SUN (Baltimore), June 8, 1923, at 23, col. 5; *First Hanging in "Pen" Will Be Girl's Assailant,* SUN (Baltimore), Apr. 19, 1923.

26. N.D. Laws, ch. 99, at 119–22 (1903); *John Rooney Protested His Innocence on the Scaffold,* FARGO FORUM, Oct. 17, 1905, at 1, 6; *Rooney Sings Song on Bismarck Gallows,* GRAND FORKS DAILY HERALD, Oct. 18, 1905, at 1, col. 1; *The Last of Rooney,* BISMARCK DAILY TRIB., Oct. 20, 1905, at 2, col. 3. Even though the North Dakota legislation contained an "emergency" clause because of the "several persons in the state under sentence of death," North Dakota's governor signed the legislation into law on March 9, 1903, only after allowing William Ross to be hanged at Bottineau, North Dakota, on March 6, 1903. The governor did not want to postpone Ross's previously scheduled execution date. N.D. Laws, ch. 99, at 122 (1903); *The Hanging Bill,* FARGO FORUM, Mar. 4, 1903, at 1, col. 1; FARGO FORUM, Mar. 4, 1903, at 4, col. 5; *Rooney Is Modest,* BISMARCK DAILY TRIB., Mar. 10, 1903, at 2, col. 2; *Hanging Bill Is Signed,* BISMARCK DAILY TRIB., Mar. 10, 1903, at 1, col. 3. Although no North Dakota law required Ross to be hanged at night, he was executed at 1:15 A.M. *Hanged Cheerfully,* ST. PAUL PIONEER PRESS, Mar. 7, 1903, at 10, col. 3; *Ross Was Hanged,* FARGO FORUM, Mar. 6, 1903, at 1, col. 4; *Wm. Ross Hanged at Bottineau,* GRAND FORKS DAILY HERALD, Mar. 7, 1903, at 1, cols. 3–5.

27. *Rooney Pays the Penalty,* BISMARCK DAILY TRIB., Oct. 17, 1905, at 1; *Rooney's Last Day on Earth,* BISMARCK DAILY TRIB., Oct. 16, 1905, at 1, cols. 2–3; *John Rooney Will Be Hanged Tomorrow,* FARGO FORUM, Oct. 16, 1905, at 1, cols. 3–4; *Death Penalty,* GRAND FORKS DAILY HERALD, Oct. 17, 1905, at 1, col. 6; *Decently and in Order,* BISMARCK DAILY TRIB., Oct. 17, 1905, at 2, col. 1.

28. *Decently and in Order,* BISMARCK DAILY TRIB., Oct. 17, 1905, at 2, col. 1; BISMARCK DAILY TRIB., Oct. 16, 1905, at 2, col. 1.

29. EDWARD BAUMANN, MAY GOD HAVE MERCY ON YOUR SOUL: THE STORY OF THE ROPE AND THE THUNDERBOLT 26, 269–74, 312 (1993); Lewey Robinson, *Negro Slayer Executed, First to Die in Chair in History of Alabama,* STAR (Anniston, Ala.), Apr. 9, 1927, at 1; BOWERS, *supra* note 6, at 399; 1923 Ala. Laws 759–62; S.D. Laws, ch. 135 (1939); *Liquor Store Murder in 1945 Set Trap Which Led to Chair for George Sitts, Ex-Boxer* (undated newspaper article on file with author); *Two Officers Gunned Down, 1946* (undated article on file with author).

30. *Governor Signs Companion Bills,* PIERRE DAILY CAPITAL-J. (S.D.), Jan. 27, 1939, at 1; *Death Penalty Bill Ready for Executive O.K.,* PIERRE DAILY CAPITAL-J. (S.D.), Jan. 26, 1939, at 1; *Senate Approves Capital Punishment,* PIERRE DAILY CAPITAL-J. (S.D.), Jan. 25, 1939, at 1–2; *House Approves Capital Punishment,* PIERRE DAILY CAPITAL-J. (S.D.), Jan. 21, 1939, at 1; *Senate Puts O.K. on Code; House Passes Three Bills,* PIERRE DAILY CAPITAL-J. (S.D.), Jan. 17, 1939, at 1; *Capital Punishment,* PIERRE DAILY CAPITAL-J. (S.D.), Jan. 16, 1939, at 2; John F. Galliher, Gregory Ray, & Brent Cook, *Abolition and Reinstatement of Capital Punishment During the Progressive Era and Early 20th Century,* 83 J. CRIM. L. & CRIMINOLOGY 538, 572–73 (1992); *Death Penalty Scheduled for Action in House,* PIERRE DAILY CAPITAL-J. (S.D.), Jan. 20, 1939, at 1–2; *Capital Punishment Restored,* PIERRE DAILY CAPITAL-J. (S.D.), Jan. 20, 1939, at 2, col. 1.

31. Mass. Acts, ch. 326 (1898); MASS. HOUSE J. 611 (1898); *Death Penalty,* BOSTON GLOBE, Mar. 23, 1898, at 7, col. 1; *Passed the House,* WORCESTER DAILY SPY, Mar. 23, 1898, at 9, col. 1; *Storti Dies in the Chair,* BOSTON GLOBE, Dec. 17, 1901, at 1, cols. 5–6 (Luigi Storti electrocuted at 12:30 A.M.); *He Pays the Penalty,* BOSTON GLOBE, Dec. 24, 1901, at 1, col. 8 (Franciszek Umilian electrocuted at 12:20 A.M.); *Cassels' Life Ends,* SPRINGFIELD UNION, May 6, 1902 (John Cassels electrocuted at 12:40 A.M.); Note from Watt Espy, Director, Capital Punishment Research Project, Headland, Ala. (indicating that hangings under prior law occurred during the day); *Electrocuted at Midnight,* BOSTON EVENING TRANSCRIPT, Dec. 17, 1901, at 14, cols. 4–5; *Another Execution,* BOSTON EVENING TRANSCRIPT, Dec. 24, 1901, at 7, col. 1; BOSTON EVENING TRANSCRIPT, Apr. 14, 1898, at 4, col. 1. The Massachusetts law was passed amid agitation for the abolition of capital punishment. *E.g., Against Capital Punishment,* BOSTON EVENING TRANSCRIPT, Feb. 5, 1898, at 13, col. 3; *The Divine Right to Kill,* BOSTON EVENING TRANSCRIPT, Feb. 5, 1898, at 15, col. 6.

32. *Execution Day in "Old Mexico" as Described by a Woman,* ARK. DEMOCRAT, Sept. 5, 1913, at 7, cols. 2–3; ROBERT CHRISTOPHE, THE EXECUTIONERS: A HISTORY OF THE SANSON FAMILY, PUBLIC EXECUTIONERS IN FRANCE FROM 1688 TO 1847, at 156 (1961); PIERREPOINT, *supra* note 22, at 208; BARBARA LEVY, LEGACY OF DEATH 224–44 (1973); GEOFFREY

ABBOTT, LORDS OF THE SCAFFOLD: A HISTORY OF THE EXECUTIONER 101–2, 139, 146–47 (1991); HENRI SANSON, EXECUTIONERS ALL: MEMOIRS OF THE SANSON FAMILY FROM PRIVATE NOTES AND DOCUMENTS 1688–1847, at 104–11, 188, 232–34, 240, 243 (1962); JOHN LAURENCE, A HISTORY OF CAPITAL PUNISHMENT 174, 193, 208, 210 (1960); ALFRED MARKS, TYBURN TREE: ITS HISTORY AND ANNALS 191, 226, 266 (1908); *Leaders of Riot Are Executed,* SPOKESMAN-REVIEW (Spokane, Wash.), Apr. 15, 1909, at 14, cols. 5–6 (describing summary executions "at daybreak" in Mexico); Report of the Capital Punishment Commission, 1695–97 (1866). Capital punishment was not abolished in France until 1981. Executions in England at the Tyburn Tree gallows generally took place at midday. When executions were moved to outside the Newgate prison in 1783, executions were conducted at 9:00 A.M. Summertime executions were scheduled for 7:00 A.M. The timing of executions was changed so that the crowds would not become too restless. Steven Wilf, *Imagining Justice: Aesthetics and Public Executions in Late Eighteenth-Century England,* 52 YALE J.L. & HUMAN. 51, 53, 67 & n.38 (1993); JAMES BLAND, THE COMMON HANGMAN: ENGLISH AND SCOTTISH HANGMEN BEFORE THE ABOLITION OF PUBLIC EXECUTIONS 55–56, 110–11, 154 (1984).

33. John D. Bessler, *Televised Executions and the Constitution: Recognizing a First Amendment Right of Access to State Executions,* 45 FED. COMM. L.J. 355, 368–72 (1993); Bill Hazlett, *3rd Person Put to Death in 12 Years,* L.A. TIMES, Oct. 22, 1977, at 1, col. 6; William Rempel, *Killer of Four Executed in Indiana,* L.A. TIMES, Mar. 9, 1981, at 1, col. 5; *see* Appendix.

Chapter Five

1. *See* Chapters 3 & 4. The text of Chapter 5 is derived largely from a law review article that the author published in 1996. John D. Bessler, *The "Midnight Assassination Law" and Minnesota's Anti–Death Penalty Movement, 1849–1911,* 22 WM. MITCHELL L. REV. 577 (1996).

2. Minn. Laws 1889, ch. 20.

3. *Upon the Scaffold High,* LITTLE FALLS TRANSCRIPT (Minn.), July 19, 1889, at 3; *The Last of Bulow,* LITTLE FALLS TRANSCRIPT (Minn.), July 26, 1889, at 3, col. 5; Execution Records, Box 1 (available at the Minnesota Historical Society); *see also The Drop Falls,* DAILY PIONEER PRESS (St. Paul), July 18, 1889, at 1, col. 3 ("Sheriff Rasicot has faithfully endeavored to carry out the new Smith law to the very letter, and no one was given tickets of admission to the execution except those specifically mentioned in . . . that law."); *Hanged in Private,* ST. PAUL DISPATCH, July 19, 1889, at 1, col. 3 ("Sheriff Rasicot was firm in his determination to live up to the requirements of the Smith law, and not a single newspaper man was allowed to enter the place of execution.").

4. *The Last of Bulow,* LITTLE FALLS TRANSCRIPT (Minn.), July 26, 1889, at 3, col. 5 (referencing the editorial opinion of the *Brainerd Journal*); LITTLE FALLS TRANSCRIPT (Minn.), July 19, 1889, at 3, col. 1; ALEXANDRIA POST (Minn.), July 26, 1889, at 1, col. 4.

5. *Hanged in Private,* ST. PAUL DISPATCH, July 19, 1889, at 1, cols. 1–2; *A "Morbid" Law,* ST. PAUL DISPATCH, July 19, 1889, at 2, cols. 1–2.

6. *John Day and His Law,* LITTLE FALLS TRANSCRIPT (Minn.), July 26, 1889, at 2, col. 3; *John Day Smith Succumbs at 88,* MINNEAPOLIS TRIB., Mar. 6, 1933, at 2, cols. 4–6.

7. *Disreputable Journalism,* MARTIN COUNTY SENTINEL (Minn.), July 26, 1889, at 4, cols. 1–2.

8. *Executed,* MOORHEAD DAILY NEWS (Minn.), Sept. 20, 1889, at 1, cols. 1–3; *Execution of Thomas Brown,* MOORHEAD DAILY NEWS (Minn.), Sept. 19, 1889, at 4, col. 4; *Execution of Thomas Brown,* MOORHEAD DAILY NEWS (Minn.), Sept. 13, 1889, at 4, col. 2; *Gone to His Doom,* ST. PAUL DISPATCH, Sept. 20, 1889, at 1, cols. 1–2.

9. *Through the Trap,* ST. PAUL PIONEER PRESS, June 27, 1890, at 1, cols. 4–5; *Hanged Until Dead,* REDWOOD REVEILLE (Redwood Falls, Minn.), Oct. 17, 1891, at 3, col. 3; *Hanged Till Dead,* MINNEAPOLIS TRIB., Oct. 23, 1891, at 1, cols. 5–7; *Paid the Penalty,* PINE COUNTY PIONEER (Pine City, Minn.), June 27, 1890, at 1, 8; Execution Records, Box 1 (available at the Minnesota Historical Society). The death warrant for William Rose, signed on September 10, 1891, called for the hanging to be conducted in accordance with the John Day Smith law. Execution Records, Boxes 1 & 2 (available at the Minnesota Historical Society); THEODORE BLEGEN, MINNESOTA: A HISTORY OF THE STATE 659 (1989) (Governor William R. Merriam).

10. *Full of Horrors,* ST. PAUL PIONEER PRESS, Oct. 16, 1891, at 1, cols. 1–3; *The Death March,* MINNEAPOLIS TRIB., Oct. 16, 1891, at 1, cols. 5–6; *Hanged Until Dead, supra* note 9, at 3, col. 3; *More in Detail,* MINNEAPOLIS TRIB., Oct. 17, 1891, at 1, cols. 3–4; *Rose Twice Hanged,* ST. PAUL PIONEER PRESS, Oct. 17, 1891, at 1, cols. 1–2; *"Those Fresh Young Reporters,"* REDWOOD REVEILLE (Redwood Falls, Minn.), Oct. 31, 1891, at 3, cols. 4–5; Execution Records, Box 1 (available at the Minnesota Historical Society); *Bungling, Shocking!,* ST. PAUL GLOBE, Oct. 17, 1891, at 1, col. 1; *Dropped to Death,* ST. PAUL GLOBE, Oct. 16, 1891, at 1, col. 1; *Caught in an Old Trick,* MINNEAPOLIS TRIB., Oct. 17, 1891, at 4, col. 2; *It Sometimes Happens,* ST. PAUL PIONEER PRESS, Oct. 17, 1891, at 4, col. 2; *News of the Hanging,* ST. PAUL GLOBE, Oct. 18, 1891, at 4, col. 3; *Getting Out of a Hole,* ST. PAUL PIONEER PRESS, Oct. 19, 1891, at 4, col. 3.

11. PINE COUNTY PIONEER (Pine City, Minn.), July 4, 1890, at 1, col. 2.

12. *Rose Twice Hanged, supra* note 10, at 1, col. 2.

13. *Rosa Bray Avenged,* ST. PAUL PIONEER PRESS, Oct. 23, 1891, at 1, cols. 1–2; *Hanged Till Dead, supra* note 9, at 1, cols. 5–7; *Rose's Footsteps,* DAILY PIONEER PRESS (St. Paul), Oct. 19, 1891, at 1, cols. 1–2; Execution Records, Box 1 (available at the Minnesota Historical Society); *Goheen Is Buried,* ST. PAUL GLOBE, Oct. 24, 1891, at 1, col. 1; *Through a Trap,* ST. PAUL GLOBE, Oct. 23, 1891, at 1, col. 1; *A Change Required,* MINNEAPOLIS TRIB., Oct. 24, 1891, at 4, cols. 1–2; *Another Strangling,* ST. PAUL PIONEER PRESS, Oct. 24, 1891, at 4, col. 2.

14. MINN. HOUSE J., at 31, 107, 192, 202 (1897) (H.F. No. 1); MINN. SEN. J., at 186, 190 (1897) (H.F. No. 1); *Four Bills Introduced,* ST. PAUL PIONEER PRESS, Jan. 8, 1897, at 2, col. 4; *Salaries Must Be Reduced,* ST. PAUL PIONEER PRESS, Jan. 28, 1897, at 3, col. 4; *The House,* ST. PAUL PIONEER PRESS, Feb. 6, 1897, at 1, col. 6; *Two Houses Get Together,* ST. PAUL PIONEER PRESS, Feb. 6, 1897, at 2, cols. 3–4; *Prevented the Slaughter,* ST. PAUL PIONEER PRESS, Feb. 7, 1897, at 10, col. 3; PORTRAIT GALLERY OF THE TWENTY-NINTH LEGISLATURE OF THE STATE OF MINNESOTA 110 (1895).

15. *Ready for the Drop*, DULUTH DAILY NEWS, Oct. 19, 1894, at 1, cols. 2–5, 2; *Nearing Their End*, DULUTH NEWS TRIB., Oct. 18, 1894, at 1, col. 4; *Well Rid of Gottschalk*, ST. PAUL PIONEER PRESS, July 22, 1905, at 6, cols. 2–3; Execution Records, Box 1 (available at the Minnesota Historical Society); *The Gallows Tree Bears Its Fruit*, ST. PAUL PIONEER PRESS, Oct. 19, 1894, at 1–2; *The Debt Is Paid*, ST. PAUL PIONEER PRESS, Oct. 19, 1894, at 4, col. 2; *Last Hours of Life*, MINNEAPOLIS TRIB., Oct. 19, 1894, at 1, col. 6, at 4, col. 4; *Paid the Penalty*, MINNEAPOLIS TRIB., Oct. 20, 1894, at 3, col. 1; *see also* Chapters 3 & 4 (discussing *Holden v. Minnesota*).

16. WALTER TRENERRY, MURDER IN MINNESOTA: A COLLECTION OF TRUE CASES vi (preface), 126, 135–54 (1985); Minnesota v. Hayward, 62 Minn. 114 (1895); Minnesota v. Hayward, 62 Minn. 474 (1895); *One Juror in Addition*, ST. PAUL PIONEER PRESS, Jan. 23, 1895, at 6, cols. 1–2; *Many Were Called*, ST. PAUL PIONEER PRESS, Jan. 24, 1895, at 6, cols. 1–2; *Hayward's Salvation*, ST. PAUL PIONEER PRESS, Jan. 30, 1895, at 6, col. 1; *"He's a Liar," Says Harry*, ST. PAUL PIONEER PRESS, Mar. 3, 1895, at 3, col. 1, at 6, col. 1 (summarizing a portion of John Day Smith's role at Hayward's trial); *Hemp for Hayward*, ST. PAUL PIONEER PRESS, Mar. 9, 1895, at 1, 6 (same); *Sentenced to Be Hanged*, ST. PAUL PIONEER PRESS, Mar. 12, 1895, at 1, cols. 1–2 (same); *Harry Expects Conviction*, ST. PAUL PIONEER PRESS, Mar. 5, 1895, at 6, cols. 1–2 (John Day Smith comments on the weakness of the state's case); *Judge J. D. Smith Dies At Age 88, Funeral Tuesday*, MINNEAPOLIS J., Mar. 6, 1933, at 9, col. 2 (containing brief biographical sketch of John Day Smith); *The Smith Execution Law*, MINNEAPOLIS J., Feb. 14, 1906, at 4, col. 3. Badly overworked on the bench, Smith had to take refuge with his daughter in Berkeley, California, after suffering his "nervous breakdown." *Judge J. D. Smith Dies at Age of 88, Funeral Tuesday, supra*, at 9, 11; *John Day Smith Succumbs at 88, supra* note 6, at 2, cols. 4–6; *His Idea Started Glen Lake Farm*, MINNEAPOLIS J., Sept. 27, 1931, at 3, cols. 1–2; *Judge John Day Smith III: Jurist Suffers from a Nervous Breakdown—He Will Go to California*, MINNEAPOLIS TRIB., Feb. 22, 1911, at 9, cols. 4–5; *Judge Smith's Work Divided*, MINNEAPOLIS TRIB., Feb. 24, 1911, at 11, col. 1; MINNESOTA LEGISLATIVE MANUAL 629 (1911); JOHN DAY SMITH, CASES ON CONSTITUTIONAL LAW (1897) (preface). Smith served as a Hennepin County district court judge from January 2, 1905, until he resigned in 1913, "when it became evident that he could not resume his judicial duties" due to his "disabling illness." *Judge John Day Smith, 1845–1933*, at 1 (memorial prepared by John Day Smith's life-long friend, E. F. Waite, and presented on February 3, 1934) (available at the Minnesota Historical Society, Minneapolis Bar Association Papers 1916 to 1934); MINNESOTA LEGISLATIVE MANUAL 104 (1911); *John Day Smith Endorsed*, MINNEAPOLIS TRIB., Nov. 5, 1904, at 11, col. 7; *Brooks Leads Judicial Vote*, MINNEAPOLIS TRIB., Nov. 10, 1904, at 2, col. 3; *Holt Led the Judges*, MINNEAPOLIS J., Nov. 11, 1904, at 6, col. 2; *How Hennepin's Votes Were Cast*, MINNEAPOLIS J., Nov. 15, 1904, at 5, col. 2. After his resignation, John Day Smith's "days were spent in the retirement of semi-invalidism." "He died suddenly and peacefully at his home March 5, 1933, at the age of eighty-eight." Those who knew him best believed that Judge Smith's breakdown in 1911 was due to overwork. *Judge John Day Smith, 1845–1933, supra*, at 1, 5–6.

17. *Judge J. D. Smith Dies at Age of 88, Funeral Tuesday, supra* note 16, at 9, 11; *Hanging Hayward,* ST. PAUL PIONEER PRESS, Dec. 3, 1895, at 6, col. 2; *Death Warrant for Hayward,* ST. PAUL PIONEER PRESS, Dec. 8, 1895, at 6, cols. 4–5; *A Noose Ready for His Neck,* MINNEAPOLIS TRIB., Dec. 8, 1895, at 1, 11; *Hayward's Death Warrant,* MINNEAPOLIS TRIB., Dec. 8, 1895, at 3, col. 3; *Hayward's Latest Trick,* ST. PAUL PIONEER PRESS, Dec. 10, 1895, at 1–2; *John Day Smith Pleads,* MINNEAPOLIS TRIB., Dec. 10, 1895, at 4, col. 2; Execution Records, Box 1 (available at the Minnesota Historical Society).

18. TRENERRY, *supra* note 16, at 152; *The Awful Curse of a Brother,* MINNEAPOLIS TRIB., Dec. 9, 1895, at 2, col. 2; *Hayward's Latest Trick, supra* note 17, at 1–2; *Has But a Single Day to Live,* MINNEAPOLIS TRIB., Dec. 10, 1895, at 1, 3; *Waning!,* MINNEAPOLIS TRIB., Dec. 11, 1895, at 2–3; *Watchers Outside,* ST. PAUL PIONEER PRESS, Dec. 11, 1895, at 2, cols. 5–6; Execution Records, Box 1 (available at the Minnesota Historical Society).

19. *"I Die Game," Says Harry,* ST. PAUL PIONEER PRESS, Dec. 11, 1895, at 1–2; *The Wages of Sin,* MINNEAPOLIS TRIB., Dec. 11, 1895, at 1, cols. 1–7; *Hanging Hayward, supra* note 17, at 6, col. 2; *Hayward Is Laid to Rest,* ST. PAUL PIONEER PRESS, Dec. 12, 1895, at 6, cols. 2–4; *The Sorrow of His Mother,* MINNEAPOLIS TRIB., Dec. 12, 1895, at 1, 7; *The Hayward Gallows,* MINNEAPOLIS TRIB., Dec. 15, 1895, at 16, cols. 5–6; *The Voice of Hayward,* MINNEAPOLIS TRIB., Dec. 18, 1895, at 7, col. 4; *Judge John Day Smith, 1845–1933, supra* note 16, at 3, 6 (referencing Smith's religiosity); *Exit Hayward,* ST. PAUL PIONEER PRESS, Dec. 11, 1895, at 4, col. 2; *A Good Law,* MINNEAPOLIS TRIB., Dec. 12, 1895, at 6, col. 1.

20. *John Day Smith—Part II,* ECCO NEWS, at 11 (Sept. 1979) (available at the Minneapolis Public Library, Special Collections); TRENERRY, *supra* note 16, at 223–26 (listing nine of the ten executions); *Crawford Calmly Goes to Execution,* DAILY PIONEER PRESS (St. Paul), Dec. 6, 1905, at 11, col. 3; *Paid the Penalty,* SHERBURNE COUNTY STAR NEWS (Elk River, Minn.), Dec. 7, 1905, at 5, cols. 3–4; SHERBURNE COUNTY STAR NEWS (Elk River, Minn.), Dec. 14, 1905, at 5, col. 2; *Crawford's Day of Doom,* DAILY PIONEER PRESS (St. Paul), Dec. 5, 1905, at 10, col. 2; *Hanged,* MINNEAPOLIS TRIB., Dec. 5, 1905, at 1, col. 7; *The Revenge of a Newspaper,* MINNEAPOLIS J., Dec. 5, 1905, at 1, col. 4; *Sheriff to Obey the Law,* ST. PAUL DISPATCH, Feb. 10, 1906, at 24, col. 4; BLEGEN, *supra* note 9, at 457–58 (discussing Governor John A. Johnson's gubernatorial administration); Execution Records, Box 2 (available at the Minnesota Historical Society). Legislative attempts to move executions to the state prison at Stillwater always failed. *E.g.,* MINN. HOUSE J., at 263, 529–30, 536, 600–601, 621–22, 638, 1589 (1903) (H.F. No. 285); MINN. SEN. J., at 493–95, 840, 1369 (1903) (H.F. No. 285); *Murderers May Be Electrocuted,* DULUTH NEWS TRIB., Mar. 6, 1903, at 1, col. 1. For example, in 1899, a bill was introduced in the Minnesota House of Representatives to conduct executions at the state prison before the hour of sunrise. *Introduction of Electrocution,* ST. PAUL DISPATCH, Jan. 5, 1899, at 9, col. 3; MINN. HOUSE J., at 33, 212 (1899); *Execution of Murderers,* ST. PAUL DISPATCH, Feb. 7, 1899, at 3, col. 4 ("The . . . bill provides the hanging shall occur within the walls of the [state] prison between sundown and sunrise, within an enclosure screened from public gaze."). However, the house voted to

"indefinitely postpone" that legislative proposal on February 28, 1899. MINN. HOUSE J., at 212, 435 (1899).

21. *Pryde Will Hang,* BRAINERD DISPATCH (Minn.), July 17, 1896, at 4, col. 5; *Execution of John E. Pryde,* BRAINERD DISPATCH (Minn.), July 24, 1896, at 1; *John E. Pryde Is Hanged,* DAILY PIONEER PRESS (St. Paul), July 23, 1896, at 4, col. 7; Execution Records, Box 1 (available at the Minnesota Historical Society); *Kelly's Expiation,* ST. PAUL PIONEER PRESS, Mar. 23, 1897, at 1, col. 7; *Sentenced to Death,* ST. PAUL PIONEER PRESS, Jan. 8, 1897, at 5, col. 1; *John Moshik Dies,* MINNEAPOLIS J., Mar. 18, 1898, at 2, cols. 2–5; *Lemke's Murder Is Avenged,* DAILY PIONEER PRESS (St. Paul), Mar. 18, 1898, at 6, cols. 1–3; *Oleson Dies on the Gallows,* ST. PAUL PIONEER PRESS, Mar. 20, 1903, at 6, col. 4; *A Life for a Life,* AITKIN AGE (Minn.), Mar. 24, 1903, at 4, col. 1; *Henderson Prays for Prisoners,* DULUTH NEWS TRIB., Mar. 2, 1903, at 5, col. 1; *Slayer of Ida M'Cormack Dies Upon the Scaffold,* DULUTH NEWS TRIB., Mar. 6, 1903, at 1, cols. 5–7; *Dies at End of Noose,* DAILY PIONEER PRESS (St. Paul), Mar. 6, 1903, at 1, col. 7; *Chounard, A Wife Murderer, Dies,* MINNEAPOLIS J., Aug. 30, 1904, at 5, col. 2.

22. *Wallert Is Hanged,* THE HUB (Gaylord, Minn.), Apr. 15, 1901, at 6, col. 5; *Wallert Hanged,* DAILY PIONEER PRESS (St. Paul), Mar. 29, 1901, at 1, col. 5; *Wallert Hanged,* THE HUB (Gaylord, Minn.), Mar. 29, 1901, at 4, cols. 2–3; *Rosa Mixa Is Avenged,* WEEKLY VALLEY HERALD (Chaska, Minn.), Feb. 20, 1902, at 1, cols. 1–5; *Tapper Pays the Penalty,* ST. PAUL PIONEER PRESS, Feb. 18, 1902, at 10, col. 3; *Ott Is Hanged,* MINNEAPOLIS TRIB., Oct. 28, 1898, at 1, col. 5; *Joe Ott Hung,* GRANITE FALLS J. (Minn.), Oct. 20, 1898, at 5, cols. 4–6; GRANITE FALLS J. (Minn.), Oct. 27, 1898, at 4, cols. 2–3 (picture of the scaffold on which Joseph Ott was hung); MINNEAPOLIS TRIB., Oct. 21, 1898, at 3, cols. 2–3 (same); Execution Records, Box 1 (available at the Minnesota Historical Society) (affidavit of Yellow Medicine County Sheriff Joseph Schwalier, dated Oct. 20, 1898, states that the execution took place "between the hours of one and two o'clock in the morning" on October 20, 1898); *John Day Smith—Part II, supra* note 20, at 11.

23. *No Last Resting Place for Gottschalk's Body,* ST. PAUL PIONEER PRESS, July 22, 1905, at 1, cols. 2–3; *Well Rid of Gottschalk, supra* note 15, at 6, cols. 2–3; *Gottschalk His Own Executioner,* ST. PAUL PIONEER PRESS, July 20, 1905, at 1, cols. 6–7; *Gottschalk's End to Be the Gallows,* ST. PAUL PIONEER PRESS, May 12, 1905, at 1, 3; *Fix Early Date for Hanging,* ST. PAUL PIONEER PRESS, May 15, 1905, at 2, col. 1; *Gottschalk to Be Hanged Aug. 8,* ST. PAUL PIONEER PRESS, May 16, 1905, at 2, col. 2; *see also State Executions,* ST. PAUL PIONEER PRESS, Feb. 2, 1907, at 6, col. 2 ("It was freely asserted and was apparently substantiated by evidence that one sheriff in this county had issued a large enough quantity of tickets of admission to the approaching show to make it economical to print them. Only the suicide of the condemned man prevented a carnival.").

24. *Executions at Penitentiary,* ST. PAUL PIONEER PRESS, Aug. 10, 1905, at 2, col. 6; *Well Rid of Gottschalk, supra* note 15, at 6, cols. 2–3.

25. *Williams Is Doomed to Gallows,* ST. PAUL PIONEER PRESS, May 20, 1905, at 1, col. 7; TRENERRY, *supra* note 16, at 160, 163 (*citing* ST. PAUL DISPATCH, May 12, 1905); Minnesota v. Williams, 96 Minn. 351, 354 (1905); *Must Face the Gallows,* ST. PAUL DISPATCH,

Feb. 12, 1906, at 7, cols. 2–3 (noting that a federal district court judge refused to grant Williams's application for a writ of habeas corpus).

26. *Newspaper Indicted for Giving News,* ST. PAUL PIONEER PRESS, Mar. 3, 1906, at 1, col. 7; *Must Face the Gallows, supra* note 25, at 7, cols. 2–3; *Governor Will Quiz Miesen,* ST. PAUL PIONEER PRESS, Feb. 14, 1906, at 3, col. 2.

27. *Sheriff to Obey the Law,* ST. PAUL DISPATCH, Feb. 10, 1906, at 24, col. 4; *Must Face the Gallows, supra* note 25, at 7, cols. 2–3.

28. *Goes to Gallows in Dead of Night,* MINNEAPOLIS J., Feb. 13, 1906, at 6, col. 2; ST. PAUL DISPATCH, Feb. 12, 1906, at 1 (diagram depicting Williams's route to the gallows); *Sheriff to Obey the Law, supra* note 27, at 24, col. 4 (picture of gallows in the sub-basement); *Displayed His Nerve to the Very Last,* ST. PAUL DISPATCH, Feb. 13, 1906, at 3, cols. 2–5; Execution Records, Box 2 (available at the Minnesota Historical Society) (affidavit of Sheriff Anton Miesen, dated Feb. 14, 1906, states that the hanging occurred at "12:31 A.M. in the basement of the County Jail"); *Sheriff Will Kill Williams,* ST. PAUL PIONEER PRESS, Feb. 12, 1906, at 4, col. 7.

29. *Williams Is Hanged at County Jail,* ST. PAUL PIONEER PRESS, Feb. 13, 1906, at 1, col. 7; *Displayed His Nerve to the Very Last, supra* note 28, at 3, cols. 2–5; *This Is Murder: I Am Innocent,* ST. PAUL DAILY NEWS, Feb. 13, 1906, at 1, col. 1. The *St. Paul Daily News* also printed Williams's last words, which were: "Gentleman, you are witnessing an illegal hanging. This is a legal murder. I am accused of killing Johnny Keller. He was the best friend I ever had, and I hope I meet him in the other world. I never had improper relations with him. I am resigned to my fate. Goodbye." *Id.*

30. *Displayed His Nerve to the Very Last, supra* note 28, at 3, col. 2; *Sheriff's Tea Party,* ST. PAUL DISPATCH, Feb. 14, 1906, at 10, col. 2.

31. *The Smith Execution Law,* MINNEAPOLIS J., Feb. 14, 1906, at 4, col. 3.

32. *What Should Result,* ST. PAUL DISPATCH, Feb. 28, 1906, at 10, col. 1; *see also An Unsafe Law and the Remedy,* ST. PAUL PIONEER PRESS, Mar. 6, 1906, at 6, col. 2.

33. *Well Rid of Gottschalk, supra* note 15, at 6, cols. 2–3 ("It is to be regretted that the last legislature did not pass that bill for the execution of all criminals at Stillwater, where the high character of the wardens would, as in New York State, be a guarantee that no seekers after sensation and none but those directly concerned in the execution would be present."); *Death by Electricity,* ST. PAUL PIONEER PRESS, Feb. 24, 1907, at 1, col. 7 (editorial section) ("The bill provides that all the executions shall take place at the state prison. A bill covering that feature was introduced some weeks ago by F. B. Phillips of St. Paul.").

34. *Governor Will Quiz Miesen, supra* note 26, at 3, col. 2; MINNESOTA LEGISLATIVE MANUAL 5–6 (1911) (obituary of Governor Johnson). The article entitled "The Only Newspaper Man Who Witnessed the Hanging," published in the *St. Paul Daily News,* reported that the execution was witnessed by thirty-two persons. ST. PAUL DAILY NEWS, Feb. 13, 1906.

35. *Won't Do a Thing to the Sheriff,* ST. PAUL PIONEER PRESS, Feb. 15, 1906, at 3, col. 3; *Newspaper Indicted for Giving News, supra* note 26, at 1, col. 7.

36. St. Paul Herald, Mar. 16, 1918, at 1, col. 1 (obituary of Anton Miesen); *Death Penalty Decried by State's Executive*, Minneapolis J., Feb. 25, 1906, at 7, col. 2; *St. Paul Newspapers Procure Indictments*, Minneapolis J., Mar. 4, 1906, at 5, col. 1; *Won't Do a Thing to the Sheriff, supra* note 35, at 3, col. 3. For whatever reason, Governor Johnson did not mention the subject of capital punishment in his annual message to the Minnesota legislature in 1907. *See* Inaugural Message of Governor John A. Johnson to the Legislature of Minnesota (available at the Minnesota Historical Society, Governors' Speeches and Messages).

37. *Protest to Prosecutor*, St. Paul Dispatch, Feb. 15, 1906, at 4, col. 2; *Goes After Papers*, St. Paul Pioneer Press, Feb. 20, 1906, at 2, col. 3; Trenerry, *supra* note 16, at 160; Men of Minnesota 53 (1902) (John W. Finehout); St. Paul City Directory (Volume D–K) (R. L. Polk & Co.'s 1906 ed.) (Emil W. Helmes listed as "Asst Corporation Atty" in "City Hall").

38. *Goes After Papers, supra* note 37, at 2, col. 3; *Newspaper Indicted for Giving News, supra* note 26, at 1, col. 7 ("Although the John Day Smith law has been in force for seventeen years, this is the first indictment of a newspaper under it, and as far as the records show the first time that the courts have taken notice of its violation, though the newspapers of the state have printed detailed accounts of every hanging that has taken place in the state since the law was passed."); *Newspapers Indicted*, Minneapolis J., Mar. 3, 1906, at 7, col. 4.

39. *Seeking to Curb Press*, St. Paul Dispatch, Mar. 3, 1906, at 7, col. 2; *Newspapers Indicted, supra* note 38, at 7, col. 4; *Newspaper Indicted for Giving News, supra* note 26, at 1, col. 7. The actual indictments can be found at the Minnesota Historical Society. Criminal Register I (Ramsey County), File No. 4695 (State of Minnesota v. Pioneer Press Co.), File No. 4696 (State of Minnesota v. Dispatch Prtg. Co.), File No. 4697 (State of Minnesota v. Daily News Publishing Co.).

40. *An Unsafe Law and the Remedy, supra* note 32, at 6, col. 2; *St. Paul Newspapers Procure Indictments, supra* note 36, at 5, col. 1.

41. *An Unsafe Law and the Remedy, supra* note 32, at 6, col. 2; *Newspaper Indicted for Giving News, supra* note 26, at 1, col. 7.

42. *Pioneer Press Enters Plea*, St. Paul Pioneer Press, Mar. 4, 1906, at 1, col. 4 (editorial section); St. Paul Pioneer Press, Mar. 3, 1906, at 6, col. 3.

43. *Seeking to Curb Press, supra* note 39, at 7, col. 2; *Papers Demur*, St. Paul Dispatch, Mar. 5, 1906, at 6, col. 1; State of Minnesota v. Pioneer Press Co., Case No. 100–173 (Certified Case), at 1–2, 4–9 (available at the Minnesota State Law Library); *Pioneer Press Enters Plea, supra* note 42, at 1, col. 4; *Papers to Test Law*, St. Paul Pioneer Press, Mar. 6, 1906, at 7, col. 4.

44. *Validity of Law Attacked*, St. Paul Dispatch, Mar. 10, 1906, at 9, col. 3.

45. *Muzzle Law Not Constitutional*, St. Paul Pioneer Press, Mar. 11, 1906, at 1, col. 7 (editorial section); Criminal Register I (Ramsey County), File No. 4695 (case certification), File No. 4696 (Demurrer to Indictment), File No. 4697 (Demurrer to Indictment).

46. *Muzzle Law Not Constitutional, supra* note 45, at 1, col. 7; *Validity of Law At-tacked, supra* note 44, at 9, col. 3; State of Minnesota v. Pioneer Press Co., Case No. 100–173 (Respondent's Brief), at 15, 21 (available at the Minnesota State Law Library). In a coincidental twist of fate, that same day in an unrelated case Judge John Day Smith, the author of the newspaper muzzle law, held a twenty-two-year-old newsboy in con-tempt of court for creating a disturbance in his courtroom. *Young Prisoner Affronts Court,* ST. PAUL PIONEER PRESS, Mar. 10, 1906, at 5, col. 7.

47. State of Minnesota v. Pioneer Press Co., Case No. 100–173 (Certified Case), at 2–3, 9–16 (available at the Minnesota State Law Library); *Muzzle Law Is Sustained,* ST. PAUL PIONEER PRESS, Apr. 17, 1906, at 2, cols. 5–6; *Law Is Held to Be Legal,* ST. PAUL DISPATCH, Apr. 16, 1906, at 1, col. 7; *Validity of Law Upheld by Court,* ST. PAUL DAILY NEWS, Apr. 16, 1906, at 1, col. 3; *Justice Bunn on the Bench,* ST. PAUL DISPATCH, Mar. 1, 1911, at 11, col. 1; Criminal Register I (Ramsey County), File Nos. 4696 & 4697 (case chronologies indicate that the cases against the *St. Paul Dispatch* and the *St. Paul Daily News* were stayed pending a final determination of the *Pioneer Press*'s case); *see also* TREN-ERRY, *supra* note 16, at 165.

48. State of Minnesota v. Pioneer Press Co., Case No. 100–173 (Brief of Appellant), at 12–16, 24 (available at the Minnesota State Law Library).

49. State of Minnesota v. Pioneer Press Co., Case No. 100–173 (Respondent's Brief), at 7–8, 15, 21 (available at the Minnesota State Law Library).

50. State v. Pioneer Press Co., 110 N.W. 867 (Minn. 1907); *Must Not Tell About Hangings,* ST. PAUL PIONEER PRESS, Feb. 22, 1907, at 5, col. 4.

51. *Newspapers Lose Appeal,* ST. PAUL DISPATCH, Feb. 21, 1907, at 1, col. 1 ("Today's decision sustains Judge Bunn and the case will now revert to the district court to be tried on its merits."); *Lid Forced Down on All Executions,* ST. PAUL DAILY NEWS, Feb. 21, 1907, at 3, col. 1; Criminal Register I (Ramsey County), File No. 4695 (containing case chronology, List of Jurors, Verdict, and Judgment); Criminal Register I (Ramsey County), File Nos. 4696 & 4697 (containing case chronologies).

52. *Publicity and Hangings,* ST. PAUL PIONEER PRESS, Feb. 23, 1907, at 6, col. 2; *see supra* note 20 (discussing attempts to move executions to Stillwater).

53. *To Abolish Capital Punishment,* ST. PAUL DISPATCH, Jan. 19, 1893, at 8, col. 1; MINN. HOUSE J., at 149, 371 (1891) (H.F. No. 222); *In the House,* DAILY PIONEER PRESS (St. Paul), Feb. 3, 1891, at 2, cols. 1–3; *Capital Punishment,* DAILY PIONEER PRESS (St. Paul), Feb. 27, 1891, at 2; MINN. HOUSE J., at 84 (1893) (H.F. No. 126); *Weary Legislators,* ST. PAUL PIONEER PRESS, Jan. 20, 1893, at 1, col. 1; MINN. HOUSE J., at 593–94, 889 (1893); *Capital Punishment,* MINNEAPOLIS J., Mar. 24, 1893, at 4, col. 3; ST. PAUL DIS-PATCH, Mar. 24, 1893, at 3, col. 4; ST. PAUL DISPATCH, Mar. 25, 1893, at 2, col. 3; MINN. SEN. J., at 620, 995 (1893); MINN. HOUSE J., at 64, 367, 581 (1895) (H.F. No. 94); *In the House,* ST. PAUL PIONEER PRESS, Jan. 24, 1895, at 1, col. 2; *Hemp for Hayward,* ST. PAUL PIONEER PRESS, Mar. 9, 1895, at 1, cols. 1–2; *Some May Be Woodchucks,* ST. PAUL PIONEER PRESS, Mar. 31, 1895, at 8, col. 1; MINN. HOUSE J., at 204, 221, 322–23, 330 (1895) (H.F. No. 371); *Will Please H. Hayward,* ST. PAUL PIONEER PRESS, Feb. 17, 1895, at 2, cols. 1–2; *Unfruitful Session,* ST. PAUL PIONEER PRESS, Mar. 3, 1895, at 9, cols. 1–2; *Hayward May*

Hang, ST. PAUL PIONEER PRESS, Mar. 5, 1895, at 6, cols. 3–4; MINN. HOUSE J., at 59, 120, 219–20 (1897) (H.F. No. 63); *House Will Work To-Day*, ST. PAUL PIONEER PRESS, Jan. 16, 1897, at 1–2; *Arbitration Commended*, ST. PAUL PIONEER PRESS, Jan. 29, 1897, at 3, cols. 2, 5; *We Will Still Hang*, ST. PAUL PIONEER PRESS, Feb. 10, 1897, at 2, cols. 3–5; WILLIAM P. EVERTS JR., STOCKWELL OF MINNEAPOLIS: A PIONEER OF SOCIAL AND POLITICAL CON-SCIENCE 69–72 (1996).

54. MINN. HOUSE J., at 104, 1007, 1119 (1901) (H.F. No. 114); *New House Bills*, MIN-NEAPOLIS J., Jan. 29, 1901, at 12, col. 2; *To Remove Death Penalty*, MINNEAPOLIS J., Jan. 29, 1901, at 12, col. 4; MINNESOTA LEGISLATIVE MANUAL 696 (1901); MINN. SEN. J., at 98 (1905) (S.F. No. 48); *Senate Session Remarkable for Nothing But New Measures*, MIN-NEAPOLIS J., Jan. 24, 1905, at 9, cols. 3–4; MINNESOTA LEGISLATIVE MANUAL 661, 677 (1905); MINN. HOUSE J., at 166 (1905) (H.F. No. 199); *Short Session*, MINNEAPOLIS J., Feb. 7, 1905, at 4, cols. 5–6; *Death Penalty Decried by State's Executive*, MINNEAPOLIS J., Feb. 25, 1906, at 7, col. 2; MINN. HOUSE J., at 166, 799, 1061–62, 1141, 1662 (1905) (H.F. No. 199). In the senate, Senator Alley's bill was referred to the Senate Judiciary Com-mittee, which reported it back on February 15 with the recommendation that it be amended to provide that the sentence for first-degree murder shall be death unless the judge or jury determined otherwise. That amendment was adopted, and the senate rec-ommended the bill's passage on February 21. MINN. SEN. J., at 98, 207–8, 238, 313, 1279 (1905); *Punishment for Murder*, MINNEAPOLIS J., Feb. 21, 1905, at 5, col. 1; *May Abolish Hanging*, MINNEAPOLIS J., Feb. 15, 1905, at 9, col. 4. As amended, Senator Alley's bill, al-though it never went any further, passed the senate on March 2 by a vote of 44–4. *Leg-islative Doings Today*, MINNEAPOLIS J., Mar. 2, 1905, at 4, col. 6; *Legislative Proceedings*, MINNEAPOLIS TRIB., Mar. 2, 1905, at 4, col. 5; *Bills Passed*, ST. PAUL PIONEER PRESS, Mar. 3, 1905, at 2, col. 6.

55. *Bills Introduced*, ST. PAUL PIONEER PRESS, Feb. 1, 1907, at 2, col. 2; *Bill to Abol-ish Death Penalty*, ST. PAUL PIONEER PRESS, Mar. 6, 1907, at 4, col. 3; *State Executions*, ST. PAUL PIONEER PRESS, Feb. 2, 1907, at 6, col. 2; *Hangings at State Prison*, ST. PAUL PI-ONEER PRESS, Feb. 1, 1907, at 2, col. 7; MINN. HOUSE J., at 161, 301, 1380–81, 1400, 1901 (1907) (H.F. No. 190); *Sheriff the Hangman*, ST. PAUL PIONEER PRESS, Apr. 13, 1907, at 5, col. 2; MINNESOTA LEGISLATIVE MANUAL 671 (1907) (containing brief biographical sketch of Frederick B. Phillips).

56. *In the House*, MINNEAPOLIS TRIB., Feb. 21, 1907, at 8, cols. 4–5 ("H.F. 473— Wright—Providing for the execution of criminals at the state penitentiary."); *Death by Electricity*, supra note 33, at 1, col. 7 ("A bill changing the method of execution of mur-derers introduced in the house last week by F. B. Wright of Minneapolis, provides that all executions shall be done with the electric chair."); *Bill to Abolish Death Penalty*, supra note 55, at 4, col. 3; MINN. HOUSE J., at 376, 1381–82, 1942 (1907) (H.F. No. 473); *Bills Introduced*, ST. PAUL DISPATCH, Feb. 20, 1905, at 5, cols. 5–6; *Bills Introduced*, ST. PAUL PIONEER PRESS, Feb. 21, 1907, at 5, col. 5; MINNESOTA LEGISLATIVE MANUAL 672 (1907) (containing brief biographical sketch of Fred B. Wright).

57. MINN. HOUSE J., at 551, 586–87, 1239 (1907) (H.F. No. 657); *Would Abolish Cap-ital Punishment*, MINNEAPOLIS TRIB., Mar. 7, 1907, at 9, col. 5; *Bills Introduced*, ST. PAUL

PIONEER PRESS, Mar. 7, 1907, at 4, col. 4; *To Stop Hangings*, ST. PAUL PIONEER PRESS, Mar. 8, 1907, at 2, col. 2; *Gallows Stay in Minnesota*, ST. PAUL PIONEER PRESS, Apr. 9, 1907, at 5, col. 3; MINNESOTA LEGISLATIVE MANUAL 675 (1907) (containing brief biographical sketch of Clarence B. Miller).

58.   MINN. HOUSE J., at 101, 386, 783 (1909); *Would Abolish Death Penalty*, ST. PAUL PIONEER PRESS, Jan. 20, 1909, at 6, col. 5; *Anti-Hanging Bill Again*, ST. PAUL DISPATCH, Jan. 19, 1909, at 5, col. 2; MINNESOTA LEGISLATIVE MANUAL 721–22 (1909) (containing brief biographical sketches of C. M. Bendixen and George A. MacKenzie); *Would Abolish Hanging*, ST. PAUL DISPATCH, Feb. 11, 1909, at 3, col. 2; *Death Penalty to Remain*, ST. PAUL DISPATCH, Mar. 9, 1909, at 3, cols. 4–5; *Will Not Abolish Hanging*, ST. PAUL PIONEER PRESS, Mar. 10, 1909, at 8, col. 6; Memorial of George MacKenzie, Dec. 6, 1948 (available at Nicollet County Historical Society).

59.   *To Abolish Death Penalty*, ST. PAUL DISPATCH, Dec. 10, 1910, at 9, col. 2; MEN OF MINNESOTA 186 (1915) (Richard D. O'Brien).

60.   Inaugural Message of Governor Adolph O. Eberhart to the Legislature of Minnesota (1911) (available at the Minnesota Historical Society, Governors' Speeches and Messages); MINN. SEN. J., at 14 (1911); MINN. HOUSE J., at 19–20 (1911); *Eberhart Address Longest on Record*, MINNEAPOLIS J., Jan. 4, 1911, at 1, col. 1.

61.   *Ask Inquiry Into Governor's Delay*, MINNEAPOLIS J., Feb. 23, 1911, at 1, col. 7; MINNESOTA LEGISLATIVE MANUAL 674 (1911) (containing brief biographical sketch of George A. MacKenzie); *Facts About Minnesota Lawmakers*, MINNEAPOLIS J., Jan. 8, 1911, at 2, col. 5 (George A. MacKenzie); *Daily News Calls Roll on House and Senate*, ST. PAUL DAILY NEWS, Apr. 19, 1911, at 1, 3; MINN. HOUSE J., at 44, 232–33 (1911) (H.F. No. 2); *Opposes Death Sentence*, MINNEAPOLIS J., Feb. 11, 1911, at 3, cols. 6–7.

62.   MINN. HOUSE J., at 512–13 (1911); *House Votes to Abolish Hanging*, ST. PAUL PIONEER PRESS, Mar. 1, 1911, at 8, col. 6; *House Votes to Abolish Hanging*, MINNEAPOLIS J., Mar. 1, 1911, at 10, col. 1; *Capital Punishment Rapped by the House*, MINNEAPOLIS TRIB., Mar. 1, 1911, at 1, col. 4; *Death Penalty Abolished*, MINNEAPOLIS J., Apr. 19, 1911, at 15, col. 5; Session Weekly (Minnesota Legislature), Feb. 28, 1992, at 12.

63.   *House Votes to Abolish Hanging*, ST. PAUL PIONEER PRESS, Mar. 1, 1911, at 8, col. 6; MINNESOTA LEGISLATIVE MANUAL 698 (1911) (Knutson); MINN. HOUSE J., at 125, 145, 235–36, 471, 514, 1796 (1911) (H.F. No. 143); *House Votes to Abolish Hanging*, MINNEAPOLIS J., Mar. 1, 1911, at 10, col. 1; *Capital Punishment Rapped by the House*, supra note 62, at 1, col. 4. Representative Keefe's bill later died in the Senate Judiciary Committee. MINN. SEN. J., at 474, 476, 1553 (1911) (H.F. No. 143).

64.   *House Votes to Abolish Hanging*, ST. PAUL PIONEER PRESS, Mar. 1, 1911, at 8, col. 6; *Pass Measure to Abolish Hanging*, ST. PAUL PIONEER PRESS, Apr. 19, 1911, at 1, col. 4; *O'Malley's Life Saved; Hanging Is Abolished*, MINNEAPOLIS TRIB., Apr. 19, 1911, at 7, col. 2; *Death Penalty Abolished*, supra note 62, at 15, col. 5; *Important Bills Passed on Last Legislative Day*, ST. PAUL PIONEER PRESS, Apr. 19, 1911, at 1, cols. 6–7; MINN. SEN. J., at 1366 (1911); Gen. Laws of the State of Minn., ch. 387 (1911); *Faint Praise by Governor*, ST. PAUL DAILY NEWS, Apr. 19, 1911, at 2, col. 2.

65.   MINNEAPOLIS J., Apr. 20, 1911, at 1, cols. 4–6.

66. Even after Minnesota's "midnight assassination law" took effect, alcohol consumption still took place on execution day. *Hanged in Private,* ST. PAUL DISPATCH, July 19, 1889, at 1, cols. 1–3.

67. *See supra* text accompanying notes 8 and 29.

68. TRENERRY, *supra* note 16, at 167.

Chapter Six

1. Richard Dieter, *Secondary Smoke Surrounds the Capital Punishment Debate,* 13 CRIM. JUST. ETHICS 2, 82–84 (Winter/Spring 1994) (citing Gallup poll results from June 26, 1991); Roper Center for Public Opinion Research, Univ. of Conn. (NBC News/Wall Street Journal poll) (survey conducted on May 15–19, 1992); Roper Center for Public Opinion Research, Univ. of Conn. (poll conducted by ABC News/Washington Post on April 22–26, 1992); Transcript, "All Things Considered," Sept. 26, 1994, at 24; Conference, *The Death Penalty in the Twenty-First Century,* 45 AM. U. L. REV. 239, 310 (1995); *see also* THE DEATH PENALTY IN AMERICA: CURRENT CONTROVERSIES 17, 91 (Hugo Adam Bedau ed., 1997) (showing public opinion data on death penalty from 1936 to 1994).

2. James Dao, *New York Revives Death Penalty After 18 Years,* N.Y. TIMES, Mar. 8, 1995, at 1, col. 3; Conference, *supra* note 1, at 242; *Senators Vote to Condemn Bombing, Cheer White House,* MINNEAPOLIS STAR-TRIB., Apr. 26, 1995, at 7A; Lucy Howard & Ned Zeman, *1-800-Death,* NEWSWEEK, July 8, 1991, at 6; Ronald J. Tabak, *Politics and the Death Penalty: Can Rational Discourse and Due Process Survive the Perceived Political Pressure?,* 21 FORDHAM URB. L.J. 239, 254 (1994).

3. *Willie Brown Now Supports Death Penalty,* S.F. EXAMINER, Aug. 25, 1993, at A4; David Margolick, *Legal Scholar on Death Row Fights to Halt Own Execution,* N.Y. TIMES, Mar. 5, 1990, at A1, col. 5, & B6, col. 3; *The Politics of Death,* ECONOMIST, Mar. 24, 1990, at 26; Dao, *supra* note 2, at 1, col. 3; James Dao, *New York Senate Approves Revival of Death Penalty,* Mar. 7, 1995, at A1, col. 3, & B5, cols. 5–6; Jim Sleeper, *Mario Brothers?,* NEW DEMOCRAT, Aug./Sept. 1994, at 11.

4. Robert M. Bohm, *American Death Penalty Opinion, 1936–1986: A Critical Examination of the Gallup Polls, in* ROBERT M. BOHM, THE DEATH PENALTY IN AMERICA: CURRENT RESEARCH 114, 117–18 (1991); Betty B. Fletcher, *The Death Penalty in America: Can Justice Be Done?,* 70 N.Y.U. L. REV. 811, 815 (1995); Appendix (listing the date of Gary Gilmore's death); Furman v. Georgia, 408 U.S. 238 (1972); FRANKLIN ZIMRING & GORDON HAWKINS, CAPITAL PUNISHMENT AND THE AMERICAN AGENDA 26, 30, 97 & n.13, 141 (1986); Michael Mello, *Adhering to Our Views: Justices Brennan and Marshall and the Relentless Dissent to Death as a Punishment,* 22 FLA. ST. U. L. REV. 591, 599 (1995); J. Mark Lane, *"Is There Life Without Parole?": A Capital Defendant's Right to a Meaningful Alternative Sentence,* 26 LOY. L.A. L. REV. 327, 328 (1993); James W. Marquart & Jonathan R. Sorensen, *A National Study of the* Furman-*Commuted Inmates: Assessing the Threat to Society from Capital Offenders, reprinted in* THE DEATH PENALTY IN AMERICA: CURRENT CONTROVERSIES, *supra* note 1, at 162–75 (a "List of Persons on Death Row at the Time of *Furman,"* prepared by the NAACP Legal Defense Fund, contains over 600 names of inmates whose capital sentences were set aside by the *Furman* ruling).

5. *Furman,* 408 U.S. at 244 (Douglas, J., concurring); *Furman,* 408 U.S. at 258–63 (Brennan, J., concurring); U.S. CONST. amend. VIII (emphasis added); *Furman,* 408 U.S. at 258 (Brennan, J., concurring) *(citing* Robinson v. California, 370 U.S. 660 (1962); Gideon v. Wainwright, 372 U.S. 335 (1963); Malloy v. Hogan, 378 U.S. 1 (1964); Powell v. Texas, 392 U.S. 514 (1968)).

6. Weems v. United States, 217 U.S. 349 (1910); *Furman,* 408 U.S. at 265–66, 269 (Brennan, J., concurring) *(citing* Trop v. Dulles, 356 U.S. 86 (1958)); *Furman,* 408 U.S. at 329 (Marshall, J., concurring); Gregg v. Georgia, 428 U.S. 153, 173 (1976); Stanford v. Kentucky, 492 U.S. 361, 369, 377 (1989) (footnote omitted); Coker v. Georgia, 433 U.S. 584, 592 (1977) (plurality opinion); McCleskey v. Kemp, 481 U.S. 279, 300 (1987) *(quoting Gregg,* 428 U.S. at 173). *See generally* Lawrence A. Vanor, Note, *The Decency of Capital Punishment for Minors: Contemporary Standards and the Dignity of Juveniles,* 61 IND. L.J. 757, 763 (1986) (discussing objective indicia); Penry v. Lynaugh, 492 U.S. 302, 330–31 (1989).

7. *Furman,* 408 U.S. at 293 (Brennan, J., concurring); *Furman,* 408 U.S. at 309–10 (Stewart, J., concurring); *Furman,* 408 U.S. at 313 (White, J., concurring); Robert J. Sech, *Hang 'Em High: A Proposal for Thoroughly Evaluating the Constitutionality of Execution Methods,* 30 VAL. U. L. REV. 381, 385 n.29 (1995) (discussing *Furman).*

8. JOHN H. ELY, DEMOCRACY AND DISTRUST: A THEORY OF JUDICIAL REVIEW 65 (1980); ZIMRING & HAWKINS, *supra* note 4, at 38–39, 44; *Gregg,* 428 U.S. at 179–80, 195, 206–7.

9. *Gregg,* 428 U.S. at 232 (Marshall, J., dissenting) (emphasis in original); *Furman,* 408 U.S. at 361 & nn.144–45 (Marshall, J., concurring).

10. Emanuel Margolis, *Habeas Corpus: The No-Longer Great Writ,* 98 DICK. L. REV. 557 (1994); Joseph L. Hoffmann, *Starting from Scratch: Rethinking Federal Habeas Review of Death Penalty Cases,* 20 FLA. ST. U. L. REV. 133, 134–35 (1992); BLACK'S LAW DICTIONARY 638 (5th ed. 1979); Barefoot v. Estelle, 463 U.S. 880, 887 (1983); Teague v. Lane, 489 U.S. 288 (1989); Tabak, *supra* note 2, at 245; Stephen Bright, *The Electric Chair and the Chain Gang: Choices and Challenges for America's Future,* 71 NOTRE DAME L. REV. 845, 850 n.15 (1996); Coleman v. Thompson, 509 U.S. 722 (1991).

11. Franklin Zimring, *Inheriting the Wind: The Supreme Court and Capital Punishment in the 1990s,* 20 FLA. ST. U. L. REV. 7, 13–14 (1992); Nicole Veilleux, *Staying Death Penalty Executions: An Empirical Analysis of Changing Judicial Attitudes,* 84 GEO. L.J. 2543, 2550–52, 2554–55 (1996); McCleskey v. Kemp, 481 U.S. 279, 312 (1987); Penry v. Lynaugh, 492 U.S. 302 (1989); WELSH WHITE, THE DEATH PENALTY IN THE NINETIES: AN EXAMINATION OF THE MODERN SYSTEM OF CAPITAL PUNISHMENT 5 (1991); Chapter 1; Katherine Bishop, *After a Night of Court Battles, a California Execution,* N.Y. TIMES, Apr. 22, 1992, at A1; Herrera v. Collins, 506 U.S. 390 (1993); Robert A. Burt, *Disorder in the Court: The Death Penalty and the Constitution,* 85 MICH. L. REV. 1741, 1782–83, 1791–92, 1811 (1987); *Chief Justice Endorses Powell Committee Report on Habeas Reform in Capital Cases,* [Apr.–Sept.] Crim. L. Rep. (BNA) No. 47, at 1159 (May 23, 1990); Christopher E. Smith & Avis A. Jones, *The Rehnquist Court's Activism and the Risk of Injustice,* 26 CONN. L. REV. 53 (1993); Bright, *supra* note 10, at 849–50; Margolis, *supra* note 10, at 557.

12.   Antiterrorism and Effective Death Penalty Act of 1996, Pub. L. No. 104–132; *Law: Innocent Dead Men Walking?*, NAT'L L.J., May 20, 1996, at A1, A20–21; *Arguments Before the Court*, 64 U.S.L.W. 3813–15 (June 11, 1996); Linda Greenhouse, *Justices, With Rare Speed, Agree to Review New Law on Appeals*, N.Y. TIMES, May 4, 1996, at 1, 8; Felker v. Turpin, 116 S. Ct. 2333 (1996).

13.   Roper Center for Public Opinion Research, Univ. of Conn. (Gallup Poll conducted on June 26–29, 1991); Michael Radelet & Michael Mello, *Death-to-Life Overrides: Saving the Resources of the Florida Supreme Court*, 20 FLA. ST. U. L. REV. 195, 208 (1992); Douglas Shuit, *Death Penalty Draws Little Debate During This Political Season*, L.A. TIMES, Apr. 15, 1992, at B2; *Capital Punishment Gaining Favor As Public Seeks Retribution*, CORRECTIONS TODAY, Aug. 1990, at 180-81; Thomas B. Edsall, *3 Democrats Now Willing to Support Death Penalty*, WASH. POST, Jan. 23, 1992, at A14; Keith Love, *Bush Backers Have Horton Victims Speak*, L.A. TIMES, Oct. 8, 1988, at 23, col. 4; Richard Cohen, *William Horton's Furlough*, WASH. POST, July 8, 1988, at A23, col. 3.

14.   Greg Lucas, *Bill Would End Execution of Retarded*, S.F. CHRON., Mar. 5, 1993, at A22; Sharon Schmicke & Conrad deFiebre, *Get-Tough Federal Laws Are Having Little Effect on Crime in Minnesota*, MINNEAPOLIS STAR-TRIB., Nov. 17, 1996, at A17; Tabak, *supra* note 2, at 282 n.87; Edsall, *supra* note 13, at A14; *Lawyer: Execution a Disgrace*, N.Y. NEWSDAY, May 4, 1992, at 3; Conference, *supra* note 1, at 282–83; David Johnston & Steven Holmes, *Experts Doubt Effectiveness of Crime Bill*, N.Y. TIMES, Sept. 14, 1994, at A1 & A12; Bright, *supra* note 10, at 847.

15.   Paul Whitlock Cobb, Note, *Reviving Mercy in the Structure of Capital Punishment*, 99 YALE L.J. 389, 394 n.26 (1989); *Arkansas Gubernatorial Candidates in Close Race*, N.Y. TIMES, Oct. 27, 1982, at B10, col. 3; Peter Applebome, *Arkansas Execution Raises Questions on Governor's Politics*, N.Y. TIMES, Jan. 25, 1992, at 8, cols. 1–6; Tabak, *supra* note 2, at 296–97; Bright, *supra* note 10, at 847; Katherine Q. Seelye, *Dole Tours Death Chamber in San Quentin and Calls for Speedier Executions*, N.Y. TIMES, Mar. 24, 1996, at 14, cols. 1–5.

16.   Violent Crime Control and Law Enforcement Act of 1994, Pub. L. No. 103–322; Johnston & Holmes, *supra* note 14, at A1 & A12; Conference, *supra* note 1, at 279 & n.125; Bright, *supra* note 10, at 847, 852–53; *Recent Developments: The New Federal Death Penalties*, 22 AM. J. CRIM. L. 293, 294 n.6 (1994); Marcia Coyle, *Death Resource Centers Reborn as Private Groups*, NAT'L L.J., Jan. 15, 1996, at A9, col. 1; *As Executions Mount, So Do Infamous Last Words*, N.Y. TIMES, July 31, 1994, at E7, col. 1; Neil A. Lewis, *G.O.P. to Challenge Judicial Nominees Who Oppose Death Penalty*, N.Y. TIMES, Oct. 15, 1993, at A26; THE DEATH PENALTY IN AMERICA: CURRENT CONTROVERSIES, *supra* note 1, at 244, 310–11. Pro–death penalty rhetoric among members of Congress is prevalent. For example, while still a member of Congress, U.S. Senator Alan Simpson of Wyoming said enthusiastically, "Let's fry 'em fast." Pennsylvania Senator Arlen Spector concurs: "I'm delighted that executions can be speeded up. Cases that have taken to 17 years can be taken care of in a year." Seymour Simon, *What Price Justice? The Case Against the Death Penalty*, CHI. TRIB., Sept. 2, 1990, at 19.

17.   William J. Bowers, Margaret Vandiver, & Patricia H. Dugan, *A New Look at Public Opinion on Capital Punishment: What Citizens and Legislators Prefer,* 22 AM. J. CRIM. L. 77, 135, 141 (1994); Dao, *supra* note 2, at 1, col. 3; Gail Diane Cox, *Voters Tough on Criminals,* NAT'L L.J., Nov. 21, 1994, at A6, col. 3; Hugh Dellios, *Shortcuts Sought to Death Penalty,* CHI. TRIB., May 7, 1995, at 23, cols. 5–6; Thomas A. Fogarty, *Kansas: New to Death Penalty,* DES MOINES REG., Jan. 29, 1995, at 1; *Senate OKs Quicker Appeals Process,* CLEVE. PLAIN DEALER, Mar. 31, 1995, at 6-B, cols. 1–4; *News Local & National,* COLUMBUS DISPATCH, Nov. 9, 1994, at 1B; Tabak, *supra* note 2, at 281 n.84; Stephen B. Bright & Patrick J. Keenan, *Judges and the Politics of Death: Deciding Between the Bill of Rights and the Next Election in Capital Cases,* 75 B.U. L. REV. 759, 763–64 (1995); Conference, *supra* note 1, at 283–84; REV. JESSE JACKSON, LEGAL LYNCHING: RACISM, INJUSTICE & THE DEATH PENALTY 43 (1996); THE DEATH PENALTY IN AMERICA: CURRENT CONTROVERSIES, *supra* note 1, at 123–24.

18.   Bright & Keenan, *supra* note 17, at 761–62, 779–80.

19.   Bowers, Vandiver, & Dugan, *supra* note 17, at 141 n.105 (*citing* Melinda G. Hall, *Constituent Influence in State Supreme Courts: Conceptional Notes and a Case Study,* 99 J. POL. 1117, 1120–23 (1987)); CODE OF JUDICIAL CONDUCT, Canon 3(A)(1) (1972); Bright & Keenan, *supra* note 17, at 761; SISTER HELEN PREJEAN, DEAD MAN WALKING: AN EYE-WITNESS ACCOUNT OF THE DEATH PENALTY IN THE UNITED STATES 10, 46, 247 (1994) (*citing* THE DEATH PENALTY IN AMERICA 68 (Hugo Adam Bedau ed., 3d ed. 1982) (over 2,000 death sentences were vacated on constitutional grounds from 1967 to 1982)). A study conducted by James Liebman of Columbia University found that 42 percent of the 357 habeas corpus petitions filed in federal court between July 1976 and June 1991 resulted in reversals of convictions or death sentences. David Margolick, *Death Row in Texas Has a Shortage of Lawyers,* MINNEAPOLIS STAR-TRIB., Jan. 3, 1994, at 4A, col. 2; Margolis, *supra* note 10, at 604 n.279, 605 (citing Liebman's study).

20.   Bright & Keenan, *supra* note 17, at 766 & n.35; Michael Radelet, *Rejecting the Jury: The Imposition of the Death Penalty in Florida,* 18 U.C. DAVIS L. REV. 1409, 1410 n.6, 1412–13 (1985); Scott Erlich, *The Jury Override: A Blend of Politics and Death,* 45 AM. U. L. REV. 1403, 1405, 1447 (1996); Radelet & Mello, *supra* note 13, at 196, 213; Spaziano v. Florida, 468 U.S. 447 (1984); Linda Greenhouse, *Judges May Overrule Juries, Court Rules,* N.Y. TIMES, Feb. 23, 1995, at A12; Harris v. Alabama, 115 S. Ct. 1031 (1995); Conference, *supra* note 1, at 255; Michael Mello & Ruthann Robson, *Judge Over Jury: Florida's Practice of Imposing Death Over Life in Capital Cases,* 13 FLA. ST. U. L. REV. 31, 31–33, 59–60 & n.144 (1985); Ronald Tabak, *The Death of Fairness: The Arbitrary and Capricious Imposition of the Death Penalty in the 1980s,* 14 N.Y.U. REV. L. & SOC. CHANGE 797, 820 (1986); Ruth E. Friedman & Bryan A. Stevenson, *Solving Alabama's Capital Defense Problems: It's a Dollars and Sense Thing,* 44 ALA. L. REV. 1 n.67 (1992) (*citing* Tracking Project, Alabama Capital Representation Resource Center, Montgomery, Alabama (1992) ("Nearly a quarter of the defendants sent to Alabama's death row arrived there after a jury had recommended the life-without-parole option.")).

21.   *Texas Executes Vermont Man in Slaying During Hitchhiking,* N.Y. TIMES, Aug. 2, 1994, at A19, col. 1; Bright & Keenan, *supra* note 17, at 793–94, 812–13.

22. Cobb, *supra* note 15, at 393 & nn.24–25 (citations omitted); Hugo Bedau, *The Decline of Executive Clemency in Capital Cases*, 18 N.Y.U. REV. L. & SOC. CHANGE 255, 263–64 (1990); Bruce Ledewitz & Scott Staples, *The Role of Executive Clemency in Modern Death Penalty Cases*, 27 U. RICH. L. REV. 227 (1993); Michael Radelet & Barbara Zsembik, *Executive Clemency in Post-*Furman *Capital Cases*, 27 U. RICH. L. REV. 289, 290 (1993); James Brooke, *Utah Debates Firing Squads in Clash of Past and Present*, N.Y. TIMES, Jan. 14, 1996, at 10, col. 5.

23. Cobb, *supra* note 15, at 394 (*citing* Woman on Death Row Creates Political Stir in North Carolina, BOSTON GLOBE, Sept. 7, 1984, at 2, col. 2; *Carolina Slayer Fails in Her Bid for a Reprieve*, N.Y. TIMES, Sept. 28, 1984, at A1, col. 2; *First Woman Is Executed in U.S. Since 1962*, N.Y. TIMES, Nov. 3, 1984, at A46, col. 1); ZIMRING & HAWKINS, *supra* note 4, at 99, 126–27; Ledewitz & Staples, *supra* note 22, at 229 n.7; Daniel T. Kobil, *The Quality of Mercy Strained: Wresting the Pardoning Power from the King*, 69 TEX. L. REV. 569, 605, 607–8 & nn.232–34 (1991) (citing sources).

24. EDMUND G. (PAT) BROWN & DICK ADLER, PUBLIC JUSTICE, PRIVATE MERCY 163 (1989); Herrera v. Collins, 506 U.S. 390 (1993) (*quoting* KATHLEEN D. MOORE, PARDONS: JUSTICE, MERCY, AND THE PUBLIC INTEREST 131 (1989)); Joseph B. Schimmel, *Commutation of the Death Sentence: Florida Steps Back from Justice and Mercy*, 20 FLA. ST. U. L. REV. 253, 254–55, 262 (1992) (listing various constitutional provisions); Ledewitz & Staples, *supra* note 22, at 228 (*citing* PA. CONST. art. IV, § 9); Kobil, *supra* note 23, at 605 & nn.232–34 (*citing* National Governors' Ass'n Center for Policy Research, Guide to State Clemency Among the American States (1988)); *60 Minutes: Life or Death* (CBS television broadcast of Jan. 21, 1990, reporting on Roemer's denial of clemency); *Louisiana Executes Man Who Killed at Age 17*, N.Y. TIMES, May 19, 1990, § 1, at 9, col. 1).

25. PREJEAN, *supra* note 19, at 158, 169–74.

26. *Terms Commuted for 8 Abused Women*, CHI. TRIB., Feb. 20, 1991, at A15; Howard Schneider, *Md. to Free Abused Women; Schaefer Commutes 8 Terms, Citing Violence*, WASH. POST, Feb. 20, 1991, at A1; Alan Johnson, *Celeste Commutes Death Sentences of Eight Killers*, COLUMBUS DISPATCH, Jan. 11, 1991, at A1; Isabel Wilkerson, *Ohio Frees 25 Battered Women Who Fought Back*, DETROIT FREE PRESS, Dec. 22, 1990, at A1; Toney Anaya, *Clemency and Pardons Symposium: Statement by Toney Anaya on Capital Punishment*, 27 U. RICH. L. REV. 177, 178–82 (1993).

27. JOAN JACOBY, THE AMERICAN PROSECUTOR: A SEARCH FOR IDENTITY 37–38 (1980) (tracing the transition from appointive to elective prosecutors); Transcript, "All Things Considered," Capital Punishment Series, at 24 (Sept. 26, 1994); Transcript, "All Things Considered," Capital Punishment Series, at 23–24 (Sept. 28, 1994); Reynolds Holding, *Texas County Proud to be Capital of Capital Punishment*, S.F. CHRON., Aug. 16, 1993, at A3; Gary Taylor, *Death Works Double-Time in the Lone Star State*, NAT'L L.J., Oct. 3, 1994, at A7; Tamar Lewis, *Who Decides Who Will Die? Even Within States, It Varies*, N.Y. TIMES, Feb. 23, 1995, at A13, cols. 1–2; Tina Rosenberg, *The Deadliest D.A.*, N.Y. TIMES MAG., July 16, 1995, at 22; Mumia Abu-Jamal, *Teetering on the Brink: Between Death and Life*, 100 YALE L.J. 993 (1991).

28. Tabak, *supra* note 20, at 799 (*citing* Jason DeParle, *Quirky System Picks Who Dies*, TIMES-PICAYUNE (New Orleans), Apr. 7, 1985, at A1 & A16); Rachel L. Swarns, *In Clash on Death Penalty Case, Pataki Removes Bronx Prosecutor*, N.Y. TIMES, Mar. 22, 1996, at 1, 16; James Traub, *The Life Preserver*, NEW YORKER, Apr. 8, 1996, at 47–48.

29. Kenneth Bresler, *Seeking Justice, Seeking Election, and Seeking the Death Penalty: The Ethics of Prosecutorial Candidates Campaigning on Capital Convictions*, 7 GEO. J. LEGAL ETHICS 941, 944 nn.14, 16–19 (1994) (*citing* Michael Oreskes, *The Political Stampede on Execution*, N.Y. TIMES, Apr. 4, 1990, at A16; Dan Balz, *Politicians Tout Death Penalty: Candidates Hoping to Establish Credentials as Crime Fighters*, S.F. CHRON., Mar. 5, 1990, at A7; John Balzar, *Van de Kamp TV Ads Focus on Death Row, Will Air Today*, L.A. TIMES, Mar. 25, 1990, at A3); Transcript, "All Things Considered," Capital Punishment Series, at 26 (Sept. 26, 1994); Helen Dewar, *Democrats Show Tilt Toward Death Penalty*, CORRECTIONS TODAY, July 1990, at 156; WENDY LESSER, PICTURES AT AN EXECUTION 26 (1993); Shuit, *supra* note 13, at B2.

30. DONALD CABANA, DEATH AT MIDNIGHT: THE CONFESSION OF AN EXECUTIONER 191–93 (1996); *Warden Quits to Avoid Role of Executioner*, HOUSTON POST, Jan. 5, 1924, at 1–2; JAMES W. MARQUART, SHELDON EKLAND-OLSON, & JONATHAN R. SORENSEN, THE ROPE, THE CHAIR, AND THE NEEDLE: CAPITAL PUNISHMENT IN TEXAS, 1923–1990, at 15 (1994); I. Reed Payne, Roger T. Pray, & Louis F. Damis, *Utah Stress Education Program Helps Staff Deal With Executions*, CORRECTIONS TODAY, July 1990, at 160–68.

31. Rosenberg, *supra* note 27, at 21 (discussing prosecutors who frequently seek death sentences); Colman McCarthy, *Sister Helen Prejean Keeps the Faith*, MINNEAPOLIS STAR-TRIB., June 5, 1996, at A13, col. 3; CABANA, *supra* note 30, at 17 (dust jacket contains quote from Sister Helen Prejean).

32. Steven P. Garvey, *Politicizing Who Dies*, 101 YALE L.J. 187 n.1 (1991); Taylor, *supra* note 27, at A7, col. 3; William J. Bowers, *The Capital Jury Project: Rationale, Design, and Preview of Early Findings*, 70 IND. L.J. 1043, 1094–95, 1097 (1995); Scott Burgins, *Jurors Ignore, Misunderstand Instructions*, A.B.A. J., May 1995, at 30–31; Caldwell v. Mississippi, 472 U.S. 320, 328–29 (1985); Taylor v. State, 666 So. 2d 36 (Ala. Ct. App. 1994), *aff'd*, 666 So. 2d 73 (Ala. 1995).

33. PREJEAN, *supra* note 19, at 53–57; Henry v. State, 136 P. 982, 988–89 (Okla. Crim. App. 1913).

34. *Joyce Hanged*, PUEBLO CHIEFTON (Colo.), Jan. 18, 1891, at 1, col. 3; *Without a Tremor*, ROCKY MT. NEWS, Jan. 18, 1891, at 1, col. 3; *Joyce's Days Ended*, REPUBLICAN (Denver), Jan. 18, 1891; *Cronin Hanged*, HARTFORD COURANT, Dec. 18, 1894, at 1; *Cronin's Last Day*, HARTFORD TIMES, Dec. 17, 1894, at 1–2; *Paid the Penalty*, HARTFORD TIMES, Dec. 18, 1894, at 1–2; *Cronin*, HARTFORD TIMES, Dec. 18, at 6, col. 2; *Seng to Hang May 24th*, NATRONA COUNTY TRIB. (Wyo.), May 29, 1912, at 8, col. 5; PREJEAN, *supra* note 19, at 78, 101, 103; Lance Gurwell, *Domestic News*, United Press International, July 30, 1992 (BC cycle) (LEXIS); Jon Nordheimer, *Gilmore Is Executed After Stay Is Upset; 'Let's Do It!' He Said*, N.Y. TIMES, Jan. 18, 1977, at 1–2; Carol Castaneda, *Wanted in Utah: Volunteers for Firing Squad*, U.S.A. TODAY, Dec. 12, 1995 ("The shooters will stand behind a curtain or wall with gunports, hidden from witnesses. They'll stand in the dark

and aim their .30 caliber rifles to a lighted area. One will have a blank so the executioners won't know who fired the fatal shot."); Sech, *supra* note 7, at 390 n.50 (one of five Utah marksmen "receives a blank shot in order to prevent any single member of the group from feeling personal guilt for the killing"); STEPHEN TROMBLEY, THE EXECUTION PROTOCOL 106, 216 (1992); Kathy Walt, *After 100 Executions, Interest Seems to Have Waned,* SAN DIEGO UNION-TRIB., Oct. 8, 1995, at A33. During the Civil War, the guns of soldiers performing firing squad executions of deserters were sometimes loaded with blanks to minimize soldiers' personal guilt. ROBERT I. ALOTTA, CIVIL WAR JUSTICE: UNION ARMY EXECUTIONS UNDER LINCOLN 41 (1989).

35. Reuters Ltd., May 26, 1979 (PM cycle) (LEXIS); Thomas Slaughter, *Domestic News,* Associated Press, May 26, 1979 (BC cycle) (LEXIS); *Man Who Killed His Baby Goes Willingly to Chair,* ORLANDO SENTINEL, Aug. 26, 1993, at B1; Chris Lavin, *Trooper's Killer Is Put to Death,* ST. PETERSBURG TIMES, July 22, 1992, at 4B ("the anonymous executioner, his head . . . covered by a black veil, began the execution"); *Scene of Silhouettes and Shadows,* SEATTLE TIMES, May 27, 1994, at A1 & A5; *Delaware Readies Gallows as Rare Form of Execution Draws Near,* WASH. POST, Jan. 21, 1996, at B1 & B4; GEOFFREY ABBOTT, LORDS OF THE SCAFFOLD: A HISTORY OF THE EXECUTIONER 26, 96 (1991); BARBARA LEVY, LEGACY OF DEATH 9 (1973); A HANGMAN'S DIARY: BEING THE JOURNAL OF MASTER FRANZ SCHMIDT PUBLIC EXECUTIONER OF NUREMBERG, 1573–1617, at 43–44, 47 (Albrecht Keller ed., 1928); ROBERT CHRISTOPHE, THE EXECUTIONERS: A HISTORY OF THE SANSON FAMILY, PUBLIC EXECUTIONERS IN FRANCE FROM 1688 TO 1847, at 27 (1961); Gerald Robin, *The Executioner: His Place in English Society,* 15 BRIT. J. SOC. 234–36 & n.8 (1964); JAMES BLAND, THE COMMON HANGMAN: ENGLISH AND SCOTTISH HANGMEN BEFORE THE ABOLITION OF PUBLIC EXECUTIONS 1, 3–4, 16, 111, 119–20, 131 (1984); ROBERT G. ELLIOTT, AGENT OF DEATH: THE MEMOIRS OF AN EXECUTIONER 286–87 (1940); E. ROY CALVERT, CAPITAL PUNISHMENT IN THE TWENTIETH CENTURY 99, 172–73 (1930).

36. WILBERT RIDEAU & RON WIKBERG, LIFE SENTENCES: RAGE AND SURVIVAL BEHIND BARS 305–18 (1992); FLA. STAT. ANN. § 945.10(1) (West Supp. 1995) ("[t]he identity of the executioner" is "confidential"); ILL. ANN. STAT. ch. 38, para. 119–5(e) (Smith-Hurd Supp. 1992); MONT. CODE ANN. § 46–19–103 (1993) ("[t]he identity of the executioner must remain anonymous"); N.J. STAT. ANN. § 2C:49–7(a) (West Supp. 1995) ("[t]he names of the execution technicians shall not be disclosed"); N.Y. Laws, art. 22-B, § 660 (1995) ("[t]he names of the execution technician or technicians shall never be disclosed").

37. David Lawrence Abney, Capital Punishment in Arizona (1863–1963) 22 (Aug. 1988) (Master's Thesis, Arizona State University); ALBERT PIERREPOINT, EXECUTIONER: PIERREPOINT 69 (1974); ELLIOTT, *supra* note 35, at 14, 138; ZIMRING & HAWKINS, *supra* note 4, at 112, 121–22.

38. Nat Hentoff, *"This Dismal Spectacle,"* WASH. POST, Dec. 30, 1995, at A19; ELLIOTT, *supra* note 35, at 299–302, 309, 315.

39. Furman v. Georgia, 408 U.S. 238, 362–63 & nn.145–147 (1972) (Marshall, J., concurring) (*citing* Gold, *A Psychiatric Review of Capital Punishment,* 6 J. FORENSIC SCI. 465, 466 (1961); ARTHUR KOESTLER, REFLECTIONS ON HANGING 164 (1957)).

40. Robert M. Bohm, *Death Penalty Opinions: A Classroom Experience and Public Commitment*, 60 SOC. INQUIRY 285, 286 (1990); Robert M. Bohm, *The Effects of Classroom Instruction and Discussion on Death Penalty Opinions: A Teaching Note*, 17 J. CRIM. JUST. 123 (1989); Robert M. Bohm, Louise J. Clark, & Adrian F. Aveni, *Knowledge and Death Penalty Opinion: A Test of the Marshall Hypotheses*, 28 J. RES. CRIME & DELINQ. 360, 369, 378–82 (Aug. 1991); Robert M. Bohm, Ronald E. Vogel, & Albert A. Maisto, *Knowledge and Death Penalty Opinion: A Panel Study*, 21 J. CRIM. JUST. 29, 30 (1993); Robert M. Bohm & Ronald E. Vogel, *A Comparison of Factors Associated with Uninformed and Informed Death Penalty Opinions*, 22 J. CRIM. JUST. 125 (1994); Austin Sarat & Neil Vidmar, *Public Opinion, the Death Penalty, and the Eighth Amendment: Testing the Marshall Hypothesis*, 1976 WIS. L. REV. 171.

41. Bowers, Vandiver, & Dugan, *supra* note 17, at 78. For example, a 1991 CNN/Gallup Poll showed support for capital punishment at 76 percent. PREJEAN, *supra* note 19, at 116 (citing other poll results in the endnotes); Richard Dieter, Sentencing for Life: Americans Embrace Alternatives to the Death Penalty (The Death Penalty Information Center, Apr. 1993), *reprinted in* THE DEATH PENALTY IN AMERICA: CURRENT CONTROVERSIES, *supra* note 1, at 116–26. In some state polls, support for capital punishment drops even further when life imprisonment is offered as an alternative. For instance, in New York, only 19 percent of respondents favored the death penalty over life imprisonment without the possibility of parole plus restitution. THE MACHINERY OF DEATH: A SHOCKING INDICTMENT OF CAPITAL PUNISHMENT IN THE UNITED STATES 70–71 (1995); *see also* Tabak, *supra* note 2, at 280 n.80 (citing other polls).

42. Roper Center for Public Opinion Research, Univ. of Conn. (poll conducted on June 28, 1989, by Yankelovich Clancy Shulman and sponsored by *Time* and CNN); William Bowers, *Capital Punishment and Contemporary Values: People's Misgivings and the Court's Misperceptions*, 27 LAW & SOC'Y REV. 157, 172 (1993) (showing opposition in some states to executing mentally retarded persons at 66 to 73 percent); Roper Center for Public Opinion Research, Univ. of Conn. (Gallup poll) (1,500 respondents); Bohm, *supra* note 4, at 137; Bowers, Vandiver, & Dugan, *supra* note 17, at 81; Deborah W. Denno, *"Death Is Different" and Other Twists of Fate*, 83 J. CRIM. L. & CRIMINOLOGY 437, 446 (1992) (citing Gallup Poll results from 1991); George Gallup, "The Death Penalty," Gallup Reports 244 & 245 (Jan./Feb. 1986), at 10–16 (*cited in* PREJEAN, *supra* note 19, at 116); *see also* THE DEATH PENALTY IN AMERICA: CURRENT CONTROVERSIES, *supra* note 1, at 85, 106–7 (listing other poll results); John D. Bessler, *Who Said, "Only the Good Die Young?,"* THE BULLY PULPIT, Fall 1988 (copy on file with author) (discussing the death penalty as applied to juveniles).

43. William J. Bowers, *The Death Penalty's Shaky Support*, N.Y. TIMES, May 28, 1990, at A21; Bowers, *supra* note 42, at 162–64, 167–70; Bowers, Vandiver, & Dugan, *supra* note 17, at 79–80 & n.8, 88–92, 102–4, 106, 142–46, 149; Edmund F. McGarrell & Marla Sandys, *The Misperception of Public Opinion Toward Capital Punishment: Examining the Spuriousness Explanation of Death Penalty Support*, 39 AM. BEHAVIORAL SCI. 500 (1996); THE DEATH PENALTY IN AMERICA: CURRENT CONTROVERSIES, *supra* note 1, at 85, 87; Phoebe C. Ellsworth & Samuel R. Gross, *Hardening of the Attitudes: Americans' Views*

on the Death Penalty, reprinted in THE DEATH PENALTY IN AMERICA: CURRENT CON-TROVERSIES, *supra* note 1, at 99.

44. Joseph Giarratano, *"To the Best of Our Knowledge, We Have Never Been Wrong": Fallibility vs. Finality in Capital Punishment,* 100 YALE L.J. 1005, 1009 (1991) (*citing* Tabak & Lane, *The Execution of Injustice: A Cost and Lack-of-Benefit Analysis of the Death Penalty,* 23 LOY. L. REV. 59, 102 (1989)); *Alabama Death-Row Inmate Is Set Free,* MIN-NEAPOLIS STAR-TRIB., Mar. 3, 1993, at 7A; Mark Hansen, *The Murder Case that Unrav-eled,* A.B.A. J., June 1993, at 30–31; Hugo Adam Bedau & Michael L. Radelet, *Miscar-riages of Justice in Potentially Capital Cases,* 40 STAN. L. REV. 21, 71–73, 81 (1987); SELECTED LETTERS OF CHARLES DICKENS 215 (D. Paroissien ed., 1985); Dirk Johnson, *Back to Family From Life on Death Row,* N.Y. TIMES, Sept. 25, 1994, at 10; MICHAEL RADELET, HUGO ADAM BEDAU, & CONSTANCE PUTNAM, IN SPITE OF INNOCENCE: ER-RONEOUS CONVICTIONS IN CAPITAL CASES 272 (1992); Staff Report, Subcommittee on Civil and Constitutional Rights, House Judiciary Committee, 103d Congress, 1st Sess. (Oct. 21, 1993), *Innocence and the Death Penalty: Assessing the Danger of Mistaken Execu-tions, reprinted in* THE DEATH PENALTY IN AMERICA: CURRENT CONTROVERSIES, *supra* note 1, at 344–60; JACKSON, *supra* note 17, at 45, 71.

45. Mark Curriden, *Would Public Executions Curb Crime?,* ATLANTA CONST., July 31, 1994, at 3R; Sam Howe Verhovek, *With Practice, Texas Is the Execution Leader,* N.Y. TIMES, Sept. 5, 1993, at 6E, col. 4 (citing FBI statistics); JACKSON, *supra* note 17, at 99; Anne Cronin, *Execution and Murder: Looking Hard at America's Deadly Numbers Game,* N.Y. TIMES, Dec. 4, 1994, at 1E; Tom Kuntz, *Killings, Legal and Otherwise, Around the U.S.,* N.Y. TIMES, Dec. 4, 1994, at E3; Sonia Rosen & Stephen Journey, *Abolition of the Death Penalty: An Emerging Norm of International Law,* 14 HAMLINE J. PUB. L. & POL'Y 163, 176 (1993); Clifford Krauss, *Now, How Low Can Crime Go?,* N.Y. TIMES, Jan. 28, 1996, at E5; Dick Lehr, *Death Penalty Foes Seek a New Debate, See Stronger Case,* BOSTON GLOBE, Jan. 10, 1993, at 1; MICHAEL RADELET & MARGARET VANDIVER, CAPITAL PUN-ISHMENT IN THE UNITED STATES: AN ANNOTATED BIBLIOGRAPHY (1988) (no U.S. crim-inologist in the past fifteen years claimed to find data indicating that the death penalty is a greater deterrent than lengthy imprisonment); THE DEATH PENALTY IN AMERICA: CURRENT CONTROVERSIES, *supra* note 1, at 127–34; Conference, *supra* note 1, at 277 nn.119–20 (discussing the deterrence issue); William C. Bailey & Ruth D. Peterson, *Murder, Capital Punishment, and Deterrence: A Review of the Literature, in* THE DEATH PENALTY IN AMERICA: CURRENT CONTROVERSIES, *supra* note 1, at 135–61. In 1987, im-mediately after Louisiana executed eight people, the murder rate in New Orleans rose over 16 percent. PREJEAN, *supra* note 19, at 110.

46. Bright, *supra* note 10, at 847 & n.6; PREJEAN, *supra* note 19, at 9; Steven A. Holmes, *Ranks of Inmates Reach One Million in a 2-Decade Rise,* N.Y. TIMES, Oct. 28, 1994, at 9, cols. 2–4; Steven A. Holmes, *Prisons Replacing Military as Nation's Hot Growth Area,* MINNEAPOLIS STAR-TRIB., Nov. 13, 1994, at 17A; Fox Butterfield, *Prison Population Rises, But Rate Slows,* MINNEAPOLIS STAR-TRIB., Jan. 22, 1997, at A8, col. 1.

47. Sentencing for Life: Americans Embrace Alternatives to the Death Penalty (a report by The Death Penalty Information Center, Washington, D.C.) (Apr. 1993),

reprinted in THE DEATH PENALTY IN AMERICA: CURRENT CONTROVERSIES, *supra* note 1, at 116–26; JACKSON, *supra* note 17, at 50; PREJEAN, *supra* note 19, at 142–44; Lane, *supra* note 4, at 335–42, 362–65; Theodore Eisenberg & Martin T. Wells, *Deadly Confusion: Juror Instructions in Capital Cases,* 79 CORNELL L. REV. 1 (1993); Bowers, *supra* note 42, at 157, 167–69; Craig Haney, *Taking Capital Jurors Seriously,* 70 IND. L.J. 1223, 1231 (1995); Marla Sandys, *Cross-Overs—Capital Jurors Who Change Their Minds About the Punishment: A Litmus Test for Sentencing Guidelines,* 70 IND. L.J. 1183, 1218 (1995); Simmons v. South Carolina, 512 U.S. 154 (1994); *see also* THE DEATH PENALTY IN AMERICA: CURRENT CONTROVERSIES, *supra* note 1, at 180–81 (citing data showing time actually served in prison by convicted murderers versus perception of how much time Americans believe convicted murderers spend in prison).

48. *Is There a Lawyer in the House?,* UTNE READER, Nov./Dec. 1992, at 94; Stephen Bright, *Counsel for the Poor: The Death Sentence Not for the Worst Crime but for the Worst Lawyer,* 103 YALE L.J. 1835, 1843, 1853, 1855–57, 1867, 1868 nn.51, 191 (1994); Conference, *supra* note 1, at 287, 302 & nn.149, 207; John D. Bessler, *The Public Interest and the Unconstitutionality of Private Prosecutors,* 47 ARK. L. REV. 511, 513 & n.9 (1994); Bright & Keenan, *supra* note 17, at 802; THE DEATH PENALTY IN AMERICA: CURRENT CONTROVERSIES, *supra* note 1, at 243, 245; David Margolick, *Death Row in Texas Has a Shortage of Lawyers,* MINNEAPOLIS STAR-TRIB., Jan. 3, 1994, at 4A, col. 1; Marcia Coyle, *Death Resource Centers Reborn as Private Groups,* NAT'L L.J., Jan. 15, 1996, at A9, col. 1; *ABA Votes for Death Penalty Moratorium,* MINNEAPOLIS STAR-TRIB., Feb. 4, 1997, at 1, cols. 2–5.

49. Burt, *supra* note 11, at 1787; JACKSON, *supra* note 17, at 100–101, 137; Tabak, *supra* note 20, at 814–15 (*citing* Lockhart v. McCree, 476 U.S. 162, 171–73 (1986)); McCleskey v. Kemp, 481 U.S. 279, 300 (1987); Witherspoon v. Illinois, 391 U.S. 510, 519, 522 & n.15 (1968); LA. CODE CRIM. PROC. ANN. art. 905.6 (West 1984). In Nevada, a panel of three judges sentences the defendant if the jury is not unanimous. In other states— Arizona, Idaho, Montana, and Nebraska—the trial judge alone may impose a death sentence. Tabak, *supra* note 20, at 820 (*citing* NEV. REV. STAT. §§ 175.554, 175.556 (1981); ARIZ. REV. STAT. ANN. § 13-703 (Supp. 1983–84); IDAHO CODE § 19-2515 (1979); MONT. CODE ANN. § 046-18-301 (1983); NEB. REV. STAT. § 029-2520 (1979)).

50. Bright, *supra* note 48, at 1836, 1878; THE MACHINERY OF DEATH: A SHOCKING INDICTMENT OF CAPITAL PUNISHMENT 102 (1995); JACKSON, *supra* note 17, at 102–3; David C. Baldus, *Keynote Address: The Death Penalty Dialogue Between Law and Social Science,* 70 IND. L.J. 1033, 1057 (1995); Dorothy O. Lewis et al., *Psychiatric, Neurological, and Psychoeducational Characteristics of 15 Death Row Inmates in the United States,* 143 AM. J. PSYCHIATRY 838 (1986); Malcolm Gladwell, *Damaged,* NEW YORKER, Feb. 24/Mar. 3, 1997, at 132–47; THE DEATH PENALTY IN AMERICA: CURRENT CONTROVERSIES, *supra* note 1, at 29, 75.

51. *Capital Punishment Is as Old as History,* L.A. TIMES, Jan. 17, 1977, pt. 1, at 10; PUNISHMENT AND THE DEATH PENALTY: THE CURRENT DEBATE 103 (Robert M. Baird & Stuart E. Rosenbaum eds., 1995); Fletcher, *supra* note 4, at 812–13; Callins v. Collins, 114 S. Ct. 1127, 1130 (1994) (Blackmun, J., dissenting) (denial of certiorari); Conference,

supra note 1, at 258–59; THE DEATH PENALTY IN AMERICA: CURRENT CONTROVERSIES, *supra* note 1, at 31–32, 55–56.

52.   PREJEAN, *supra* note 19, at 129–30, 260; DALLAS MORNING NEWS, Mar. 8, 1992; PUNISHMENT AND THE DEATH PENALTY, *supra* note 51, at 109; Conference, *supra* note 1, at 245 & n.13 (referencing studies showing that "it costs a jurisdiction approximately three times as much to have capital punishment than to use the punishment of life in prison without parole"); Radelet & Mello, *supra* note 13, at 213; Lynn Adelman, *Con: Wisconsin Should Not Reverse 140 Years of History by Reinstating the Death Penalty,* WIS. LAW., Oct. 1993, at 25, 62; Baldus, *supra* note 50, at 1035; Richard C. Dieter, Millions Misspent: What Politicians Don't Say About the High Costs of the Death Penalty (The Death Penalty Information Center, Fall 1994), *reprinted in* THE DEATH PENALTY IN AMERICA: CURRENT CONTROVERSIES, *supra* note 1, at 410–10.

Chapter Seven

1.   WENDY LESSER, PICTURES AT AN EXECUTION 172 (1993); Anne Cronin, *Execution and Murder: Looking Hard at America's Deadly Numbers Game,* N.Y. TIMES, Dec. 4, 1994, at 1E (containing the picture of Ruth Synder); EDWARD BAUMANN, MAY GOD HAVE MERCY ON YOUR SOUL: THE STORY OF THE ROPE AND THE THUNDERBOLT 392–96 (1993) (containing a picture of James "Mad Dog" Morelli dying in the electric chair); ROBERT G. ELLIOTT, AGENT OF DEATH: THE MEMOIRS OF AN EXECUTIONER 186–87, 190–91 (1940).

2.   Garrett v. Estelle, 424 F. Supp. 468, 469–70 (N.D. Tex. 1977); *see* Chapter 1.

3.   *Garrett,* 424 F. Supp. at 469, 471–73; U.S. CONST. amend. I.

4.   Associated Press, Jan. 13, 1977 (AM cycle) (LEXIS); Associated Press, Jan. 6, 1977 (AM cycle) (LEXIS); Associated Press, May 25, 1977 (AM cycle) (LEXIS).

5.   Pell v. Procunier, 417 U.S. 817 (1974); Saxbe v. Washington Post Co., 417 U.S. 843 (1974); Garrett v. Estelle, 556 F.2d 1274, 1278–79 (5th Cir.), *cert. denied,* 438 U.S. 914 (1978); Richard Carelli, Associated Press, July 3, 1978 (PM cycle) (LEXIS); Gil Santamarina, *The Case for Televised Executions,* 11 CARDOZO ARTS & ENT. L. REV. 101, 108 (1992); *Covering Executions,* NEWS MEDIA & L., Oct. 1977, at 9.

6.   Halquist v. Department of Corrections, 783 P.2d 1065 (Wash. 1989) (en banc).

7.   Jon Nordheimer, *Lawyers Making Last Bids Today to Save Gilmore,* N.Y. TIMES, Jan. 14, 1977, at A12, col. 5; *Firing Squad Executes Gilmore,* L.A. TIMES, Jan. 18, 1977, pt. 1, at 18, col. 3; *Gilmore Execution Leads to Utah Lawsuits over Press Access to Executions,* NEWS MEDIA & L., Oct. 1977, at 9–10; James Brooke, *Utah Debates Firing Squads in Clash of Past and Present,* N.Y. TIMES, Jan. 14, 1996, at 10, col. 5; NORMAN MAILER, THE EXECUTIONER'S SONG 1020–24 (1979); *see* Chapter 6.

8.   Kearns-Tribune v. Utah Bd. of Corrections, 2 Media L. Rep. (BNA) 1353, 1354 (D. Utah 1977); David Johnston, *Court Battle Fails to Halt Execution,* L.A. TIMES, Jan. 17, 1977, pt. 1, at 1, col. 6.

9.   Nordheimer, *supra* note 7, at A12, col. 5; William Greider, *"Today . . . Gilmore Has Quiet,"* WASH. POST, Jan. 18, 1977, at A1, cols. 4–6, & A4, col. 1 (FAA ruling); *Execution of Gilmore Stayed,* WASH. POST, Jan. 17, 1977, at A1, col. 1, & A3, col. 1 ("Scores of reporters and television camera crews had gathered outside the Utah State Prison for

an all-night vigil, awaiting word that Gilmore had been shot to death."); David John-ston, *Utah Fights to Overturn U.S. Judge's 10-Day Delay,* L.A. TIMES, Jan. 17, 1977, pt. 1, at 1; *Death Watch in Salt Lake City,* TIME, Jan. 24, 1977, at 51; L.A. TIMES, Jan. 14, 1977, pt. 1, at 2, col. 4.

10. Jon Nordheimer, *Gilmore Faces Execution at Dawn; 2 Appeals to Supreme Court Fail,* N.Y. TIMES, Jan. 17, 1977, at 48, col. 6; Jon Nordheimer, *Gilmore Is Executed After Stay Is Upset; 'Let's Do It!' He Said,* N.Y. TIMES, Jan. 18, 1977, at 1, col. 4, & 21, cols. 3–5; Jon Nordheimer, *Plane Scatters Gilmore's Ashes as Utah Begins Return to Normal,* N.Y. TIMES, Jan. 19, 1977, at A14, cols. 1–2; *A Partial Transcript of Remarks by Witness to Gilmore Execution,* N.Y. TIMES, Jan. 18, 1977, at 21, cols. 1–2; Johnston, *supra* note 8, at pt. 1, at 1, col. 6; L.A. TIMES, Jan. 14, 1977, pt. 1, at 2, col. 4; David Johnston, *Gilmore Sedated, Annoyed by Guards' "Death Watch,"* L.A. TIMES, Jan. 17, pt. 1, at 10, cols. 1–3; Greider, *supra* note 9, at A1, cols. 4–6, & A4, cols. 1–3; Deborah W. Denno, *Is Electro-cution an Unconstitutional Method of Execution? The Engineering of Death Over the Cen-tury?,* 35 WM. & MARY L. REV. 551, 687–88 (1994); *see also* Carol Castaneda, *Wanted in Utah: Volunteers for Firing Squad,* U.S.A. TODAY, Dec. 12, 1995, at 3A.

11. *Firing Squad Executes Gilmore, supra* note 7, pt. 1, at 18, col. 2; Johnston, *supra* note 8, pt. 1, at 1, col. 6; Greider, *supra* note 9, at A1, cols. 4–6, & A4, cols. 1–3.

12. *N.C. High Court Refuses Request for TV Execution,* Reuters, Ltd., May 18, 1994 (BC cycle) (LEXIS); *Newsmakers,* HOUSTON CHRON., Mar. 10, 1993, at A2; Lawson v. Dixon, 22 Media L. Rep. (BNA) 1839 (4th Cir. June 13, 1994).

13. Lawson v. Dixon, Court File No. 198P94-2 (Supreme Court of North Carolina, May 31, 1994) (WESTLAW, NC-CS database); Lawson v. Dixon, 22 Media L. Rep. (BNA) 1839 (4th Cir. June 13, 1994).

14. *Justices Deny Donahue Appeal to Videotape Execution,* Reuters, Ltd., June 14, 1994 (BC cycle) (LEXIS); *Killer of Texas Grocery Manager Is Executed,* WASH. POST, June 15, 1994, at A26; John Carmody, *The TV Column,* WASH. POST, June 16, 1994, at C6; *Donahue Seeks High Court Help,* WASH. POST, June 11, 1994, at A2.

15. George Gordon, *Is This the First Step Back to Public Execution,* Associated News-papers Ltd (Daily Mail), June 16, 1994 (LEXIS); *Pay-TV Executions Have No Takers,* COM. APP. (Memphis), Apr. 4, 1994, at 2A (LEXIS).

16. *Public Execution Denied,* WASH. POST, May 24, 1990, at C4; Gordon, *supra* note 15 (John Thanos requested a televised execution); Kenneth Soo, *Regional News,* United Press International, Apr. 4, 1984 (AM cycle) (LEXIS) (prison officials denied condemned child killer Arthur Frederick Goode's request for a televised execution); *Domestic News,* United Press International, Apr. 2, 1984 (AM cycle) (LEXIS) (same); Ferguson v. State, 417 So. 2d 631, 635–36 (Fla. 1982). For an argument that private execution laws violate death row inmates' First Amendment rights, see Roderick C. Patrick, Note, *Hiding Death,* 18 NEW ENG. J. CRIM. & CIV. CONFINEMENT 117 (1992).

17. Sharon Herbaugh, *Prison Board Decides Against Televising Executions,* Associated Press, Mar. 12, 1984 (PM cycle) (LEXIS); *Domestic News,* Associated Press, Feb. 25, 1984 (AM cycle) (LEXIS).

18. Charles Aldinger, *Washington Dateline,* Reuters Ltd., June 14, 1985 (PM cycle) (LEXIS); S. 1155, 102d Cong., 1st Sess. (1991); Jonathan Sherman, *Pictures at an Execution,* N.Y. TIMES, May 3, 1991, at A31 ("In 1985 . . . Senator Mark Hatfield of Oregon suggested that the public would turn against the death penalty once it peered into the execution chamber."); 137 Cong. Rec. S6667 (daily ed. May 23, 1991) (statement of Senator Hatfield); Michael Madow, *Forbidden Spectacle: Executions, the Public and the Press in Nineteenth Century New York,* 43 BUFF. L. REV. 461, 557–58 (1995).

19. Ray Sotero, *TV Station Sues State to Allow TV Coverage of Execution,* Gannett News Service, Oct. 25, 1990 (LEXIS); 1991 Ga. H.B. 110, *available in* LEXIS, Genfed Library, Bills File (introduced on January 15, 1991); Robert McDaniel, *Regional News,* United Press International, Apr. 22, 1981 (BC cycle) (LEXIS); Bill Halldin, *House Panel Foresees Call for TV Executions,* TAMPA TRIB., July 9, 1991, at 1.

20. *Judiciary Committee Rejects Plan to Televise Executions,* United Press International, Feb. 17, 1983 (BC cycle) (LEXIS).

21. Greg Lucas, *State Assembly Defeats Bill to Allow Televising of Executions,* S.F. CHRON., May 30, 1991, at A23; Greg Lucas, *Televised Executions Bill Dies: Assembly Votes It Down for a Second Time,* S.F. CHRON., Sept. 4, 1991, at A14; Jerry Gillam, *Assembly Panel OKs Bill on Televised Executions,* L.A. TIMES, May 11, 1991, at B6, col. 1; Jerry Gillam, *Bill to Permit TV Coverage of Executions Fails in Assembly,* L.A. TIMES, May 30, 1991, at A27, col. 5.

22. *Executions on TV Worry Legislators,* L.A. TIMES, Jan. 17, 1977, pt. 1, at 3, cols. 5–6.

23. Betty Wilson, *Is There an Electric Chair in Minnesota's Future?,* MINN. J.L. & POL., Feb. 1995, at 8; Robert Whereatt, *Carlson Reconsiders Death Penalty Stance,* MINNEAPOLIS STAR-TRIB., Nov. 3, 1994, at 2B; MINN. H.F. No. 1700 (copy on file with author); MINN. HOUSE J., at 3542 (1995); Session Weekly (Minnesota Legislature), May 5, 1995 (discussing proposed amendment to the judiciary finance bill); Patricia Lopez Baden, *House OKs Crime Bill Without Death Penalty,* MINNEAPOLIS STAR-TRIB., May 3, 1995, at 2B; Jim Ragsdale, *Death Penalty Amendment Voted Down in House,* ST. PAUL PIONEER PRESS, May 3, 1995, at 1B & 6B; MINN. HOUSE J., at 3542–52 (1995); Minnesota House of Representatives, Tape Recording of May 2, 1995 (copy on file with author) (containing legislative debate regarding Representative Bettermann's proposed amendment seeking to authorize capital punishment); Members Directory, Minnesota Legislature, 79th Sess. 1995–1996, at 81, 83, 103 (containing brief biographical sketches of Representatives Ron Abrams, Hilda Bettermann, and Dee Long).

24. Md. House Bill 1149 (1994); Testimony of H. Mark Stichel before the Maryland House of Delegates Judiciary Committee (Mar. 3, 1994), at 1, 5–7 (copy on file with author); Telephone Interview with H. Mark Stichel, Piper & Marbury, Baltimore (Jan. 10, 1996); Thomas Hardy & Rob Karwath, *Philip Asks to Go Tough on Killers,* CHI. TRIB., Feb. 5, 1993, at D6; Michael Moline, *Candidate Calls for Vote on Televised Execution,* United Press International, Feb. 21, 1986 (AM cycle) (LEXIS).

25. *Judge Invites TV to Film Execution,* COM. APP. (Memphis), Nov. 25, 1994, at 2A (LEXIS); James Ewinger, *Judge's Order Draws Spotlight; Vatican Faults Edict to Televise Execution,* CLEVE. PLAIN DEALER, Nov. 29, 1994, at 1B (LEXIS).

26. Alan Cooper, *4th Circuit Rejects Electrocution Challenge,* NAT'L L.J., Feb. 1, 1993, at 7; Tim Cox, *Bunch Executed,* United Press International, Dec. 10, 1992 (BC cycle) (LEXIS); G. L. Marshall, *Court Approves Videotaping of Execution,* United Press International, Dec. 10, 1992 (BC cycle) (LEXIS).

27. Marcia Coyle, *Inmate Wants Execution Taped,* NAT'L L.J., Feb. 21, 1994, at 3; *In re* Thomas, 155 F.R.D. 124 (D. Md. 1994); Sabra Chartrand, *Given a Push, Maryland Alters Its Death Penalty,* N.Y. TIMES, Mar. 25, 1994, at B18; Release and Waiver of John Thanos dated Oct. 21, 1993 (copy on file with author); *In re* Petition of Donald Thomas, Misc. No. 93–95 (U.S. Dist. Ct. Md.) (Opposition to Petition for Discovery), at 7–8 (copy on file with author); *Maryland Inmate OKs Taping of His Execution,* CHI. SUN-TIMES, Feb. 14, 1994, at 8; Telephone Interview with H. Mark Stichel, Piper & Marbury, Baltimore (Dec. 21, 1995); *In re* Petition for Donald Thomas, Misc. No. 93–95 (U.S. Dist. Ct. Md.) (Memorandum in Opposition to Motion for Reconsideration and to Vacate Order), at 2–3 (copy on file with author); *In re* Petition for Donald Thomas, Misc. No. 93–95 (U.S. Dist. Ct. Md.) (Motion for Reconsideration and to Vacate Order), at 1–2 (copy on file with author); Md. House Bill 498 (1994).

28. Welton W. Harris II, *It's Over,* INDIANAPOLIS NEWS, Dec. 8, 1994, at A1; Nancy Armour, *Brink's Guard Killer Dies in Electric Chair,* Associated Press, Dec. 8, 1994 (PM cycle) (LEXIS); Mary Dieter, *A Search for "Some Meaning"; Inmate Hoped Death Would Bring Change,* COURIER-J. (Louisville), Dec. 9, 1994, at 1A; STATE J.-REG. (Springfield, Ill.), Dec. 8, 1994, at 2; Ellis Wayne Felcher & Larry Grant Lonchar v. Tony Turpin, Case No. 5:96-CV-425-4(DF) (D. Ga. Nov. 12, 1996); Ellis Wayne Felcher & Larry Grant Lonchar, Case No. 5:96-CV-311-2(DF) (D. Ga. Nov. 12, 1996).

29. Campbell v. Blodgett, 982 F.2d 1356, 1357–65 (9th Cir. 1993); BNA's DIRECTORY OF STATE & FEDERAL COURTS, JUDGES & CLERKS (1995–1996 ed.), at 4.

30. GEORGE COMSTOCK, TELEVISION AND THE AMERICAN CHILD ix (1991); Margaret S. Andreasen, *Evolution in the Family's Use of Television: Normative Data from Industry and Academe, in* TELEVISION AND THE AMERICAN FAMILY 24 (Jennings Bryant ed., 1990); HERBERT H. HOWARD, MICHAEL S. KIEVMAN, & BARBARA A. MOORE, RADIO, TV, AND CABLE PROGRAMMING 178 (1994) (62.9 percent of households subscribed to cable television in 1993).

31. Don R. Le Duc, *Recognizing the Interests of the Public in Broadcast Programming,* 6 NOTRE DAME J.L., ETHICS & PUB. POL'Y 75, 82 n.25 (1992); A. C. Nielsen Co., Nielsen Report on Television 8 (1990); COMSTOCK, *supra* note 30, at 56; Rod Granger, *Cable Viewers Want Big 3, Study Finds,* ELECTRONIC MEDIA, May 6, 1991, at 8 (*citing* Roper Organization, America's Watching: Public Attitudes Towards Television); Elliot E. Slotnick, *Television News and the Supreme Court: A Case Study,* 77 JUDICATURE 21, 22 (1993) (television is the main or only source of news for most Americans); Jeff Angeja, Note, *Televising California's Death Penalty: Is There a Constitutional Right to Broadcast Executions?,* 43 HASTINGS L.J. 1489, 1501 (1992); William C. Bailey & Ruth D. Peterson, *Capital Punishment*

and Non-Capital Crimes: A Test of Deterrence, General Prevention, and System-Overload Arguments, 54 ALB. L. REV. 681, 692 n.51 (1990); Vanderbilt Television News Archive, Television News Index and Abstracts (Jan. 1976–Dec. 1987); OXBRIDGE COMMUNICATIONS, INC., THE STANDARD PERIODICAL DIRECTORY 1127–28 (13th ed. 1990); Richard Weizel, *From New Words, New Worlds,* N.Y. TIMES, May 3, 1992, § 13CN, at 1 (U.S. Department of Education figures); Kurt Andersen, *The Outsider,* NEW YORKER, Mar. 31, 1997, at 47.

32. Roper Organization, Trends in Attitudes Towards Television and Other Media: A Twenty-Four Year Review 4 (1983).

33. *Nightline,* "Making the Death Penalty Visible" (ABC television broadcast, May 24, 1991); Julia Keller, *"Witness" Makes Viewers Pay to Watch,* COLUMBUS DISPATCH, Feb. 13, 1994, at 4G; Howard Rosenberg, *TV: A Witness for the Execution,* L.A. TIMES, May 19, 1990, at F1 (*L.A. Law* episode); Ray Loynd, *"Shoot the Picture" Graphic on Death Row,* L.A. TIMES, Sept. 8, 1990, at F13 (review of *Somebody Has to Shoot the Picture*).

34. John D. Bessler, *Televised Executions and the Constitution: Recognizing a First Amendment Right of Access to State Executions,* 45 FED. COMM. L.J. 355, 367 n.57 (1993).

35. SISTER HELEN PREJEAN, DEAD MAN WALKING: AN EYEWITNESS ACCOUNT OF THE DEATH PENALTY IN THE UNITED STATES 42, 68, 94, 197, 214–15 (1994); *Let TV Cameras Show Executions,* USA TODAY, July 18, 1990, at 6A (opinion).

36. Herb Haines, *Flawed Executions, the Anti–Death Penalty Movement, and the Politics of Capital Punishment,* 39 SOC. PROB. 125, 127 (1992); Elwood McIntyre, *A Farmer Halts the Hangman: The Story of Marvin Bovee,* WIS. MAG. HIST., Autumn 1958, at 3–12; Alexander T. Pendleton & Blaine R. Renfert, *A Brief History of Wisconsin's Death Penalty,* WIS. LAW., Aug. 1993, at 26–30.

37. John Carmody, *The TV Column,* WASH. POST, June 16, 1994, at C6; Transcript #1104, CNN (*Crossfire*), June 1, 1994 (LEXIS); LESSER, *supra* note 1, at 40, 106.

38. Michael Schwarz, *TV in the Death Chamber: A News Story Like Any Other,* N.Y. TIMES, May 17, 1991 ("many prominent death penalty supporters—including law enforcement officers like Joseph Russoniello, former United States Attorney for California's Northern District—have publicly said that putting executions on television will enhance their deterrent effect"); PREJEAN, *supra* note 35, at 235; James Gill, *On Publicly Televising Executions,* TIMES-PICAYUNE (New Orleans), May 19, 1995, at B7; *Mayor Suggests Televised Executions to Cut Down on Murders,* United Press International, Apr. 26, 1991 (LEXIS); Steven Stack, *Publicized Executions and Homicide, 1950–1980,* 52 AM. SOC. REV. 532, 532 (Aug. 1987).

39. Haines, *supra* note 36, at 132; Bailey & Peterson, *supra* note 31, at 691; William C. Bailey, *Murder, Capital Punishment, and Television: Execution Publicity and Homicide Rates,* 55 AM. SOC. REV. 628 (1990); Stack, *supra* note 38, at 533, 538; *see, e.g.,* WASH. POST, Feb. 26, 1991, at A4, col. 2 (execution of Lawrence Buxton). News coverage is even more limited outside of the state where an execution occurs. None of the twenty-five executions in Alabama between 1950 and 1965 were even reported in the *Charleston News and Courier.* Stack, *supra* note 38, at 534 n.4.

40. William J. Bowers & Glenn L. Pierce, *Deterrence or Brutalization: What Is the Effect of Executions?,* 26 CRIME & DELINQ. 453–484 (1980); *see also* William Bailey & Ruth

Peterson, *Murder, Capital Punishment, and Deterrence: A Review of the Evidence and an Examination of Police Killings,* 50 J. SOC. ISSUES 53 (1994); William J. Bowers, *The Effect of the Death Penalty Is Brutalization, Not Deterrence, in* KENNETH C. HAAS & JAMES A. INCIARDI, CHALLENGING CAPITAL PUNISHMENT: LEGAL AND SOCIAL SCIENCE APPROACHES 55 (1988); Stephen J. Kim, *"Viewer Discretion Is Advised": A Structural Approach to the Issue of Television Violence,* 142 U. PA. L. REV. 1383, 1387, 1390 & nn.15, 28 (1994).

41. David P. Phillips, *The Deterrent Effect of Capital Punishment: New Evidence on an Old Controversy,* 86 AM. J. SOC. 139, 144 (1980); Stack, *supra* note 38, at 533; Bowers, *supra* note 40, at 72 & n.12. For additional articles on Phillips's study, see Wayne Kobbervig, James Inverarity, & Pat Lauderdale, *Deterrence and the Death Penalty: A Comment on Phillips,* 88 AM. J. SOC. 161 (1982); Hans Zeisel, *Comment on the Deterrent Effect of Capital Punishment,* 88 AM. J. SOC. 167 (1982) (critique of Phillips's study); David P. Phillips, *The Fluctuation of Homicide After Publicized Executions: Reply to Kobbervig, Inverarity, and Lauderdale,* 88 AM. J. SOC. 165 (1982); David P. Phillips, *Deterrence and the Death Penalty: A Reply to Zeisel,* 88 AM. J. SOC. 170 (1982).

42. Bailey, *supra* note 39, at 628; Stack, *supra* note 38, at 532, 536, 538. *But see* William Bailey & Ruth Peterson, *Murder and Capital Punishment: A Monthly Time-Series Analysis of Execution Publicity,* 54 AM. SOC. REV. 722 (1989) (criticizing Stack's study). In 1990, Steven Stack published a related study of thirty South Carolina executions that occurred between 1950 and 1963. That study found that the homicide rate in South Carolina fell 17.5 percent in months with publicized executions. Steven Stack, *Execution Publicity and Homicide in South Carolina: A Research Note,* 31 SOC. Q. 599 (1990). This study produced results that were at odds with an earlier study. David R. King, *The Brutalization Effect: Execution Publicity and the Incidence of Homicide in South Carolina,* 57 SOC. FORCES 683 (1978).

43. Bowers, *supra* note 40, at 50, 57, 69–81 & n.25; William C. Bailey & Ruth D. Peterson, *Murder, Capital Punishment, and Deterrence: A Review of the Literature, in* THE DEATH PENALTY IN AMERICA: CURRENT CONTROVERSIES 147 (Hugo Adam Bedau ed., 1997). Phillips even conceded that "within five or six weeks of a publicized execution, the drop in homicides is cancelled by an equally large rise in homicides." *Id.* at 70.

44. George F. Will, *Capital Punishment and Public Theater,* WASH. POST, May 12, 1991, at C7; Thomas Sowell, *Televised Executions? Media Bias at 11,* DETROIT NEWS, July 22, 1991, at 10A; Anthony Lewis, *Their Brutal Mirth,* N.Y. TIMES, May 20, 1991, at A15; Ernest van den Haag, *The Ultimate Punishment: A Defense,* 99 HARV. L. REV. 1662, 1667 n.22 (1986).

45. Julia W. Schlegel, *The Television Violence Act of 1990: A New Program for Government Censorship,* 46 FED. COMM. L.J. 187, 197–98 (1994); John P. Murray, *The Impact of Televised Violence,* 22 HOFSTRA L. REV. 809, 812 (1994); Max Frankel, *The Murder Broadcasting System,* N.Y. TIMES MAG., Dec. 17, 1995, at 46, 48.

46. Schlegel, *supra* note 45, at 197; GEORGE COMBE, THOUGHTS ON CAPITAL PUNISHMENT 14 (1847); ARIZ. REV. STAT. ANN. § 13-705 (1989) ("nor shall any minor be allowed to witness the execution"); CAL. PENAL CODE § 3605 (West. Supp. 1993) ("nor can any person under 18 years of age be allowed to witness the execution"); CONN. GEN.

STAT. ANN. § 54-100 (West 1985) ("such other adults, as the prisoner may designate"); LA. REV. STAT. ANN. § 15:570 (West 1992) ("[n]o person under the age of eighteen years shall be allowed within the execution room during the time of execution"); MO. ANN. STAT. § 546.740 (Vernon Supp. 1992) ("no person under twenty-one years of age shall be allowed to witness the execution"); NEV. REV. STAT. § 176.355 (1991) (director of the department of prisons shall invite "not less than six nor more than nine reputable citizens over the age of 21 years, to be present at the execution"); N.J. STAT. ANN. § 2C:49-7(a) (West Supp. 1992) ("six adult citizens"); N.M. STAT. ANN. § 31-14-15 (Michie 1984) (no person "under age" is allowed to witness an execution); PA. STAT. ANN. tit. 61, § 2125 (Supp. 1992) ("six reputable adult citizens selected by such warden"); S.D. CODIFIED LAWS ANN. § 23A-27A-36 (1988) ("[t]he warden . . . shall not permit the presence of any person under the age of eighteen years, unless a relative, and no relatives of tender years shall be admitted"); UTAH CODE ANN. § 77-19-11(7)(b) (1990) ("[a]ny person younger than 18 years of age may not attend"); ALA. CODE § 15-18-83(b) (1982); OHIO REV. CODE ANN. § 2949.25(E) (Baldwin 1992); OHIO ADMIN. CODE § 5120-9-54(A)(5)-(6) (1989); TEX. CRIM. PROC. CODE ANN. § 43.20 (West 1979).

47. van den Haag, *supra* note 44, at 1667 n.22.

48. Will, *supra* note 44, at C7 ("[s]olemnity should surround any person's death"); Steve Keeva, *Watching a Killer Die: A California TV Station Sues to Televise Execution*, 76 A.B.A. J. 24, 25 (1990); *Texan Executed by Injection for Murder in 1977*, N.Y. TIMES, Dec. 5, 1986, at A18, cols. 1–5; *Texas Murderer Is Executed After Top Court Rejects Plea*, N.Y. TIMES, Dec. 19, 1986, at A30, cols. 1–2.

49. Seth Rosenfeld, *Warden Afraid of Revenge on Guards If Executions on TV*, S.F. EXAMINER, Mar. 28, 1991, at A5; Katherine Bishop, *Judge Weighs TV Coverage of Execution*, N.Y. TIMES, June 5, 1991, at A22, cols. 1–3.

50. Tom Matthews & Peter Greenberg, *Gilmore's Countdown*, NEWSWEEK, Jan. 24, 1977, at 35; *The Harris Survey* (Louis Harris & Assoc.), *cited in* THE DEATH PENALTY IN AMERICA 92 (Hugo A. Bedau ed., 3d ed. 1982); FRANKLIN ZIMRING & GORDON HAWKINS, CAPITAL PUNISHMENT AND THE AMERICAN AGENDA 17 (1986); Lauren R. Reskin, *Majority of Lawyers Support Capital Punishment*, A.B.A. J., Apr. 1985, at 44; Yankelvich Clancy Shulman, *Views on the American Scene: Executions and Television*, 23 NAT'L J. 1828 (July 20, 1991); *Allow Television Cameras in Death Chamber? Don't Execute Criminals on TV, Most Callers Say*, ORLANDO SENTINEL, May 7, 1991, at A7; Gary N. Howells, Kelly A. Flanagan, & Vivian Hagan, *Does Viewing a Televised Execution Affect Attitudes Toward Capital Punishment?*, 22 CRIM. JUST. & BEH. 411, 412 (1995).

51. S.C. CODE ANN. § 24-3-550 (Law. Co-op. Supp. 1992); S.D. CODIFIED LAWS ANN. § 23A-27A-34 (1988).

52. *Man Who Killed Foster Mother Is Executed by Lethal Injection*, ST. LOUIS POST-DISPATCH, July 28, 1993, at 1B (Frederick Lashley executed for crime he committed when he was seventeen); Bill Walsh, *Supreme Court Was Sawyer's Last Hope for Life*, TIMES-PICAYUNE (New Orleans), Mar. 5, 1993, at A1 (Robert Sawyer executed despite strong evidence of mental retardation and brain damage); *Florida Inmate Dies in Electric Chair*, COURIER-JOURNAL (Louisville), July 28, 1990, at 6A (at the May 4, 1990, ex-

ecution of Jesse Tafero, "fire, smoke and sparks spewed" from his head); Bessler, *supra* note 34, at 412.

53. Howells, Flanagan, & Hagan, *supra* note 50, at 411; THE DEATH PENALTY IN AMERICA: CURRENT CONTROVERSIES, *supra* note 43, at 41 (listing by jurisdiction the minimum age authorized for capital punishment).

54. David Lawrence Abney, Capital Punishment in Arizona, 1863–1963 (Aug. 1988) (Master's Thesis, Arizona State University). Five states—Georgia, Kentucky, Maryland, New Mexico, and Tennessee—currently prohibit the execution of mentally retarded inmates. Greg Lucas, *Bill Would End Execution of Retarded,* S.F. CHRON., Mar. 5, 1993, at A22.

55. Andrew Freinkel, Cheryl Koopman, & David Spiegel, *Dissociative Symptoms in Media Eyewitnesses of an Execution,* 151 AM. J. PSYCHIATRY 1335 (1994); *Witness to the Execution,* PSYCHOLOGY TODAY, May/June 1995, at 12. *But see* Steven Ornish, *Witnessing an Execution,* 152 AM. J. PSYCHIATRY 1404 (1995) (letter to the editor criticizing the study conducted by Freinkel, Koopman, and Spiegel).

56. Lance Williams, *Trial to Open on Executions on TV,* S.F. EXAMINER, Mar. 24, 1991, at A23, col. 2; Plaintiff's Trial Brief at 24, KQED, Inc. v. Vasquez, 18 Media L. Rep. (BNA) 2323 (N.D. Cal. 1991) (No. C90-1383RHS); *The Vietnam War: The Executioner,* NEWSWEEK, Nov. 13, 1978, at 70; Robin Oakley, *New Death Penalty Debate Likely,* TIMES (London), Feb. 13, 1990, at 9 (*citing* ROGER HOOD, THE DEATH PENALTY: A WORLDWIDE PERSPECTIVE (1989)); *see also* THE DEATH PENALTY: AMNESTY INTERNATIONAL REPORT 35, 40, 49, 52, 58, 63–64, 75, 102, 143, 150–51, 165, 167–68, 175, 179 (1979) (referencing public executions in China, Equatorial Guinea, Ethiopia, Haiti, Iraq, Kuwait, Morocco, Nigeria, Saudi Arabia, Somalia, Syria, Tanzania, Thailand, Uganda, and Yemen Arab Republic).

57. *Death Penalty Popular in Japan, But Rare Recently,* N.Y. TIMES, May 29, 1995, at 2, cols. 1–4; Leigh Bienen, *Criminal Homicide in Western Nigeria, 1966–1972,* 18 J. AFRICAN L. 57, 65 (1974); Leigh Bienen, *The Determination of Criminal Insanity in Western Nigeria,* 14 J. MOD. AFRICAN STUD. 220, 225 n.1 (1976); Shigemitsu Dando, *Toward the Abolition of the Death Penalty,* 72 IND. L.J. 7, 10 (1996); THE DEATH PENALTY: AMNESTY INTERNATIONAL REPORT, *supra* note 56, at 52–54, 70–71, 85 (noting that executions in Rhodesia were conducted without public notification and that the names of persons executed in Bangladesh are not published).

58. Howard Rosenberg, *TV: A Witness for the Execution,* L.A. TIMES, May 19, 1990, at F1 (quoting University of California, Berkeley professor and media critic Ben Bagdikian) ("'increase savagery'"); Lewis, *supra* note 44, at A15.

59. Sable Communications v. FCC, 492 U.S. 115, 128 (1989) (*quoting* Bolger v. Youngs Drugs Prods. Corp., 463 U.S. 60, 73 (1983)); Butler v. Michigan, 352 U.S. 380, 383 (1957). A *New York Times* poll recently reported that 84 percent of parents have forbidden their children to watch or listen to a particular television program because the parents objected to its content. Sixty-four percent said they had done so in the previous six months. Elizabeth Kolbert, *Americans Despair of Popular Culture,* N.Y. TIMES, Aug. 20, 1995, sec. 2, at 1, 23.

60. Jef I. Richards & R. Bruce Easter, *Televising Executions: The High-Tech Alternative to Public Hangings,* 40 UCLA L. REV. 381, 410 (1992); Amy Wallace & David Beasley,

McCorquodale Dies in State's Electric Chair, ATLANTA CONST., Sept. 22, 1987, at 1A, col. 6, & 7A, cols. 1–4; Brandenburg v. Ohio, 395 U.S. 444, 447 (1969). This whole line of argument further assumes, erroneously, that all prisoners are opposed to capital punishment. A recent study of 307 inmates found that "the majority of inmates, both violent and nonviolent inmates alike," favor capital punishment. Approximately 53 percent of inmates in North Carolina and South Carolina and 63 percent of inmates in Illinois support capital punishment for some crimes. Dennis Stevens, *Research Note: The Death Sentence and Inmate Attitudes,* 38 CRIME & DELINQ. 272, 278 (1992).

61. Plaintiff's Post-Trial Brief at 23–24, KQED, Inc. v. Vasquez, 18 Media L. Rep. (BNA) 2323 (N.D. Cal. 1991) (No. C90–1383RHS); *Solicitor Calls for Televised Executions in Prisons,* United Press International, Mar. 12, 1985 (AM cycle) (LEXIS). In KQED's lawsuit, KQED's lawyer, William Bennett Turner, accused the state of "trying to restrict the general public to what's fit for prisoners to see instead of blacking out the prisoners' television, which the warden can do." State Deputy Attorney General Karl Mayer conceded that it might be initially feasible to block the telecast of an execution within the prison. However, he argued that "the videotape could be shown in the future when something is going on in the prison, when there is tension over some other issue, and further incite them." Bishop, *supra* note 49, at A22, cols. 1–3.

62. LESSER, *supra* note 1, at 166–68; Plaintiff's Post-Trial Brief at 22–23 & n.18, KQED, Inc. v. Vasquez, 18 Media L. Rep. (BNA) 2323 (N.D. Cal. 1991) (No. C90–1383RHS); MARSHALL H. MCLUHAN, UNDERSTANDING MEDIA (1964) (title of first chapter).

63. Nat Hentoff, *Governor Pataki: Why Not Televise Executions?,* VILLAGE VOICE, Mar. 28, 1995, at 22. Death penalty referenda are not uncommon. For instance, in Oregon, a referendum seeking to abolish capital punishment failed in 1958 but was later approved in 1964. Two years later, Colorado voters approved the death penalty by a wide margin, and in 1970, approximately 64 percent of Illinois voters approved of capital punishment in a referendum. Furman v. Georgia, 408 U.S. 238, 438–39 (1972) (Powell, J., dissenting); Katherine H. Waldo, *The 1984 Death Penalty Initiatives: A State Constitutional Analysis,* 22 WILLAMETTE L. REV. 285, 288 (1986) (*citing* Hugo A. Bedau, *Capital Punishment in Oregon, 1903–64,* 45 OR. L. REV. 1 (1965)); *see also* John F. Galliher, Gregory Ray, & Brent Cook, *Abolition and Reinstatement of Capital Punishment During the Progressive Era and Early 20th Century,* 83 J. CRIM. L. & CRIMINOLOGY 538, 562, 569 (1992) (citing other referenda on capital punishment).

64. ZIMRING & HAWKINS, *supra* note 50, at 3–5, 12–15, 21–22, 143; William A. Schabas, *International Law and the Death Penalty,* 22 AM. J. CRIM. L. 250 (1994); THE DEATH PENALTY IN AMERICA: CURRENT CONTROVERSIES, *supra* note 43, at 78–83 (listing nations that have abolished or retained capital punishment).

65. Holden v. Minnesota, 137 U.S. 483 (1890); Jerome Tao, Note, *First Amendment Analysis of State Regulations Prohibiting the Filming of Prisoner Executions,* 60 GEO. WASH. L. REV. 1042, 1046 n.20 (1992).

66. Wilkerson v. Utah, 99 U.S. 130 (1879) (*cited in Furman,* 408 U.S. at 322 (Marshall, J., concurring)); *Furman,* 408 U.S. at 297, 303 (Brennan, J., concurring); Michael Mello, *Adhering to Our Views: Justices Brennan and Marshall and the Relentless Dissent to*

Death as a Punishment, 22 FLA. ST. U. L. REV. 591 (1995); Glass v. Louisiana, 471 U.S. 1080, 1086 n.12 (1985).

67. Bessler, *supra* note 34, at 355, 433–35 (arguing that private execution laws are unconstitutional); William Bennett Turner & Beth S. Brinkmann, *Televising Executions: The First Amendment Issues,* 32 SANTA CLARA L. REV. 1135 (1992) (arguing that the prohibition on cameras in execution chambers in California is unconstitutional); Richards & Easter, *supra* note 60, at 381, 419 (arguing in favor of televising executions on a First Amendment basis); Tao, *supra* note 65, at 1042, 1045 (arguing that prohibitions against the filming of executions are unconstitutional content-based restrictions on First Amendment freedoms); Angeja, *supra* note 31, at 1491 (arguing that television reporters have a right of access to execution chambers based on the First Amendment); Dane A. Drobny, Note, *Death TV: Media Access to Executions Under the First Amendment,* 70 WASH. U. L.Q. 1179, 1181 (1992) (arguing that the press does not have a First Amendment right to attend or televise an execution); Patrick D. Filbin, Note, *"Pictures at an Execution,"* 9 THOMAS M. COOLEY L. REV. 137, 137–38 (1992) (examining arguments behind televising executions and asserting that there is not a constitutional right of media access to executions); Philip R. Wiese, *Popcorn and Primetime vs. Protocol: An Examination of the Televised Execution Issue,* 23 N.U. L. REV. 257 (1996) (developing an argument against televised executions using an Eighth Amendment argument); Patrick, *supra* note 16, at 117, 119 (stating that the government's prohibition of public executions violates the impermissible ends doctrine of Shapiro v. Thompson, 394 U.S. 618 (1969) and the "rational relation" test of Turner v. Safley, 482 U.S. 78 (1978)); Comment, *Broadcasters' News-Gathering Rights Under the First Amendment:* Garrett v. Estelle, 63 IOWA L. REV. 724, 729 (1978) (criticizing the Fifth Circuit's 1977 decision in *Garrett* upholding a Texas ban on cameras in the execution chamber); Katherine A. Mobley, Case Note, 11 CREIGHTON L. REV. 1031, 1052 (1978) (arguing that "graphic information about executions must be made available to the public"); *see also* David Sternbach, *Hanging Pictures: Photographic Theory and the Framing of Images of Execution,* 70 N.Y.U. L. REV. 1100 (1995) (discussing theories of photographic representation in the context of execution proceedings); 2 JESSE CHOPER ET AL., THE SUPREME COURT: TRENDS AND DEVELOPMENTS 197 (1981).

68. U.S. CONST. amend. I; Sable Communications v. FCC, 492 U.S. 115, 126 (1989); Boos v. Barry, 485 U.S. 312, 321 (1988); Geoffrey Stone, *Content-Neutral Restrictions,* 54 U. CHI. L. REV. 46, 47–48 (1987); Geoffrey Stone, *Content Regulation and the First Amendment,* 25 WM. & MARY L. REV. 189, 189–90 (1983).

69. Police Dept. of Chicago v. Mosley, 408 U.S. 92, 95–96 (1972) (*quoting* New York Times Co. v. Sullivan, 376 U.S. 254, 270 (1964)).

70. Cohen v. California, 403 U.S. 15 (1971); Texas v. Johnson, 491 U.S. 397, 408–9, 414 (1989) (*quoting* Terminiello v. Chicago, 337 U.S. 1, 4 (1949)).

71. Pell v. Procunier, 417 U.S. 817 (1974); Saxbe v. Washington Post Co., 417 U.S. 843 (1974); Branzburg v. Hayes, 408 U.S. 665, 681 (1972).

72. Potter Stewart, *Or of the Press,* 26 HASTINGS L.J. 631, 633–34 (1975); Houchins v. KQED, Inc., 438 U.S. 1, 17 (1978) (Stewart, J., concurring) (*quoting* Branzburg v. Hayes, 408 U.S. 655, 726 (1972), and Estes v. Texas, 381 U.S. 532, 539 (1965)).

73. LEONARD LEVY, THE EMERGENCE OF A FREE PRESS xii, 200, 291 (1985).

74. Turner & Brinkmann, *supra* note 67, at 1157 & n.107 (emphasis in original).

75. Zacchini v. Scripps-Howard Broadcasting Co., 433 U.S. 562, 581 (1977) (Powell, J., dissenting); Cable News Network v. American Broadcasting Cos., 518 F. Supp. 1238, 1245 (N.D. Ga. 1981).

76. *Furman,* 408 U.S. at 303 (Brennan, J., concurring); Cruzan v. Director, Mo. Dept. of Health, 497 U.S. 271, 310 (1990) (Brennan, J., dissenting). Even if legislators were to grant death row inmates a privacy right, the public's right to know would still be largely protected because many death row inmates would likely consent to televised executions. Twenty-one of twenty-nine death row inmates responding to a survey conducted by the Florida House of Representatives reportedly favored televised executions. Richards & Easter, *supra* note 60, at 419 & n.164; USA TODAY, Sept. 13, 1991. Obviously, a select number of official witnesses, including prison officials and community and press representatives, would have to be allowed to attend any execution, even if a state legislature were to legitimize a prisoner's right-to-privacy claim.

77. Pell v. Procunier, 417 U.S. 817 (1974); Saxbe v. Washington Post Co., 417 U.S. 843 (1974); *see* Chapter 3.

78. Richmond Newspapers v. Virginia, 448 U.S. 555, 564–65, 569, 571–72, 580 (1980) (plurality opinion of Burger, C.J.) (*quoting* The 1677 Concessions and Agreements of West New Jersey, *reprinted in* SOURCES OF OUR LIBERTIES 180, 188 (Richard L. Perry ed., 1959)) (alteration by court).

79. *Richmond Newspapers,* 448 U.S. at 587–88, 592 (emphasis in original) (*quoting In re* Oliver, 333 U.S. 257, 270 (1948), and New York Times Co. v. Sullivan, 376 U.S. 254, 270 (1964)).

80. Chandler v. Florida, 449 U.S. 560 (1981); David Harris, *The Appearance of Justice: Court TV, Conventional Television, and Public Understanding of the Criminal Justice System,* 35 ARIZ. L. REV. 785, 800 & n.119 (*citing* Radio-Television News Directors Ass'n, Summary of Expanded Media Coverage of State Courtroom Proceedings (1993)); Ronald K. L. Collins & David M. Skover, *Paratexts,* 44 STAN. L. REV. 509, 512 & nn.14–15 (1992); *see also* Richard H. Frank, *Cameras in the Courtroom: A First Amendment Right of Access,* 9 COMM/ENT L.J. 749, 752 & n.15 (1987); Henry Reske, *Rally for Court Cameras Falls Short,* A.B.A. J., Mar. 1995, at 30; *No More Cameras in Federal Courts,* A.B.A. J., Nov. 1994, at 28; Linda Greenhouse, *Disdaining a Sound Bite, Federal Judges Banish TV,* N.Y. TIMES, Sept. 25, 1994, at 4E; Harry F. Rosenthal, *TV Executives Upset by Decision to Bar Cameras from Courtroom* (undated article on file with author). Many members of the U.S. Supreme Court have been downright paranoid about the presence of television cameras in the courtroom. The Supreme Court itself refuses to allow oral arguments to be filmed, with Chief Justice Rehnquist and predecessor Warren Burger both opposing the idea. At a U.S. House of Representatives subcommittee meeting in March 1996, Justice David Souter told legislators: "The day you see a camera coming into our courtroom, it's going to roll over my dead body." Ronald Goldfarb, *The Invisible Supreme Court,* N.Y. TIMES, May 4, 1996, at 15, col. 2.

81. Harris, *supra* note 80, at 786–87, 800, 823 & nn.18, 23, 119, 284 (*citing* Richard Zoglin, *Justice Faces a Screen Test,* TIME, June 17, 1991, at 62 (Court TV began broadcasting in 1991)).

82. Estes v. Texas, 381 U.S. 532 (1965); First Nat'l Bank of Boston v. Bellotti, 435 U.S. 765, 791–92 (1978).

83. Sharon Herbaugh, *Prison Board Decides Against Televising Executions,* Associated Press, Mar. 12, 1984 (PM cycle) (LEXIS).

84. *Helping a Man Kill Himself, As Shown on Dutch TV,* N.Y. TIMES, Nov. 13, 1994, at E7.

Conclusion

1. *See* Appendix.

2. PHILIP MACKEY, HANGING IN THE BALANCE: THE ANTI-CAPITAL PUNISHMENT MOVEMENT IN NEW YORK STATE, 1776–1861 (1982).

3. Public Acts of Conn., Ch. CXXXVII, § 3 (1889–1899) (restricting attendance to "adult males"); E. ROY CALVERT, CAPITAL PUNISHMENT IN THE TWENTIETH-CENTURY 115–16, 118 (1930).

4. State v. Pioneer Press Co., 110 N.W. 867, 868 (Minn. 1907); 36 U.S.C. § 174(a) (1994) ("It is the universal custom to display the flag only from sunrise to sunset on buildings and on stationary flagstaffs in the open. However, when patriotic effect is desired, the flag may be displayed twenty-four hours a day if properly illuminated during the hours of darkness."). States have similar laws. For example, the New York state flag cannot be displayed at night "except on special occasions." Likewise, a Texas flag "normally should not be displayed outdoors earlier than sunrise or later than sunset." Only if the Texas flag is "properly illuminated" may the flag fly in darkness. N.Y. EXEC. LAW ch. 18, art. 19, § 403 (McKinney 1994); TEX. CIV. STAT. art. 6139c (1994).

5. Colman McCarthy, *Sister Helen Prejean Keeps the Faith,* MINNEAPOLIS STAR-TRIB., June 5, 1996, at A13, cols. 1–2.

6. Howard Rosenberg, *TV: A Witness for the Execution,* L.A. TIMES, May 19, 1990, at F1; Anna Quindlen, *TV Executions Will Force Us to Look Death in the Eye,* CHI. TRIB., May 21, 1991, Perspective Section, at 19; Gary N. Howells, Kelly A. Flanagan, & Vivian Hagan, *Does Viewing a Televised Execution Affect Attitudes Toward Capital Punishment?,* 22 CRIM. JUST. & BEH. 411, 414 (1995); Harris v. Alabama, 115 S. Ct. 1031, 1038 (1995) (Stevens, J., dissenting); Scott Erlich, *The Jury Override: A Blend of Politics and Death,* 45 AM. U. L. REV. 1403, 1435 n.224 (1996); Alex Kozinski, *Tinkering with Death,* NEW YORKER, Feb. 10, 1997, at 48, 52.

7. Neil Nussbaum, *"Film at Eleven . . ."—Does the Press Have the Right to Attend and Videotape Executions?,* 20 N.C. CENT. L.J. 121 (1992).

Appendix

1. Debbie Salamone, *Jerry White Pays Ultimate Price for '81 Murder,* ORLANDO SENTINEL, Dec. 5, 1995, at A1.

2. *Killers Executed in Separate Cases,* N.Y. TIMES, Apr. 16, 1986, at B9, col. 1.

3. Rhonda Cook, *Child's Killer Is Executed,* ATLANTA CONST., May 18, 1995, at 4C.

4. *Vietnam Veteran Is Put to Death in Florida,* N.Y. TIMES, Apr. 23, 1986, at A10, cols. 4–6; *Judge Refuses to Block Execution in Florida,* N.Y. TIMES, Apr. 22, 1986, at A10, col. 6.

5. *Florida Executes Second Man for Murder of a Store Owner,* N.Y. TIMES, May 21, 1986, at A19, cols. 1–4.

6. *Daugherty Execution Makes Him "Free,"* United Press International, Nov. 8, 1988, *available in* LEXIS, News Library, UPI File; *Florida Executes Killer of 4 Women,* N.Y. TIMES, Nov. 8, 1988, at B22, cols. 4–6.

7. Judi Villa, *Jeffers Dies Cursing His Executioners,* ARIZ. REPUBLIC, Sept. 14, 1995, at A1.

8. *Arizona Man Executed in Texas,* United Press International, Dec. 11, 1995, *available in* LEXIS, News Library, UPI File.

9. *Vietnamese Man Executed in Texas,* United Press International, Dec. 7, 1995, *available in* LEXIS, News Library, UPI File.

10. Michael Graczyk, *Texas Executes 100th Inmate, Killer of 17-Year-Old Cashier,* Associated Press, Oct. 4, 1995, *available in* WESTLAW, DIALOG-GW Library, AP-NEWS File.

11. Tracy Everbach, *Man Who Killed Officer in '88 Is Executed,* DALLAS MORNING NEWS, Dec. 7, 1995, at 37A.

12. Michael Graczyk, *Inmate Executed for Robbery in Which 2 Men Killed,* HOUSTON CHRON., Dec. 13, 1995, *available in* WESTLAW, Allnews Library.

13. *Florida Inmate Dies in Electric Chair,* COURIER-J. (Louisville), July 28, 1990, at 6A; *Killer, 38, Is Executed in Florida,* N.Y. TIMES, July 28, 1990, at 9, cols. 2–3.

14. *Three Murderers Die in Triple Execution,* COLUMBIAN (Vancouver, Wash.), Aug. 4, 1994, at C2.

15. David Beasley & Amy Wallace, *Mitchell Dies in Georgia's Electric Chair,* ATLANTA CONST., Sept. 2, 1987, at 1A, col. 1, & 6A, cols. 1–6; Amy Wallace, *Convicted Killer Scheduled to Die in Chair Tonight,* ATLANTA CONST., Sept. 1, 1987, at 19A, col. 1, & 21A, cols. 3–6.

16. Amy Wallace & David Beasley, *McCorquodale Dies in State's Electric Chair,* ATLANTA CONST., Sept. 22, 1987, at 1A, col. 6, & 7A, cols. 1–4.

17. Amy Wallace & W. Steven Ricks, *Messer Is Executed for Kidnap-Murder of 8-Year-Old Niece,* ATLANTA CONST., July 29, 1988, at 1A, col. 6, & 8A, cols. 1–4.

18. David Beasley & Scott Thurston, *Convicted Murderer Mulligan Executed,* ATLANTA CONST., May 16, 1987, at 1A, cols. 1–3, & 10A, cols. 1–4.

19. David Beasley, *Tucker Dies Calmly After Wink, Smiles,* ATLANTA CONST., May 30, 1987, at 5A, cols. 4–5.

20. *Three Murderers Die in Triple Execution, supra* note 14, at C2.

21. *2 Killers Executed in Arkansas,* ST. LOUIS POST-DISPATCH, May 12, 1994, at 10A.

22. *Alabama Killer Is Executed as High Court Rejects Pleas,* L.A. TIMES, Apr. 23, 1983, pt. 1, at 3, cols. 1–2.

23. *Arkansas Electrocutes Killer of Police Officer,* N.Y. TIMES, June 19, 1990, at A17, cols. 1–4.

24. June Arney & Laura Lafay, *Executed Inmate Had Hidden Gun,* DAYTON DAILY NEWS, May 27, 1995, at 3A.

25. *2 Killers Executed in Arkansas, supra* note 21, at 10A.

26. *Stockton Executed,* ROANOKE TIMES & WORLD NEWS, Sept. 28, 1995, at A1.

27. *Killer Executed After Clinton Denies Clemency,* N.Y. TIMES, May 8, 1992, at A17, cols. 1–2; Cathleen Decker, *Inmate Is Executed After Clinton Denies Clemency Plea,* L.A. TIMES, May 8, 1992, at A32, cols. 1–6.

28. *Arkansas Inmate Fairchild Executed,* United Press International, Aug. 31, 1995, *available in* LEXIS, News Library, UPI File.

29. *2 Inmates Executed in a Day,* N.Y. TIMES, Jan. 26, 1995, at A17, col. 4.

30. *British-Born Killer Put to Death in Ga.,* CHARLESTON DAILY MAIL, Apr. 8, 1995, at 3A.

31. *White Supremacist Executed for Murdering 2 in Arkansas,* N.Y. TIMES, Apr. 21, 1995, at A16.

32. *Arkansas Executes Killer of 16; Texas Kills Inmate by Injection,* N.Y. TIMES, June 26, 1990, at A21, cols. 1–2.

33. *Three Murderers Die in Triple Execution, supra* note 14, at C2.

34. R. B. Fallstrom, *Missouri Man, 33, Executed for Killing,* ST. LOUIS POST-DIS-PATCH, Oct. 22, 1992, at 8A, cols. 5–6.

35. *Murderer Is Executed in Missouri After Supreme Court Lifts a Stay,* N.Y. TIMES, May 12, 1990, at 10, cols. 5–6.

36. *Man Who Killed Wife, Two Stepdaughters Is Executed,* VIRGINIAN-PILOT (Nor-folk), Oct. 20, 1995, at B7.

37. *Georgia Executes Killer of Soldier,* N.Y. TIMES, Dec. 9, 1993, at B18.

38. *Florida Executes Man Who Killed During Robbery,* N.Y. TIMES, May 10, 1993, at A20, col. 1; *Court Lifts Johnson's Stay of Execution,* United Press International, May 7, 1993, *available in* LEXIS, News Library, UPI File.

39. Peter Applebome, *Arkansas Execution Raises Questions on Governor's Politics,* N.Y. TIMES, Jan. 25, 1992, at 8, cols. 1–6; Hugh Aynesworth, *Execution in Arkansas Draws Clinton to State,* WASH. TIMES, Jan. 24, 1992, at A4.

40. *Prisoner Is Executed in Georgia: Objections Were Made by a Juror, and Lawyers Who Said He Was Retarded,* PHIL. INQUIRER, Apr. 1, 1994, at A4.

41. Frank Green, *Inmate Executed for Killing 2 People,* RICHMOND TIMES-DISPATCH, Nov. 14, 1995, at B1.

42. *Pennsylvania Execution Is 1st in 33 Years,* L.A. TIMES, May 3, 1995, at A14.

43. *Organizer of Death-Row Escape Is Executed in a Virginia Prison,* N.Y. TIMES, Oct. 13, 1984, at 19, cols. 1–3.

44. *Virginia Executes Killer of Woman,* N.Y. TIMES, Aug. 31, 1989, at A22, col. 4.

45. *Virginia Executes Killer of 3 Women,* N.Y. TIMES, Dec. 14, 1990, at A26, col. 4.

46. *Killer Is Put to Death in Virginia After Inmates Riot in His Support,* N.Y. TIMES, Apr. 19, 1985, at A16, cols. 4–5.

47. *Two Men Convicted of Murder Are Executed in Virginia and Texas,* N.Y. TIMES, June 26, 1985, at A18, cols. 3–6.

48. *Convicted Killer Is Put to Death in Virginia,* N.Y. TIMES, July 7, 1987, at B6, cols. 1–4.

49. *Earl Clanton Jr. Dies In Virginia Electric Chair,* WASH. POST, Apr. 15, 1988, at D7, col. 1.

50. *Virginia Electrocutes Killer of an Elderly Woman,* N.Y. TIMES, July 20, 1990, at A12, cols. 3–5.

51. *Man Is Put to Death in Virginia for Rape and Murder of Girl,* N.Y. TIMES, July 25, 1991, at B8, col. 6.

52. *Ex-Navy Officer Executed in Enlisted Woman's Death,* ORLANDO SENTINEL, June 18, 1993, at A12.

53. *Virginia Sends Man to the Electric Chair for Couple's Slaying,* N.Y. TIMES, Sept. 17, 1992, at A18, col. 4; Sue Anne Pressley, *Slayer Says Goodbye, Smiling,* WASH. POST, Sept. 16, 1992, at A1, cols. 2–4, & A17, cols. 1–3.

54. Ann Gibson, *Inmate Executed for Killing Sheriff's Deputy,* Associated Press, Oct. 18, 1990, *available in* LEXIS, News Library, AP File; *Virginia Executes Killer of Deputy,* N.Y. TIMES, Oct. 18, 1990, at A22, col. 1.

55. *Virginia Man Executed for Rape, Murder,* WASH. POST, Dec. 17, 1993, at D6, cols. 3–4.

56. *Virginia Executes Killer of 2 Store Clerks,* SUN-SENTINEL (Ft. Lauderdale), Mar. 4, 1994, at 6A.

57. David Reed, *Murderer, Rapist Edward Fitzgerald Executed in Va.,* WASH. POST, July 24, 1992, at B4, cols. 1–2.

58. G. L. Marshall, *Death Row Breakout Artist Executed,* United Press International, Aug. 22, 1991, *available in* LEXIS, News Library, UPI File; *Executions Carried Out in Virginia and Missouri,* N.Y. TIMES, Aug. 23, 1991, at D18, cols. 4–6.

59. *Virginia Executes Man Who Killed 5 in '84 Crime Spree,* N.Y. TIMES, Mar. 20, 1993, at 7, col. 1; *Time Running Out for Condemned Killer,* United Press International, Mar. 18, 1993, *available in* LEXIS, News Library, UPI File.

60. *Murderer Put to Death in Virginia,* N.Y. TIMES, Apr. 28, 1994, at A19, col. 1.

61. Joe Taylor, *Disabled Death-Row Inmate Executed in Virginia's Electric Chair,* Associated Press, Jan. 20, 1993, *available in* LEXIS, News Library, AP File; Joe Taylor, *Disabled Killer Visits with Family as Execution Nears,* Associated Press, Jan. 19, 1993, *available in* LEXIS, News Library, AP File.

62. Bill Montgomery, *Stevens Executed for '77 Murder of Kidnapped Cabbie,* ATLANTA CONST., June 30, 1993, at C1, col. 1, & C4, col. 1; *Murderers Are Put to Death in Texas and Georgia,* N.Y. TIMES, June 30, 1993, at B7, cols. 1–3.

63. Jeanne Cummings, *Henry Willis Put to Death for Murder,* ATLANTA CONST., May 19, 1989, at A1, col. 6, & A15, cols. 1–6; Jeanne Cummings, *13 Years Later, Officer's Killer Facing Execution,* ATLANTA CONST., May 18, 1989, at B1, cols. 5–6, & B6, cols. 2–4.

64. Tim Cox, *Bunch Executed; Videotape Order Overturned at Last Minute,* United Press International, Dec. 10, 1992, *available in* LEXIS, News Library, UPI File.

65. Celestine Bohlen, *Va. Executes Coppola After High Court Intervenes,* WASH. POST, Aug. 11, 1982, at 1, col. 1.

66. Peter Applebome, *Virginia Executes Inmate Despite Claim of Innocence*, N.Y. TIMES, May 21, 1992, at A20, cols. 3–6.

67. *Virginia Man Dies in Electric Chair*, N.Y. TIMES, Aug. 1, 1986, at D17, cols. 1–3.

68. *Moser Execution Set for 10 P.M. Tonight*, PR Newswire, Aug. 16, 1995, *available in* LEXIS, News Library, PRNEWS File; *Pennsylvania Executes Man Who Killed Family*, Reuters, Ltd., Aug. 16, 1995, *available in* LEXIS, News Library, REUNA File.

69. *Executed in Alabama*, WASH. TIMES, Apr. 29, 1995, at A3; *Alabama Executes Man for Ax Murder*, N.Y. TIMES, Apr. 29, 1995, at 9, col. 5.

70. Susan Leonard, Abraham Kwok, & Pamela Manson, *Arizona Executes Multiple Murderer*, ARIZ. REPUBLIC, Apr. 14, 1993, at A1; Abraham Kwok, Pamela Manson, & Susan Leonard, *Time, Appeals Run Out for Killer*, ARIZ. REPUBLIC, Apr. 14, 1993, at A1.

71. Carolyn Tuft, *Killer Put to Death in Decade-Old Murders*, ST. LOUIS POST-DISPATCH, July 27, 1995, at 3B.

72. *Satellite Woes*, PHOENIX GAZ., Oct. 6, 1993, at A6; *State Executes Killer of Two*, ST. LOUIS POST-DISPATCH, Oct. 6, 1993, at 4B.

73. Jim Mosley, *More Executions Are Foreseen*, ST. LOUIS POST-DISPATCH, Jan. 7, 1989, at 1A, cols. 3–6, & 4A, cols. 1–2; Jim Mosley & Terry Ganey, *Ashcroft Refuses to Block Execution*, ST. LOUIS POST-DISPATCH, Jan. 6, 1989, at 1A, cols. 1–3.

74. *Missouri Performs Smith's Execution "Professional Way,"* ST. LOUIS POST-DISPATCH, Jan. 19, 1990, at 3A, cols. 2–5.

75. Jacob Wolf, *Laughing Killer Executed*, United Press International, May 17, 1990, *available in* LEXIS, News Library, UPI File; Tim Bryant, *Killer Is Executed; 2 Others Near Date*, ST. LOUIS POST-DISPATCH, May 18, 1990, at 14A, cols. 1–2; *Louisiana Man Is Put to Death in 1977 Killing of a State Trooper*, N.Y. TIMES, May 18, 1990, at A17, cols. 1–2; E. J. Dionne Jr., *Capital Punishment Gaining Favor as Public Seeks Retribution*, WASH. POST, May 17, 1990, at A12, cols. 1–6.

76. Timothy Egan, *For the First Time Since '65, A State Uses Its Gallows*, N.Y. TIMES, Jan. 6, 1993, at A10, cols. 1–4.

77. *Missouri Executes Two-Time Killer at Potosi Prison*, ST. LOUIS POST-DISPATCH, Jan. 28, 1993, at 11A, col. 4.

78. *Convicted Murderer Robert Wayne Sawyer Executed*, United Press International, Mar. 5, 1993, *available in* LEXIS, News Library, UPI File; *Killer Described as Retarded Is Put to Death in Louisiana*, N.Y. TIMES, Mar. 6, 1993, at 9, col. 1.

79. *Execution of Insane Killer Draws Criticism*, OTTAWA CITIZEN, May 13, 1995, at H10.

80. *Alabama Executes Man in Death of a Widow*, N.Y. TIMES, May 27, 1989, at 24, cols. 1–4.

81. *Missouri Executes Man Convicted of Killing 5*, N.Y. TIMES, Sept. 1, 1990, at 20, cols. 1–4.

82. *Louisiana Executes Murderer*, N.Y. TIMES, July 23, 1991, at A16, cols. 1–2.

83. Stephen Kirkland & Tim Bryant, *Man Who Killed Foster Mother Is Executed by Lethal Injection*, ST. LOUIS POST-DISPATCH, July 28, 1993, at 1B; Stephen Kirkland, *Court*

Refuses to Block Execution, ST. LOUIS POST-DISPATCH, July 28, 1993, at 3B; *Missouri Executes Murderer,* ST. LOUIS POST-DISPATCH, July 29, 1993, at 3B, col. 1.

84. William Rempel, *Killer of Four Executed in Indiana,* L.A. TIMES, Mar. 9, 1981, at 1, col. 5; Graham Stewart, Reuters, Ltd., Mar. 9, 1981, *available in* LEXIS, News Library, REUNA File.

85. *Murderer of Girl Is Put to Death in Louisiana,* N.Y. TIMES, July 31, 1987, at B8, cols. 4–6.

86. *Byrne Was 100th Person Executed Since Return of Capital Punishment,* Associated Press, June 14, 1988, *available in* LEXIS, News Library, AP File.

87. *Illinois Executes Slayer of Couple, Its First Death Penalty in 28 Years,* N.Y. TIMES, Sept. 13, 1990, at A22, cols. 3–4.

88. James Minton, *Ward's Execution Low-Key, But Affects Observers,* ADVOCATE (Baton Rouge), May 17, 1995, at 1B.

89. Kristina Sauerwein, *Serial Killer Executed after Eating Steak-and-Shrimp Dinner,* ST. LOUIS POST-DISPATCH, Nov. 30, 1995, at 3B.

90. *Baldwin Is Executed at Angola,* TIMES-PICAYUNE (New Orleans), Sept. 10, 1984, at 1, cols. 1–2, & 3, cols. 1–4; Associated Press, Sept. 10, 1984, *available in* LEXIS, News Library, AP File.

91. Alex Martin, *Second Killer Is Executed as State Thins Death Row,* TIMES-PICAYUNE (New Orleans), June 10, 1987, at B1, cols. 2–5, & B2, cols. 1–2.

92. *Missouri Killer Executed,* United Press International, Aug. 23, 1991, *available in* LEXIS, News Library, UPI File; *Executions Carried Out in Virginia and Missouri,* N.Y. TIMES, Aug. 23, 1991, at D18, cols. 4–6.

93. Nancy Armour, *Brink's Guard Killer Dies in Electric Chair,* Associated Press, Dec. 8, 1994, *available in* LEXIS, News Library, AP File; Welton W. Harris II, *It's Over,* INDIANAPOLIS NEWS, Dec. 8, 1994, at A1.

94. James Hodge, *Sonnier Executed for Double Murder,* TIMES-PICAYUNE (New Orleans), Apr. 5, 1984, at 1, cols. 1–5, & 4, cols. 1–3.

95. Alex Martin, *Murderer Is 3rd to Die in La. Chair This Week,* TIMES-PICAYUNE (New Orleans), June 12, 1987, at A1, cols. 4–5, & A4, col. 3.

96. Bill Grady, *Killer Offers a Cryptic Message as Death Closes In,* TIMES-PICAYUNE (New Orleans), Mar. 16, 1988, at B8, cols. 1–6.

97. *Alabama Man, 43, Is Executed for Killing Girl with Pipe Bomb,* N.Y. TIMES, Aug. 19, 1989, at 8, cols. 5–6.

98. *Lowry Meets with Campbell, Refuses to Stop Execution,* SEATTLE TIMES, May 26, 1994, at A1; *Campbell Hanged,* SEATTLE TIMES, May 27, 1994, at A1, col. 1, & A4, cols. 1–6; *Washington Hangs Murderer; Texas Executes Officer Killer,* N.Y. TIMES, May 28, 1994, at 8, cols. 1–2.

99. *Louisiana Killer Is Put to Death,* N.Y. TIMES, Dec. 29, 1984, at 5, cols. 1–4.

100. *Inmate Executed in Alabama Prison,* N.Y. TIMES, Mar. 22, 1986, at 16, col. 1.

101. *Man Who Called His Trial Unjust Is Executed for Mississippi Killing,* N.Y. TIMES, June 22, 1989, at A14, cols. 3–4.

102. Susan Blaustein, *Witness to Another Execution,* HARPER'S MAGAZINE, May 1994, at 61.

103. Jason DeParle, *Rapid Rejection of Appeals May Signal Change in Courts,* TIMES-PICAYUNE (New Orleans), Mar. 1, 1984, at 1, 4.

104. *Louisiana Marchers Support and Protest a Killer's Execution,* N.Y. TIMES, Jan. 5, 1985, at 6, col. 6.

105. *Man Is Executed in Louisiana,* ST. PETERSBURG TIMES, June 8, 1987, at 3A; Alex Martin, *Berry's Execution Ends 2–1/2 Year Halt to Deaths in State,* TIMES-PICAYUNE (New Orleans), June 7, 1987, at A1, cols. 5–6, & A4, cols. 5–6.

106. *Embezzler Who Killed Secretary Dies in Louisiana's Electric Chair,* N.Y. TIMES, Aug. 24, 1987, at D9, cols. 1–2.

107. *Slayer of Five Boys Is Executed in Utah,* N.Y. TIMES, June 11, 1988, at 8, col. 6.

108. *Texas Inmate Executed for Killing in Burglary,* N.Y. TIMES, Aug. 12, 1992, at A20, col. 1; Kathy Fair, *Convicted Killer Executed for Slaying in '83 Burglary,* HOUSTON CHRON., Aug. 12, 1992, at A19.

109. *Texas Executes Man Who Had Mother Killed,* Reuters, Ltd., June 29, 1993, *available in* LEXIS, News Library, REUNA File; *Murderers Are Put to Death in Texas and Georgia,* N.Y. TIMES, June 30, 1993, at B7, cols. 1–3.

110. *Holland Executed for S&L Slayings,* HOUSTON POST, Aug. 12, 1993, at A27, cols. 5–6.

111. Peter Conney, *A Texas Execution Sets Modern Record,* PHIL. INQUIRER, Sept. 1, 1993, at A14.

112. *Two Killers Executed While a Third Seeks a Stay,* N.Y. TIMES, Oct. 31, 1984, at A14, cols. 1–5.

113. *Prisoner in Texas Dies for Murder,* N.Y. TIMES, May 16, 1985, at A20, col. 1.

114. Alex Martin, *Wingo Executed for 1982 Killings,* TIMES-PICAYUNE (New Orleans), June 16, 1987, at A1, cols. 4–6, & A4, cols. 1–2.

115. *Ex-Singer Executed in Texas for Contract Killing,* N.Y. TIMES, Sept. 21, 1989, at A27, cols. 1–5.

116. *Killer Is Put to Death in Texas After Court Turns Down Appeal,* N.Y. TIMES, July 19, 1990, at A20, col. 1.

117. *Inmate Says "Let's Do It, Man" Before Execution,* HOUSTON POST, Nov. 12, 1991, at A13.

118. Kathy Fair, *Killer Laughs Before His Execution,* HOUSTON CHRON., Nov. 20, 1992, at A34.

119. *James Executed for Murdering Woman Abducted from High Island Bar in '85,* HOUSTON POST, Sept. 3, 1993, at A30.

120. *Murderer Dies in Gas Chamber,* L.A. TIMES, Sept. 2, 1983, at 20, col. 3.

121. Donna Gehrke, *Convicted Killer Executed,* Associated Press, June 19, 1986, *available in* LEXIS, News Library, AP File; *Texas Murderer Is Put to Death,* N.Y. TIMES, June 19, 1986, at A20, col. 1.

122. *Three Inmates Executed in Same Day,* Associated Press, Aug. 28, 1987, *available in* LEXIS, News Library, AP File; *3 Executions Held in One Day; 2 Stayed,* L.A. TIMES,

Aug. 28, 1987, at 2, col. 5; *One Day, Three Executions: Alabama, Florida and Utah*, N.Y. TIMES, Aug. 29, 1987, at 9, cols. 1–2.

123.   Douglas Freelander, *'74 Prison Hostage Crisis Figure Cuevas Dies by Lethal Injection*, HOUSTON POST, May 23, 1991, at A25, cols. 2–3.

124.   *Texas Inmate Executed*, WICHITA EAGLE, Jan. 22, 1992, at 3A.

125.   *Garrett Gets Lethal Injection for 1981 Rape, Slaying of Nun*, HOUSTON POST, Feb. 11, 1992, at A9, cols. 2–3.

126.   *Killer Dies by Injection in Huntsville*, HOUSTON POST, May 7, 1992, at A34, col. 6.

127.   *Snow Hits East; Much More to Come*, ST. PETERSBURG TIMES, Dec. 11, 1992, at A18.

128.   *Ariz. Inmate Is Executed; Had Killed Pregnant Fiancee*, PHIL. INQUIRER, Mar. 4, 1993, at A12, col. 6; Abraham Kwok, *Brewer's Transition to Death Imperceptible to Witnesses*, ARIZ. REPUBLIC, Mar. 4, 1993, at A7.

129.   *Mexican National's Execution Draws Angry Remarks, Protests*, HOUSTON CHRON., Mar. 26, 1993, at A34.

130.   *Texas Executes Second Brother in Good Samaritan Slaying*, Reuters, Ltd., July 30, 1993, *available in* LEXIS, News Library, REUNA File; *2nd Man Executed in "Good Samaritan" Case*, HOUSTON POST, July 30, 1993, at A25, cols. 2–5.

131.   *Texan Is Executed for Killing of Six*, N.Y. TIMES, Mar. 4, 1987, at D22, col. 3.

132.   *Convicted Killer Executed in Alabama*, United Press International, July 13, 1990, *available in* LEXIS, News Library, UPI File; *Inmate Executed in Alabama for 1976 Murder of Woman*, N.Y. TIMES, July 14, 1990, at 7, cols. 1–2.

133.   *Texas Executes Ex-Lawyer for Courthouse Slayings*, ORLANDO SENTINEL, Sept. 21, 1994, at A12.

134.   *Texas Executes Man Who Recanted Murder Confession*, Reuters, Ltd., Jan. 4, 1995, *available in* LEXIS, News Library, REUNA File.

135.   *Man Who Murdered His Father-in-Law Executed in Indiana*, N.Y. TIMES, Oct. 17, 1985, at A22, col. 1.

136.   Douglas Freelander, *Wicker Executed for Burying Woman Alive*, HOUSTON POST, Aug. 26, 1986, at 1A, cols. 1–5; *Texas Executes Killer of College Student*, CHI. TRIB., Aug. 27, 1986, at C4.

137.   *Texas and Mississippi Executions Bring Total to 83 Since '76 Ruling*, N.Y. TIMES, July 9, 1987, at A16, cols. 3–4.

138.   *Mail-Order Murderer Is Executed*, HOUSTON POST, May 22, 1992, at A33, col. 6.

139.   *Alabama Executes Nun's Killer; Inmate Is Put to Death in Texas*, N.Y. TIMES, Nov. 20, 1992, at A21; Dennis Cauchon, *Controversy Grows as Execution Nears in Alabama Case*, U.S.A. TODAY, Nov. 19, 1992, at 10A.

140.   *Killer Executed for 1985 Abduction-Slaying*, HOUSTON POST, Mar. 31, 1994, at A27.

141.   *Texas Executes a Guard's Killer Who Was Convicted in Two Trials*, N.Y. TIMES, May 4, 1994, at A19, cols. 1–2; *Inmate Executed in 1978 Holdup*, HOUSTON POST, May 3, 1994, at A17, cols. 3–4.

142.   *Texan Is Executed for Deadly Robbery*, N.Y. TIMES, Sept. 17, 1994, at 10, col. 3.

143.   *Texas Executes Man Convicted of Woman's Kidnap, Murder*, Reuters, Ltd., Feb. 7, 1995, *available in* LEXIS, News Library, REUNA File.

144. Bill Hazlett, *3rd Person Put to Death in 12 Years*, L.A. TIMES, Oct. 22, 1979, at 1, col. 6.

145. *Police Officer's Killer Executed*, S.F. CHRON., Mar. 12, 1986, at 26, col. 3.

146. *Texas Murderer Is Put to Death*, N.Y. TIMES, June 10, 1986, at A25, col. 1.

147. *Texan Executed by Injection for Murder in 1977*, N.Y. TIMES, Dec. 5, 1986, at A18, cols. 1–5.

148. *Convict in Mississippi, Professing Innocence, Is Executed for Murder*, N.Y. TIMES, May 21, 1987, at A24, cols. 3–4.

149. *Murderer Executed in Alabama*, L.A. TIMES, Nov. 17, 1989, at P2; *Murderer of Woman Is Executed*, N.Y. TIMES, Nov. 18, 1989, at 33, cols. 2–4.

150. *State Executed Killer—Murdered Man at Houston Grocery*, HOUSTON POST, Feb. 26, 1991, at A17, col. 6.

151. *Execution in Texas*, Newsday, June 18, 1991, *available in* LEXIS, News Library, NEWSDY File.

152. *Killer of Store Clerk Who Feared for Life Is Executed in Texas*, N.Y. TIMES, Oct. 6, 1994, at A14, col. 1.

153. *Texan Who Killed Ex-Wife and Her Niece Is Executed*, N.Y. TIMES, Jan. 18, 1995, at A16, col. 5.

154. *Texas Executes Convicted Killer of Pregnant Woman*, Reuters, Ltd., Feb. 21, 1995, *available in* LEXIS, News Library, REUNA File.

155. *Killers Executed in Separate Cases*, N.Y. TIMES, Apr. 16, 1986, at B9, col. 1.

156. Douglas Freelander, *Final Appeal Fails; Williams Executed*, HOUSTON POST, May 28, 1987, at 1A, cols. 1–2, & 10A, cols. 1–4.

157. *Texas and Mississippi Executions Bring Total to 83 Since '76 Ruling*, *supra* note 137, at A16, cols. 3–4.

158. *Texas Executes "Meanest" Killer*, N.Y. TIMES, Sept. 23, 1992, at A25, cols. 5–6; Kathy Fair, *Quiet Execution Ends Man's Violent Life*, HOUSTON CHRON., Sept. 23, 1992, at A14.

159. *Kelly Executed for 1980 Slaying of Waco Convenience Store Clerk*, HOUSTON POST, Aug. 20, 1993, at A20.

160. *Texas Inmate Dies by Injection*, COM. APP. (Memphis), Aug. 24, 1993, at A5; *Around the Nation: Texas, California Executions*, WASH. POST, Aug. 25, 1993, at A9.

161. *Killer of Texas Grocery Manager Is Executed*, WASH. POST, June 15, 1994, at A26.

162. *Texas Executes Vermont Man in Slaying During Hitchhiking*, N.Y. TIMES, Aug. 2, 1994, at A19, col. 1.

163. *Texas Executes Convicted Murderer*, Reuters, Ltd., Feb. 16, 1995, *available in* LEXIS, News Library, REUNA File.

164. *Oklahoma Executes Killer Once Shielded by Cuomo*, CHI. TRIB., Mar. 21, 1995, at N7.

165. *Texas Executes Convicted Killer*, United Press International, June 21, 1995, *available in* LEXIS, News Library, UPI File.

166. *Texas Execution Is Third in the Nation in a Week*, N.Y. TIMES, Jan. 17, 1985, at A13, cols. 1–5.

167. *Texan Is Executed for Burning Woman to Death*, N.Y. TIMES, Aug. 21, 1986, at A17, cols. 1–3.

168. *Executed in Texas,* WASH. TIMES, May 19, 1993, at B6; *Texas Executes Woman's Slayer,* N.Y. TIMES, May 19, 1993, at A13, cols. 1–2.

169. Dan McGrath, *Chill of Death Settles Over San Quentin,* SACRAMENTO BEE, Aug. 25, 1993, at A2; Sandra Gonzales, *Killer's Appeals Turned Down, Execution of Mason Expected to Proceed at 12:01 A.M. Tuesday,* SAN JOSE MERCURY NEWS, Aug. 21, 1993, at 1A.

170. *Texas Executes Inmate for Rape-Slaying in 1986,* ORLANDO SENTINEL, June 22, 1995, at A10; *Texas Executes Convicted Killer,* United Press International, June 21, 1995, *available in* LEXIS, News Library, UPI File.

171. Bill Montgomery & Hall Straus, *Ivon Stanley Dies in State's Electric Chair,* ATLANTA CONST., July 12, 1984, at 1A, col. 5, & 16A, cols. 1–5.

172. *Two Killers Executed While a Third Seeks a Stay, supra* note 112, at A14, cols. 1–5.

173. *Killer in $25 Robbery Is Executed,* N.Y. TIMES, Aug. 23, 1986, at 7, cols. 3–4.

174. *Texan Is Put to Death by Injection for Killing Woman in a Robbery,* N.Y. TIMES, Dec. 8, 1989, at A24, cols. 3–4.

175. Michael Graczyk, *State Executes Man for Killing Security Guard,* AUSTIN AM.-STATESMAN, Sept. 19, 1995, at B3.

176. Dan Moran, *Arsenic Killer's Quiet Death,* ST. LOUIS POST-DISPATCH, Sept. 21, 1995, at 1.

177. *Texas Slayer Says Goodby to Dad, Then Is Executed,* L.A. TIMES, May 15, 1986, at 2, cols. 1–2.

178. Richard Boyd, *Lowenfield Denies Murders as He Goes to Chair,* TIMES-PICAYUNE (New Orleans), Apr. 14, 1988, at A20, cols. 1–6.

179. *Man Put to Death for Texas Murder,* N.Y. TIMES, May 25, 1989, at A23, col. 1.

180. *Convicted Killer Executed in Texas,* Reuters, Ltd., May 4, 1993, *available in* LEXIS, News Library, REUNA File.

181. *Texas Executes Man for 1980 Murder; 12th in 1994,* Reuters, Ltd., Nov. 22, 1994, *available in* LEXIS, News Library, REUWLD File.

182. *San Antonio Man Put to Death for '86 Killing,* AUSTIN AM.-STATESMAN, Aug. 15, 1995, at B4.

183. *Georgia Convict Is Executed for 3 Fatal Beatings in 1974,* N.Y. TIMES, Mar. 20, 1985, at A19, cols. 5–6.

184. *Man Halted Appeal, Is Executed,* N.Y. TIMES, Apr. 22, 1990, at 27, cols. 1–3.

185. *Oklahoma Man, 41, Electrocuted in Georgia in Death of Shop Clerk,* N.Y. TIMES, Feb. 21, 1985, at A18, cols. 1–2.

186. *Texan Put to Death for a Murder Committed at 17,* N.Y. TIMES, Sept. 12, 1985, at A19, cols. 1–3.

187. *Slayer of Aged Woman Executed in Louisiana After Appeals Fail,* N.Y. TIMES, July 21, 1987, at A15, cols. 1–2.

188. *Texas Man Executed for 1978 Beating Death,* N.Y. TIMES, Mar. 23, 1989, at A19, col. 1; Douglas Freelander, *State Executes Leon King for '78 Slaying,* HOUSTON POST, Mar. 22, 1989, at A5, cols. 2–5.

189. Peter Applebome, *2 Electric Jolts in Alabama Execution,* N.Y. TIMES, July 15, 1989, at 6, cols. 1–3.

190. *Alabama Executes Man in Contract Killing of Wife,* Reuters, Ltd., Mar. 20, 1992, *available in* LEXIS, News Library, REUNA File.

191. *Execution in "Samaritan" Case,* N.Y. TIMES, July 2, 1993, at A11, cols. 3–4.

192. *Barnard Executed for 1980 Slaying,* HOUSTON POST, Feb. 2, 1994, at A15.

193. *Georgian, Asserting Innocence, Put to Death,* N.Y. TIMES, Jan. 10, 1985, at A19, cols. 1–4.

194. *Bonham Executed for 1981 Murder,* HOUSTON CHRON., Sept. 28, 1993, at A11.

195. *Texas Serial Rapist Executed for 1981 Killing,* Associated Press, Dec. 6, 1994, *available in* LEXIS, News Library, AP File.

196. Janan Hanna, *State Ranks 2nd in '95 Executions,* CHI. TRIB., May 18, 1995, at 7.

197. Charles Howe, *Arizona Killer Dies in Gas Chamber,* S.F. CHRON., Apr. 7, 1992, at A2; *Arizona Conducts First Execution in 29 Years,* N.Y. TIMES, Apr. 7, 1992, at A25, cols. 1–3.

198. *Beavers Executed in Abduction-Slaying,* HOUSTON POST, Apr. 4, 1994, at A15, cols. 1–2.

199. *2 Texas Killers Are Executed in 88 Minutes,* N.Y. TIMES, Feb. 1, 1995, at A19, col. 1; Michael Graczyk, *Executed Pair Served Combined 29 Years,* AUSTIN AM.-STATESMAN, Feb. 1, 1995, at B4.

200. *Man Put to Death for Texas Murder,* N.Y. TIMES, Sept. 11, 1987, at A21, col. 1.

201. Michael Graczyk, *Convicted Killer Put to Death,* Associated Press, Nov. 3, 1988, *available in* LEXIS, News Library, AP File.

202. *Texan Executed by Lethal Injection for 1981 Slaying of Brother-in-Law,* HOUSTON POST, May 17, 1990, at A26, cols. 1–3; *Louisiana Man Is Put to Death in 1977 Killing of a State Trooper,* N.Y. TIMES, May 18, 1990, at A17, cols. 1–2; E. J. Dionne Jr., *Capital Punishment Gaining Favor as Public Seeks Retribution,* WASH. POST, May 17, 1990, at A12, cols. 1–6.

203. *Officer's Killer Executed by Lethal Injection,* HOUSTON POST, May 27, 1994, at A33; *Washington Hangs Murderer; Texas Executes Officer Killer,* N.Y. TIMES, May 28, 1994, at 8, cols. 1–2.

204. *Oklahoma Killer Is Executed After 15 Years on Death Row,* AUSTIN AM.-STATESMAN, July 2, 1995, at B2.

205. James Webb, *Illinois Executes 6-Year-Old's Killer,* PEORIA J. STAR, Nov. 23, 1995; *Convicted Child Killer Executed,* TELEGRAPH HERALD (Dubuque, Iowa), Nov. 22, 1995, at B6.

206. *Killer Put to Death in Texas,* N.Y. TIMES, July 10, 1985, at A11, cols. 1–2.

207. *Two Killers Executed in Neighboring States,* United Press International, June 26, 1990, *available in* LEXIS, News Library, UPI File; *Arkansas Executes Killer of 16; Texas Kills Inmate by Injection,* N.Y. TIMES, June 26, 1990, at A21, cols. 1–2.

208. *Jernigan Executed for Slaying Man During Break-In,* HOUSTON POST, Aug. 5, 1993, at A20.

209. *Texas Murderer Is Executed After Top Court Rejects Plea,* N.Y. TIMES, Dec. 19, 1986, at A30, cols. 1–2.

210. *35-Year Hiatus Ends As Nebraska Puts a Killer to Death,* N.Y. TIMES, Sept. 3, 1994, at 8, col. 4; Peter Hernon, *Acquaintance of Convict Not at Execution,* ST. LOUIS POST-DISPATCH, Sept. 3, 1994, at 4B.

211. *Execution Denounced,* St. Louis Post-Dispatch, May 7, 1995, at 6C.

212. *Delaware Executes Killer,* Wash. Post, Mar. 18, 1995, at A2; *Delaware Executes Man for '92 Killing,* N.Y. Times, Mar. 18, 1995, at 7, col. 1.

213. *Oklahoma Killer Is Put to Death,* N.Y. Times, Sept. 11, 1990, at B12, col. 4.

214. *Execution Over, But Doubts Linger,* Rocky Mt. News, Jan. 23, 1992, at 10.

215. *Delaware Executes a Convicted Killer After Supreme Court Clears Way,* Phil. Inquirer, June 23, 1994, at B7; *Delaware Executes Participant in Double Murder,* Reuters, Ltd., June 23, 1994, *available in* LEXIS, News Library, REUNA File.

216. Scott Charton, *Missouri Executes Man Who Murdered Relative,* St. Louis Post-Dispatch, Nov. 16, 1995, at 4B.

217. *Murderer Executed in Georgia After Appeals Fail,* N.Y. Times, Dec. 13, 1984, at A18, cols. 1–5.

218. Michael Graczyk, *Fort Worth Man Executed for Slaying,* Austin Am.-Statesman, June 8, 1995, at B11.

219. *Slayer Autry Professed Love as He Died,* L.A. Times, Mar. 14, 1984, at 2, cols. 1–3.

220. *Oklahoma Executes Man Convicted in '77 Slaying,* N.Y. Times, Mar. 11, 1992, at A16, cols. 4–6; *Second Execution in 26 Years Held in Oklahoma,* United Press International, Mar. 10, 1992, *available in* LEXIS, News Library, UPI File.

221. *Texas Executes Murderer of Bar Manager,* N.Y. Times, Apr. 27, 1994, at A18, cols. 5–6; *Convicted Murderer Executed for 1982 Slaying of Bar Manager,* Houston Post, Apr. 26, 1994, at A15, cols. 5–6.

222. Alex Rodriguez & Lou Ortiz, *2 Killers Executed,* Chi. Sun-Times, Mar. 22, 1995, at 1; *Executed in Illinois,* Wash. Times, Mar. 23, 1995, at A3.

223. *Tube Springs Leak,* Chi. Trib., Dec. 14, 1988, at C18; Douglas Freelander, *Houstonian's Killer Gets Fatal Injection—2nd Man Spared,* Houston Post, Dec. 13, 1988, at A3, cols. 5–6.

224. *"It's Over. That's Fine," Wife Says After Execution,* Times-Picayune (New Orleans), Apr. 1, 1984, at 12, cols. 1–2.

225. *First Idaho Execution in 36 Years: A Killer Who Used a Baseball Bat,* N.Y. Times, Jan. 7, 1994, at A20, cols. 1–2; *Idaho Executes First Man Since 1957,* Baltimore Sun, Jan. 7, 1994, at 6A; Jack Broom, *Record Number Executed in 1993, South Favors Death Penalty,* Times-Picayune (New Orleans), Jan. 9, 1994, at A7; Marty Trillhaase, *Wells Executed, Death Penalty Resumes After 36-Year Gap,* Idaho Falls Post Reg., Jan. 6, 1994, at A1.

226. *Phillips Executed in Iris Siff's Death,* Houston Post, Dec. 15, 1993, at A29, cols. 3–4.

227. *Murderer of Three Women Is Executed in Texas,* N.Y. Times, Mar. 14, 1985, at A22, cols. 1–6.

228. *Addict Is Executed in Texas for Slaying of 2 in Robbery,* N.Y. Times, June 25, 1987, at A24, cols. 1–2.

229. *White Gets Lethal Injection After 14 Years on Death Row,* Houston Post, Apr. 23, 1992, at A38, cols. 5–6.

230. *Gacy Executed by Lethal Injection for 33 Murders,* Wash. Post, May 10, 1994, at A6, cols. 1–3; *Glitch with Gacy Fuels Fire of Execution Foes,* Com. App. (Memphis), May 11, 1994, at 2A.

231. *Man Executed for Inmate Bomb Death,* L.A. TIMES, Sept. 7, 1991, at A17, col. 1; David Margolick, *Rarity for U.S. Executions: White Dies for Killing Black,* N.Y. TIMES, Sept. 7, 1991, at 1, cols. 1–2, & 11, col. 1.

232. Paul W. Valentine, *Execution of Thanos Went "Like Clockwork,"* WASH. POST, May 18, 1994, at D1.

233. David W. MacDougall, *Adams Dies Proclaiming His Faith,* POST & COURIER (Charleston, S.C.), Aug. 19, 1995, at A17; *Executed in South Carolina,* WASH. TIMES, Aug. 19, 1995, at A2.

234. *Three Inmates Executed in Same Day, supra* note 122; *3 Executions Held in One Day; 2 Stayed, supra* note 122, at 2, col. 5; *One Day, Three Executions: Alabama, Florida and Utah, supra* note 122, at 9, cols. 1–2.

235. *"I'm Sorry," Says a Killer of 4 Just Before He's Put to Death,* N.Y. TIMES, Apr. 28, 1990, at 10, cols. 1–3.

236. *Texas Slayer Dies in First Execution of Year,* N.Y. TIMES, Jan. 31, 1987, at 28, cols. 1–5.

237. *Louisiana Killer Dies in Electric Chair,* L.A. TIMES, Dec. 14, 1983, pt. 1, at 5, col. 1; Dan Even, *Domestic News,* Associated Press, Dec. 14, 1983, *available in* LEXIS, News Library, AP File.

238. Dan Balz, *Execution in Texas Rekindles Debate,* WASH. POST, Dec. 8, 1982, at 1, 8.

239. *Executed in Missouri,* WASH. TIMES, Dec. 7, 1995, at A6.

240. *Convicted Murderer Is Executed,* N.Y. TIMES, Sept. 19, 1991, at B11, cols. 1–2.

241. *Texas Killer Executed,* United Press International, June 1, 1995, *available in* LEXIS, News Library, UPI File.

242. *Louisiana Man Is Put to Death in 1977 Killing of a State Trooper,* N.Y. TIMES, May 18, 1990, at A17, cols. 1–2.

243. *Two Men Convicted of Murder Are Executed in Virginia and Texas,* N.Y. TIMES, June 26, 1985, at A18, cols. 3–6.

244. Scott Charton, *Inmate on Death Row for 12 Years Executed,* ST. LOUIS POST-DISPATCH, July 22, 1993, at 2B, cols. 3–5.

245. *Convicted Killer of Bryan Couple Gets Lethal Injection,* HOUSTON POST, Feb. 29, 1992, at A23, col. 1.

246. *"Punishment Fits Crime": Killer of Teen-age Girl Dies of Injection,* HOUSTON POST, May 21, 1992, at A27, cols. 1–2.

247. *Executed in Texas,* WASH. TIMES, Apr. 7, 1995, at A9.

248. *Executed in Illinois,* WASH. TIMES, Mar. 23, 1995, at A3.

249. *Utah Executes Man for His Role in 1974 Robbery That Left 3 Dead,* N.Y. TIMES, July 31, 1992, at A14, cols. 1–3; Ted Olsen, *Utah Man Executed After Last-Minute Appeals Refused,* Reuters, Ltd., July 30, 1992, *available in* LEXIS, News Library, REUNA File; United Press International, July 30, 1992, *available in* LEXIS, News Library, UPI File.

250. *Executed in Oklahoma,* WASH. TIMES, Aug. 12, 1995, at A3.

251. *2 Texas Killers Are Executed in 88 Minutes, supra* note 199, at A19, col. 1; Graczyk, *supra* note 199, at B4.

252. *Killer of Medical Student Dies in Electric Chair in Louisiana,* N.Y. TIMES, July 25, 1987, at 9, cols. 1–3.

253. *Murderer Is Executed in Nevada,* N.Y. TIMES, June 20, 1989, at A18, cols. 1–2.

254. *Nevada Executes Man in Homosexual Killings,* N.Y. TIMES, June 24, 1989, at 24, cols. 1–4.

255. *Confessed Murderer of 13 Is Executed in Nevada,* N.Y. TIMES, Dec. 7, 1985, at 28, cols. 1–5.

256. *North Carolina Killer Executed After Appeal Fails,* N.Y. TIMES, Sept. 20, 1986, at 7, cols. 4–5.

257. *2 Inmates Executed in a Day, supra* note 29, at A17, col. 4.

258. Estes Thompson, *Ingle Dies Asking for Forgiveness,* HERALD-SUN (Durham, N.C.), Sept. 23, 1995, at A3.

259. William Schmidt, *Woman Executed in North Carolina,* N.Y. TIMES, Nov. 2, 1984, at A1, col. 4, & A20, cols. 4–6.

260. *Man Is Put to Death for Double Slaying During Crime Spree,* N.Y. TIMES, Oct. 24, 1992, at 7, cols. 1–2; *Murderer Executed in North Carolina,* COURIER-J. (Louisville), Oct. 24, 1992, at 4A.

261. *Killer of 3 Policemen Is Executed,* N.Y. TIMES, Mar. 17, 1984, at 11, cols. 1–2.

262. *Killer Executed After Losing Videotape Request,* N.Y. TIMES, June 16, 1994, at A23; *No TV Death for Killer,* NEWSDAY, June 16, 1994, at A25.

263. *Murderer Executed in North Carolina,* S.F. CHRON., Oct. 19, 1991, at C10.

264. *Executed in Montana,* WASH. TIMES, May 11, 1995, at A12.

265. *Texas Puts Murderer of FBI Secretary to Death,* Reuters, Ltd., June 21, 1995, *available in* LEXIS, News Library, REUNA File.

266. *Around Texas and Southwest,* DALLAS MORNING NEWS, Mar. 24, 1993, at 14D.

267. Peter Applebome, *Georgia Inmate Is Executed After "Chaotic" Legal Move,* N.Y. TIMES, Sept. 26, 1991, at A18, cols. 1–4.

268. Rob Meckel & Douglas Freelander, *Execution Delay "3-Ring Circus," Prosecutor Says,* HOUSTON POST, Jan. 8, 1988, at 8A, cols. 5–6.

269. *Prosecutors Sure Ellis Execution Justified Despite Lawyers' Claims,* HOUSTON POST, Mar. 4, 1992, at A15, cols. 1–2.

270. Kathy Fair, *Final Appeal Fails; Herrera Is Executed,* HOUSTON CHRON., May 13, 1993, at A32.

271. *Former Altar Boy Executed in S. Carolina,* L.A. TIMES, Jan. 12, 1985, pt. 1, at 3, cols. 1–3; *Condemned Man Rejects Further Appeals Efforts,* N.Y. TIMES, Jan. 11, 1985, at A8, col. 6.

272. *South Carolina Executes Killer; Age Stirs Protest,* N.Y. TIMES, Jan. 11, 1986, at 6, col. 1.

273. *Killer Executed at Texas Prison,* N.Y. TIMES, Dec. 12, 1994, at A8, cols. 5–6.

274. Katherine Bishop, *After Night of Court Battles, a California Execution,* N.Y. TIMES, Apr. 22, 1992, at A1, cols. 2–4, & A22, cols. 1–5; Katherine Bishop, *Foes of Execution Fear California May Set Tone,* N.Y. TIMES, Apr. 21, 1992, at A14, cols. 1–2.

275. *Oklahoma Killer Is Put to Death,* N.Y. TIMES, Mar. 14, 1992, at 7, col. 1; *Oklahoma Executes Second Murderer in a Week,* United Press International, Mar. 13, 1992, *avail-*

able in LEXIS, News Library, UPI File; *Second Execution This Week Set in Oklahoma,* United Press International, Mar. 12, 1992, *available in* LEXIS, News Library, UPI File.

276. *Florida Executes Man in '81 Slaying,* N.Y. TIMES, Apr. 25, 1991, at B9, col. 1.

277. *Florida Executes Convicted Killer,* N.Y. TIMES, Nov. 20, 1990, at B9, col. 3.

278. *Florida Executes Informer's Killer,* N.Y. TIMES, June 26, 1991, at A19, col. 1.

279. Ron Word, *Killer of Two Executed in Florida's Electric Chair,* Associated Press, July 21, 1992, *available in* LEXIS, News Library, AP File; *Escapee Who Killed 2 Is Executed in Florida,* N.Y. TIMES, July 22, 1992, at A13, cols. 1–4.

280. *Antone Executed, Forgives Authorities for "Ignorance,"* L.A. TIMES, Jan. 26, 1984, at 2, cols. 3–4.

281. Bill Lohmann, *Domestic News,* United Press International, Apr. 5, 1984, *available in* LEXIS, News Library, UPI File; *2 Convicted Killers Die in a Single Day,* N.Y. TIMES, Apr. 6, 1984, at A14, col. 1; Carl Schoettler, *Florida's Death Row Inmate Loves Execution's Publicity,* TIMES-PICAYUNE (New Orleans), Apr. 5, 1984, at 5, cols. 4–6.

282. Jesus Rangel, *Confessed Murderer of 3 Executed in Florida,* N.Y. TIMES, July 14, 1984, at A24, cols. 1–6.

283. *Asserting Innocence, Convict Dies in Florida Electric Chair,* N.Y. TIMES, Sept. 21, 1984, at A17, cols. 1–2.

284. *Former Florida Prison Guard, 31, Is Electrocuted as Killer of Girl, 8,* N.Y. TIMES, May 5, 1989, at A16, cols. 1–3.

285. *Slayer of Tampa Boy Electrocuted in Florida,* N.Y. TIMES, Mar. 7, 1985, at A28, cols. 2–5.

286. *Florida Executes Killer of 12,* N.Y. TIMES, Apr. 22, 1993, at A22, cols. 4–6.

287. *Black Man Executed in Florida, Asserting Race Led to Verdict,* N.Y. TIMES, May 11, 1984, at A17, col. 1.

288. *Florida Executes Killer of Officer,* N.Y. TIMES, Jan. 31, 1985, at A21, col. 1.

289. *3 Executions Held in One Day; 2 Stayed, supra* note 122, at 2, col. 5; *One Day, Three Executions: Alabama, Florida and Utah, supra* note 122, at 9, cols. 1–2.

290. *Florida Executes Killer of Woman,* N.Y. TIMES, Apr. 23, 1994, at 9, col. 1; *Newswatch on the Nation,* BALTIMORE SUN, Apr. 22, 1994, at 3A.

291. *Slayer Is Electrocuted in Florida,* N.Y. TIMES, June 21, 1984, at A18.

292. Patrick May, *Florida Executes Killer After 14-Year Appeal,* TIMES-PICAYUNE (New Orleans), Mar. 16, 1988, at A8, cols. 2–3.

293. *Florida Executes Convict for Killing Store Owner,* N.Y. TIMES, Sept. 22, 1990, at 24, cols. 1–5.

294. *Killer of 2 Police Officers Executed in Florida,* N.Y. TIMES, May 5, 1990, at 26, cols. 1–4.

295. *Student's Killer Executed,* N.Y. TIMES, May 13, 1992, at A19, col. 1; Jim Ross, *Martin Dies in Electric Chair,* ST. PETERSBURG TIMES, May 13, 1992, at 1B.

296. *Nevada Murderer Is Put to Death,* N.Y. TIMES, June 4, 1990, at A21, col. 1.

297. Jon Nordheimer, *Bundy Is Put to Death in Florida After Admitting Trail of Killings,* N.Y. TIMES, Jan. 25, 1989, at A1, cols. 5–6, & A2, cols. 3–6.

298. *Florida Killer Executed, Just as He Wished,* CHI. TRIB., Aug. 26, 1993, at 4M; *Man Who Killed His Baby Goes Willingly to Chair,* ORLANDO SENTINEL, Aug. 26, 1993, at B1.

299. *Florida Prisoner Dies for Slayings,* N.Y. TIMES, May 30, 1985, at D23, cols. 1–2.

300. Scott Thurston, *Tucker Is 2nd Executed in State in 7 Days,* ATLANTA CONST., May 23, 1987, at 1A, col. 6, & 18A, cols. 1–3.

301. Jon Nordheimer, *Gilmore Is Executed After Stay Is Upset; "Let's Do It!" He Said,* N.Y. TIMES, Jan. 18, 1977, at 1 & 21.

302. Tracy Thompson & Sam Hopkins, *A Calm Smith Is Executed,* ATLANTA CONST., Dec. 16, 1983, at 1, col. 2.

303. *Delaware Carries Out First Execution Since '46,* N.Y. TIMES, Mar. 15, 1992, at 17, cols. 1–6.

304. *Shotgun Killer Is Executed in Delaware,* ARIZ. REPUBLIC, Sept. 1, 1993, at A9.

305. *Florida Executes Slayer of Furniture Store Owner,* N.Y. TIMES, Nov. 9, 1984, at A18, cols. 4–6.

306. *Father Who Murdered 2 of His Children Executed,* N.Y. TIMES, Sept. 8, 1984, at 6, cols. 3–5.

307. Jim Galloway & Tracy Thompson, *Bowden Executed Day After "Mildly Retarded" Ruling,* ATLANTA CONST., June 25, 1986, at A1 & A11.

308. *Florida Killer Recites Psalm, Is Electrocuted,* L.A. TIMES, Dec. 1, 1983, at 1, col. 3.

309. Doug Nurse, *Killer Apologizes, Then Dies for Crime,* TAMPA TRIB., Dec. 6, 1995, at 1.

310. Wayne King, *Florida Executes Killer as Plea Fails,* N.Y. TIMES, May 26, 1979, at 1, col. 1; Thomas Slaughter, *Domestic News,* Associated Press, May 26, 1979, *available in* LEXIS, News Library, AP File; Reuters, Ltd., May 26, 1979, *available in* LEXIS, News Library, REUNA File.

311. *Miami Torture-Murderer Executed,* United Press International, July 18, 1995, *available in* LEXIS, News Library, UPI File.

312. *Murderers Are Executed in Delaware, Arizona,* BOSTON GLOBE, Mar. 4, 1993, at 20, cols. 1–4; Reid Kanaley, *Murderer James Red Dog Is Executed in Delaware,* PHIL. INQUIRER, Mar. 4, 1993, at B1, cols. 4–6, & B4, cols. 1–3; *Two Who Wanted to Die Are Executed,* ST. PETERSBURG TIMES, Mar. 4, 1993, at 7A.

313. *Other News to Note,* HOUSTON POST, Sept. 15, 1993, at A11.

Additional Sources

The photograph on the cover depicts the lynching of Frank McManus in Minneapolis on May 28, 1882, for molesting a four-year-old girl. The photograph, taken by H. R. Farr, was obtained from the Minnesota Historical Society in St. Paul, Minnesota.

The epigraphs on page 3 come from *John Day and His Law,* LITTLE FALLS TRANSCRIPT (Minn.), July 26, 1889, at 2, col. 3, and from LOUIS MASUR, RITES OF EXECUTION: CAPITAL PUNISHMENT AND THE TRANSFORMATION OF AMERICAN CULTURE, 1776–1865, at 110 & n.36 (1989) (*citing* THOMAS UPHAM, THE MANUAL OF PEACE 234–35 (1836)).

The sources for the illustration captions are as follows. *The hanging of Rainey Bethea: see* Chapter 2. *John Day Smith:* Minnesota Historical Society, Gallery of Prominent Men. *The hanging of William Taylor:* Letter from Harriet C. Frazier, Sept. 14, 1996 (verifying identity of picture); 1 Complete History of Sullivan County, 1836 to 1990, at 254–63, 276–78 (1977); Letter from State Historical Society of Missouri, Aug. 16, 1996 (confirming that D. S. Cole is pictured and listed in the 1896 atlas of Carroll County); *William P. Taylor Hanged for Murder of the Meeks,* ST. LOUIS POST-DISPATCH, Apr. 30, 1896, at 1, cols. 1–3; *Scenes and Incidents,* ST. LOUIS POST-DISPATCH, Apr. 30, 1896, at 8, cols. 2–3; *Taylor's Crime,* ST. LOUIS POST-DISPATCH, Apr. 30, 1896, at 8, col. 3; *Taylor's Wish Not Granted,* ST. LOUIS POST-DISPATCH, May 1, 1896, at 3, col. 2; *His Life the Penalty,* DAILY CITIZEN (Pueblo, Colo.), May 1, 1896; *Bodies Under the Straw,* MASTER DETECTIVE, July 1937, at 16–21, 51–54; *see also* Photographs of Taylor's Execution obtained from Watt Espy and the Missouri Historical Society. *The hanging of Henry Wirz:* WILLIAM MARVEL, ANDERSONVILLE: THE LAST DEPOT 246–47, 308 (1994) (that book also contains this photograph); JAMES McPHERSON, BATTLE CRY OF FREEDOM: THE CIVIL WAR ERA 796–803 (1988); HISTORICAL TIMES ILLUSTRATED ENCYCLOPEDIA OF THE CIVIL WAR 544, 837 (Patricia Faust ed., 1986). *The lynching of Henry Smith: Burned at the Stake,* DAILY PICAYUNE (New Orleans), Feb. 2, 1893, at 1, cols. 5–6; *The Paris, Tex. Horror,* DAILY PICAYUNE (New Orleans), Feb. 3, 1893, at 1, col. 4. *Cartoon:* MINNEAPOLIS J., Apr. 20, 1911, at 1, cols. 4–6.

~ BIBLIOGRAPHIC ESSAY

I consulted hundreds of primary and secondary sources in the course of writing this book. The primary sources consisted largely of state codes, session laws, court briefs and opinions, newspapers, and legislative journals, testimony, and reports. A small number of gubernatorial messages and original execution records also were reviewed. The secondary sources consisted of books, magazines, master's and doctoral theses, and academic journal articles in the fields of criminology, history, law, political science, psychology, and sociology. Because the notes contain citations to the material that was actually incorporated into the book, the creation of a full-blown bibliography would be redundant. However, at the publisher's suggestion, I have added this bibliographic essay to provide readers with information about my research methodology and the scope of my research efforts. The citations in the endnotes themselves are modeled after the format suggested in A UNIFORM SYSTEM OF CITATION (16th ed. 1996), which is also commonly referred to as "The Bluebook."

In writing the book, I first attempted to identify all the American laws requiring private, nighttime executions. The modern-day laws were easily identified by reviewing current state statute books, but identifying the early American laws mandating private, nighttime executions required considerable work. The citations for the first private execution laws in America were found in *The Executioner's Song: Is There a Right to Listen?*, 69 VA. L. REV. 373, 375–80 (1983). However, additional efforts were made to identify amendments to these laws and other private execution laws by consulting more secondary sources and reviewing various statutory compilations from all fifty states. Because no one secondary source had ever compiled a list of laws requiring nighttime executions, I relied upon my own review of more than a hundred state statutory compilations from the mid-1800s to the early 1900s to create this list. Only a few state session laws, which are produced annually, were reviewed, as conducting an exhaustive review of various session laws would have involved hundreds, if not thousands, of hours of additional work. Many state session laws do not contain indexes, making a review of them cumbersome and particularly time-consuming.

Once the relevant private and nighttime execution laws were identified, I attempted to ascertain the legislative intent behind certain of these laws, first by obtaining the house and senate journal entries for each of the bills that eventually became law, and then reviewing contemporary newspaper articles describing the legislative action and the purpose for it. The house and senate journal entries themselves were usually of little value for obtaining substantive information because they frequently indicate only when actions were taken on a bill, such as when the bill was introduced. In some cases, the journals also give the vote totals for and against motions on a bill or final passage of the bill itself. The house and senate journal entries usually do not indicate why a bill was introduced or what reasons legislators gave for voting for or against the legislative proposal.

Copies of house and senate journal entries and other legislative history materials were obtained from the following institutions: the Arkansas Supreme Court Library in Little Rock, the Colorado Supreme Court Library in Denver, the Connecticut State Library in Hartford, the Northwestern University School of Law Library in Chicago, the Indiana State Library in Indianapolis, the Kentucky State Law Library in Frankfort, the Maine State Historical Society in Portland, the Maryland State Law Library in Annapolis, the Commonwealth of Massachusetts State Library in Boston, the Minneapolis Public Library, the Nicollet County Historical Society in St. Peter, Minnesota, the University of Minnesota Law School Library in Minneapolis, the William Mitchell College of Law in St. Paul, the Minnesota Historical Society in St. Paul, the State Historical Society of Missouri in Columbia, the Thormodsgard Law Library at the University of North Dakota in Grand Forks, the Supreme Court of Ohio in Columbus, the State Library of Ohio in Columbus, the Ohio Historical Society in Columbus, the McKusick Law Library at the University of South Dakota in Vermillion, the Legislative Reference Library in Austin, Texas, and the University of Virginia Law Library in Charlottesville. Maryland Penitentiary records, kept by Warden Vernon L. Pepersack and containing useful historical information on Maryland's execution practices, were obtained from H. Mark Stichel, a lawyer at Piper & Marbury in Baltimore.

Once I determined the effective dates for relevant state laws, I identified the first or first few executions that occurred in those states after the laws took effect. This was done by contacting Watt Espy, the Director of the Capital Punishment Research Project in Headland, Alabama. Espy has spent more than twenty-five years documenting American executions and has identified nearly 19,000 people who have been legally executed since 1608 in what is now the United States. After providing him with the effective dates for these laws, Espy provided me with information about the first executions that took place after these laws took effect in the following states: Ohio (1885), Colorado (1889), Indiana (1889), New York (1889), Connecticut (1893), Massachusetts (1898), North Dakota (1903), Wyoming (1905), Virginia (1908), Arkansas (1913), Maryland (1923), Texas (1924), Alabama (1927), South Dakota (1939), Kentucky (1944), and Louisiana (1952). The dates in parentheses indicate the year in which the relevant private and/or nighttime execution law took effect. An appendix in William Bowers's book, *Legal Homicide: Death as Punishment in America, 1864–1982* (1984), also assisted me in identifying pertinent execution dates.

Finally, nineteenth- and early twentieth-century newspapers were painstakingly reviewed to research the history of relevant laws or particular executions. The following pre-1970s newspapers were consulted: Arkansas, *Arkansas Democrat* (1913), *Arkansas Gazette* (1913); Colorado, *Pueblo Chiefton* (1889–91), *Rocky Mountain News* (1889–91); Connecticut, *Hartford Courant* (1893–94), *Hartford Times* (1893–94), *New Haven Register* (1893–94); District of Columbia, *Washington Post* (1923); Illinois, *Chicago Tribune* (1885, 1889); Indiana, *Indianapolis News* (1889, 1894); Louisiana, *Daily Picayune* (1893), *Times-Picayune* (1952); Maryland, *Baltimore Sun* (1922–23); Massachusetts, *Boston Evening Transcript* (1898, 1901), *Boston Globe* (1898, 1901), *Springfield Republican* (1898, 1901), *Worcester Daily Spy* (1898); Missouri, *St. Louis Post-Dispatch* (1896, 1937); New York, *New York Times* (1936–37); North Dakota, *Bismarck Daily Tribune* (1903, 1905), *Fargo Forum* (1903, 1905), *Grand Forks Herald* (1903, 1905); Ohio, *Akron Daily Beacon* (1885), *Cleveland Herald* (1885), *Cleveland Plain Dealer* (1885), *Daily Ohio State Journal* (1885), *Morrow County Sentinel* (1885); South Dakota, *Pierre Daily Capital-Journal* (1939); Texas, *Austin American-Statesman* (1923–24), *Houston Chronicle* (1924), *Houston Post* (1923–24); Virginia, *Richmond Evening Journal* (1908), *Richmond News Leader* (1908), *Richmond Times-Dispatch* (1908); Washington, *Seattle Post Intelligencer* (1909), *Spokesman-Review* (1909); Wyoming, *Cheyenne Daily Leader* (1905), *Natrona County Tribune* (1905, 1912).

In researching the history of Minnesota's "midnight assassination law" and that state's abolitionist movement, the following Minnesota newspapers also were consulted: *Aitkin Age* (1903), *Alexandria Post* (1889), *Brainerd Dispatch* (1896), *Daily Minnesotian* (1854–55), *Duluth News Tribune* (1894, 1903), *Fergus Falls Weekly Journal* (1888), *Freeborn County Standard* (1861), *Granite Falls Journal* (1898), *The Hub* (1901), *Hutchinson Leader* (1919), *Little Falls Transcript* (1889), *Mankato Weekly Record* (1862), *Martin County Sentinel* (1889), *Minneapolis Journal* (1885, 1889, 1893, 1898, 1901, 1904–6, 1908, 1911–12, 1919, 1931, 1933), *Minneapolis Tribune* (1872–73, 1876–77, 1879, 1881, 1889–91, 1894–96, 1898, 1904–5, 1907–8, 1911, 1933), *Minnesota Daily* (1911), *Minnesota Democrat*

(1854), *Minnesota Pioneer* (1853–55), *Minnesota Republican* (1854–55), *Moorhead Daily News* (1889), *Pine County Pioneer* (1890), *Pioneer & Democrat* (1858–61, 1872), *Red Wing Argus* (1868), *Redwood Reveille* (1891), *Sherburne County Star News* (1905), *St. Anthony Express* (1854), *St. Paul Daily News* (1906–7, 1911), *St. Paul Dispatch* (1868–69, 1877, 1879, 1889, 1893, 1899, 1901, 1905–7, 1909–11), *St. Paul Globe* (1891, 1901, 1903), *St. Paul Herald* (1918), *St. Paul Pioneer Press* (1865, 1868–69, 1872–77, 1879, 1881–83, 1885, 1888–91, 1893–98, 1901–3, 1905–9, 1911), *St. Peter Tribune* (1868), *Weekly Valley Herald* (1902).

I examined these newspapers on microfilm page by page for select dates during the years listed in parentheses to find information about particular legislative actions or specific executions. For pertinent legislative actions, such as the introduction, amendment, or passage of a bill, I reviewed all the articles and editorials in the relevant newspaper on the specific date and for a few days or a week on either side of the legislative act. Likewise, when researching the history of a particular execution, I reviewed the applicable dates in the newspaper not only for stories or editorials describing the execution itself, but for news items that were published in the days leading up to or after the event took place. This process was used to ensure that any available information about an execution or a particular legislative action was retrieved. Because I used a huge number of newspapers and news service reports published after 1970 in my research, I do not list them here; they are cited in the notes to this book and may be obtained at public libraries or from WESTLAW or LEXIS databases. Any further inquiries about the sources consulted should be directed to the author via the publisher, Northeastern University Press.

∾ INDEX